T0390922

# TRADE POLICY FLEXIBILITY AND ENFORCEMENT IN THE WTO

The World Trade Organization (WTO) is an incomplete contract among sovereign countries. Trade policy flexibility mechanisms are designed to deal with contractual gaps, which are the inevitable consequence of this contractual incompleteness. Trade policy flexibility mechanisms are backed up by enforcement instruments which allow for punishment of extra-contractual conduct.

This book offers a legal and economic analysis of contractual escape and punishment in the WTO. It assesses the interrelation between contractual incompleteness, trade policy flexibility mechanisms, contract enforcement, and WTO Members' willingness to cooperate and to commit to trade liberalization. It contributes to the body of WTO scholarship by providing a systematic assessment of the weaknesses of the current regime of escape and punishment in the WTO, and the implications that these weaknesses have for the international trading system, before offering a reform agenda that is concrete, politically realistic, and systemically viable.

SIMON SCHROPP is an international trade analyst for Sidley Austin LLP, a leading law firm in international trade law and WTO litigation. He has previously worked for the WTO Secretariat and as a research fellow investigating legal and economic issues of the WTO.

# CAMBRIDGE INTERNATIONAL TRADE AND ECONOMIC LAW

As the processes of regionalization and globalization have intensified, there have been accompanying increases in the regulations of international trade and economic law at the levels of international, regional, and national laws.

The subject matter of this series is international economic law. Its core is the regulation of international trade, investment, and cognate areas such as intellectual property and competition policy. The series publishes books on related regulatory areas, in particular human rights, labor, environment, and culture, as well as sustainable development. These areas are vertically linked at the international, regional, and national level, and the series extends to the implementation of these rules at these different levels. The series also includes works on governance, dealing with the structure and operation of related international organizations in the field of international economic law, and the way they interact with other subjects of international and national law.

*Books in the series:*

*Trade Policy Flexibility and Enforcement in the WTO: A Law and Economics Analysis*
Simon A. B. Schropp

*The Multilaterization of International Investment Law*
Stephan W. Schill

# TRADE POLICY FLEXIBILITY AND ENFORCEMENT IN THE WORLD TRADE ORGANIZATION

## A Law and Economics Analysis

SIMON A. B. SCHROPP

CAMBRIDGE
UNIVERSITY PRESS

# CAMBRIDGE
## UNIVERSITY PRESS

University Printing House, Cambridge CB2 8BS, United Kingdom

Cambridge University Press is part of the University of Cambridge.

It furthers the University's mission by disseminating knowledge in the pursuit of education, learning and research at the highest international levels of excellence.

www.cambridge.org
Information on this title: www.cambridge.org/9780521761208

First published 2009

*A catalogue record for this publication is available from the British Library*

ISBN 978-0-521-76120-8 Hardback

*To my parents, for their love and unquestioning support, and to my sister Lena, for being her*

# CONTENTS

# FIGURES

# ABBREVIATIONS

| | |
|---|---|
| AoA | Agreement on Agriculture |
| AB | Appellate Body |
| ABM | Agreement on Anti-Ballistic Missiles |
| AD | antidumping |
| ADA | Antidumping Agreement |
| Art./Arts. | article(s) |
| BoP | balance of payments |
| CCC | Pareto-efficient complete contingent contract |
| CvD | countervailing duty |
| DDA | Doha Development Agenda |
| DG | Directorate General |
| DR | default rule(s) |
| DS | dispute settlement |
| DSB | Dispute Settlement Body |
| DSM | Dispute Settlement Mechanism |
| DSU | Dispute Settlement Understanding |
| EBC | efficient "breach" contract |
| EC | European Communities |
| EEC | European Economic Communities |
| EU | European Union |
| GATS | General Agreement on Trade in Services |
| GATT | General Agreement on Tariffs and Trade |
| GPA | Agreement on Government Procurement |
| GSP | Generalized System of Preferences |
| ILC | International Law Commission |
| ILO | International Labour Office |
| ILP | Agreement on Import Licensing Procedures |
| IMF | International Monetary Fund |
| IO | industrial organization |
| IP | intellectual property |
| IR | international relations |
| IT | information technology |

| | |
|---|---|
| ITO | International Trade Organization |
| L&E | law and economics |
| LDC | least developed country/countries |
| LR | liability rule(s) |
| MFN | most-favored nation |
| NGO | non-governmental organization |
| NVC | non-violation complaint(s) |
| OMA | orderly marketing agreements |
| PD | prisoners' dilemma |
| PR | property rule(s) |
| PROF | politically realistic objective function(s) |
| R&D | research and development |
| ROO | Agreement on Rules of Origin |
| RPT | reasonable period of time |
| SALT | Strategic Arms Limitations Treaty |
| SCM | Agreement on Safeguards and Countervailing Measures |
| SG | safeguard |
| SGA | Agreement on Safeguards |
| SIG | special interest group |
| SPS | Agreement on Sanitary and Phytosanitary Measures |
| TBT | Agreement on Technical Barriers to Trade |
| TC | transaction costs |
| TOT | terms of trade |
| TPRM | Trade Policy Review Mechanism |
| TRIMs | Agreement on Trade-Related Investment Measures |
| TRIPS | Agreement on Trade-Related Intellectual Property Rights |
| UCC | United States Uniform Commercial Code |
| UR | Uruguay Round |
| USTR | United States Trade Representative |
| VCLT | Vienna Convention on the Law of Treaties |
| VER | voluntary export restraint(s) |
| WTO | World Trade Organization |

# ACKNOWLEDGEMENTS

"Build a house, beget a son, plant a tree, write a book." It is said that these are four essential things every man should accomplish during his lifetime. Writing a book certainly can be a solitary, frustrating, and self-deprecating process at times. Yet it does not have to be this way, especially if one receives as generous a support as I did during the completion of this book. It is thanks to the following outstanding individuals that I now could – in theory – turn my full and undivided attention to more tangible projects, such as planting trees or constructing houses.

Petros Mavroidis was my cosmopolitan PhD advisor – twice. Petros not only worked "like a dog" on earlier drafts of this book; he also has been a never-ending source of support and inspiration to me. At St. Gallen University, Heinz Hauser was the best "Doktorvater" I could have hoped for: patient yet demanding, stern yet just, supportive yet always straightforward. His comments on this book were extremely helpful to me.

During my time at Columbia University and the Graduate Institute, Geneva, I was fortunate to work with a number of distinguished WTO scholars. Patrick Low was not only a brilliant boss at the WTO; he also showed great flexibility and patience in accepting me as his *impromptu* PhD student. Cédric Dupont supported me in all stages of the process and saw to providing my funding for over two years. Joost Pauwelyn has been a great teacher and it was a privilege to have collaborated with him on several exciting academic projects. Henrik Horn was there for me when help was most needed (and most appreciated). I am indebted to Richard Baldwin, Jagdish Bhagwati, Chad Bown, Richard Gardner, and Merit Janow.

Alexander Keck and Marc Bacchetta at the WTO; Manfred Elsig, Mirko Abbritti, Kornel Mahlstein, and Philip Stucki at the Graduate Institute; and Frieder Roessler, Niall Meagher, and Tom Sebastian of the Advisory Center of WTO Law provided valuable academic input and moral support.

I wish to thank Scott Andersen, Todd Friedbacher, Nicolas Lockhart, and Andy Shoyer of Sidley Austin LLP for giving me the opportunity to work in such a stimulating and fun environment, and for granting me the time and intellectual latitude to engage in various academic extravaganzas.

Last but not least, things indubitably would have gone South without the unquestioning support and loving care of my family and friends. Without aiming to be exhaustive, I would like to express my profound gratitude to Andreas Moll, Ladane Nasseri, Johanna von Braun, Nico Tyabji, Tim and Marc Stog, SCG, Benvenuto Salm-Reifferscheidt, Dominic Furlong, and whoever it was that invented *Ramazotti*. This book is dedicated to my parents Helga and Peter, and to my sister Lena, in love and eternal gratitude.

Simon Arnd Benedikt Schropp
Geneva

# FOREWORD

The study of WTO dispute settlement has been attracting increasing interest in law and economics scholarship: in part, as a reaction to the largely impressionistic early legal literature, which had decided on the effectiveness of the new regime on scarce evidence; in part, because of the characteristics of the new regime – compulsory third party adjudication is not the paradigmatic adjudication process in international relations. There is already an impressive body of literature that addresses a series of questions relating to the participation of various WTO Members in proceedings; the impact of third parties on the outcome; the legal capacity of the various participants as an explanatory variable for success in proceedings; the propensity of complainants to prevail; the decision to litigate, and the connected decision to move from one stage of the proceedings to the next. The predictive power of the various models employed varies, and some would argue that it is probably too early to have robust empirical evidence for many of them.

The study of remedies occupies a prominent place within this body of literature. The original contributions, which saw nothing wrong with the WTO system, gave way to more skeptical views over time. There are few empirical papers and lack of transparency often makes this study difficult. Simon Schropp is on top of the literature, and this volume displays it in excellent manner. However, this is not all that the author does. Borrowing from contract theory, he places enforcement in a wider context where a player deviates from the contract (ab)using its safeguards clauses and/or without invoking them.

There should be little doubt that, in light of the de facto prospective nature of remedies in the WTO, WTO Members have an incentive, for political economy reasons, to abuse recourse to, say, safeguards, and thus to provide their domestic industry with the necessary "breathing space." Indeed, bad-faith behaviour is probably exacerbated by the fact that WTO adjudicating bodies have interpreted the safeguard clause in a very restrictive manner, de facto depriving potential users of an important instrument.

More generally, we are still far away from developing a comprehensive theory of disputes – there are no models predicting when disputes will occur in a setting like the WTO. Contract incompleteness is probably a contributing factor, but in and of itself no reason for a dispute: for one, the trading partners can always go back to the table and negotiate further; unless one takes the view that some of the GATT provisions are obligationally incomplete, it should be that heavy negotiating costs dictate adjudication over renegotiation.

Schropp's work is one of the first that tries to shed light on these questions. The author provides both a framework for analysis for all these questions, as well as his own proposals to help trading partners deal with the various problems identified in this volume. The outcome is a very welcome input to an ongoing discussion regarding the shaping of the multilateral trading system. Having set himself high standards with his first work, his subsequent steps in this area will be eagerly anticipated.

Petros C. Mavroidis
*New York City*
Edwin B. Parker
*Professor of Law at Columbia Law School,*
*New York*

# Introduction: trade policy flexibility in the WTO – vice or virtue?

> But to my mind, though I am native here
> And to the manner born, it is a custom
> More honour'd in the breach than the observance
>
> William Shakespeare, Hamlet, Act I, Scene 4

This study deals with the rational design of trade policy flexibility and remedies in the World Trade Organization (WTO). It examines whether, and under what circumstances, contractual non-performance (or escape) may be considered *more honour'd* than the *observance* of previously made trade commitments, at what cost for the breaching Member, and with what effect for the global trading order.

The WTO[1] is a multilateral trade agreement and as such the international equivalent of a contract.[2] It lies in the nature of a trade accord that governments accept far-reaching trade liberalization concessions, which severely limit their domestic policy discretion in the future. Prior to the conclusion of the Agreement, countries did not possess full knowledge of the nature, probability of occurrence, or impact of future events. Nor were they able to anticipate the possible trade policies and instruments that their trade partners might concoct in the course of the contractual performance. Asymmetrical information settings, uncertainty over future environmental contingencies, bounded rationality,

---

[1] Throughout the course of this study, the terms "WTO" or "the Agreement" will be used interchangeably as shorthand for the bundle of multilateral contracts that are known as the Uruguay Round Agreements. These Agreements include the Marrakech Agreement ("WTO Agreement" or "WTO Charter"), and all the treaties mentioned in Annexes 1–4 to the Marrakech Agreement.

[2] The WTO Appellate Body (AB) in *Japan – Alcoholic Beverages*, WT/DS 8,10,11/AB/R: 16, expressly stated that "the WTO Agreement is a treaty – *the international equivalent of a contract*" (emphasis added).

limited resources, or mishap, or a mix of the above, at the time of its conclusion make the WTO an inherently incomplete contract.[3]

A defining feature of incomplete contracts is that they contain gaps: important contingencies (eventualities, future conditions, or "states of nature") are not considered in the terms of the original contract, and thus are not exhaustively and unambiguously specified *ex ante*, i.e. at the time the parties concluded the contract. *Ex post*, during the performance phase of the contract, gaps may leave gains from trade unrealized. This, in return, may create room for "regret" (Goetz and Scott 1981) whenever unanticipated and unforeseen developments, or shocks, occur.[4] In the context of international trade a shock, such as a protectionist backlash within a country, may seriously threaten some domestic import-competing sector or export industry, and therewith jeopardize welfare and/or employment of certain groups of society, or economic growth and social cohesion at large. Performance as previously agreed upon may then no longer be either desirable for the affected WTO Member nor mutually efficient.[5]

---

[3] The insight that the WTO contract is incomplete in important aspects is neither original nor particularly new. This view of the WTO has recently gained acceptance and acknowledgment among WTO scholars (e.g. Downs and Rocke 1995; Dunoff and Trachtman 1999; Ethier 2001a; Hauser 2000; Hauser and Roitinger 2003, 2004; Herzing 2005; Horn, Maggi and Staiger 2006; Lawrence 2003; MacLeod 2006; Mavroidis 2007; Rosendorff 2005; Rosendorff and Milner 2001, to name only a few). There is a rapidly expanding literature that discusses or models the WTO as an incomplete trade accord between sovereign nations. (Recent contributions include Bagwell 2007; Bagwell and Staiger 2005b; Ethier 2001a; Horn, Maggi, and Staiger 2006; Howse and Staiger 2005; Kucik and Reinhardt 2007; Lawrence 2003; Rosendorff 2005.)

[4] A signatory experiences regret whenever an *ex ante* envisioned transaction value is not realized in the light of the newly revealed information. An unanticipated contingency arises which, had it been known to signatories at the outset of negotiations, would have changed the content of the original contract. Mahoney (1999, p. 117) aptly states: "A contract is an exchange of promises ... and the parties enter into it because each values the thing received more than the thing foregone. These values are based on expectations about the future because some or all of the contractual performance will occur in the future. When the future diverges from what a party expected, he may conclude that the performance he will receive under the contract is no longer more valuable than the performance he must provide. He has ... experienced a 'regret contingency' and now would prefer not to perform and not to receive the promised performance from the other party."

[5] To grasp the concept of *ex post* regret, consider the simple example of a fixed-price contract that obliges one party to produce and the other party to buy a product. An earthquake destroys the production facilities and makes delivery as prescribed extremely costly: the producer will prefer not to perform; by means of a side payment to the buyer (exceeding the latter's personal value of the good) both parties can be made better off by not conducting the envisaged transaction (see Shavell 1980, note 4).

When drafting the original accord, signatories to any trade agreement have shown a profound interest in allowing shock-ridden Members to withdraw from previously made concessions rather than forcing them to rigidly observe the letter of the contract. But how exactly should rules of flexibility be organized and designed? Should a shock-afflicted party be allowed to withdraw fully or partially, temporarily or permanently, at any point in time or under strict preconditions, at its own discretion or with prior consent of the affected party/parties? What is the appropriate price for such deviation from contractual obligations? And how can rules of flexibility be credibly enforced against opportunistic and ill-meaning abuse?

This study is primarily concerned with two issues: first, why are the current WTO flexibility mechanisms flawed? Second, how should they better be organized instead? While many commentators remain largely conjectural about the imminence of the WTO's problems in its system of contractual escape and dispute settlement, we aim to provide a structured, differentiated, and comprehensive approach towards the issue of trade policy flexibility in multilateral trade agreements. In the course of this study, starting with the next chapter, we will assess exactly where the WTO system of *ex post* escape is at fault, with what effect, and how it should be improved.

Meanwhile, by way of an introduction to the topic of trade policy flexibility and enforcement in the WTO, this chapter proceeds as follows: section 1.1 briefly reviews some major concerns that commentators have voiced about the way trade policy flexibility and enforcement are currently organized in the WTO. Section 1.2 establishes the ground-rules for any successful system of flexibility in trade agreements. In particular, it addresses the intricate connection between any rule of contractual *ex post* adjustment of concessions, the remedies for doing so, and the initial willingness of signatories to cooperate in trade matters. Section 1.3 summarizes the objective of this study and formulates its central research questions. It is followed by a reader's guide to this book. Then, in section 1.4. we present an overview of this study's content and summarize some of the key findings. Section 1.5 provides a short literature review, describing in particular in which aspects our approach to the topic of trade policy flexibility and enforcement differs from WTO scholarship.

## 1.1 Trade policy flexibility in the WTO: a system at fault

The framers of the WTO were acutely aware of the presence of contractual gaps and the inevitable uncertainty in the economic environment.

To that end, the WTO contract provides countries with a means of departing from previously agreed obligations. In order to seize gains from regret and to deflate the build-up of domestic pressure against trade liberalization, the WTO contract includes certain trade policy flexibility instruments that permit one party (the "injurer") to (partially) default, i.e. to step back from ("modify or withdraw") contractual performance obligations it had previously agreed to. The injurer can do so if certain preconditions are met, most notably that of compensating the parties affected by such back-tracking behavior (the "victims").[6]

The WTO provides for several formal, de iure, trade policy flexibility mechanisms.[7] Examples in the General Agreement on Tariffs and Trade (GATT)[8] are Art. XII (*Restrictions to Safeguard the Balance of Payments*, applicable to developed countries only), Art. XVIII (infant industry protection and balance of payments crises; applicable to developing countries only), Art. XIX (*Emergency Actions on Imports of Particular Products*, also known as the "safeguards clause"), Art. XXVIII (*Modification of Schedules*, also known as tariff renegotiation), and – arguably – Arts. XX and XXI (*General Exceptions* and *Security Exceptions*).[9] As our analysis in Chapter 4 will show, common to these de iure flexibility mechanisms are rather high levels of conditionality (enactment preconditions and scope of application),[10] as well as relatively modest indemnity payments to the

---

[6]  No positive or negative connotations are implied in calling the parties "injurer" and "victim." Consistent with standard law and economics (L&E) literature, the terms injurer and victim are used as roles (or "types") that signatories can assume throughout the performance phase of a contract: injurers are parties that long for *ex post* adjustments, and victims are parties affected by any of the injurer's subsequent decisions.

[7]  Trade policy flexibility tools are sometimes also called "opt-outs," "trade contingency measures," "safety valves," or "escape clauses." Later on in the study we will explain why none of these terms is sufficient in capturing the entire realm of trade policy flexibility mechanisms.

[8]  Similar examples of trade policy flexibility instruments can be found in other WTO Agreements, such as the General Agreement on Trade in Services (GATS), the Agreement on Technical Barriers to Trade (TBT), or the Agreement on Agriculture (AoA).

[9]  Whether GATT Arts. XX and XXI should really be seen as flexibility mechanisms will be discussed at p. 218 below.

[10]  The level of conditionality of a flexibility instrument is composed of two elements, the first being enactment thresholds. Enactment thresholds are contingency-related preconditions that the injurer has to surpass before making use of a flexibility mechanism. Enactment costs are sunk, and compensation payments do not form part of conditionality-related costs. The second element of conditionality is the scope of application, the contractual deployment strings attached to the use of a trade policy flexibility mechanism. The ease of use of a flexibility instrument is thus a function of the level of both conditionality and scope of application.

affected victim countries (in some cases, such as under GATT Arts. XII, XV, XX, or XXI, victims are not compensated at all).

In addition to these de iure escape clauses there are various informal, de facto, flexibility tools available to WTO Members. Trade policy tools such as voluntary export restrictions (VERs), orderly marketing agreements (OMAs), antidumping (AD) and countervailing duty (CvD) measures, subsidies, or a violation of the Agreement are frequently used by WTO Members as ways to escape initially made trade liberalization commitments. Resort to these instruments is often in contravention of the letter of the law, or at least the spirit of the Agreement. Given that these de facto trade policy flexibility mechanisms happen more or less in the shadow of the law, their use is hence characterized by lower enactment costs, far-reaching scope of application (especially in the case of violation of the Agreement), and indemnity payments (damages) that are strictly lower than commensurate with the damage caused.[11]

The way trade policy flexibility is currently organized in the WTO raises a string of serious systemic issues.[12] As an example: why do certain WTO Members prefer the use of AD and CvD measures over the use of the designated escape clause of GATT Art. XIX, what are the consequences of such behavior, and what can be done to reverse this trend (see e.g. Barfield 2001; Barton *et al.* 2006; Blonigen and Bown 2003; Bown 2001; Finger, Hall and Nelson 1982; Finger, Ng and Wangchuck 2001; Messerlin 2000; Palmeter 1991b)?

Next, what is the logic of sanctioning legal escape options and contractual defection in the same manner? Note that the WTO applies the same remedy – substantially equivalent damages – to legitimate non-performance (e.g. GATT Arts. XIX, XXVIII) as well as to a violation of the Agreement (DSU Art. 22.4).

Further, what is the WTO's rationale for having a whole arsenal of *substitutive* escape clauses that have overlapping scopes of application? In a given situation, a Member has the choice of resorting to GATT Arts. XIX or

---

[11] As will be shown later in more detail, many informal escape mechanisms, such as AD and CvD measures, do not provide for any compensation of victims at all. Even utilizing "violation-cum-retaliation" as an escape mechanism (i.e. breaching the Agreement, losing a trade litigation, and withering retaliatory measures enacted by the victim) does not add up to commensurate damages due to the way dispute panels have interpreted Art. 22.4 of the Understanding on Rules and Procedures Governing the Settlement of Disputes (DSU).

[12] Many of these issues have been addressed by WTO scholarship; some have already been subject to litigation in high-profile WTO disputes. We leave a detailed discussion for later chapters (especially Chapters 5 and 6).

XXVIII, VERs/OMAs, an AD measure (under GATT Art. VI and the Antidumping Agreement (ADA)), or violation of the Agreement. Various flexibility mechanisms only differ in their level of conditionality and the compensation payable to the victims. It is thus evident that an injuring country will always go for the escape instrument which promises "most mileage," i.e. the fewest enactment costs, the lowest compensation, and the largest scope of application. As a consequence, instead of engaging in legal contractual escape in situations where *ex post* adjustment is mutually beneficial, Members act opportunistically and opt for informal protectionist escape instruments. They engage in de facto escape such as antidumping or countervailing duty actions, and risk losing the ensuing disputes (see e.g. Bown 2001, 2002a, 2002b, 2004; Finger 1998; Finger, Ng, and Wangchuck 2001; Lawrence 2003; Roitinger 2004; Schropp 2005; Sykes 1991).

Another concern is the limited scope of existing de iure escape clauses. Numerous scholars have argued that de facto breaches of WTO obligations often occur because of the rigidity connected to the enactment of formal escape mechanisms, such as GATT Art. XIX. Mavroidis (2006) states that the more rigid and "expensive" (in terms of remedies) contractual safeguards are, the less they are used. According to Mavroidis, WTO Members are more likely to violate the WTO treaty if rigid safeguards deny them the necessary "breathing space."[13] The current WTO safeguards regime allegedly does not address Members' needs for policy flexibility (see also Horn and Mavroidis 2003; Roitinger 2004; Sykes 2003). As became clear in the course of the *EC – Hormones* case,[14] the European Communities, for political or health reasons, wished to step back from a commitment they had made under the Agreement on Sanitary and Phytosanitary Measures (SPS). This endeavor, however, is not considered in any formal WTO escape clause. Hence, lacking any official means of withdrawing from existing concessions, the EC claimed to see no alternative to maintaining its violation of the Agreement.

In summary: while it is well-established that contractual escape mechanisms are an indispensable feature of multilateral trade agreements, it is the contention of many WTO pundits (trade practitioners, international lawyers, economists, and international relations scholars

---

[13] The *US – Steel* case, for example, patently revealed that Art. XIX safeguards and violation of the Agreement can be used as ready substitutes (*Definitive Safeguard Measures on Imports of Certain Steel Products*, WT/DS 248, 249, 251, 252, 253, 254, 258, 259).

[14] *Measures Affecting Livestock and Meat (Hormones)*, WT/DS 26 and 48, and *Continued Suspension of Obligations in the EC – Hormones Dispute*, WT/DS 320 and WT/DS 321.

alike) that the current system of trade policy flexibility in the WTO does not provide for adequate contractual escape, and therefore is profoundly flawed. In the course of this study we will show that the current system sets the wrong incentives for injurers, and undercompensates victims of escape. This situation may consequently lead, or already have led, to excessive breach, undercommitment (less-than-ideal *ex ante* trade liberalization concessions) by WTO Members, and an atmosphere of mistrust within the Organization. As a result, disgruntled and disillusioned Members have resorted to retaliatory strategies within and outside the realm of the WTO (e.g. retaliatory antidumping or retaliatory litigation). It could even be argued that the flawed system of trade policy flexibility and enforcement has resulted in a destabilization of the entire multilateral world trading system.

## 1.2 Some definitional groundwork: connecting issues of breach, remedies, and commitment level in incomplete contracts

But why exactly is the current system of WTO flexibility mechanisms flawed and what can be done to remedy the situation? One can only grasp the full extent of the flexibility debate if it is preceded by a discussion of the intricate connection between trade policy flexibility, contract breach, enforcement, and *ex ante* commitments. Figure 1.1 prepares some

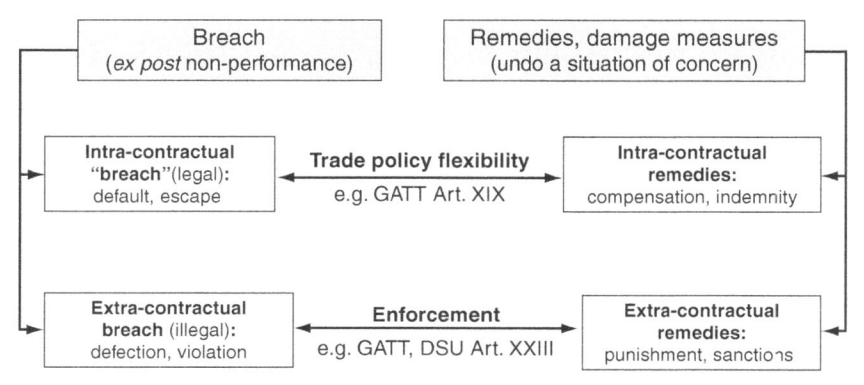

**Figure 1.1** Non-performance (breach and remedies) in incomplete contracts
Note: This chart depicts the relationship between *ex post* non-performance (breach) and the remedies such breach entails. Depending on whether the breach is intra-contractual (legal), or extra-contractual (illegal), a breach-cum-remedy combination is either called a "trade policy flexibility mechanism" or an "enforcement instrument."

definitional groundwork. It captures our general understanding of breach and remedies in trade contracts. In particular, it illustrates the important interlinkage between *ex post* adjustment (non-performance) and enforcement in incomplete contracts.

Most contracts, no matter how trivial the underlying transaction is or how well the agreement specifies the rights and obligations of the signatories, have implicit or explicit rules of non-performance, that is about breach and remedies. Whilst the definitional terms are not entirely satisfactory, *breach*[15] and *remedies*[16] will be used in a generic sense so as to delineate any form of contractual *ex post* adjustment, and any behavior towards undoing a situation of concern, respectively.

*Ex post* non-performance, or breach, of previously agreed contractual commitments can occur in two ways: first, if non-performance is contractually specified and therefore legitimate ("breach"), this arrangement – called escape, default, or excuse from obligations – forms an integral part of the contract. Non-performance as agreed upon then represents intra-contractual, permissible, behavior, not a violation of the terms of the accord. Generally, escape rules can be organized as opt-out mechanisms, or as renegotiation clauses.

A second non-performance possibility is constituted by extra-contractual, illegal, behavior. As a convention, we call this behavior *defection* or *violation of the contract* (other terms would be infringement, reneging, deviation, or contractual misdemeanor).

---

[15] The term *breach* is somewhat misleading, since in everyday terminology it bears the connotation of extra-contractual, illegal behavior. Yet in contract theory, breach is often used to describe lawful opt-out clauses, or liability rules, which allow the injurer to unilaterally decide on contractual performance and non-performance at its discretion. In order to avoid confusion, we will use breach as a generic term for any kind of non-performance. Whenever the word is used as an intra-contractual sense (such as in "efficient breach"), we will put it in quotation marks ("breach").

[16] Following standard contract-theoretical terminology, the term *remedy* is used in a comprehensive sense, so as to cover any action aimed at undoing unanticipated behavior by one contracting party. It is the generic term encompassing intra-contractual remedies (compensation, indemnity) and extra-contractual sanctions (punishment). Our understanding of the term "remedy" is notably different from the customary extra-contractual connotation it bears in the WTO literature, or, for that matter, in public international law in general, as spelled out in the ILC Draft on State Responsibility (see Grané 2001; Mavroidis 2000; Vazquez and Jackson 2002). In the WTO context the notation "remedies" is usually used in a narrow sense as legally sanctioned responses pursuant to *non-compliance* by the injuring WTO Member whose practices have been multilaterally condemned (Mavroidis 2005). DSU remedies, narrowly defined, are comprised of the WTO legal "countermeasures," namely retaliation and tariff compensation (Mavroidis 2000, p. 800).

Every act of contractual non-performance is necessarily connected to a remedy rule, or a rule of damage. As Figure 1.1. demonstrates, there are intra- and extra-contractual remedies payable to the victim of a violating measure. Those remedies in connection with legitimate escape clauses will be called *compensation* or *indemnity*. Extra-contractual remedies will be termed *punishment* or *sanctions*.[17] In general, remedies are placed on a continuum ranging from zero to infinitely high, or coercive, damages.

In the context of a multilateral trade agreement, such as the WTO, a combination of a rule of intra-contractual non-performance and the accompanying remedy procedure together establish a *trade policy flexibility instrument*. A trade flexibility tool is to be defined as any intra-contractual, legal provision that legitimizes *ex post* discretion in the form of a departure from performance as promised.[18] (Trade policy flexibility has also been termed "structured defection" (Rosendorff 2005), "selective disengagement" (Rodrik 1997, chapter 5), or "safety valve" in the literature).

Extra-contractual breach behavior and the subsequent punishment will be bundled together in the term *enforcement*. The WTO deals with issues of enforcement mainly in GATT/GATS Arts. XXIII and DSU Arts. 21 and 22, although some Agreements feature their own dispute settlement clauses (e.g. the Agreement on Safeguards and Countervailing Measures (SCM); or the Agreement on Agriculture (AoA)).

With these definitions of breach and remedies in place, we can now move on to a discussion of the tight interlinkage between mechanisms of escape and enforcement provisions, as well as that between the

---

[17] It should be noted that we use the words *punishment* and *sanction* in their customary contract-theoretical, objective, connotation. Neither term is part of the official WTO vocabulary. The DSU speaks of "suspension of concessions or other obligations," and "damages," or "trade effects," respectively. However, in WTO matters, the term *sanctions* has evolved into a colloquialism for the countermeasure of retaliation. This is not how we will use this expression.

[18] We use a broad notion of "trade policy flexibility." Our understanding of the term differs from some conventional definitions that depict trade policy flexibility as "the ability of governments to decide *unilaterally* when to introduce new *temporary import restrictions* after an international trade agreement has been concluded" (Roitinger 2004, p. 1, emphasis added). The difference is thus threefold: first, in this study, trade policy flexibility mechanisms are not reduced to liability rules, i.e. to those instruments assigning the discretion to injurers; secondly, we do not discriminate between temporary and permanent flexibility; thirdly, non-performance is not limited to ex post import restrictions, but more generally to all agreed-upon contractual behavior (e.g. retreat from a non-reciprocated obligation, such as a notification requirement).

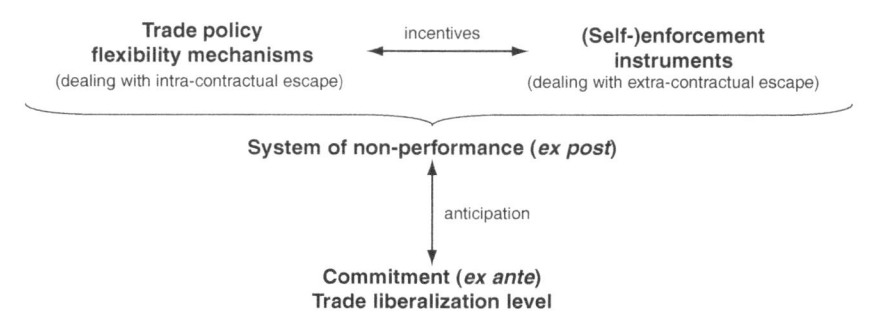

**Figure 1.2**  Commitment, breach, and trade policy flexibility in incomplete contracts
Note: This chart shows how trade policy flexibility mechanisms, enforcement instruments and *ex ante* trade liberalization commitments are linked in incomplete contracts: a proper enforcement scheme encourages shock-ridden signatories to use de iure flexibility mechanisms in situations of *ex post* regret. In anticipation of a functioning system of non-performance, all contracting parties are well-inclined to cooperate and thus are willing to undergo extensive up-front commitments. Whenever the system of trade policy flexibility of enforcement is defective, signatories can be assumed to cut down their pre-contractual concessions.

contractual system of non-performance and *ex ante* commitment. Figure 1.2 illustrates this interrelationship.

The intuition here is rather straightforward: the more incomplete a contract, the more important is the careful design of viable escape mechanisms (presuming functioning enforcement).[19] The availability and the quality of the negotiated flexibility mechanism(s) have an immediate impact on extra-contractual breach behavior of shock-affected parties (which we call "injurers" for shorthand). Whenever permissible intra-contractual behavior is mis-specified,[20] injurers under pressure may look for legal loopholes, and

---

[19]  If, hypothetically, a contract were complete, that is, specified in detail all possible contingencies and prescribed comprehensive plans of actions, flexibility mechanisms would be superfluous. Every *ex post* non-performance would then by definition be extra-contractual, i.e. deviating, punishable behavior. Conversely, the more incomplete a contract, the more flexibility arrangements gain prominence.

[20]  Escape clauses can be said to be mis-specified or ill-defined whenever they are too lax, too restrictive, or too ambiguous. Flexibility instruments are too rigid if they do not allow signatories to seize regret contingencies, are too expensive to enact, too restrictive in application scope, display ambiguous language, or fail to anticipate certain contingencies completely. They are too lax if they permit injurers to opt out inefficiently often, i.e. more frequently than a hypothetical complete contingent contract would permit. Ambiguous and ambivalent language result from poorly described contingencies and their outcomes.

resort to illegal actions – either hoping not to get caught, or because the punishment faced in the aftermath will be smaller than the expected gains from non-performance. Alternatively, if escape mechanisms are not available when needed, injurers may exit the agreement (or rather, refrain from signing it in the first place). Another real problem occurs when intra-contractual remedies are such that they over- or undercompensate the victim. Overcompensatory escape clauses are "under"-enacted, whereas undercompensatory ones are used too often compared to what a hypothetical first-best contract would stipulate.

Next to the organization of contractual flexibility, the design of the available enforcement provisions is a second critical aspect in incomplete contracts. The reaction to extra-contractual behavior in violation of the letter of the contract crucially determines the incentives for potential injurers: whenever enforcement remedies are too lenient, injurers may decide to violate the Agreement, instead of choosing intra-contractual default – as they should.

As a result of the interplay of flexibility tools and enforcement rules, three general dangers relating to the system of non-performance loom large: (i) that of opportunism on part of the injurer; (ii) that of regret contingencies not seized by the injurer; and (iii) that of insufficient compensation paid to the victim. All those potential pitfalls can be expected to have serious repercussions on the *ex ante* commitment that signatories are willing to make.

Applied to the WTO context, the extent to which a country agrees to liberalize trade *ex ante* is a direct reaction to the quality and design of the contractual system of non-performance.[21] Intuitively, if a Member country is not allowed to react to unforeseen developments in a certain industry or sector, it may not be willing to liberalize that sector in the first place. Similarly, if a WTO Member expects to be compensated inadequately for suffering from another Member's protectionist back-tracking, the former will be hesitant to liberalize in the first place.

Prior to the conclusion of the WTO contract, no country possesses full knowledge of the nature and impact of future events, or of the possible trade policies and instruments that its partners might concoct. Nor can it

---

[21] *Ex ante* commitments define the gains to be had from cooperation. In the case of a trade agreement, *ex ante* commitment can be defined as the scale and scope of trade liberalization concessions or, more generally, as the composition and level of international trade cooperation. This assertion will not remain unchecked, but will be subject to a substantial analysis in Chapter 4.2.

anticipate whether these contingencies will make it victim or injurer. At the beginning of contract negotiations, every prospective Member of a trade agreement is thus faced with a non-trivial dilemma: in the presence of uncertainty over the future, it wants to seize future regret, that is, it has a preference for *ex post* adjustment mechanisms. Yet at the same time, each Member wishes to avoid falling prey to opportunistic defections, and therefore tends to favor contractual rigidity.[22] The best a signatory can do to address this conundrum is to evaluate the efficiency, feasibility, and credibility of the negotiated system of trade policy flexibility and enforcement. It will shape its up-front trade liberalization commitments accordingly.

Any well-crafted system of trade policy flexibility must fulfill three crucial criteria: first, trade policy flexibility must allow injurers to seize post-contractual regret and consequently reap all available efficiency gains from non-performance. Secondly, at the same time, injuring Members must compensate the victim countries such that they agree to maximize the scale and scope of their *ex ante* commitment. Thirdly, the enforcement provisions flanking this arrangement must protect the existing system of trade policy flexibility from abuse; opportunism in the form of an inefficient breach must be effectively deterred. In short, any system of trade policy flexibility and enforcement must strive to mimic the outcome (*not* the substance) of the Pareto-efficient complete contingent contract, the unachievable contracting ideal of a trade agreement. The ultimate goal of flexibility is to provide for contractual escapes in exactly those instances where the hypothetical complete contract would mandate non-performance.

## 1.3   Objectives of the study

Addressing this intricate relationship between *ex ante* willingness to cooperate in trade matters and a contract's non-performance design,

---

[22] A prospective WTO Member thus faces what Ethier (2001a, p. 5) calls the "reciprocal-conflict problem," which he describes as follows: "Each country is aware, *ex ante*, that it may find itself, *ex post*, harmed by a policy that some trading partner wishes to make. So the former will want a recognized punishment procedure as a deterrent. But that country will also be aware, *ex ante*, that it might find, *ex post*, itself in a position where it would be costly not to take some policy action that would harm a partner. This is the *reciprocal-conflict problem*: every country knows that it might turn out to be either the accuser or the accused. Thus it is in no country's best interest, *ex ante*, to agree that, *ex post*, either the accuser should be unconstrained in its ability to punish or the accused should be unconstrained in its ability to proceed without punishment."

this study intends to provide a systematic and comprehensive examination of trade policy flexibility and enforcement mechanisms of the WTO. To that end, the following string of research questions form the core of this study:

(1) What is the optimal design of trade policy flexibility and enforcement in an incomplete multilateral trade agreement? How should flexibility in a multilateral trade agreement (such as the WTO) best be organized, given the initial negotiation context with all its actors, preferences, trade-offs, and constraints? Important issues that arise are:

    (a) Is it prudent for WTO Members to allow for *ex post* escape at all, or would signatories not rather be better off with a mandatory contract performance obligation?

    (b) Is it practical to have multiple escape mechanisms with overlapping scopes of application?

    (c) Should Members allow for temporary deviation from all previously agreed commitments or should diverse contractual obligations be treated differently?

    (d) Is trade policy flexibility in the WTO best organized as a ready-to-use escape mechanism that allows any injuring party to (partially) opt out of its contractual performance obligation at any point in time, or is it more prudent to structure trade policy flexibility as *ex post* renegotiations between injurer and victim ("buy-out")?

    (e) Should a high level of conditionality (preconditions and mandated scope of application) be in place for the enactment of trade flexibility tools?

    (f) In case *ex post* discretion is apposite: Which intra-contractual remedies are to be awarded to the victim of such a back-tracking measure? Should the victim be put in as good a position as if the injurer had performed? Should the *status quo ante* the breach be re-established, or rather the *status quo ante* the contract?[23] Alternatively, should the victim rather receive a fair share of the actual efficiency gains generated from the injurer's temporary withdrawal from his contractual obligations?

    (g) Finally, what kind of *enforcement* mechanisms, accompanied by which extra-contractual remedies, should be in place to protect those flexibility rules of the game?

---

[23] We shall demonstrate below that these options correspond to the expectation, the reliance, and the restitution damage measure, respectively.

(2) Once we have a clear picture what system of non-performance rational trade negotiators can be expected to draft in the first place, we can proceed by asking various subsequent research questions: What is the contractual logic, and what are the flaws of the existing regime of trade policy flexibility and enforcement in the WTO today? How does the contemporary system of contractual non-performance perform compared to the hypothetical benchmark established under point (1)?[24] This includes the discussion of issues such as:

   (i) Is the regime for escape, as currently designed, compatible with injurers' flexibility strategies and victims' compensation needs?

  (ii) What kind of loopholes encumber the system? Is the regime's enforcement system a stringent and effective protection belt against opportunistic deviation?

 (iii) What are the expected dynamic *ex ante* effects on signatories' trade liberalization commitments entailed by the current system of *ex post* flexibility and enforcement?

(3) After having assessed how an optimally shaped system of contractual non-performance should be designed (under point (1)) and how the contemporary WTO system compares to this benchmark (under point (2)), the logical next question is: Which concrete reform steps should be taken towards improving trade policy flexibility and enforcement in the WTO?

## 1.4   A reader's guide to this study

This book is addressed to all those readers interested in systemic aspects of the WTO and in the inherent logic of international trade cooperation. It is written for WTO delegates, trade practitioners, NGO activists and advocates, trade lawyers, WTO scholars and graduate students in the fields of international trade, political economy, or international economic law – given that these individuals share an interest in the economics of WTO

---

[24] We believe that if one is to comprehend what is wrong with breach and remedies in the WTO today, one must assess what system of non-performance rational trade negotiators can be expected to draft in the first place. Sykes (2000, p. 348) confirms: "[F]rom the perspective of academics interested in the positive political theory of the WTO and of international relations in general, it is important to understand what [institutional framework] WTO members have fashioned for themselves. If we are to theorize successfully about the rules of the game, we must understand the *nature* of those rules at the outset."

law. Although we have tried to cut back on jargon, basic knowledge of fundamental economic concepts, or at least an appreciation thereof, is essential for the understanding of the study. The reader should be acquainted with concepts like preferences, (expected) payoffs, equilibria, incentives, efficiency, and the Pareto principle. The study contains several graphs as well as formal descriptions, but in no instances are technical skills indispensable for the reader's comprehension or the book's core substance. Graphs and formulas are aimed at illustrating and facilitating the intuition behind our argumentation, and the reader should not be put off by them.

The study is divided into three parts. Part I (An introduction to incomplete contracting) consists of Chapters 2 and 3. It is a basic coverage of contracting, incomplete contracts, and the nature of flexibility mechanisms. Part I is essential, because it provides the reader with an important conceptual framework. It is difficult to properly examine the quality of the WTO's contemporary system of non-performance without having a clear idea why people or countries cooperate via contracts, what the nature of incomplete contracts is, why incompleteness exacerbates the drafting and conclusion of a contract, and what kinds of general gap-filling strategies contracting parties can apply to remedy this incompleteness.

Part II (Theorizing about the WTO as an incomplete contract) is comprised of Chapters 4 and 5. It is a comprehensive contract-theoretical examination of the WTO. In particular, the current system of trade policy flexibility and enforcement in the WTO is scrutinized for flaws and inconsistencies. Part III of the study (Chapters 6 and 7) bears the title "Flexibility and enforcement in the WTO: towards an agenda for reform." In this final part we perform a "hypothetical bargain analysis" (Scott 1990, p. 598) of the WTO contract: we speculate what institutional system of non-performance a group of sophisticated, forward-looking, and reasonably rational trade negotiators would design at the outset of trade cooperation negotiations, given the context that negotiations are embedded in.[25] In other words, we rewrite the non-performance regime of the WTO in a manner that makes political-economic sense, while retaining the basic contextual givens and principles of the international trading order. This

---

[25] The most striking contextual constraints, which rational trade negotiators are initially faced with, are domestic political pressure, uncertainty about the future, and the need for the agreement to be self-enforcing in the absence of a supra-national enforcer of rights and obligations.

hypothetical bargain analysis results in a positive benchmark for trade policy flexibility and enforcement, and hence constitutes a positive basis for a detailed reform agenda of the current WTO system.

Although we would advise against doing so, time-constrained readers may want to skip parts of the more theoretical background in Chapters 2, 3 and 4. However, such readers should make sure to look at sections 2.2 (Basics of contracting: creating rules), 3.1 (A categorization of contractual incompleteness), and 3.2.2. (Seizing regret: drafting flexibility mechanisms). Chapter 4 is an incomplete-contract analysis of the WTO. Readers less interested in finding out about the identity and objectives of WTO contracting parties, the rationale for concluding a trade agreement, and the nature of contractual incompleteness may choose to skip this section of the study. Section 4.2 (Primary rules of contracting: basic entitlements in the WTO) should, however, be looked at.

Let us now summarize the individual chapters of the book and highlight some of the main findings.

Chapter 2 deals with the nature of contracts in general. We blend approaches from economic contract theory and law and economics (L&E) theories of contracting to discuss why individuals choose to structure interpersonal cooperation by means of written contracts. Defining a contract as "enforceable commitment over time," we review the essence of contractual design ("contracting") and highlight the intricate connection between signatories' willingness to cooperate and contract enforcement.

Special consideration is attributed to the issue of contract design. We find that any process of contracting necessarily consists of three consecutive steps: (i) setting out the level of ambition and defining the entitlements to be traded (entitlement choice or "primary rules of contracting"); (ii) determining the scope for *ex post* discretion (providing intra-contractual rules of flexibility, "secondary rules"); and (iii) fixing rules of enforcement ("tertiary rules").

Chapter 3 is entitled "Incomplete contracting, and the essence of flexibility." We review the sources and nature of contractual incompleteness, and transactors' strategies of overcoming them. *Ex post*, contractual incompleteness creates room for regret contingencies that signatories need to address. We analyze various strategies for coping with contractual incompleteness that reasonably rational actors may choose. Two basic strategic trajectories suggest themselves to contracting parties: one towards trying to complete the contract, and the other to embracing contractual incompleteness.

Flexibility mechanisms are designed with the intention of embracing contractual incompleteness by efficiently seizing gains from *ex post* regret. Flexibility provisions are secondary rules of contracting, i.e. rules of entitlement protection. In Chapter 3 we show that there are two kinds of contractual flexibility mechanisms: contingency measures and default rules, where contingency measures are special cases of default rules.[26] These rules are central, because they apply to all previously unspecified (unanticipated, unforeseen, unforeseeable) situations of contractual regret.

Any contractual flexibility tool must be complemented by an intra-contractual remedy or compensation award. We pay special attention to the optimal design of contractual remedies, since they determine the injurer's incentives to breach *ex post* and victims' willingness to cooperate *ex ante*. Chapter 3 ends with a characterization of the achievable first-best flexibility design of any incomplete contract: an efficient "breach" contract is able to replicate exactly the outcome of a complete contingent contract – it is the best *ersatz* contract signatories can possibly craft.

Although it may not seem so at first glance, Chapter 3 prepares the theoretical ground for the rest of the study. It also establishes a frame of reference of how parties can tackle regret contingencies caused by the inevitable incompleteness of contracts. Only if one has an idea which gap-filling strategies lend themselves to fight which types of incompleteness, will one appreciate why flexibility mechanisms are such important contracting elements. In the same vein, the intricacies of rational flexibility design can only be understood in the light of the respective contracting context. Thus, we firmly believe that we can only properly appraise the WTO framers' choice of gap-filling and trade policy flexibility, if we possess a solid grasp of the nature of contractual incompleteness, and the nature of contracting under real-life imperfections.

Chapter 4 is a contract-theoretical examination of the WTO Agreement. We discuss the essence of the WTO contract (reason for contracting, exchanged entitlements, rules of entitlement protection and the contractual system of enforcement) and demonstrate why the WTO is a *necessarily* incomplete contract.

We start by reviewing what trade scholarship deems the most important rationales for the conclusion of multilateral trade agreements. We do not confine ourselves to economic motivations for contracting, but

---

[26] Default rules (also known as backstop, fallback, gap-filling, supplementary, or background rules) are imperatives "that define the parties' obligation in the absence of any explicit agreement to the contrary" (Craswell 1999, p. 1).

also take notice of what international relations and legal scholars have contributed in this area. We largely concur with mainstream trade economics that the WTO was accomplished with the paramount aim of overcoming international market access externalities. Yet we establish a second(ary) motivation for entering into a trade contract: countries wish to make the trade in goods and services more efficient by setting regulatory minimum standards and basic rules of conduct.

Reasons for contracting aside, the scope of traded entitlements (primary rules of contracting) goes well beyond that of merely regulating the mutual exchange of market access: the WTO is far more than the tariff-liberalization treaty that many scholars, economists in particular, like to characterize it as. Rather, we argue that WTO signatories exchange a whole range of logically distinct rights and obligations, i.e. entitlements. The WTO is introduced as a multi-issue, multi-entitlement contract of highest complexity. The most important entitlement exchanged in the WTO contract is the right to reciprocal trade, or "market access entitlement," in which countries commit to granting the right to compete fairly in each other's markets. However, other WTO commitments are traded in the WTO contract, namely basic auxiliary entitlements and minimum standard entitlements which are subsumed under the term "multilateral entitlements." The different nature of different WTO entitlements is imperative for examining the existing and designing the optimal contractual rules of entitlement protection and enforcement (Chapters 5 to 7 deal with these issues).

Chapter 5 looks at the contemporary system of trade policy flexibility and enforcement in the WTO and discusses its flaws and problems. The verdict is not enthusiastic. Currently, the WTO does not adequately address Members' needs for contractual escape. The de iure system of escape and enforcement is rather dubious: the available escape clauses display too many preconditions and an insufficient scope of application. The contractual default rules are underdeveloped. DSU enforcement remedies are systemically undercompensatory, they are too weak to deter violations of the Agreement. Injuring Members can afford to seek legal loopholes to satisfy their (oftentimes opportunistic) escapist ambitions. We find that the informal WTO trade policy flexibility regime practically annihilates the de iure rules, and thus defies much of what contract theory has to say about efficient entitlement protection. *Violation-cum-retaliation* is the de facto default rule for all WTO entitlements. This can be expected not only to crowd out *ex ante* trade liberalization commitments and create significant discontent among WTO Members, but also tends to destabilize the WTO in the long run.

Chapter 6 pieces together the lessons learned from Parts 1 and 2 and conducts a hypothetical bargain analysis of the WTO contract. Following Chapter 5's systematic assessment of why the non-performance regime in the current-day WTO is flawed, Chapter 6 theorizes about the organization and design of an efficient flexibility and enforcement regime that reasonably rational trade negotiators could be expected to negotiate. How should the various entitlements traded in the WTO ideally be protected – and at what costs for the party engaging in contractual escape? Much of the discussion focuses on the optimal trade policy flexibility regime of the salient market-access entitlement, i.e. the reciprocal right to compete fairly in trade partners' markets. We find evidence that when it comes to trade policy flexibility, an unconditional liability rule backed by expectation damages clearly Pareto-dominates both a rule of inalienability and a renegotiation requirement.[27] Chapter 6 also deals with the relationship between trade policy flexibility mechanisms and enforcement provisions: escape and enforcement are not rationally designed as mutual *substitutes*, but as strategic *complements*. In an incomplete contract, enforcement is the second line of defense of entitlement protection.

On the basis of this comprehensive analysis of the WTO as an incomplete contract, Chapter 7 lays out an agenda for reform which would precipitate a more efficient and viable system of flexibility and enforcement in the WTO. Briefly, the WTO should evolve into an efficient "breach" contract, which would involve three major changes in the current Agreement:

(1) Institute a liability rule of default for the market access entitlement. This could be achieved by turning the safeguards clause of GATT Art. XIX (and GATS Art. X) into a simple, non-contingent liability rule of flexibility. That way, WTO Members could react to unforeseen contingencies by unilaterally opting out of previously made trade concessions. For the liability-rule regime to work, WTO Members need binding third party arbitration, the procedures of which have to be contractually specified. The intra-contractual

---

[27] Only the contractual remedy of the expectation damage measure is apt to satisfy the strict efficient "breach" criterion. Expectation damages place the victim in as good a position as it would have been had the injurer performed, and as such constitutes the replacement value of the deal.

remedy tied to the unconditional liability rule must amount to the expectation damage measure and is payable to the victim(s) in the form of tariff compensation.

(2) Introduce an unambiguous default rule for all other entitlements, for example by adding an Art. X*bis* to the WTO Charter. This article would demand a specific performance duty (a property rule), a rule of inalienability, or a rule of liquidated damages, depending on the nature of the multilateral entitlement.

(3) Reorganize the WTO enforcement regime regulated by DSU Art. 22. This article could be remodeled so as to establish a two-tier system of enforcement. Tier one, an inner protective belt of contractual entitlements, is aimed at dealing with welfare-enhancing good faith trade disputes (that emerge due to contractual ambiguity, interpretative problems, or unintentional contract infringements), and at solving them in an amicable manner. Remedies at this stage are strictly commensurate to the damage caused. Tier two, the outer layer of protection, mandates punitive and collective punishment. After all, contract enforcement must protect against extra-contractual behavior, not invite it. Given that there is always an efficient safety valve in place for benevolent injurers thanks to the presence of default rules and the first tier of enforcement, WTO enforcement must protect WTO Members against contractual misdemeanor by means of effective penalties.

## 1.5 A brief survey of the literature on trade policy flexibility and enforcement in the WTO

This study seeks to provide a thorough examination of non-performance in the WTO. In this regard, there is a sizeable gap in the literature. We believe that our approach to trade policy flexibility is more comprehensive than many contributions to WTO research on the topic. Figure 1.3 illustrates this schematically: established strands of literature (numbered from 1 to 7) have each highlighted *some* aspects of the triangular relationship between trade policy flexibility, enforcement, and *ex ante* trade liberalization, but have not addressed the inherent interrelationships in a comprehensive manner. The systemic links between trade policy flexibility mechanisms and enforcement instruments, as well as their effect on the pre-contractual trade liberalization commitment of signatories, has not yet been clearly demonstrated.

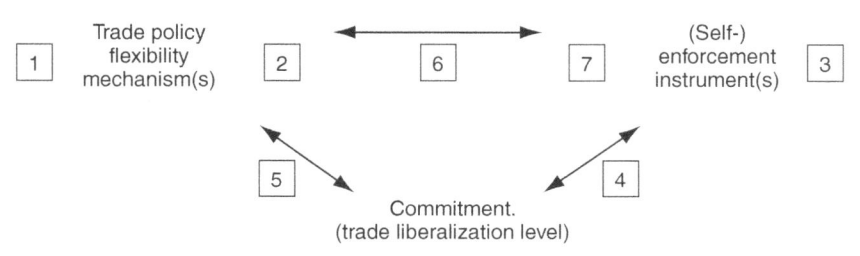

**Figure 1.3** Locating the existent WTO literature on trade policy flexibility
Note: This figure revisits Figure 1.2. Various strands of WTO literature have dealt with issues of trade policy flexibility, self-enforcement, and *ex ante* commitment. Most approaches are selective in that they either focus exclusively on one issue (1, 2, 3, 7), or on a bilateral relationship (4, 5, 6). The numbers hereby stand for strands of literature (explained in the text).

**Strand 1: descriptive assessments of trade policy flexibility**   Kleen (1989), Finger (1998), and Roitinger (2004), among others, have described and compared over twenty WTO provisions that Members can use as escape mechanisms. However, these sources (with the notable exception of Roitinger 2004) are mainly descriptive in nature. They tell us little about the deeper rationale of trade policy flexibility, or how (and on what basis) to compare and assess the merits of various different mechanisms in the contract. The studies are elusive in explaining how these mechanisms relate to WTO enforcement rules, and how they affect signatories' *ex ante* willingness to cooperate. Without these systemic links and without any notable *theory* of trade policy flexibility, purely descriptive assessments of trade policy flexibility tools should be seen as insufficient, and ought to be complemented.

**Strand 2: literature on single trade policy flexibility tools**   Various contributions have focused exclusively on description and analysis of a single escape tool. They set out far-reaching reform suggestions (e.g. Finger 2002; Lee and Mah 1998; and Sykes 2003 on safeguards; Sykes 1989 on countervailing duties; Barfield 2005; Lindsey and Ikenson 2003; Messerlin 2000; and Palmeter 1991a on antidumping). For our purpose, however, these studies are of limited added value, since there is presumably a high degree of substitutability between individual de iure and de facto flexibility instruments. It makes little sense to base reform proposals for a particular escape tool on an isolated analysis, since any effect intended by such proposals risks being undone by a rational injurer through an evasion maneuver towards another escape mechanism.

**Strand 3: literature on enforcement and WTO dispute settlement**  There is an abundance of literature on systemic flaws in and challenges to WTO enforcement and dispute settlement.[28] Scholars have found fault with various aspects of the current system of WTO dispute settlement, such as:

(a) *participation*: Are developing countries targeted excessively by industrialized countries? Why are least developed countries under-represented in WTO dispute settlements?
(b) *adjudication*: Have dispute settlement panels exceeded their mandate in WTO litigation? Has the dispute settlement system become too legalized? Is there a lack of transparency in dispute settlement?
(c) *implementation*: What are the systemic flaws of the current retaliation and compensation regimes? Are there alternative enforcement remedies?
(d) *arbitration*: Have DSB arbitrators correctly calculated damage awards when interpreting the level of nullification and impairment?

This literature does not usually take a systemic view, but isolates relevant enforcement concerns from those of trade policy flexibility. One could also argue that these sources often presuppose (treat as implicit) a clear conception of what constitutes right and wrong behavior, and that any contractual gaps should always be filled by dispute panels according to those normative guidelines. Reform demands in this tradition are frequently shaped by the respective author's normative judgment, rather than a coherent view of the nature of the contract or of signatories' preferences.

**Strand 4: theories of trade cooperation and self-enforcement**  There is unanimity in the literature that in the absence of a supra-national authority any contract among sovereign nations must necessarily rely on self-enforcement. In trying to explain the rationale for trade cooperation, early work on the GATT and subsequently the WTO has solely

---

[28]  The WTO World Trade Report 2007 (WTO 2007, chapter II.D.3.c) contains an exhaustive review of the relevant literature. We will take up some of the concerns again in section 5.4 at p. 234 below.

dealt with self-enforcement. Issues of rules and the organization of trade agreements were neglected (Staiger 1995). Scholars modeled the GATT/ WTO as a standard infinitely repeated prisoners' dilemma in which cooperation is sustained by the deterrent threat of the grim-trigger strategy of retaliation.[29] Although these formal economic models accommodate the intricate relationship between enforcement and *ex ante* commitments (e.g. Bagwell and Staiger 2002b, chapter 6), they nevertheless abstracted from reality when assuming a stationary (static) environment. These early models presented trade agreements as fully efficient and complete contracts that never needed renegotiation or modification. Consequently, trade agreements in formal models of this kind never witnessed deviation, and were free of any kind of disputes (cf. Keck and Schropp 2008, section B).[30]

Starting with the works of economists like Copeland (1990); Dixit (1987); and Kovenock and Thursby (1992), and international relations (IR) scholars like Downs and Rocke (1995), the WTO literature added realism by moving away from the assumption of a stationary environment. The aforementioned authors integrated the notion of uncertainty concerning future events, and consequently introduced *contractual incompleteness* (the logical nexus between uncertainty and incompleteness will be shown in Chapter 3). This prompted trade scholars to examine the role of trade policy flexibility mechanisms in trade agreements.[31] However, the focus of this strand of scholarship was on the stability-enhancing role of (exogenously given) trade policy flexibility mechanisms. Authors conjectured and/or proved that escape-clause-induced negotiation equilibria Pareto-dominate other arrangements without contractual safety valves. Flexibility mechanisms were thus proven to successfully decrease the breakdown risk of the trade game and to add to the stability of the world trading system (see e.g. Goldstein *et al.* 2000; Herzing 2005; Koremenos, Lipson, and Snidal 2001; Rosendorff 2005; Rosendorff and Milner 2001).

While this literature is important in establishing the rationale for trade policy flexibility mechanisms in trade agreements, it fails on four

---

[29] See e.g. Bagwell, Mavroidis, and Staiger 2005, Bagwell and Staiger 1999; 2002a; 2002b; 2005b; Bown 2002a; Dixit 1987; Ethier 2004a; Johnson 1953.

[30] To be more precise, in these models disputes are equivalent to the breakdown of the system: under a fully efficient trade agreement any deviation from the specified terms is necessarily opportunistic and thus automatically provokes the grim-trigger response.

[31] See at p. 266 below for modeling details.

accounts for the purpose of this study. First, it remains largely elusive about the impact of trade policy flexibility on *ex ante* commitments (with the notable exception of Herzing 2005). Secondly, the formal models assume the presence of one (exogenously given) single escape mechanism, namely an unconditional liability-type opt-out. Thirdly, they take the WTO contract to consist uniquely of reciprocal *tariff*-reduction commitments. Lastly, these approaches fail to differentiate between an intra-contractual escape clause, and violation of the WTO Agreement. In short, they take violation of the contract to be just another opt-out mechanism. These contributions to WTO scholarship thus fail to discuss the crucial issues of the nature of the contract, the escape clause design, and how trade policy flexibility relates to enforcement and links back to *ex ante* commitments.

**Strand 5: linking trade flexibility and commitment level**   Scholars of this category have examined the systemic link between trade policy flexibility and commitment level, or level of trade liberalization. Whereas scholars in strand 4 of the literature have studied the stability-enhancing qualities of trade policy flexibility, this literature takes a different route. It assesses the beneficial character of escape clauses in capturing contractual regret in incomplete contracts, and how these provisions consequently shape the *ex ante* willingness of governments to liberalize trade in the first place.[32] Examples of this line of research include Ethier 2001a; 2002; Herzing 2005; Mahlstein and Schropp 2007; Roitinger 2004; Schwartz and Sykes 2002b; and Sykes 1991. These studies discuss the incentive-compatibility constraints posed by intra-contractual remedies. In other words, these contributions bring in the concerns of *victims* of flexibility mechanisms by raising attention to the fact that adequate compensation for the victim is important.

Ethier (2001a); Herzing (2005, Chapter 3); Mahlstein and Schropp (2007), and Sykes (1991) formally calculate the optimal remedies payable to a victim of *ex post* contractual escape. These authors go on to discuss the dynamic relationship between *ex ante* trade liberalization

---

[32] See e.g. Sykes (1991, p. 279) who states: "[I]n the absence of an escape clause, trade negotiators may decline to make certain reciprocal concessions for fear of adverse political consequences in the future. But with an escape clause in place the negotiators will agree on a greater number of reciprocal concessions, knowing that those concessions can be avoided later if political conditions so dictate."

commitments and *ex post* flexibility.[33] Schwartz and Sykes (2002a) assess the impact of trade policy flexibility design on *ex ante* trade liberalization commitments, but their analysis is too narrow in that it only broaches issues in connection with DSU enforcement (i.e. violation of the Agreement as informal opt-out). Roitinger (2004) offers a thorough review of trade flexibility in the WTO, although the author's criteria for comparing the effectiveness of different escape mechanisms (2004, chapter 2.2) seem somewhat arbitrary. In addition, his examination of the connection between *ex ante* trade liberalization and *ex post* flexibility remains largely suggestive. None of the papers mentioned analyze the relationship between enforcement and trade flexibility in sufficient detail.

**Strand 6: theories linking trade policy flexibility to enforcement**   WTO scholars have linked the issue of trade policy flexibility to that of DSU enforcement. Approaches assessing the political economy of protectionism in the WTO seek to explain the trade-off by escapist Member governments as that between enacting some trade policy flexibility mechanism, and a blatant violation of the Agreement, given the constraint set presented by the contemporary WTO system (examples include Anderson 2002; Barton *et al.* 2006; Bown 2002b; Finger 1991; Finger, Hall and Nelson 1982; Rosendorff 1996; Schropp 2005; Sykes 1989; Tharakan 1995). This line of research is paralleled by more formal work in international economics which endogenizes governments' choices between *one* specific escape mechanism and defecting from the Agreement. Models in this line of research explain players' protectionist incentive structures when deciding whether to utilize AD measures or to violate the Agreement (see e.g. Bloningen and Bown 2003; Bown 2001; and Martin and Vergote 2004), or whether to enact safeguard action or opt for violation-cum-retaliation (see e.g. Bown 2002a).

This literature sensitizes readers to the systemic link between trade policy flexibility and enforcement, but must be supplemented for the following reasons. First, it presupposes a notion of the contract: it explains governments' choices within the existing system without discussing why the system is the way it is, and how things can be improved. Secondly, some of the formal work may just as well be termed "models of

---

[33] All of these approaches, however, consider only one flexibility mechanism, namely GATT Art. XIX or violation of the Agreement, respectively. Also, all models reduce complexity by representing the WTO as a reciprocal tariff-reduction contract.

protectionism," because the authors allege that injurers wish to seize legal loopholes only in order to opportunistically opt out of the system. The welfare-enhancing value of non-performance (seizing regret), as dealt with in strand 5, is hardly ever addressed. Finally, all approaches remain conjectural at best, when it comes to the intricate systemic effects of protectionist opt-out on the expected commitment level of WTO signatories.

**Strand 7: the compliance vs. rebalancing debate**  The so-called compliance/rebalancing debate involved some of the most prominent WTO scholars from the fields of international economics, L&E, international relations, and international trade law. In a nutshell, the debate circles around the purpose and objective of WTO enforcement and the general "bindingness" of WTO dispute panel rulings and recommendations: whereas some scholars argue for a "pay-or-perform" system of rebalancing, advocates of the rival camp opine that the main objective of WTO remedies is to induce compliance with the rulings and recommendations of the dispute panels. The compliance/rebalancing debate as led by WTO scholars for the last decade,[34] focused too narrowly on issues of WTO enforcement. It missed the opportunity to discuss the WTO's system of non-performance more broadly, and can be said to have hit a dead-end. Schropp (2007b) documents in detail why this discussion did not tackle (let alone resolve) the underlying issues of trade policy flexibility, enforcement, and trade liberalization concessions.

---

[34] The compliance-rebalancing controversy has essentially been led by Bello 1996; Palmeter and Alexandrov 2002; Schwartz and Sykes 2002b; Sykes 2000 on the rebalancing side, and by Charnovitz 2001; 2002a; 2002c; Jackson 1997b; 2004; and Pauwelyn 2000 on the compliance side of the debate. Numerous other papers allude to the debate but do not add substantial insights.

# PART I

## An introduction to incomplete contracting

The aim of Part 1 of the book is to give a guided tour through the realm of interpersonal contracting. Covering the whole range of contracts, we try to carve out what we believe to be the central characteristics and properties of contracts at large. The topic of contracting is hence treated in a fairly generalist manner. We will demonstrate that a contract is determined by its context, including the identity of transactors, the nature of contingencies, the entitlements traded, the entitlement-specific transaction costs, the number of players, the time-horizon of a contract and the frequency of interaction. When negotiating the contractual framework, signatories must adapt their contractual design to the context of the situation. To judge whether they did a good, mediocre, or bad job of that, it is vital to understand the nature of the underlying contract in the first place.

Chapter 2 provides an introduction to the nature of contracts in general. We will focus on complete contracts and on the contracting ideal, the Pareto-efficient complete contingent contract. Chapter 3 discusses the nature of contractual incompleteness, and presents signatories' available strategies for overcoming the inevitable incompleteness that besets all real-life contracts. Special emphasis is thereby put on the optimal design of default rules, which can be phrased as liability rules, property rules, or rules of inalienability.

# 2

# Complete contracts and the contracting ideal

In order to comprehend the intricacies of *incomplete* contracting, we should first get a grasp of *complete* contracting and the overall nature of contracts. This chapter represents a general law and economics (L&E) view on complete contracts and on contract design. We will deal with contracts in the most general way so as to include all sorts and types of contract, from simple handshake barters to national constitutions or sophisticated covenants with thousands of pages and hundreds of signatories. It should be acknowledged that owing to the diversity of real-life contracts, a general introduction to complete contracting is a daunting task, and one that necessarily implies painting with a broad brush.

The difficulties of generalization notwithstanding, all contracts share some fundamental properties. It is these commonalities we intend to concentrate on here in order to distill the essence of contracts, i.e. to filter out the common characteristics, motivations, and principles of contractual relationships.[1] We will examine what constitutes a contract, why parties enter into contracts, and what determines signatories' *ex ante* willingness to cooperate in a self-enforcing contract (section 2.1). Next, we will assess the basic design of contracts (section 2.2), and distinguish different kinds of contracts (section 2.3). Finally, the contracting ideal of the Pareto-efficient complete contingent contract as the unachievable first-best will be introduced in section 2.4.

## 2.1 Contracts: enforceable commitment over time

Among the many definitions of a contract in the L&E and economics literature, the essence of a contractual exchange is best captured as "an enforceable mutual commitment over time" (Craswell 1999, p. 18; Dunoff and Trachtman 1999, p. 30). This definition integrates the

---

[1] Note that the following introduction is but *one view* on the principles of contractual logic and the inherent trade-offs connected with forming contracts. Other authors may put the emphasis elsewhere. But this introduction suffices to prepare the ground for later chapters.

three features that are essential to understanding contracts: the time dimension, commitment (or cooperation) as the currency of the agreement, and credible (effective) enforcement.

### 2.1.1    Timing

In contrast to an instant barter, swap, or a spot-transaction where a good or service is handed over instantaneously in return for another good, service, or money (a concept economists usually refer to as "transaction"), the points in time between agreement/consent and delivery in a contract necessarily diverge. By default the subject of exchange (the transacted "item" or "good") in a contract is *not* a commodity, merchandise, natural resource, or service, but a *promise of future delivery*: a commitment.[2]

### 2.1.2    Commitment: cooperative intent and assurance

The essence of a contract, hence, is not the exchange of goods and services per se, but rather the promise thereof. Credible commitments are the currency of a contract. A commitment is constituted by two salient components: the *motivational/cooperative* aspect and the *assurance/enforcement* aspect.

The motivational aspect can be called the "contractual intent," or what Schwartz (1992, p. 284) calls "substantive goals" of an agreement. Every contract is concluded for a purpose, and this purpose is cooperation in some issue area or another. Cooperation is geared towards increasing the welfare of not just one, but of all the signatory parties, by means of reaping the ensuing gains from trade.[3] Contracting parties usually engage in a cooperative relationship with other actors with one or a combination of the following objectives:

---

[2]  Craswell (1999, p. 18) submits: "There is an important difference between permitting free exchange and permitting binding promises. An exchange can take place instantaneously, but a promise necessarily involves a commitment to act in a certain way at some time in the future. Once this temporal element is recognized, it can be seen that enforcing promises does not simply transfer existing goods from one owner to another. Instead, the enforcement of promises creates a new good."

[3]  Throughout this study (except when expressly noted otherwise), we endorse the tenet of "rational," as opposed to "constrained," choice. This is to say, we take a strictly Paretian view of contracting: signatories are believed to strive for maximization of their own, private welfare. Mutual interaction then leads to a maximization of the absolute gains of interaction. The (bounded) rationality of all actors prevents contracting parties from entering into agreements that are harmful, abusive, or coercive to an individual transactor in the short or long term.

(1) Minimizing transaction costs: contracts significantly reduce pre-contractual transaction costs.[4] By concluding a contract, signatories can reap efficiencies through avoiding *ex ante* sorting, searching, information gathering, and bargaining costs in contexts where additional information serves merely to redistribute rather than to expand the available surplus (Kenney and Klein 1983; Masten 1999). In a repeated-interaction setting (as opposed to a one-off exchange), for example, considerable transaction costs may be saved through the conclusion of a contract, since parties dispense themselves from having to rebargain the terms of a contractual exchange over and over again.

(2) Engaging in risk transfer: in risk-transfer transactions, the contractual objective is to shift risk to the less risk-averse transactor or low-cost risk bearer (cf. Masten 1999, p. 27). Throughout this study we will assume risk-neutral actors. Therefore, issues of risk transfer will be neglected in all future considerations.

(3) Reaping interpersonal gains from trade: probably the most important reason for concluding contracts is the aim of achieving direct transaction efficiencies created by the handing over of goods and services at some future point in time. Transaction efficiencies are generated *ex post* through the conversion of the promise (the delivery of a good, a service, money, a concession, risk transfer, etc.) into a transaction. As in an on-the-spot barter, *ex post* transaction efficiencies are reaped as long as each party values the item/good received more than the item/good foregone (Mahoney 1999, p. 117).

The second component defining a credible commitment is assurance. Since in a contract the moments of consent and delivery by definition diverge, assurance against other actors' defection is an important factor for contracting parties. Before entering into the contract and making a binding promise containing far-reaching commitments, each party will assess the risk of the other party's contractual non-performance, and want to take the necessary precautions against such incidents.[5] Most

---

[4] For the purpose at hand, "transaction costs" (TC) is a general term for all those real-life costs that signatories must incur when cooperating. Such costs include pre-contractual sorting and searching, information gathering, and processing costs, costs of bargaining, as well as post-contractual litigation, enforcement, and policing costs. Early work on transaction costs dates back to Coase 1937 and Williamson 1979; 1985. See more on TC at p. 62 below.

[5] Masten (1999, p. 26) points out: "Without some form of assurance that others will, when the time comes, uphold their end of the bargain, individuals will justifiably be reluctant to

importantly, deliberate violation of the letter or spirit of the agreement terms, or *ex post* opportunism, has to be contractually anticipated and forestalled.[6] To this end, rational and far-sighted parties tend to give the contract additional structure over and above a mere specification of their envisioned terms of trade. Schwartz (1992, p. 284) refers to those contractual clauses that specify the "parties' desire to achieve substantive goals in the best way" as "contracting" clauses. Contracting clauses hence only have an indirect, secondary significance for the agreement.

### 2.1.3  *Effective enforcement and the link between commitment and enforcement*[7]

Enforcement is the third key feature of contracts, next to timing and commitment. Every contract needs to be enforceable, whether it is a quasi-instant barter, such as the purchase of a candy bar (where only a few seconds lie between consent and conversion of the promise), a more complicated employment contract, or a complex long-term, repeated-interaction treaty (such as a multilateral trade agreement). Enforcement is the *sine qua non* of contracts, giving effect to the mutual commitment and deterring defection. Without enforcement the contract is likely to break down, or, more probably, is not concluded in the first place.

Enforcement is a function of "enforcement capacity" and "enforce-ability" (see WTO 2007, section II.C.5). *Enforcement capacity* is the ability to reciprocate credibly against violation of any terms of the contract; it is the capability to sanction contractual misdemeanors. Punishment can thereby be exercised by the affected party itself, by a neutral third party,[8] by society at large, or through collective enforce-ment enacted by a circle of affected or concerned parties (such as the membership of a multilateral contract). Enforcement instruments can vary from physical (incarceration), to economic (penalty fees), or emotional (reputation loss, withdrawal of affection) measures.

---

make investments, forgo opportunities, or take other actions necessary to realize the full value of exchange."

[6] Opportunism has been defined as "self-interest seeking with a guile" by Williamson (1985, p. 47; see also Williamson 1979, p. 234, note 3). A more precise definition is "inefficient redistribution" (Cohen 1999, p. 90): in contrast to a lump-sum transfer, opportunism is always welfare-depreciating.

[7] This section draws heavily on Keck and Schropp (2008).

[8] Third party enforcement may be called "court-and-copper" enforcement, since constitutional states require that a judiciary determines a legal infringement, and an executive (police) enforces the law.

*Enforceability* of a contract is another vital determinant of enforcement. Typically, issues of observability, verifiability, and quantifiability feature prominently when it comes to enforceability. *Observability* is the property that contract infringements can be detected in the first place, either by the affected party itself, or by a third party (say, an attorney or prosecutor). *Verifiability* is concerned with the issue of whether the contract can actually be enforced as written or agreed upon: a violation or infringement is verifiable if the affected party can point to a clause in the contract and prove its contravention. This presupposes that such a clause is actually mentioned explicitly in the contract and can be interpreted unambiguously (i.e. that the contract does not contain a gap). Also it presupposes that the violation can be conclusively proven to a neutral third party.[9] *Quantifiability* is the ability of the aggrieved party (or a court)[10] to calculate or quantify the harm suffered as a result of the contract breach. In a way, quantifiability is verifiability of damage incurred by the victim of a contract violation.

Another – maybe more intuitive – way of thinking about the two dimensions enforceability and enforcement capacity is the following: contractual enforcement is composed of two phases – a *dispute* or litigation phase, and a *punishment* or remediation phase (if the measure in question is in violation of the contract). The litigation phase features issues of enforceability, while the remediation phase deals with issues of enforcement capacity.

An important aspect of contracts is the intricate link between the quality of enforcement on the one hand, and the level of *ex ante* commitment, or cooperation, on the other. Cooperation rarely is a binary issue, but rather a matter of degrees.[11] For illustrative purposes consider Figure 2.1. The horizontal axis shows various degrees of cooperation $(C)$,[12] where $(C^{max})$ is the point of full cooperation and $(C^N)$ is the point where no contract

---

[9] As to the difference between observability and verifiability, see Schwartz 1992, p. 279: "[I]nformation is observable when it is worthwhile for the parties to know it, but the cost of proving it to a third party exceed the gains; information is verifiable when it is both observable and worth proving to outsiders."

[10] The word "court" is used as shorthand for an impartial, independent decision-maker or a group of decision-makers. By the actions of a court (be it adjudication, arbitration, or monitoring), we mean to include proceedings by a jury, an arbitrator, an expert agency, a dispute panel, and so forth.

[11] Think about a commercial bank assessing how much credit it should give to a client: as much as the client asks for, less than that, or nothing at all?

[12] We define cooperation loosely here so as to encompass many forms of interpersonal collaboration and across many issue areas.

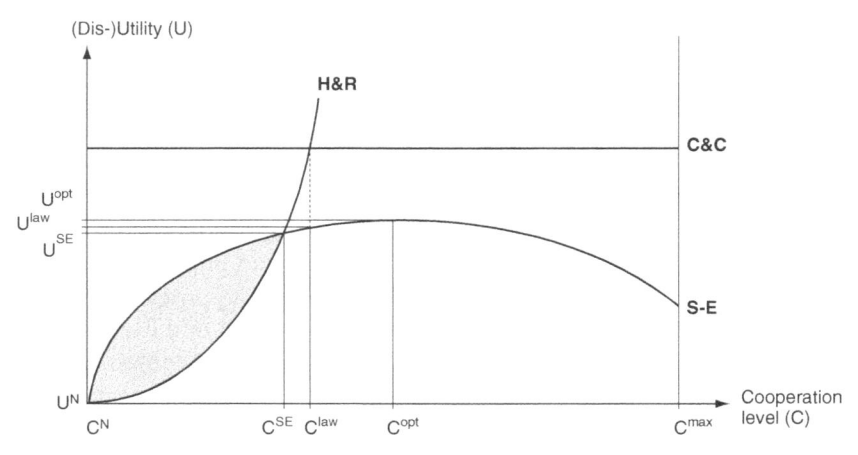

**Figure 2.1**    Enforcement constraint in contracts
Source: Keck and Schropp 2008, Figure 1.
Note: This chart shows trade-offs and constraints from the point of view of an injuring party. H&R is "hit-and-run". The H&R curve represents the discounted benefits of defecting from the terms of the initial contract. S-E is "self-enforcement". The S-E curve represents the expected costs (disutility) of defection in a self-enforcing agreement. Under a "grim trigger" enforcement strategy, those costs are tantamount to the foregone discounted value from future cooperation. C&C is "external 'court-and-copper' enforcement". The C&C line is the expected disutility from defection (here, a liquidated damage clause) in a contract enforceable by a third party. Utility level $U^{opt}$ corresponds to the optimal level of cooperation ($C^{opt}$).

exists.[13] The vertical axis depicts the excess (dis-)utility generated by the contract. Along this axis we display gains reaped over and above a non-cooperative situation, and costs of being punished for having defected. Point $U^N$ in the origin corresponds to the Nash-cooperation point $C^N$ in absence of a contract. Suppose a contract between two players.[14] The contractual intent, i.e. reason for contracting, is of no consequence here. Assume, however, that we are dealing with a long-term contract of repeated interaction (such as an employment contract).

[13]  Note that point $C^N$ in Figure 2.1 represents the Nash-level of cooperation, which is the degree of cooperation with no contract in place. The cooperation at the Nash-level may well be positive and different from a zero transaction-level.
[14]  For simplicity, parties are assumed to be symmetrical: only one contractor thus needs to be examined; incentives and actions by the other party are identical. This is without loss of generality. In a model with multiple actors the enforcement can be represented as a two-player game, namely between a player "X" and a player "rest of the world."

Each contracting party has an immediate incentive to cheat on a contract by deviating optimally from the initial terms of the agreement. The short-term benefit from defection ("hit-and-run" advantage) is the additional one-shot utility the injurer enjoys from defecting over and above the gain from cooperating as promised.[15] It is a short-term benefit only, since it merely stretches from the moment of defection to the moment this violation is detected or enforced.[16] The hit-and-run benefit (if seized by the potential defector) is by definition an opportunistic, hence inefficient, redistribution of welfare to the detriment of the potential victim (not pictured). This raises the central concern of contracting parties as they design a mutual agreement: how can rule-obedience, that is, continuous commitment to cooperation, be safeguarded? Issues of enforcement come into play.

Two enforcement mechanisms are depicted in Figure 2.1. First, in the absence of a central enforcement instance (such as a court) to deal with the case, and if parties interact repeatedly over time, the best a victim can do to enforce the contract is to engage in *self*-enforcement: the victim retaliates by exiting the agreement and returning to the non-cooperative past (threat of "grim trigger").[17] The curve S-E represents the injurer's

---

[15]  In line with conventional L&E literature, we define "victim" and "injurer" as shorthand for the different types of actors participating in the contractual exchange that unfolds after the parties have signed a contract. The two terms are understood as *roles*, not as *conditions*. During the performance of the contract any contracting party wishing to modify the content of the contract or to withdraw, assumes the role of the injurer, independently of whether it actually acts upon its impulse (e.g. by partially withdrawing from its obligations) or not. Equivalently, the role of the victim is that of the player affected by the other party's desire to modify or withdraw. Both terms are non-judgmental and are free of welfare implications to the players (a victim is not necessarily worse off by assuming that role). For the ease of reading, and to avoid misunderstandings, the injurer throughout this study will be referred to as "he," while the victim carries the personal pronoun "she."

[16]  The convex curvature of line H&R in Figure 2.1 is intuitive: the curve is flat and equal to zero at $C^N$, where the contracted cooperation is equivalent to the situation without agreement. The higher the agreed-upon level of cooperation (i.e. the higher the *ex ante* commitment), the more a one-time defection pays off – increasing marginal returns from defection. The convexity of the curve is not necessary. Bagwell and Staiger (2002b, p. 102) supply some arguments in favor of this curvature for the case of a trade agreement/contract.

[17]  Alternative (less drastic) punishment rules are of course possible, for example the "tit-for-tat" strategy of enforcement, where the victim of a defection retaliates for exactly one round and then returns to cooperative behavior. It is sometimes argued that tit-for-tat retaliation produces more stable outcomes than the grim-trigger strategy (e.g. Axelrod 1984; Axelrod and Keohane 1986; Oye 1986). For the situation at hand, however, the retaliation strategy chosen by the victim, or agreed to by both signatories, is inconsequential, since it may be assumed that the nature of resumed cooperation is linked to the history of players' choices. On the latter issue, see e.g. Ludema (2001).

disutility (opportunity costs of reprisal), that is, the expected discounted value of future cooperation that the injurer foregoes by exiting the cooperation game.[18] The discounted value of cooperation is the sum of all future per-period gains from having concluded a contract (as opposed to having no contract at all).[19]

The potential defector balances the short-term incentive to cheat against the long-term cost incurred by such cheating, once the victim retaliates by suspending cooperation indefinitely: gains and losses approach zero if the contract stipulates little cooperation, since this practically replicates the non-cooperative Nash outcome. If the contract specifies greater cooperation (levels above $C^N$), short-term defection gains and long-term opportunity costs begin to rise. As the agreed-upon cooperation increases, the costs of reprisal first exceed the hit-and-run gains from one-time defection. The two curves intersect at $C^{SE}$, which can be defined as the most-cooperative level of concessions that can be sustained through self-enforcement. Beyond this point, the gains from one-time infringement of the agreement exceed all the compiled future gains of cooperation. It is thus evident that it would be foolish (irrational) for the injuring party to comply beyond a cooperation level of $C^{SE}$ due to its binding incentive constraint. Anticipating the injurer's behavior, it is equally irrational for the victim to agree to a more cooperative deal, even though its welfare-optimal level of cooperation would equally be $C^{opt}$ (due to symmetry of the players). Hence, without a central enforcer only the range between $C^N$ and $C^{SE}$ is self-enforceable, yielding an additional utility in the range between $U^N$ and $U^{SE}$. The levels of cooperation and the according utility range of the contract that are achievable under self-enforcement are represented by the grey area.

---

[18] Indeed, the defector's expected disutility from defection is identical to the sum of forfeited future benefits from cooperation that the injurer forsakes by having defected once and therefore having prompted the grim-trigger response.

[19] The concave curvature of the S-E curve in Figure 2.1 is intuitive: more cooperation in every round is beneficial up to some optimal point $C^{opt}$. After that point additional commitments in the form of more cooperation display declining (possibly even negative) returns. This is so, for example, because of a loss of freedom and sovereignty caused by overly zealous levels of cooperation. Bagwell and Staiger (2002b, p. 102) give the intuition for concavity of long-term cooperation gains in the case of trade agreements. The S-E curve also goes through the origin: the more the negotiated commitment approaches the no-contract level, the smaller are the future gains from cooperation.

To understand a second mechanism of enforcement,[20] take a look at the line C&C in Figure 2.1: if there is a central enforcer – a Court to detect/verify an infringement, as well as Coppers (policemen) to enforce the court's verdict – that is capable of and willing to implement the contract under pain of penalty, contracting parties conclude their agreement in the "shadow of the law."[21] Under these circumstances parties can agree to a more far-reaching cooperation (between $C^N$ and $C^{law}$), because any defection will immediately be discovered and punished. For the injurer, punishment results in a utility amounting to the difference between the H&R gain and the C&C punishment, which is negative everywhere below the cut-off point $C^{law}$. Hence, third-party enforcement can yield a higher mutual utility than the self-enforcement mechanism ($U^{law}$ instead of $U^{SE}$).[22]

Now consider Figure 2.2. It demonstrates that the efficient enforcement range is substantially dependent on both enforcement capacity and enforceability. Under a self-enforcement regime a victim's enforcement capacity is directly dependent on the injurer's time-value,[23] the victim's enactment costs of retaliation,[24] as well as the latter's general ability to cause (political, economic, social, emotional) harm to the injurer. Weak enforcement factors may skew the injurer's opportunity-cost curve downwards (shown as the move from the dotted S-E to the solid S-E' in Figure 2.2).

---

[20] Other kinds of enforcement than the grim trigger and external punishment are not considered here. They are just variants or combinations of the two mechanisms explained.

[21] Think of line C&C in Figure 2.1 as a liquidated damages clause stipulating that the victim is entitled to a flat-rate amount of $X$ units of money whenever the other party reneges from its contract obligations. Alternatively, suppose a judge applies a law protecting the victim party and is assisted by a policeman who gives effect to the verdict. The shadow of the law effectively stretches from $C^N$ to $C^{law}$, i.e. over the entire contracting space. Beyond $C^{law}$, however, no contract is probable, since the gains of defection are more attractive than taking the losses of legal punishment.

[22] However, this does not mean that the shadow of the law is always able to safeguard an optimal mutual cooperation $C^{opt}$, possibly because the law cannot enforce every little detail of the contract.

[23] The injurer's time-value, or discount factor, describes how much the injurer is interested in the current period as opposed to future periods. In the extreme case in which the injurer is only interested in today's utility and not at all in the future, a grim trigger strategy has no deterrent effect. Therefore, no agreement would be signed.

[24] Any costs connected with enacting a sanction mitigate the victim's power (and willingness) to retaliate. It is sometimes argued that a grim-trigger strategy is costly to apply for the victim, since it is not only the defecting party that foregoes future benefits of cooperation, but also the punishing party (Dixit 1987; Downs and Rocke 1995; Klimenko, Ramey, and Watson 2002).

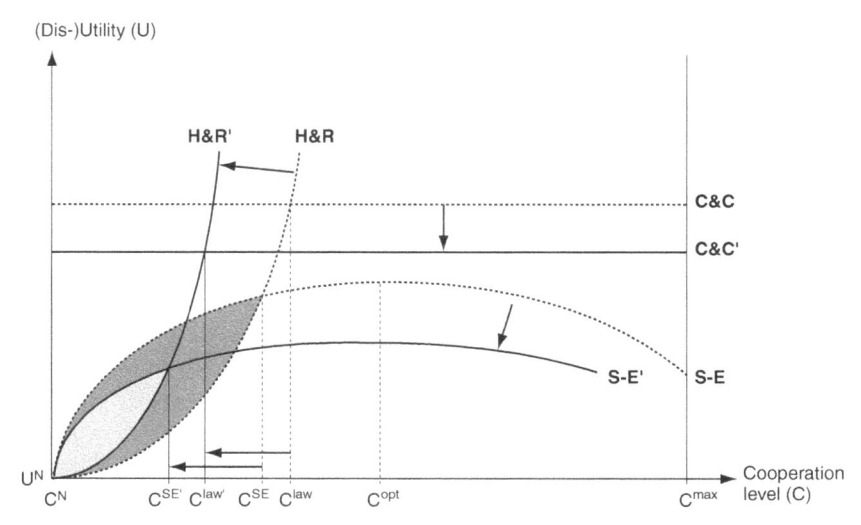

**Figure 2.2**    Importance of enforcement capacity and enforceability in contracts
Source: Keck and Schropp 2008, Figure 2
Note: The general set-up of this chart is analogous to Figure 2.1. The graph illustrates
the impact of weak enforcement capabilities on players' willingness to enter into
contractual obligations. Spurious enforceability skews the H&R curve to the left.
Inadequate enforcement capacity on the part of the victim skews the self-enforcement
curve S-E and the C&C curve down. Insufficient enforcement (intersection of H&R'
and S-E' curves) results in less self-enforceable contracts (lightly shaded, instead of
darkly shaded area) and deficient third party enforcement (intersection of H&R' and
C&C' instead of H&R and C&C).

Enforceability plays a role in shaping the short-term hit-and-run
curve: insufficient observability, verifiability, and quantifiability make
one-time defection more attractive (the H&R curve gets skewed to the
left, as illustrated in the move from the dotted line to the solid H&R'
curve). For every level of cooperation, defection pays off more due to a
higher defection utility.

The result of inefficient enforcement depicted in Figure 2.2 is a
smaller self-enforcement range. Therefore, less cooperative contracts
are possible in the first place in comparison to a situation of full
enforcement: whereas the intersection of the dotted H&R and S-E
curves produces a larger enforcement range (the darkly shaded area),
the scenario with insufficient enforcement (intersection of H&R' and

S-E$'$ curves) results in much less enforceable contracts (lightly shaded area). Moving away from the self-enforcement case, enforcement capacity and enforceability are equally crucial for contracts concluded in the shadow of the law: when "court-and-copper" enforcement capacity is weak, the dotted C&C line shifts down to the solid C&C$'$ line. Imperfect detection and conviction of contractual deviation causes a leftward shift of the H&R curve. Hence, under weak third-party enforcement, the possible contract range shifts to the left from $C^{law}$ in Figure 2.1 to $C^{law'}$.

Figures 2.1 and 2.2 are meant to illustrate three important points about contractual enforcement. First, the level of commitment or cooperation that a contracting party is willing to undergo is crucially dependent on its ability to enforce the terms of the agreement. A party that rationally anticipates the difficulties of punishing defective behavior by its contracting partner is not willing to make excessive *ex ante* cooperation commitments, even though it ideally would want to do so.

Secondly, it is the *most reluctant transactor*, i.e. the party with the lowest enforcement capabilities, that will set the terms of the deal (such as the level of mutual trade liberalization, cf. Ethier 2001b). Any mutual deal (if not coercive) is decided by the party least willing to give concessions. The most reluctant liberalizer (victim or injurer) can effectively decide on the common level of exchange: neither will a weak victim concede to "deeper" cooperation than it can sustain, nor will its stronger contract partners give additional concessions for free.[25]

Thirdly, the schematic representation above shows that (self-)enforcement is a *process* much more than it is an *act* of punishment. It is a lengthy dispute activity consisting of a litigation/adjudication phase and a punishment/remediation phase. Enforcement is a function of both enforceability and enforcement capacity. Whenever either aspect is deficient, contracting parties react by scaling down their ambitions; their willingness to cooperate shrinks. Having all the enforcement

---

[25] Another way of saying this is that a mutual deal is struck at *that* level of cooperation where the first contracting party hits its *participation constraint* (Bagwell and Staiger 2002a, chapter 4). This constraint is then binding for all parties, since any deviation from that cooperation level (even if other signatories would favor it) necessarily brings Pareto deterioration for at least one of the signatories. If parties are uncertain about their future roles and the frequency of being victim or injurer, they must assess the probability of becoming victim or injurer *ex ante*.

capacity in the world may not help the victim much if the injurer cannot be proven guilty of his defection from the letter (or the spirit) of the contract.

The fact that enforceability is an equally important ingredient of enforcement, as is enforcement capacity, has unfortunately been neglected by contract theory. The self-enforcement literature usually conveniently presupposes a complete or at least a comprehensive contract,[26] one where every signatory knows at all times what constitutes right and what is wrong behavior, and is able to immediately observe and punish defection. Difficulties in observing defection, the presence of a violation investigation, and issues of litigation are notably neglected.[27] Those models therefore reduce contract enforcement to punishment and remediation – the H&R curve in Figures 2.1 and 2.2 is assumed to be fixed.

Traditional WTO scholarship such as Bagwell and Staiger (1999; 2002b) is no exception to this standard contract theory: as we will show in more detail at p. 149 below, externality-based theories of trade agreements (terms-of-trade school and political externalities school) presuppose a complete contract, and reduce WTO enforcement to remediation. This is due to the rigid set of assumptions that underlie the externality-based models of trade cooperation (see Keck and Schropp 2008, section B). In their basic form, these models largely assume away those imperfections that may occur during the contracting phase and during the performance phase of the trade agreement. That way, these models can afford to focus on enforcement capacity (the shadow of the grim trigger), while disregarding issues of enforceability – verifiability, observability, and quantifiability. Therefore, albeit helpful for carving out a rationale for trade cooperation, those models of trade agreements suppress all real-life problems occurring during and after the conclusion of a multilateral contract (cf. WTO 2007, section II.C.1). This omission of dealing with issues of enforceability is consequential for questions of contractual incompleteness in general, as we will show in the next chapter.

---

[26] On the distinction between complete and comprehensive contracts, see at p. 85 below.

[27] This is due to the rigid set of assumptions that usually underlie the models of cooperation, namely a stationary environment and zero transaction costs. Economic theories of contracts largely single out one, and ignore (i.e. model away) all other real-life imperfections that may occur during the contracting phase (i.e. before the contract is signed) and/or during the performance phase of the trade agreement. This renders unnecessary any treatment of disputes, enforceability, and the need for courts.

### 2.1.4   Concluding remarks on the definition of contracts

To conclude this section on the nature of contracts, four important observations can be derived from the above definition of a contract.

First, contracts differ from simple coordination activities, since contracts solve a problem. Whereas in some coordination games parties can easily join forces so as to reap mutual transaction efficiencies, or synergies, contracting parties have partially conflicting interests, namely those of cheating the other party for their own benefit.[28] Contracts are thus largely concluded with the objective of hedging against misdemeanor, and to forestall (or limit) the opportunistic behavior of signatories.

Secondly, commitment is valuable (Hviid 1999, p. 48). The *ex ante* effect of contracts is of immense significance: commitment effectuates a present transfer, not of goods and services, but of *rights* and *duties*. Commitment can be assumed to have a value over and above the pure spot-contract or transaction value, and is hence socially useful. A transfer of rights and duties produces efficiency gains in its own right, independently of whether it is efficient to actually carry out the promise *ex post* or not (Craswell 1999, p. 18). The more effectively opportunism is contained and transaction efficiency reaped, the bigger is the exchanged "good," i.e. the higher is each party's *ex ante* willingness to cooperate and to engage in an exchange in the first place.[29] The scale and scope of each party's *ex ante* commitments (i.e. the size of the promise) are thus a direct function of the other party's inclination and possibilities to defect, which is equivalent to saying that it is

---

[28] A commonly utilized distinction in the structure of strategic games is that between collaboration problems and coordination problems (Martin 1993; Stein 1983). Briefly, in collaboration games (such as the prisoners' dilemma), parties have partially conflicting interests, namely those of acting opportunistically by cheating the other party. Opportunism is not a problem in the simplest versions of coordination games (such as the "battle-of-the-sexes" game). Coordinating parties join forces so as to reap mutual transaction efficiencies or synergies, and no party gains from defecting. We will have more to say on the collaboration/coordination distinction at pp. 54, 160, 189 below.

[29] For example, if I know that the defection risk of my contracting partner is close to zero, I will be willing to trade more bushels of wheat at an agreed price and a specified point in time. I might even add bushels of oats to the deal. However, if I must assume that my contracting partner will probably defect at my expense, I will be hesitant to trade my entire harvest with him. The lower the risk of being cheated, the larger will be the size of the *ex ante* commitment and the more valuable will be the promise.

a function of the enforceability and enforcement capacity aspects surrounding the deal.

Thirdly, issues of assurance and enforcement are responsible for a good deal of the complexity and bargaining costs of contracts: whereas the motivation for cooperating is usually quite trivial (building a house, performing a series of duties as a manager, conducting R&D activities), it is much more difficult and time-consuming to craft contractual obligations so as to curb potential opportunism and to maximize mutual enforceability/enforcement capacity. Depending on the special situation at hand, a contract may be shaped more by assurance or by motivational issues. When the risk of opportunism is small (such as in the contract: "I will buy a bushel of wheat from my cousin John Doe for $3 tomorrow"), the assurance aspect of the contract is less salient. Increased attention can be focused on the substance of the contractual exchange (here: the quality of the wheat, or specifics of the delivery). Those kinds of contracts then resemble *coordination* rather than *collaboration* accords.

In other contractual relations, however, the underlying transaction is trivial, but the assurance aspect is central. Correspondingly, enforcement provisions assume a prominent role in the contract. Examples are incentive alignment contracts that economic principal-agent theory frequently deals with. Pure incentive-alignment contracts are nearly exclusively concerned with specifying contracting goals of the agreement, i.e. establishing the rules of the game so as to achieve maximum mutual assurance for the contracting parties.

Fourthly, the logic of joint welfare maximization of contracting parties is at the core of every contract. All rational choice contracts obey a strict Paretian logic (but see note 3). A contract is a Pareto-superior transaction (Krauss 1999, p. 783), or at least one which every signatory hopes to benefit from (given his/her available information). Each signatory maximizes his/her expected value of cooperation, given the present contextual constraints. Rational actors can safely be assumed to enter into a contractual relationship only if doing so results in an improvement of their expected short-, medium- or long-term utility. Since all sides of the deal are rational utility maximizers, it is in the interest of all contracting parties to maximize the joint gains from trade, that is, to enable them to attain the "Pareto frontier" (Schwartz and Sykes 1996; 2002b; Scott 1987). A contract on the Pareto frontier has the property that no alternative contract can increase the utility for one signatory without decreasing any other contracting party's utility.

## 2.2    Basics of contracting: creating rules

Every contract has four key stages: contract formation,[30] contract design ("rule-making" or "contracting"), contract performance,[31] and contract enforcement (cf. Masten 1999). It is in the contract design phase that signatories determine how their substantive goals will be achieved in the most effective and efficient way – they concoct the best possible governance structure.

Pursuant to the seminal 1972 article by Calabresi and Melamed, scholars realized that contracting parties are "making their own law" by assigning themselves residual ownership rights, or "entitlements": signatories mold cooperative commitments into a set of mutual rights and obligations that capture, as unambiguously as possible, the nature, extent, and limits of the agreed-upon entitlements.[32] To that end, contracting parties generally undertake three distinct phases of contract design in which they (i) define the number and nature of traded entitlements; (ii) define entitlement protection rules and remedies; and (iii) lay down enforcement rules in case of contractual defection by one party or the other (Calabresi and Melamed 1972; Pauwelyn 2006; Trachtman 2006).

### 2.2.1    *Primary rules of contracting: exchange of entitlements*

Contracting parties first define the "primary rules" of their contractual exchange. Signatories assign residual rights of ownership, or "entitlements"

---

[30] Contract formation is the stage at which two or more parties convene to assess their motivation, scope for cooperation, level of ambition, and the objective to be pursued by the mutual interaction. Contractors lay out their basic contractual intentions by loosely formalizing their substantive goals.

[31] The contract performance phase is the stage at which the agreed-to transaction occurs, and the commitments are effectuated/converted into the promised transactions. Alternatively, it is the phase where intra- or extra-contractual defection occurs. Illegitimate behavior may then trigger the enforcement phase, which can include dispute settlement/litigation and punishment as substages.

[32] Calabresi and Melamed (1972, p. 1090) characterize the nature of contractual entitlements as mutual commitments that allocate ownership rights between signatories within a specific area of contractual exchange. Entitlements are "social compacts" that define which party will be entitled to prevail in case of conflict: an entitlement to make noise or an entitlement to have silence, an entitlement to pollute vs. an entitlement to breathe fresh air, an entitlement to trade or to restrict trade, an entitlement to non-intervention or to respect human rights, etc. Entitlements give rise to mutual obligations. "These obligations in turn cause people to behave in accordance with the compact in particular cases regardless of the existence of a dominant force" (*ibid.*).

to each other.[33] Entitlements are the essence of a contract and are formulated in the form of one or a bundle of mutual rights and obligations. Some issues around contractual entitlements are especially noteworthy.

**Substantive vs. auxiliary entitlements**    Substantive entitlements qualify the contractual intent, or the cooperative gains from trade pursued by the contract.[34] Substantive entitlements circumscribe the level of co-operation which each party is willing to concede to.[35]

Auxiliary entitlements specify ways in which the substantive goals can ultimately be achieved in the most efficient and effective manner (Macaulay 1985). Auxiliary entitlements are non-substantive rules in that they do not follow any independent contractual intent. They safeguard, facilitate, and ameliorate the contractual interaction, such as procedural requirements and timelines, codes of conduct (anticircumvention rules, transparency guidelines, reporting obligations, rules of voting, exit, or entry to the contract), exceptions or amendments to substantive entitlements, and other organizational details.[36] Auxiliary entitlements are geared towards increasing transaction efficiencies, reducing transaction costs, and improving observability, verifiability, and quantifiability.

**Bilateral vs. multilateral entitlements**    Not all entitlements concern all signatories. In a contract with many signatories, some entitlements are owed reciprocally (bilaterally), while others are owed to the entire membership, or *erga omnes partes*. For reciprocal entitlements the rights of one signatory constitute the obligations of the other. A multilateral

---

[33] Residual ownership or property rights are referred to by L&E and economics scholars as the "individual's ability to directly consume the services of an asset, or to consume it indirectly through exchange" (Barzel 1997, p. 3).

[34] Substantive entitlements define the substance of the transaction (prices, quantities, dates, and other transaction details; see Masten 1999, p. 33). Take a simple fixed-price contract, for example: both parties agree to grant the buyer an entitlement to own a product and the seller an entitlement to a certain amount of money.

[35] As pointed out before (see note 11 above), commitment is usually not a binary issue, but one of degrees. Take the example of an employment contract: although the employee obliges himself to work to the benefit of the employer, he does not wish to put all his time and effort into the contract. Also, he will promise his cooperation in some fields, but not in those, say, that involve illegal or immoral conduct.

[36] In the international context, such an organizational entitlement would be the establishment of an international organization that supports the contract and lends credence to the parties' contractual endeavors.

entitlement charges all of the contracting parties with an obligation to behave in a certain way, whereby the entitlement is not exchanged bilaterally, but owned by the entire membership.

**Dependent vs. general auxiliary entitlements**   Some auxiliary entitlements have a limited application scope; they are second-order obligations which are "pegged" to, or dependent on, a single substantive entitlement. We shall call this type "dependent auxiliary entitlements." Other auxiliary entitlements apply to multiple substantive entitlements ("basic auxiliary entitlements"). More complex settings are conceivable in which there are auxiliary entitlements of tertiary and lower order (e.g. an exception to a procedural rule).

**Level of detail**   Both substantive and auxiliary entitlements come in various levels of detail. For example, parties may grant entitlements to pollute, or to be free from pollution. They may, however, craft more meticulous covenants which define under what circumstances (and with what magnitude and effect) pollution will be allowed (Pauwelyn 2006, p. 7). In this case the entitlement "environmental pollution," owned by one party or the other, is broken down into more sensible portions. If parties so decide, the ownership to the entitlement may change.[37]

**Balance of substantive and auxiliary entitlements**   It is probably fair to say that the more complete a contract, the more and finer grained substantive entitlements it provides. Also, the ratio of substantive to auxiliary entitlements can be expected to be higher, the more complete a contract proves to be. Many real-life contracts consist of a set of very basic substantive entitlements and many auxiliary entitlements that lend additional structure to the contractual exchange. The less detailed an entitlement, the more incomplete the contract can be assumed to be (more on that below).

---

[37] A more fine-tuned contract may read: "If polluter Y stays under the legal minimum of 50 mg/m$^3$ then he has the entitlement to pollute. If Y pollutes between 50 and 100 mg/m$^3$ then he may do so, but must pay compensation to X for the damage caused. If Y wishes to exceed 100 mg/m$^3$, he must buy this entitlement from X. Any amount exceeding 250 mg/m$^3$ is prohibited." Thus, the entitlement to pollution switches from the polluter Y to the affected party X with increasing intensity of contamination. Finer-grained contract language, however, comes at non-trivial costs of contracting (Horn, Maggi, and Staiger 2006).

**Multiple entitlements**    Few, if any, contracts assign just one entitlement per signatory. Indeed, perhaps all real-life contracts encompass multiple entitlements (implicitly or explicitly), even if they only exchange a single set of substantive entitlements.[38] More complicated contracts affect more than one specific entitlement, and hence comprise a multitude of issue areas, tasks, and responsibilities.[39] In fact, the best way to understand any contract is to view it as a bundle of rights and obligations mutually consented to by all contracting parties. As we will see later on, it is important for the researcher examining a certain contract to detangle this bundle of entitlements, and to split up the contract into its constituent parts.

### 2.2.2    Secondary rules of contracting: entitlement protection

The second concern of contracting parties ("secondary rules") is to allocate *residual decision rights* that organize or prohibit *ex post* behavior during the contract performance stage. In laying down the secondary rules, parties define how each entitlement should be protected, and agree upon the adequate intra-contractual remedy if entitlements are allowed to be transferred *ex post*. Residual decision rights are different from initial entitlements, since they lay down how, and how strongly, the initial entitlement choice is to be protected from *ex post* discretion in the course of the contractual relationship. In short, the secondary rules are rules of flexibility, escape, and remedies.

Three generic types of entitlement protection are noted in the literature: inalienability, liability, and property rules of protection.

If entitlement transfer (to take, sell, or trade residual rights) is considered inefficient or immoral, a rule of inalienability (also termed

---

[38] A single-issue contract touches upon one entitlement and leaves all the other entitlements of each transactor unaffected.

[39] Think of a simple employment contract between a shop-clerk and the owner. Principal and agent exchange much more than the promises "work effort" for "money." Issues such as perquisites, social insurance, leisure, health benefits, continuing education, responsibility, job rotation, etc. are all additional promises on the employer's side. The employee, on the other hand, makes commitments over and above his job description, such as filling in for colleagues, working overtime, handling goods with accuracy and diligence, embracing responsibility, being honest, training new colleagues, planning the yearly Christmas party, etc. In short, many more rights and obligations are of relevance in a real-life contractual relationship than one might think, many of which are not even put down in writing. The point is that there are more than a single pair of entitlements (work effort and salary) affected in a seemingly simple contract.

"mandatory specific performance") is agreed upon. The protection of the initial entitlement allocation is then called absolute, and a taking of the entitlement is strictly prohibited.[40] Rules of inalienability mandate unconditional specific performance of the contractual rules.

If contracting parties generally consent to the possibility of trading or reallocating entitlements *ex post*, they determine whether to protect initial entitlements by means of a liability rule (LR) or a property rule (PR) of entitlement protection (or a mix thereof). Under a pure LR, one party (the taker or injurer[41]: he) has the option to take away parts of the other party's (the owner or victim: she) entitlement unilaterally, i.e. without the owner's prior assent. The taker can engage in unilateral appropriation (which is an expropriation of the holder of the entitlement) under the condition that he compensates the owner for damages suffered in some fashion or other – usually by paying a previously specified exercise price.

Under a property rule of protection both parties are under a "specific performance duty," i.e. a strict obligation to respect the initial entitlement distribution. In this case, the taker is directed to perform, and a failure to do so is punished so severely that he would never prefer violating the order to complying with his obligation. However, a potential taker can buy off the owner's entitlement through renegotiations. He can still avoid his commitments by securing permission from the owner, usually by paying for it. Whenever the parties come to an agreement, the owner cedes her entitlement and sells it to the taker – the transfer is thus bilateral.

A rule of entitlement protection must in all cases be accompanied by a corresponding remedy rule. Parties thereby agree on how "costly" intra-contractual non-performance by the injurer should be. There is a continuum of remedies ranging from a zero-damage payment to coercive (infinitely high) damages (Mahoney 1999). In between lie the most important damage remedies: the *restitution* remedy re-establishes the

---

[40] Political rights are an example of inalienable rights that cannot be traded: it is not legally possible to sell off your vote in a ballot.

[41] As was mentioned in Chapter 1, notes 6 and 15 above, we define "victim" and "injurer" as *roles*, not as *conditions*. This is to say that any contracting party experiencing some form of contractual regret or doubt automatically assumes the role of the "injurer" independently of whether it acts on that regret (e.g. by exercising a liability-type opt-out, engaging in renegotiations, or violating the respective agreement) or not. Equivalently, the role of the "victim" is that of the actor affected by the other party's regret or doubt. Both terms are non-judgmental and are free of welfare implications for the players (a victim is not necessarily worse off by assuming that role).

*status quo ante* the contract. The *reliance* measure obliges the injurer to re-establish the victim's *status quo ante* the "breach."[42] Expectation damages place the victim in as good a position as she would have been in had the injurer performed. The expectation remedy represents the replacement value of the deal and acts as a complete insurance policy to the victim: *ex post*, expectation damages make the victim indifferent between the injurer's performance and default. Next, *efficiency* damages are expectation damages plus the efficiency gains from non-performance (should there be any). Negotiated remedies can in principle lie anywhere between zero and coercive remedies. Their size, however, crucially depends on the underlying rule of entitlement protection.[43] Not all combinations of escape and remedy rules make sense: inalienability rules are best adhered to by coercive penalties (prison, forfeit, liquidated damages, etc.). Property-rule protection is logically accompanied by bilaterally negotiated remedies. Liability-rule protection is usually accompanied by expectation damages, a combination sometimes (unfortunately) referred to as "efficient breach."[44]

Technically, secondary rules of contracting are formulated as *dependent* auxiliary entitlements, i.e. as norms that are pegged to a specific substantive or auxiliary entitlement. A single basic entitlement can be protected by various rules of entitlement protection, whereby different

---

[42] Reliance presumably affords the victim a larger amount than the restitution rule of damage, since prior transaction efficiencies have to be accounted for. The longer the contractual relationship has been going on, the more restitution and reliance measures differ.

[43] Under an LR of entitlement protection that allows the injurer to opt out whenever he desires, negotiated remedies can potentially be close to zero. Under a PR, however, negotiated damages are strictly in between the expectation and the efficiency measures. The rational victim will not settle at a loss (and expectation damages put her in a position where she is exactly indifferent between the injurer's performance and his non-performance), and ideally would want to capture all the injurer's efficiency gains from non-performance for her willingness to "let go" of her contractual rights.

[44] It is evident by now that the nomenclature "efficient breach" for an LR-cum-expectation damages arrangement of protection is doubly misleading. First, as mentioned, if a contract specifically permits non-performance to occur, it is imprecise to speak of a "breach" of rules. Secondly, the term does not resolve the more vital question of *how* to organize non-performance efficiently – as a liability rule or a property rule. Efficient adjustment to changing circumstances and unforeseen contingencies is notably possible under both LR and PR: "To be sure, it is possible for efficient breach to occur with other remedial options [than the LR]. In particular, if specific performance is the remedy for breach a party wishing to breach can always approach the other party and attempt to negotiate a release of performance," as Sykes (2000, p. 353) points out.

protection rules come into effect under different circumstances, contingencies, or actions (see the example in note 37).

As will be shown in the next chapter, signatories' choice for entitlement protection becomes an interesting topic in incomplete contracts, that is, in those situations where the original contract contains gaps, and where *ex post* non-performance can be welfare-enhancing to both (or all) signatories to the contract. The more difficult the initial contracting context (number of traded entitlements, level of entitlement refinement, number of signatories, etc.), and the more dynamic the environment surrounding a contract, the more important – and difficult – the choice of entitlement protection rules proves to be.

### 2.2.3   *Tertiary rules of contracting: enforcement of entitlements*

After having delineated intra-contractual, permissible behavior, transactors then have to decide how to sanction extra-contractual uncooperative behavior should it nevertheless occur. These tertiary rules concern what can be called *back-up* entitlement protection: enforcement mechanisms and procedures taken in response to the illegitimate taking or destruction of an entitlement. Hereby, the parties consent to how the previously agreed-upon assignment and the rules for transfer of entitlements can or should be protected against unilateral defection. The task for the contracting parties is to make sure that a protection of rights is enforceable, and that punishment is not an empty threat. Enforcement capacity and enforceability clearly play a large role: depending on how easily the contractual rules can be thwarted through opportunistic behavior, parties are more or less willing to cooperate to the full extent. If the original primary commitments cannot be enforced, parties will scale down their original level of cooperation to a level that can be sustained by the enforcement tools at hand.[45] As Pauwelyn (2006) points out, the question of contract enforcement is especially relevant in the international realm, where usually no supra-national enforcer exists and abidance by the rules of the game cannot be taken for granted.

---

[45] Eventually, in the course of the contract design phase, one or more contracting parties may scale back their initial level of ambition. This is precisely the application of some of the last section's insights: if the governance structure is faulty (due to, say, imprecise or ambiguous language), or if one party is aware that it cannot safeguard a certain level of enforcement, it will have to reduce the level of cooperation it is willing to muster.

In summary: the outflow of the contract design phase is a set of enforceable mutual commitments in the form of a bundle of traded entitlements and entitlement protection rules. Each party knows its rights and its obligations and has given its consent to sanctions for deviating behavior.[46] The contract design phase is the most important contracting stage, since the quality of the negotiated governance structure sets the level of ambition *ex ante*, and determines signatories' behavioral patterns in the subsequent phases, namely the contract performance and enforcement phases – all sorts of *ex post* problems and challenges have to be anticipated and the governance structure adapted accordingly. This implies that the originally intended level of cooperation may have to be modified depending on how feasible or risky the attainment of the transaction goals are in light of the difficulties in later stages of contracting.

Depending on the contractual context (number of players, complexity of the exchange, longevity, market imperfections, transaction costs, information asymmetries, etc.), parties regularly need to engage in trade-offs between what is desirable and what is feasible. In particular, parties have to anticipate and adapt to environmental eventualities ("contingencies") and ensuing opportunistic party actions – and how such misdemeanor shall/can be sanctioned. As we will show in Chapter 3.2, contractual design efforts geared towards preventing opportunistic behavior can take place either by explicit wording or by contractual default rules. Since rule-making is a costly enterprise, rational parties have to engage in another trade-off: between the costs of writing contractual contingencies and the expected gain generated therefrom (Battigalli and Maggi 2002; Horn, Maggi, and Staiger 2005; 2006).

### 2.2.4   Mixed regimes of entitlement and entitlement protection

An important aspect of contracting is that of mixed regimes. We have so far stated that contract entitlements "belong" to one or the other contracting party (the injurer or the victim), and that entitlement protection is organized as a liability, property, or inalienability rule. We did so for expositional convenience only. In real life we often see mixed entitlements, and systems of mixed entitlement protection.

---

[46] Commitments are frequently implicit and not written down. Nevertheless, they have been given the consent of both parties.

## Multi-entitlement contracts and divided entitlements

Real-life contracts oftentimes feature regulations of entitlements divided between contracting parties (so-called "co-ownership"; see Kaplow and Shavell 1996b, p. 749): entitlements are not fully owned by one transacting party or the other, but are in fact shared. Think of the aforementioned example of environmental pollution: victim Y may think she has an entitlement to be "free from pollution." In reality, however, firms are allowed to pollute the environment within prescribed limits: otherwise they would not pursue their production activity. The prescribed pollution limits, or technological requirements, are expected to balance the harmfulness of pollution against the costs of its prevention.

What Kaplow and Shavell refer to as co-ownership or divided entitlement is in fact little more than a more detailed (and more accurate) definition of mutual rights and obligations. To fix the mutual balance of rights and obligations, and to carve out entitlements more finely, clear and unambiguous entitlement language has to be agreed on by contracting parties. The finer the determination of mutual entitlements, the more detailed, nuanced, and accurate the entitlement protection rules have to be.[47]

As ready alternatives to explicit entitlement definitions, contracts often provide for conditionality clauses, consisting of enactment thresholds and limitations of scope. The level of conditionality is often determined in the form of a set of prerequisites that have to be fulfilled before the contracting parties may engage in *ex post* discretion.[48] This high level of prerequisites bestows significant negotiation power, and dispute sway, on potential victims. Alternatively (or additionally) to a high enactment threshold, the scope of application of *ex post* discretion may be restricted: a measure may only be enacted once, only on Fridays, only for a limited amount of time, or only vis-à-vis a certain subset of signatories, etc.[49]

---

[47] As we stated at note 37 above, finer-grained entitlement language may bring more nuanced ownership rights.

[48] A pertinent example of a hybrid entitlement protection somewhere in between a simple liability rule and a property rule is GATT Art. XIX. Under the safeguards clause a potential injurer is faced with a substantial threshold of application: for a safeguard measure to be imposed, an enacting country must show that "i) as a result of *unforeseen development;* ii) imports in *increased quantities*; iii) have *caused* or threatened to cause; iv) *serious injury* to the domestic industry producing the v) *like product*" (see Howse and Mavroidis 2003, p. 686; Roitinger 2004, p. 102).

[49] High levels of prerequisites and restrictions on application scope may, however, entail non-trivial problems, as will be detailed below in the discussion on contingency measures of flexibility (p. 88 below).

### Rules of divided entitlement protection

Single-entitlement contracts are a rare animal. Realistically, multiple entitlements are traded in real-life contracts. Finding one-size-fits-all solutions to protect *all* traded entitlements with the same entitlement protection rule is highly unlikely. Just as the nature, context, and level of detail of entitlements vary, so will the appropriate mechanisms of protection. Signatories are hence better off protecting each exchanged entitlement by a (set of) unique rule(s) of entitlement protection. Therefore, a mixed system of entitlement protection seems the logical consequence of multi-entitlement contracts. Thus, we can expect bundles of entitlements that together constitute a contract to be protected by a mixture of the possible default rules, namely the alienability, property, or liability rule.

Closely connected to this point and the previous issue of co-ownership of entitlements is another important aspect of real-life contracting: divided entitlement protection. Many entitlements are not protected against intra-contractual non-performance by one simple liability rule whereby the injurer is permitted to cause harm at any time, provided he compensates the victim for the damage done (or a court's best estimate of it). Kaplow and Shavell (1996b), and Ayres and Talley (1995b) have shown that liability and inalienability are two points along a spectrum. In fact, inalienability can be understood as a special case of liability that uses fixed *ex ante* estimates and prohibitive damages. A property rule, in turn, is nothing but a special case of an LR with varying damage awards.[50] Consequently, there is a considerable grey area of divided entitlement protection. To see this, consider Figure 2.3.

The horizontal axis in Figure 2.3 depicts which party enjoys the power of *ex post* discretion, or in other words, who "owns" a contractual gap (not: who owns the entitlement). Post-contractual discretion can thereby reside with the injurer, with the victim, with both players (divided entitlement protection), or with none (in case of inalienability). The vertical axis represents the size of contractual remedies payable for the

---

[50] "[W]ere we to allow damages to be any quantum, then 'liability' rules and property rules would no longer be distinct: ... The conventional liability rule that we emphasized is the rule with damages equal to courts' best estimate of harm ... a liability rule with very high damages is equivalent to property rule protection of victims, and a liability rule with damages of zero is equivalent to property rule protection of injurers" (Kaplow and Shavell 1996b, pp. 724, 754).

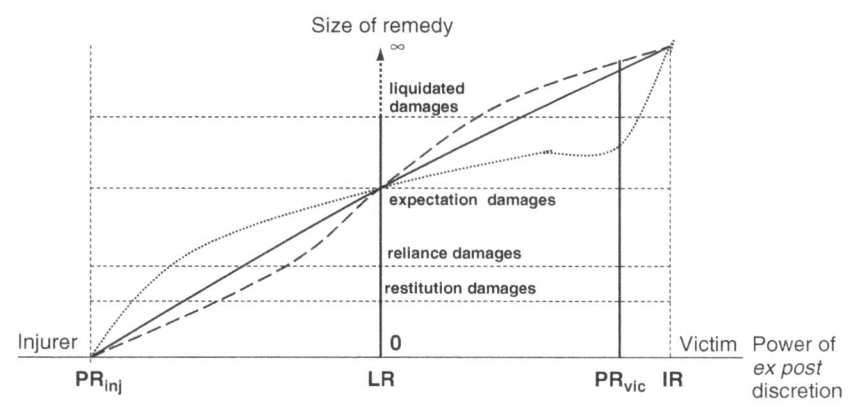

**Figure 2.3**    Divided entitlement protection: points along a continuum
Note: The horizontal axis represents the power of *ex post* discretion, which can lie with the victim, or the injurer, or with neither of them. Property rule (PR) can be granted to the injurer ($PR_{inj}$) or to the victim ($PR_{vic}$); LR is "liability rule"; IR is "inalienability rule." The vertical axis maps the size of remedies, which can range from zero to infinitely high. The curvature of the graphs is of no importance, and as such three variants are shown.

exercise of *ex post* non-performance, ranging from zero to infinitely high amounts. The curvature and progression of the remedy graph is inconsequential here, because signatories usually establish a single point on the graph in the contract, where they define a single-entitlement protection rule accompanying a particular contractual entitlement. So, for exposition purposes three possible graphs are shown in the figure. It is important to see that the two ends of the continuum are a property rule (PR) awarded to the injurer and an inalienability rule, respectively. A PR to the injurer is connected to a zero-damage rule of remedy: the victim actually has to buy off the injurer if she wishes to maintain the performance of the contract. An inalienability rule is connected with infinitely high remedies for both parties. A PR to the victim is connected with negotiated remedies: the injurer has to renegotiate his non-performance, or else be obliged to perform as promised. In between the endpoints of the continuum are liability rules (LR) with different amounts of intra-contractual remedies, with the expectation damage measure featuring most prominently here, since it exactly reimburses the victim for her damage (expectation remedies are the "replacement value" of a promise). Hence, we witness contract clauses in which compensation for damages paid by the liable party is systemically short of harm (see the reliance and restitution measures in Figure 2.3). Liability damages can also exceed harm done, in order to add a deterrent effect for future violations (so-called "liquidated damages").[51]

Examining mixed regimes has relevance for the conceptual analysis and for the understanding of particular contractual rules. When considering how property and liability rules are actually applied in real-life contracts, we realize that mixed regimes of entitlement and entitlement protection are much more prevalent than the conventional extremes.

To summarize this section on the basics of contracting: whereas in section 2.1 the "level of cooperation" was treated in the abstract, this section helps to elucidate what actually constitutes the phenomenon of cooperation: a contract consists of a bundle of entitlements, or mutual rules and obligations. These various entitlements combined determine the overall level of contractual commitment, or cooperation. *Ex ante* commitment in an entitlement will vary with the quality of its respective system of entitlement protection and enforcement. The protection of all entitlements is called the "governance structure" of a contract. The more sophisticated the system of entitlement protection, and the more effective the enforcement measures, the higher the signatories' overall level of commitment.

## 2.3    Types of contracts and alternatives to contracting

Contracts (narrowly defined as signed pieces of paper, or broadly defined as any "enforceable commitment over time") are a principal foundation of human interaction. Many different types of contracts exist, and almost as many ways to categorize them. For our purpose we want to distinguish contracts along two dimensions: the underlying problem to be solved by the contract, and the complexity of the agreement.

### 2.3.1    Collaboration vs. coordination

A contract is created to solve a problem.[52] We want to distinguish two sorts of cooperation problems and their inherent strategic game

---

[51] Signatories often opt for the *liquidated damages* measure, which is a contractually fixed (*ex ante* negotiated) indemnity (cf. Mahoney 1999, p. 27). A liquidated damages clause usually refers to a certain sum, or action, that falls due whenever one signatory deviates from its promised behavior (Masten 1999, p. 27).

[52] Without a problem, contracts would be superfluous, and a simple cooperation accord (by handshake or nod) would suffice. Negotiation and "ink costs" would notably be saved.

structures: *collaboration* and *coordination* games.[53] Generally, in co-operation games that display the collaboration *problématique* (examples are the prisoners' dilemma, or the stag hunt game[54]), parties have partially conflicting interests, namely those of acting opportunistically by cheating on the other party. Through the conclusion of a contract, cooperating parties can overcome the problem of mutual defection and welfare-depreciating opportunism.

Opportunism is less of a problem in the simplest versions of coordination games (e.g. the convention to drive on the left or the right side of the road). The problem in these games is distribution. Consider the infamous battle-of-the sexes game:[55] parties have to choose between two cooperative equilibria (whereby each player prefers a different cooperative outcome), but ultimately no party ever gains from defecting. Players can only reap mutual transaction efficiencies if they cooperate. In coordination games the conclusion of a contract (which is, after all, a costly enterprise) would seem superfluous.

However, coordination games are not generally free from disagreement. Whenever applied to a less clinical and more real-life setting than a $2 \times 2$-matrix, coordination over complex issues typically yields a vast amount of self-enforcing equilibria that two or more parties prefer to no agreement at all. But parties are in vivid disagreement on their subjective rankings of the mutually preferable agreement candidates. Different equilibria are thereby favored by different players. Parties must choose collectively one of various welfare-superior equilibria.

---

[53] See note 28 above. There are more nuanced strategic game characterizations (see e.g. Aggarwal and Dupont 1999; 2004; Ostrom 2003; Sandler 1992), which are of little added value here.

[54] The stag hunt is a game which describes a conflict between safety and social cooperation. The game lends its name to a situation described by Jean-Jacques Rousseau in which two riflemen go out on a hunt. Players simultaneously choose whether to hunt a stag or a hare. If an individual hunts down a stag, she must have the cooperation of her partner in order to succeed. An individual can get a hare by herself, but a hare is worth less than a stag. Formally, a stag hunt is a game with two pure strategy Nash equilibria, one being risk dominant, another being payoff dominant (see e.g. Skyrms 2003).

[55] In its simplest form, the battle-of-the-sexes game has the following set-up. Imagine a couple: the husband would most of all like to go to the football game; the wife would like to go to the opera. Both would prefer to go to the same place rather than different ones. If they cannot communicate, where should they go? This game has two pure strategy Nash equilibria, one where both go to the opera and another where both go to the football game. However, note that each of the Nash equilibria is deficient in some way. The two pure strategy Nash equilibria are unfair, one player consistently does better than the other.

This creates tensions and disagreement among the players. Consequently, transactors tend to argue about the distribution of gains from cooperation.[56] A contract can thus help signatories fix the negotiated distribution of expected gains in a way that is acceptable to all players, and verifiable by external third parties, such as a court.

It is often argued that, with regard to surveillance and enforcement, collaboration regimes are typically more formalized and institutionalized than coordination regimes. Fearon (1998, pp. 270, 275–276), however, points out that the collaboration/coordination dichotomy is misleading, because most contractual problems in existence have a common – mixed – strategic structure.[57] Fearon contends that most cooperative settings first involve a problem of bargaining about the distribution of future cooperation gains. This bargaining is akin to a coordination game. In a second stage, games of cooperation involve a problem of enforcement and monitoring, which is akin to a prisoners' dilemma (PD) game of collaboration. Fearon concludes that approaches which treat a PD as the key problem in contractual cooperation tend to under-estimate *ex ante* bargaining. Bargaining problems are often more important obstacles to cooperation (especially cooperation between sovereign states) than monitoring and enforcement.[58] The lesson here for our purpose at hand is that most real-life contracts solve problems of co-ordination *and* collaboration at the same time (see also Powell 1994).

### 2.3.2    Complexity of contracts and alternatives to contracting

Real-world contracts can be placed on a "complexity" continuum.[59] Contractual complexity can be characterized by the following dimensions: longevity of the contract, frequency of exchange, dynamism of the environment, contractual incompleteness, number and heterogeneity of

---

[56]   Adding realism by considering dynamism, uncertainty, and asymmetrical information about other parties' "bottom line" makes it clear that virtually all contexts of international cooperation involve such distributional conflict concerning the terms of cooperation (Fearon 1998).

[57]   Fearon's contribution underlines a point made by Snidal that "almost all international cooperation problems mix efficiency and distribution concerns" (Snidal 1997, p. 485; see also Morrow 1994).

[58]   While "a long shadow of the future may make enforcing an international agreement easier, it can also give states an incentive to bargain harder, delaying agreement in hopes of getting a better deal" (Fearon 1998, p. 270).

[59]   Contractual complexity has not been defined conclusively in the literature. We take the liberty to characterize it as noted.

players, number of cooperative goals (or "issue areas"), and the "depth" of commitments.

Along the complexity dimension we can now rank contracts from simple quasi-barters of a single good (one-off transactions displaying high contractual explicitness and completeness, as well as high environmental stability), to more complicated multi-issue contracts (like drilling a tunnel, employment contracts, R&D orders), to repeated-interaction relational contracts, to constitutions, and international organizations (displaying a multitude of heterogeneous signatories, longevity, repeated transactions, a high level of incompleteness, and significant environmental volatility).[60] Differences in complexity notwithstanding, common to all types is the contractarian logic outlined above, namely the need for substantive and contracting goals, for assigning entitlements and entitlement protection, the Paretian principle, and the four phases of contracting.

Inter-subjective cooperation is the essence of peaceful human interaction. Formal contracts are very frequent nowadays, and continuously gaining in significance. They are, however, merely a social structuring device by which individuals or groups regulate their interaction. Alternatives to (explicit, written) contracts include spontaneous barters (spot-transactions), reputation-based covenants (Masten 1999, p. 26), and integration into a firm, family, or group.[61]

## 2.4  The contracting ideal: the Pareto-efficient complete contingent contract

The quest for the very contract terms that yield optimal outcomes is the subject of a prodigious theoretical literature in economics. The

---

[60] Dunoff and Trachtman (1999, p. 17) contend: "Between spot market transaction and the formal organization there exist many types of formal contracts and informal arrangements, and even the formal organization is a nexus of contracts. Thus, the supposed dichotomy [between transactions and institutions] is, in fact, a continuum: the boundary between the transaction and the institution is blurred." International organizations are institutions founded through treaties, and therefore logically are to be understood as contracts of sorts. Following the "New Institutional Economics" strand of literature (Coase 1937; Menard 2004; North 1990; 1991; 2005; Williamson 1979; 2000), we contend that an institution is a contract, an equilibrium to a game of strategic interaction (North 1990).

[61] There is a large literature in the field of industrial organization dealing with the boundaries of the firm and with the question of when it makes sense to integrate processes within the firm instead of "contracting out" at arm's length (Grossman and Hart 1986 and references therein).

customary starting point is the concept of the "complete contingent claims contract" associated with the work of Arrow and Debreu (e.g. Hart and Holmström 1987). In a seminal contribution to contract theory, Shavell (1980) coined the term "Pareto-efficient complete contingent contract" (CCC) as the first-best benchmark for every contract – irrespective of contracted content, number of contracting parties, or situational context at hand.

A CCC is the Arrow-Debreu ideal of a contract that completely informed, perfectly rational parties would write in the absence of any contracting imperfection (such as negotiation costs, costs of information gathering, or bounded rationality; see Shavell 1980, p. 466) and in the presence of optimal enforcement capacity. It is an imaginary, hypothetical contract that provides for a complete description of every possible present and future state of the world, no matter how small the probability of the contingency. A CCC assigns rights and ownership between parties in every situation and for every contingency, spelling out exhaustively and in complete detail the exact legal rights and duties of each party including the set of instruments that a signatory may or may not use (Cohen 1999, p. 79). The fully efficient contract thereby exhausts all possible gains from trade: it is the first-best contract between trade partners (cf. also Craswell 1999; Hart and Moore 1988; Posner 1988).

The following comments illustrate the nature of the CCC.

(i) It is the property of efficiency that makes the CCC the "archetype against which to compare all realistic agreements" (Masten 1999, p. 27). The CCC is free of market imperfections, unforeseen developments, and opportunistic behavior. It maximizes joint welfare (Shavell 1980). The CCC not only satisfies the requirements of Pareto superiority, but of Pareto efficiency, too. No other contract can do better than the CCC.

(ii) The CCC takes full care of the assurance aspect of contracts (cf. section 2.1.2). Since contractual opportunism is forestalled by perfect foresight, contracting parties are prepared to maximize their *ex ante* commitments.[62] In other words, the exchanged up-front promises of contracting parties are of maximal size. Parties are willing to offer the optimal scale and scope of the contractual exchange that are needed to maximize the *ex post* gains from trade.

---

[62] This goes for symmetrical parties. In the case of asymmetrical players, mutual commitment continues, until one player achieves his/her preferred (optimal) level of cooperation. Additional mutual cooperation beyond the binding participation would invariably lead to Pareto deterioration (see note 25 above).

(iii) The CCC is a complete contract in the sense that, no matter what happens, the CCC prescribes a course of action. There is no freedom of action, no *ex post* discretion. This brings about three interrelated consequences. First, no mutually beneficial *ex post* modifications to this completely state-dependent contract can be made. A complete and conclusive set of mutual rights and obligations is in place from the beginning, and no decision at a later stage can effectuate any improvement. The contract is "renegotiation-proof" and never needs to be revised or complemented (Holmström and Tirole 1989, p. 68; Mahoney 1999, p. 119). Secondly, CCC entitlements are logically protected by a rule of inalienability – an unconditional specific performance rule backed up by prohibitively high extra-contractual remedies.[63] Indeed, since the CCC is Pareto-optimal, every contractual non-performance must by definition be opportunistic and welfare-depreciating. Thirdly, to tie in with what has been said about the primary rules of entitlements in previous sections: a CCC consists of a comprehensive set of substantive and auxiliary entitlements that assign rights of ownership to signatories in every possible state of nature ("if contingency $x$ occurs, party A is to do $y$ and party B is to do $z$"). This fine-meshed set of entitlements is protected by a general enforcement rule of inalienability.

(iv) Intra-contractual default is very well provided for in the CCC (in the form of carefully crafted primary rules of entitlement). According to the terms of the CCC, a party will typically be released from certain obligations under well-specified contingencies (the right of ownership shifts). For example, one party may be excused from having to sell its good if the factory burns down. Therefore, the statement that a party always obeys the terms of a CCC does *not* mean that the party always meets a named obligation, i.e. takes a particular action (cf. Shavell 1980, note 2).

---

[63] Shavell 1980, p. 467: "[A] Pareto efficient complete contingent contract is one to which the parties would find it in their mutual interest to be *bound* to adhere. In particular, they would wish for damages for failure to meet the terms of the contract to be set sufficiently high that the terms would always be obeyed."

# 3

## Incomplete contracting and the essence of flexibility

The Pareto-optimal complete contingent contract is a hypothetical construct that does not correspond to any contract that has ever been or will be concluded. Intuitively, writing a CCC is neither practical nor feasible: it does not appear practical, since even in a stationary world, i.e. one where environmental circumstances do not change at all, it is prohibitively costly to lay down in detail all permissible (read: joint welfare maximizing) behavior of transactors (Horn, Maggi, and Staiger 2005).[1] Even if one abstracted from the costs of negotiating and writing down a contract, writing a CCC would still be impractical.[2]

In real life, however, it is not only impractical but flat-out impossible to write a complete contract, since the future is only imperfectly foreseeable for contracting parties (Masten 1999; Shavell 1980; Craswell 1999). Clearly, the world is *not* stationary but volatile and ever-changing. A complete contingent contract would have to consider all sorts of present and future environmental or behavioral contingencies *and* prescribe in a detailed and unambiguous fashion the admissible welfare-maximizing behavior by all contracting parties. Every contingency, occurring even with the slightest probability at any point of time during the contract duration, would have to be considered and contractually fixed.

---

[1] Tirole (1994) cites a classic example of the impracticability of writing a complete contract: suppose a research and development (R&D) contract between a principal (client) and an agent (researcher). A "water-tight," complete, contract between these two parties would have to specify not only the desired outcome (say, a remedy against cancer), but also the way of achieving it – which, of course, is the whole point of an R&D contract in the first place.

[2] Assuming signatories were living in a "Coasean world," a world void of transaction costs and with infinitely rational actors, *any* initial allocation leads to an efficient outcome through renegotiation (which is an application of the Coase Theorem, see Kaplow and Shavell 1996b). Thus, wasting resources on negotiating and writing a contract in a Coasean world must be seen as a futile task (Dunoff and Trachtman 1999, p. 23).

Thus, all contracts known today are incomplete (Dixit 2007). They contain gaps, that is, they are insufficiently contingent and (in a strictly technical sense) inaccurately written. This chapter provides a structured introduction to contractual incompleteness. In particular, we will examine the reasons for, and propose a taxonomy of contractual incompleteness (sections 3.1.1 and 3.1.2). This is followed by an assessment how incompleteness affects the wellbeing of signatories (section 3.1.3). We will then discuss ways of dealing efficiently with contractual incompleteness and the regret it provokes in signatories (section 3.2). Specific focus will be placed on the design of contractual flexibility mechanisms (section 3.3). In section 3.4 we will introduce the achievable contracting ideal of an incomplete contract – the efficient "breach" contract. In place of a conclusion, section 3.5 assesses this chapter's progress towards a coherent "theory of disputes."

## 3.1   A categorization of contractual incompleteness

If we want to operationalize the concept of incompleteness and deal with it in a structured manner, three questions need to be tackled: first, what makes contracts incomplete? (section 3.1.1). Secondly, what varieties, or types, of contractual incompleteness can be distinguished, and along which logical fault-lines, or attributes? (section 3.1.2). Thirdly, what are the consequences of incompleteness for signatories? (section 3.1.3).

There is a steadily growing incomplete-contract literature, from within both the L&E and the economics disciplines.[3] However, many contract scholars have contented themselves with stating that contracts are *somehow* incomplete, without specifying what they mean by that, and what kinds of assumptions underlie this contention. Others give the statement a bit more meaning by citing "uncertainty" as the key reason for contractual incompleteness. But what exactly is implied by the term

---

[3] There is no single universally accepted definition of "incomplete contract" (Tirole 1994, p. 743). We will stick to the very rigid definition of Tirole who regards as incomplete *every* contract that is not a CCC: "A contract is incomplete if it does not exhaust the contracting possibilities envisioned in the complete contract" (*ibid.*). This definition integrates both the economists' view of incompleteness (as insufficiently contingent contracts), and the lawyers' view of missing language. For lawyers, incomplete usually means that the obligations of the parties are not clearly specified: that important terms like price, quantity, time of delivery, and quality are not written down in the contract (see Edlin and Reichelstein 1996, note 4; Ayres and Gertner 1989, note 29).

"uncertainty"? We can at least distinguish three conceptions in the contract literature: uncertainty over the future;[4] uncertainty over other players' actions, agent-type, or knowledge (asymmetrical information); and uncertainty over the meaning and scope of existing contractual provisions (e.g. textual ambiguity). While this distinction is a good point of departure, there are still a number of questions unresolved. Take the concept of "uncertainty over the future": Does this imply that players cannot fathom contingencies at all ("unforeseeability"), or that they just have not bothered to specify them ("unforeseen contingencies")? And are we referring to uncertainty over future actions, outcomes (situations), probabilities of incidence, or the identity of the party affected by future contingencies (roles/types)?

In the following two subsections, we will seek to structure the concepts of uncertainty and incompleteness, and show how the two are interlinked.

### 3.1.1    What makes contracts incomplete? Transaction costs and bounded rationality

If uncertainty is the reason for contractual gaps and hence the existence of incompleteness, it makes sense to first assess the origins of uncertainty. Two explanations as to why contractors have to cope with uncertainty (and hence leave gaps in their contracts) are mentioned in the literature: rational cost-benefit consideration due to the presence of transaction costs, and bounded rationality of signatories.

#### Transaction costs

Transaction costs (TC) serves as a general term for all those real-life costs that signatories must incur when cooperating. TC make collective human interaction cumbersome and contracting costly. When the costs of writing down contingencies exceed the benefits of doing so, signatories will rationally embrace uncertainty. Although much has been said about transaction cost economics (a strand of the literature linked to the names of Ronald Coase and Oliver Williamson), there is no consistent

---

[4] In the literature, uncertainty over future contingencies is usually conceived very broadly as the existence of unanticipated political, economic, technological, or natural contingencies (such as demand shocks, technological breakthroughs, recessions, or *force majeure*). Instead of exogenous contingencies, some scholars depict uncertainty as unknown future behavior of parties.

understanding of what the term really implies. TC seem to be a collective "bulk term" for anything that somehow produces imperfections: pre-contractual sorting and searching, or post-contractual litigation, enforcement, and policing costs, etc.[5] We suggest a slightly more concise classification, utilizing Cohen's (1999) distinction between *ex ante/ex post*, and exogenous/endogenous TC. Consistent with our usage so far, *ex ante* refers to the time prior to the conclusion of the agreement, while *ex post* refers to every point in time thereafter.

*Exogenous*, or "Coasean" TC are real-life impediments to inter-subjective interaction. Exogenous ex ante TC consist of the basket of (opportunity) costs incurred in the run-up to signing an agreement, such as sorting, searching, information gathering, and processing costs, and bargaining costs in particular. This includes negotiation costs, costs of researching probabilities, and effects of possible contingencies, legal fees, and "ink costs" (drafting and writing costs). Exogenous *ex ante* TC are impartial costs of market imperfection.

Exogenous *ex post* TC consist of renegotiation, litigation, policing, and enforcement costs. "Litigation costs" is thereby the catch-all term for information processing, research, drafting, pledging, court, lawyer, and opportunity costs in connection with conducting a litigation. Policing and enforcement costs are expenses incurred for making sure the other party sticks to the terms of the contract, and for taking appropriate action if this turns out not to be the case.

*Endogenous* transaction costs are original actions, or behavioral responses to exogenous contingencies by contracting parties. Endogenous TC are of major concern in contracting situations: they are subjective, or unilaterally provoked (hence avoidable) costs. They are also known as strategic behavior.[6] Strategic actions can occur before the contract is signed (*ex ante*) or during contract performance (*ex post*).

---

[5] Cheung (1992) has come up with a telling, but hardly helpful definition of TC as any costs that are not conceivable in a "Robinson Crusoe economy." Williamson (1985, p. 43) classifies TC along the following determinants: frequency, specificity, uncertainty, limited rationality, and opportunistic behavior. Admittedly, this classification is difficult to understand, because the criteria have overlapping content, and are on different logical abstraction levels.

[6] "Even if contracting parties could anticipate all of the possible changes in economic variables, they would have a much harder time anticipating and protecting against opportunistic behavior by the other party. At the extreme, the more a contracting party is willing to contemplate the possible opportunistic behavior of his contracting partner, the less likely he will be to want to contract with that partner at all" (Cohen 1999, p. 91).

Strategic gamesmanship can be afforded by asymmetric, or privately revealed information.[7] Yet it may also occur in situations of symmetrical information, such as when informed parties are engaging in so-called "hold-ups"[8] and "hold-outs."[9]

## Bounded rationality

An alternative, possibly complementary, explanation for the presence of contractual uncertainty is the assumption of bounded rationality. At the core of this view is the simple realization of "human contracting error." Human error unfolds in three ways. First, contracting parties regularly fail to anticipate the existence of certain future circumstances or issue areas – they lack the imagination to think about possible states of the world, be it environmental situations or human actions. Consequently, they erroneously assign a zero percent probability to a

---

[7] Asymmetric information settings may give rise to *ex ante* costs produced by "adverse selection" (hidden knowledge), or to *ex post* "moral hazard" behavior (hidden action): in standard terminology, the propensity to deviate from joint-surplus maximizing behavior in the presence of asymmetric information is called "moral hazard" when the distortion involves actions or information revelation *ex post*, and "adverse selection" where *ex ante* private information leads only those transactors with less desirable characteristics to transact (Masten 1999, p. 28). An extensive review of this earlier incomplete contract literature can be found in Hart and Holmström (1987).

[8] Hold-ups happen in situations where one or both of two trading partners make sunk relationship-specific *ex ante* investments ("reliance investments") at the time of the contract conclusion. Reliance investments enhance the efficiency of this specific trade but have considerably less outside value – they are partly sunk. These investments cannot be contractually fixed, either because they are non-verifiable by a court, or because future contingencies are imperfectly foreseen. Hold-ups then occur when one party (usually that which has made no investments) imposes contract renegotiations on the investing party. Threatening to cancel the deal, the injuring party can partially expropriate the quasi-rents generated from efficiency gains of the relationship-specific investment. Anticipating this opportunistic behavior, potential hold-up victims react with under-investment, which leads to an inefficient resource allocation and thus to an *ex post* inefficient outcome. The hold-up literature has a versatile field of application in economics (Edlin and Reichelstein 1996, p. 478).

[9] Hold-outs are a natural characteristic of dynamic bargaining problems (Rubinstein 1982 was the first to formalize the dynamic aspect of bargaining). They occur in situations where there are multiple outcomes that two (or more) parties prefer to having no agreement at all. In a sequence of offers and counter-offers one party may strategically delay the resolution of the contract in hope that the other side will make concessions. Knowing that delay is costly (it results in more time spent without the benefits an agreement would bring; it also increases the risk that one side will break off negotiations entirely and look for other trading partners), the contracting party that values the agreement more (has higher opportunity costs), is at a disadvantage and prone to being held out by the player with the lower cost for non-cooperation (see Fearon 1998, p. 278).

positive-probability contingency. Secondly, signatories assign the wrong probabilities to possible contingencies, or mis-specify their effects or magnitude. Actors often omit crucial details or neglect the dynamic effects of their contractual regulations. Thirdly, contracting parties regularly write down contradictory clauses and agree on terms that are subject to opposite interpretation.

As we will show shortly in section 3.1.2, bounded rationality may lead to inadvertent (in contrast to foreseeable) incompleteness of the contract. Although situations of factual ambiguity and accidental contract gaps are rather intuitive and per se trivial propositions, the discipline of economics is not well equipped to deal with them. In order to buy into this explanation, one must be willing to assume actors are of limited cognition and perception, and hence not fully rational.

### 3.1.2   Contractual incompleteness: a taxonomy

Ours is not the only classification of incompleteness. Other authors have come up with different categorizations.[10] However, we find these classifications to offer no analysis of incompleteness to speak of. Rather, they are incoherent strings of symptoms explaining the absence of an ideal contract. A more "complete" classification of contractual incompleteness is required, one that is rooted in rigorous and structured analysis.

If a contracting party is uncertain about the existence, nature, incidence, or effect of a relevant contingency,[11] it will not be in a position to write a complete contingent contract, try as it may. The logical nexus

---

[10]  Schwartz (1992, p. 278) notes five "causes" for contractual incompleteness: ambiguous language, undeliberate [sic!] omissions, efficiency reasons, asymmetric information, and adverse selection. Shavell (1980, p. 468) only mentions efficiency and verifiability reasons; Tirole (1994) distinguishes between unforeseeable and unforeseen contingencies that can give rise to incompleteness. Ayres and Gertner (1989, note 29) distinguish two "ways for a contract to be incomplete: a contract may fail to specify specific future contingencies [and it may be] insensitive to relevant future contingencies," even though parties' duties are fully specified. Salanié (1997, chapter 7) mentions efficiency reasons, non-verifiability and bounded rationality as possible reasons for incompleteness. Dunoff and Trachtman (1999, p. 34) allege three causes of contractual incompleteness: (i) inadequate knowledge of the future; (ii) rational cost-benefit deliberations; and (iii) asymmetrical information.

[11]  Every contract is incomplete in many ways, but only some facets of uncertainty are of issue to signatories: incompleteness is relevant (and hence needs to be addressed) only if the revelation of certain contingencies results in regret, or if it opens the floodgates to opportunism.

between uncertainty and incompleteness is that uncertainty is a *condition* to which one or more signatories are exposed, while incompleteness is the corresponding contractual *outcome*.

Yet there are really many different kinds of uncertainty that may encumber signatories during their contract formation: a party can be ill-informed or ignorant (i) of the overall existence of future contingencies; (ii) of contingency outcomes or results; or (iii) of outcome probabilities. Alternatively, or in addition to the above, (iv) a contracting party can be asymmetrically informed whether a situation of concern has actually happened at all (non-observability of contingency occurrence).

Different causes of contractual uncertainty will provoke different kinds of incompleteness. Consider Figure 3.1. It is a synopsis of how uncertainty and incompleteness are interlinked in interpersonal contracts, and presents a taxonomy of contractual incompleteness. The chart plots a decision tree along four relevant dimensions:

(i) Can a contingency be specified/forecast?
(ii) Can its outcome be defined?
(iii) Do contingencies happen with a previously known probability?
(iv) Are contingencies observable to all parties or verifiable to an outside court?

Depending on whether these criteria are fulfilled (yes (Y), poorly or not (N)), different kinds of contractual uncertainty can be distinguished.

A contract can only be called complete, if signatories are able to comprehensively specify all relevant present and future contingencies, and if all anticipated contingencies are symmetrically revealed to all parties. Consequently, the first question to address when classifying contractual incompleteness is precisely: (i) Can *all* contracting parties specify in advance *all* future contingencies, actions/policies, and events?[12] If so, the next relevant criterion is (iv) whether the contingency (once it occurs) is revealed by nature to both (all) signatories symmetrically (observable information), or whether it is private knowledge to one party only.[13] If the information is in fact observable, is it also verifiable

---

[12] An event is a bundle of concomitant environmental or behavioral contingencies.
[13] Criteria (ii) and (iii), which deal with the knowledge of outcomes and their probabilities, are hereby less relevant: if contracting parties can define every possible contractual contingency, they can *ipso facto* specify outcome and outcome probabilities.

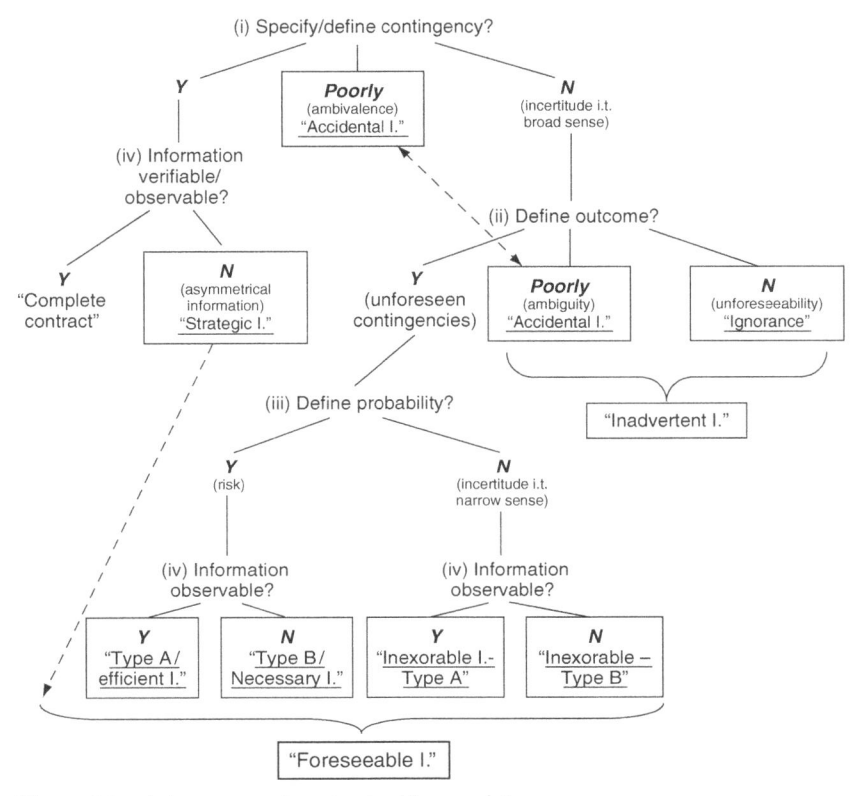

**Figure 3.1** A taxonomy of contractual incompleteness
Note: The typology of incompleteness is determined by four relevant dimensions: (i) Can a contingency be specified/forecast? (ii) Can its outcome be defined? (iii) Do contingencies happen with a previously known probability (-density)? (iv) Are contingencies symmetrically observable or verifiable? Depending on whether these criteria are fulfilled ([Y]/[Poorly]/[N]), different kinds of contractual uncertainty result.

Only the left-most branch of the uncertainty-tree leads to a complete contract; all the other types of uncertainty (underlined) inevitably lead to incompleteness in the contract. The presence of different variants of uncertainty results in various types of incompleteness. Accidental incompleteness and ignorance can be subsumed under the category "inadvertent incompleteness". The other types of incompleteness (strategic, efficient, necessary, inexorable type A/B) form the category of "foreseeable incompleteness".

by an impartial third party (see Chapter 2, note 9 for the difference between observability and verifiability)?[14] Whenever the contingency is

---

[14] The distinction between observability and verifiability only makes sense in those contractual contexts where signatories can prosecute a claim in front of a third party, e.g. a court.

not verifiable by a court or non-observable to an affected party, there must be uncertainty as to the better informed party's actions. "Asymmetrical information" in the form of moral hazard or adverse selection (see note 7) then defies the fabrication of a complete contingent contract.

If contingencies are poorly specified in the original terms of the contract, we shall call the resulting uncertainty type "ambivalence": relevant passages in the agreement referring to certain contingencies are ambiguous and subject to discussion, dispute, and potentially to opportunism.[15] This again forestalls the creation of a complete contract.

In case it is not possible for signatories to forecast or outline exactly all relevant contingencies, we shall talk of "incertitude in the broad sense." The subsequent question to tackle then is (ii) whether parties, though technically incapable of "nailing down" the nature of the contingency conclusively, can nevertheless define the likely outcome (i.e. give answer to the question, which contractual entitlement is affected and with what magnitude of disruption). Whenever neither contingency nor outcome can be specified, we shall call that type of uncertainty "unforeseeability."[16] If the outcome is poorly defined, we follow Stirling (1999) and refer to this type of uncertainty as "ambiguity." Just like ambivalence, ambiguity leads to misunderstandings, opposite interpretations, opportunism, and hence to disputes.

Whenever signatories are capable of anticipating/outlining the effect or outcome of previously unspecified states of nature, the contract displays "unforeseen contingencies." The follow-up question now is (iii) whether parties can assign a probability to (or probability density function over) the outcome. If so, we may speak of "risk" instead of uncertainty. We can further distinguish (iv) whether the contingency will be revealed symmetrically or not.[17] Whenever parties are ignorant about

---

[15] Checking for criteria (ii) to (iv) seems ineffective here, because ambivalently defined contingencies are a shaky fundament to build on. Subsequent questions (ii) to (iv) would yield equally ambivalent, i.e. uncertain, results.

[16] Whenever outcomes cannot be defined *ex ante*, their probability cannot be defined either. Question (iii) is hence not pertinent and drops out of consideration. The same goes for question (iv) concerning the revelation of a contingency. If the state of nature is not foreseeable, its revelation cannot be foreseen, either.

[17] Note that previously unspecified contingencies will automatically be non-verifiable to external third parties. Courts have a very hard time dispensing justice on issues that are not foreseen and hence not mentioned in the contract. Parties cannot point to a specific rule or obligation to prove contractual infractions.

the probability density function of the unspecified contingency, we shall call the result "incertitude in the narrow sense." Incertitude in the narrow sense then can be divided according to the revelation of the contingency (symmetrical or private revelation).

Based on this characterization of different types of uncertainty that may, singly or cumulatively, encumber the initial contract negotiations between two or more parties, we are now ready to develop a taxonomy of contractual incompleteness. Figure 3.1 distinguishes six specific, logically distinct types of contractual incompleteness.

**(1) Strategic incompleteness**  This form of contractual incompleteness is an outflow of a situation which we called "asymmetrical information" in Figure 3.1. Strategic incompleteness is given when (despite the fact that parties can comprehensively specify all relevant contingencies) some important states of nature are asymmetrically observable (revealed privately to some parties, but not to all) or non-verifiable by a neutral third party.

One party may have private knowledge of the occurrence (or magnitude) of a contingency at hand, which it can strategically withhold. When information is unobservable to one of the signatories, parties are not able to condition on it, and obviously will not even attempt to write an enforceable contract on the set of unobservable contingencies – the issue to which the information relates to is "noncontractible" (Schwartz 1992, p. 279). Alternatively, wherever the occurrence of contingencies or certain actions is observable but not verifiable, parties can informally condition on them, but are not able to write a legally enforceable contract.[18]

In other words, rational, forward-looking contractors will refrain from conditioning performance on asymmetrically revealed contingencies or actions, since the better informed party can be expected to opportunistically abuse its information edge by misrepresenting the truth. Asymmetrical information will thus result in the impossibility of writing complete contingent contracts.

---

[18]  Masten (1999, p. 28) submits: "The concern posed by non-verifiability is that, with the court no longer able to determine whether some aspect of promised performance has occurred, transactors stand to gain by strategically withholding information or by altering their behavior in ways that yield private benefits but reduce joint gains." Salanié (1997, p. 175) confirms: "It is no use conditioning the contract on a variable if nobody can settle the dispute that may arise."

Incomplete-contract theorists from the "industrial organization" (IO) discipline in economics predominantly deal with contexts that give rise to *strategic incompleteness*: a previously well-defined contingency is either asymmetrically revealed, or observable but not verifiable by an independent court. Situations of moral hazard, adverse selection, hold-out, or hold-up are the result.[19] Economists have devised ingenious strategies aimed at overcoming the strategic incompleteness of those types of contracts (see Tirole 1994 for a survey of the literature). In order to make up for asymmetrical information gaps, contract economists suggest signatories to draft elaborate payment schedules or sharing rules which either force the better-informed party to reveal its information, or which align the informed party's behavior with the interests of the less informed party/parties. These information-forcing and incentive alignment contracts, however, can only mitigate, but never make up for any welfare losses relating to the contractual incompleteness.[20]

(2) **Accidental incompleteness**   A second type of contractual imperfection can be termed as accidental incompleteness. It is caused by ambivalent/ambiguous treaty language. Whenever the nature of the contingency is mis-specified, signatories have to deal with an uncertainty that we called *ambivalence* above. Whenever the resulting outcome is poorly delineated, parties must live with an uncertainty type that we termed *ambiguity* above.

Accidental incompleteness, though probably a very common kind of contractual imperfection, is in need of further research (at least from the perspective of economics and L&E).[21] There is little theoretical work on

---

[19]   In other words, IO theorists usually assume away any imperfection except asymmetrical information. Models featuring strategic incompleteness do not assume what we termed above as uncertainty in the broad sense (see Figure 3.1). Unanticipated events of any kind are notably absent (usually because non-stationarity of the environment is assumed away). Under this type of incompleteness parties (and the court) know exactly what the environmental and contractual context is; they just don't have access to private information, cannot "see inside the other party's head."

[20]   "[C]ontracts designed to elicit voluntary performance of unverifiable actions depart from the Arrow-Debreu ideal in leaving gains from trade potentially unrealized relative to the cooperative (nonstrategic) outcome" (Masten 1999, p. 28).

[21]   When it comes to accidental gaps caused by poor specification of contingencies, and/or probabilities of outcome, the canon of economic theory has reached its limits: some pundits have argued that whenever parties accidentally or haphazardly leave contractual gaps, they cease to be rational. Tirole (1994) warns against giving up the assumption of rationality in the absence of any workable theory of "bounded rationality". He contends

how and when ambiguous, contradictory, erratic, or incoherent language emerges, and how to take precautionary measures to prevent these types of incertitude from happening.[22]

**(3) Ignorance**   This type of incompleteness stems from a type of uncertainty that we referred to as unforeseeability above. As Figure 3.1 illustrates, whenever a contingency can neither be defined nor its outcome specified, contracting parties are simply at a loss: at the time of the contract conclusion they are completely ignorant about the existence (let alone the occurrence) of a contingency – until it happens. Consequently, they are not able to protect themselves properly against the incidence of unforeseeable contingencies. We will call the resulting incompleteness *ignorance*.

By definition it is difficult to study ignorance in contracts, simply because no individual knows *ex ante* what he or she does not know. Economists feel very uncomfortable having to deal with instances of ignorance: unforeseeability is a challenge to the precept of rationality which fundamentally drives all results in economics. Contract economists claim that bounded rationality (not to speak of irrationality) is an unworkable concept,[23] given that the economics profession has made very little progress in understanding, let alone modeling it.[24] How can one assign probabilities to something one is ignorant of *ex ante*? How can one write a contract on issues that he or she is not aware of? Unforeseeable contingencies by definition do not affect contracting parties' decision-making or actions (cf. Ayres and Gertner 1989, note 34).

**(4) Inexorable incompleteness**   In Figure 3.1 we defined "incertitude in the narrow sense" as contracts where contingencies cannot be

---

that any theory of bounded rationality and human error must be able to specify when errors occur, why they occur, and what the consequences are for all signatories.

[22]   A better understanding of the concepts of ambiguity and ambivalence might be expected from social science (psychology, sociology) and linguistics.

[23]   Maskin and Tirole (1999) claim that without clear theories of how uncertainty comes about and what issues exactly contracting parties are (un)certain of, the integration of contractual uncertainty is methodologically arbitrary. Unless scholarship comes up with an explicit theory of bounded rationality and uncertainty, these two complete-contract proponents submit that full rationality and unlimited foresight is the more accurate methodological benchmark.

[24]   "Unfortunately, while many authors have insisted on the need for such an approach, little progress has been made yet" (Salanié 1997, p. 188).

specified, whose outcome can be foreseen, but not their probability. These conditions lead to what we call *inexorable* contractual incompleteness. Whenever the contingency revelation can be expected to be observable we speak of *inexorable incompleteness of type A*. A contract bestowed with asymmetrical revelation of information gives rise to *inexorable incompleteness of type B*.

We choose the nomenclature "inexorable," because this kind of incompleteness is extremely difficult to overcome. After all, how are parties supposed to deal with an event of known magnitude but unknown probability of occurrence? Potentially there exist hundreds and thousands of contingencies. Without being able to assign probabilities to contingencies, economic actors have no means of assessing expected costs and benefits. Not only signatories, but also contract theorists, are at a loss when it comes to inexorable incompleteness. Economistic logic of rational choice and utility maximization, which fundamentally relies on actors' rational cost-benefit calculations, breaks down in those situations.

**(5) Type A or efficient incompleteness**    Whenever faced with a contract situation in which there are symmetrically-revealed contingencies of known effect, magnitude, and probability distribution, signatories may *choose* incompleteness out of rational cost-benefit considerations. Parties find it too difficult to anticipate, evaluate, and write down every possible detail that the future may bring. We shall call the result *type A*, or *efficient incompleteness*.

Based on the methodology of Battigalli and Maggi (2002), Horn, Maggi, and Staiger (2005; 2006) in a formal incomplete-contract model show that in a dynamic, non-stationary world it can be both rational and efficient for contracting parties to deliberately leave contractual gaps, and to refrain from writing a fully contingent contract – even if they could do so if they wanted to. The transaction costs involved in researching, writing, and bargaining over contractual obligations and permitted instruments under the full range of possible environmental conditions just render contractual completeness impractical. The costs outweigh the benefits of doing so.[25] This is

---

[25] It is not a new insight that the TC involved in considering all contractual contingencies are prohibitive, even if their probabilities are known *ex ante*. This was argued by various authors (see e.g. Ayres and Gertner 1989, p. 92; Macneil 1978, p. 871; Shavell

typically the case when contracts are relatively complex and display a large number of low-probability contingencies that can affect the value of contractual performance.[26] Efficient incompleteness is also chosen whenever efficient responses to contingencies vary substantially but cannot easily be specified in advance (see Cohen 1999, p. 81; Hadfield 1994, note 15).

Thus, under the burden of significant transaction costs, contracting parties accept uncertainty (the term "risk," as discussed above, is more precise) over future conditions of the world and over possible responses. It is efficient and rational for signatories to conclude incomplete contracts, since it is cheaper to leave contractual gaps and to refrain from dealing with contingencies until they happen. As a result, contracting parties have to enter into *ex ante* negotiations on how to deal with unanticipated contingencies. See more on strategies of dealing with incompleteness below (section 3.2).

**(6) Type B or necessary incompleteness**  In contractual situations where both outcomes and probabilities of contingencies can be specified (albeit at a cost of doing so), but some important contingencies are privately revealed to one party, *type B* or *necessary incompleteness* is the result. Conceptually, this type of incompleteness is a combination of strategic and efficient incompleteness.[27]

Exposed to asymmetrically revealed unforeseen contingencies, contractual incompleteness is unavoidable: parties neither have the chance

---

1980, p. 468; Williamson 1985, p. 70). Horn, Maggi, and Staiger's contribution to contract theory lies in the formalization and operationalization of this important insight. The authors have devised a method to *endogenously* derive the incompleteness of the contract. They do so without having to jettison the assumption of rationality. This is a significant result, since it refutes the objections of influential "complete-contract theorists" (Masten 1999, p. 28), who are wary of embracing the concept as long as scholarship lacks an explicit theory of uncertainty and fails to operationalize it.

[26] If the probability of a contingency (or class of contingencies – an event) is low, then it may be inconvenient for signatories to bear the costs of providing for the contingency with certainty by including the respective passage in the contract. A less costly alternative for contracting parties in the expected sense may be to resolve difficulties only on the chance that they arise (cf. Shavell 1980, note 7 for a numerical example).

[27] Efficient incompleteness means living with (accepting) the risk posed by future contingencies for reasons of prohibitive endogenous transaction costs. Strategic incompleteness is caused by asymmetrical information, either between signatories or between signatories and courts. Necessary incompleteness, then, combines the insights of these two types.

of writing a complete contingent contract (as they could under efficient incompleteness) nor of devising an elaborate incentive scheme (as they could under strategic incompleteness). A contract cannot be made contingent (directly or indirectly) on something that is not foreseen (i.e. that has not been specifically provided for in the contract).

Unforeseen privately revealed contingencies, in short, provoke a kind of contractual incompleteness which is impossible to "cure" or "overcome," even if signatories are assumed to be fully rational actors (see Schwartz 1992). This will be consequential for our later examination of the WTO contracting context.

Although in real life contracting parties are frequently confronted with exactly those situations of necessary or type B incompleteness (as Schwartz 1992 convincingly shows), we submit that this is an under-researched area in contract theory (Grossman and Hart 1986; Klein 1996; Salanié 1997). As Salanié writes (1997, p. 188): "In my view, [practical approaches] should eventually study the consequences of incomplete contracting when information is asymmetric." Economic contract theory has so far been reluctant to formally tackle this kind of incompleteness (notable exceptions include Copeland 1990; Herzing 2005; Horn 2006; Hungerford 1991; Kovenock and Thursby 1992; Shavell 1980).

It now makes sense to define two super-groups of contractual incompleteness.

Ignorance and accidental incompleteness together represent what we shall call *inadvertent incompleteness*: both kinds of uncertainty result in a contractual incompleteness which is haphazard, or accidental in nature. This set of incompleteness types occurs frequently in real life (if one is willing to accept that actors are of limited or bounded rationality): signatories think they have "nailed down" an issue, i.e. specified it comprehensively and in unambiguous terms. Yet the language chosen is in fact incompletely contingent, open to opposite interpretations, or inadvertently leaves gaps that can be abused by a party acting in bad faith. It may also be the case that contingencies occur that have not been anticipated to ever happen at all.

In addition, and possibly complementary to inadvertent incompleteness, signatories may face what can be called *foreseeable incompleteness*. As Figure 3.1 shows, this term clusters strategic, efficient, necessary, and inexorable (type A and B) types of incompleteness. The idea is that reasonably rational actors (i.e. those that have trust in their contracting capabilities, but may not always be able to contractually specify in advance all possible contingencies/outcomes) will sometimes accept and anticipate incertitude as a fact of life. They foresee that incompleteness is something they must deal with, and that, for better or worse, signatories must develop strategies for dealing with incompleteness in the contract.

The difference between inadvertent and foreseeable incompleteness is that in the case of the former, parties can only *assume* that incompleteness is looming, whereas in the latter case they *know* this for a fact, and act accordingly. They can even assess the outcomes thereof. In other words, in situations of inadvertent incompleteness signatories are facing unforeseeable events, or "unknown unknowns." In situations of foreseeable incompleteness, actors are faced with what can be called "known unknowns."[28]

Before concluding this section on the classification of contractual incompleteness we have three annotations to make.

First, the above taxonomy can help researchers to understand better the nature of incompleteness of a contractual situation at hand. Different types of contractual incompleteness require different ways of dealing with them (this will be the topic of section 3.2). Researchers should not treat all forms of incomplete contracts as if they were nails to be hit with the same contracting hammer: when examining an incomplete contract situation, the researcher should be conscious of the type of underlying incompleteness that his/her subject of research is affected by. Only he or she who understands his/her problem can assess the scope and limits of different solution strategies, methods and approaches, and consequently take advantage of them. He or she will know which literature to apply, and at what "cost" of doing so (in terms of loss of explanatory scope).

---

[28] This may remind the reader of a notorious quote made by the former US Secretary of Defense, Donald Rumsfeld, given at a press conference on February 12, 2002. Certainly, his statement borders on poetry: "Reports that say that something hasn't happened are always interesting to me, because as we know, there are known knowns; there are things we know we know. We also know there are known unknowns; that is to say we know there are some things we do not know. But there are also unknown unknowns – the ones we don't know we don't know" (taken from the official transcript of the press briefing; available at www.defenselink.mil/transcripts/transcript.aspx?transcriptid=2636).

Secondly, we have shown that contractual incompleteness is caused by different types of uncertainty. Our novel taxonomy may thus help to distinguish better how different strands of contract theory have addressed issues of incompleteness, and how their results can be adopted to explain the contract under examination. Various strands of contract theory literature have dealt quite selectively with issues of uncertainty and incompleteness, for example, by taking into consideration some transaction costs and assuming away others, or by assuming complete, bounded, or reasonable rationality of actors.[29] Consequently, scholars have in fact modeled very different types of incomplete contracts: as we mentioned, industrial organization (IO) theorists usually focus on asymmetrical information settings and therewith on strategic incompleteness; some scholars applied economic tools to examining what we call efficient incompleteness; L&E scholars have more pragmatically dealt with necessary and inexorable variants of incompleteness.

The results and insights generated from various strands of contract theory do not easily carry over to just any desired contractual situation, but only to similar contracting contexts. Hence, being able to distinguish various types of incompleteness may help researchers to make accurate use of and draw upon adequate literature.

Finally, we have shown that when it comes to tackling contractual incompleteness, the technical toolkit which economics has to offer is quite scant. This goes especially for the kinds of incompleteness we termed ignorance, accidental incompleteness, inexorable incompleteness, and necessary incompleteness, because their existence may clash with the strict rationality principle cherished by many economists (see note 21).

Yet it is not the objective of our study to examine incompleteness as economists see it, but to describe how contracting parties in real life cope with contractual incompleteness. Therefore, instead of getting entangled into a theoretical discussion of the limits of actors' rationality, we favor a pragmatic approach to incompleteness: in order to be as encompassing as possible, and especially in order not to exclude the phenomena of inexorable and necessary incompleteness from our

---

[29] When reviewing the literature it was at times frustrating to find out that scholars hardly ever make explicit their underlying concept (or "type") of incompleteness. This omission makes it notoriously difficult to compare different incomplete contract models/ approaches and to assess and compare their findings.

considerations, we derail from the assumption of perfect rationality so cherished by many economists, and instead embrace the notion of *reasonably rational actors*.[30] A key tenet of the concept of reasonable rationality is that individuals are not rational supercomputers, but are not foolhardy either: important decisions are taken after careful deliberation of the costs and benefits they may entail. However, information constraints as well as the complexity of the contractual environment make the occurrence of contractual gaps inevitable. Signatories of the reasonably rational type may lapse, but are cognizant of this fact, and learn from previous errors.[31] To that effect, contracting parties try to minimize the mutual welfare losses triggered by contractual incompleteness through the best possible design of the contract.

### 3.1.3  Effects of incompleteness on contracting behavior

Pre-contractual uncertainty and the resulting incompleteness make contracting difficult. We believe that contractual incompleteness provokes three generic types of errors:

(a) ambiguous and ambivalent contract language, caused by poorly described contingencies and their outcomes;
(b) insufficient language (Type-I errors or "false positives"), which provoke gaps and give rise to legal loopholes. Type-I errors result from

---

[30] We prefer the newly-created term of "reasonable rationality" to that of "bounded rationality." The term "bounded rationality" was coined by Herbert Simon (1955), who used it to question the standard rationality assumption of orthodox economics. Over the years, however, the term has assumed a life of its own and spiraled in two connotative directions that we do not approve of: for some, bounded rationality is equivalent to *irrationality* of actors (e.g. Kahnemann 2003), while for others it is related to concepts of *constrained choice* and Bayesian updating of otherwise perfectly rational actors (e.g. Rubinstein 1998). We do not wish to maintain either of these two extreme assumptions. Actors neither are irrational, nor are they superhuman utility maximizers. Reasonably rational actors are guided by rational choice: they have complete, transitive, and continuous sets of preferences and engage in thorough cost-benefit analyses. Yet they are not perfect at doing so, and human errors in judgment, evaluation, foresight, and decision-making may slip in occasionally. In short, although actors do the best they can to act rationally, they are prone to erratic decisions.

[31] The following quote is apt in this regard: "So mistakes will be made ... Our assumption that there are no systematic mistakes means only that actors will not miscalculate in the same way every time they confront a similar set of circumstances. The subjects in our models are not systematically myopic, systematically gullible, or systematically naïve about the responses of others" (Grossman and Helpman 2001, p. 15).

the inclusion of excusable contingencies into the contract where there should not be any. In contrast to what the (error-ridden) contract may say, *ex post* non-performance does not actually lead to a mutual welfare increase, but instead opens the floodgates to opportunistic abuse by the enacting party;[32]

(c) contractual rigidity (Type-II errors or "false negatives") make the language of the contract overtly strict, or rigid. Signatories fail to foresee regret contingencies. Thus, the letter of the contract wrongly prohibits non-performance in situations where a complete contingent contract would actually have mandated welfare-enhancing *ex post* adjustment.

All three error types make contracting more difficult and thus cause transaction costs *ex ante*. Worse still, they are prone to reduce the *ex ante* cooperation level of signatories. Ambiguous language brings down the general efficiency of a contractual framework, because it instigates disputes (more on this in section 3.5 below). Type-I errors harm victims of *ex post* non-performance, whilst the Type-II errors harm injurers. In this section we want to assess in more detail how and to what extent incompleteness may impact on the contracting behavior of signatories.

Effect of incompleteness on victims' willingness to cooperate

Incomplete contracts may not sufficiently consider abusive reactions to environmental eventualities or opportunistic party conduct. They often contain legal loopholes, and mis-draw the line between intra-contractual, permissive, and extra-contractual, illegitimate behavior. The victim party is unable to tell whether an observable outcome (e.g. the quality of a contractor's performance, or a country's level of protectionism) was provoked by an outside shock (in which case the injurer's action can be seen as legitimate), or by opportunistic (and hence prohibited) behavior (see Copeland 1990). In other words, the contingency is not sufficiently observable to the victim.

---

[32] Think of the contingency measures of AD and CvD in the WTO: the ambiguities inherent in these contingent events give rise to protectionist abuse of these "unfair trade" instruments. National bureaucracies have substantial leeway to "interpret" the evidence. The porous language of ADA and SCM allows political players to "shape" the laws and regulations which govern the work of these bureaucracies (Finger, Hall, and Nelson 1982).

Alternatively, some action by the injurer is clearly discernable as opportunistic, but its enactment has not been anticipated in the letter of the agreement (or the contract language is blurry). Hence, although the injurer acts in contravention to the spirit of the contract, the victim cannot point to a specific contractual provision that explicitly outlaws such behavior. The contingency is non-verifiable and the victim cannot bring the injurer to trial for contractual misconduct.

A third option is that the injurer's action is found to be in contradiction with the contract, but the damage caused to the victim cannot easily be assessed by anyone except the victim, who has an incentive to exaggerate the magnitude of the impact.

In all three cases, the victim's ability to enforce the contract is imperfect, because efficient enforceability (observability, verifiability, quantifiability) of the contract cannot be safeguarded. Recall that enforcement is a function of enforceability and enforcement capacity (cf. at p. 32 above). So, even if a victim signatory possesses sufficient enforcement capacity to punish the injurer (or have him punished), she is likely to be hesitant to cooperate extensively, if the enforceability of the contract is porous. Figure 3.2 illustrates this point: it corresponds to Figure 2.2, but shows the contracting constraints from the victim's point of view.[33]

The "hit-and-run" curve (H&R) represents the victim's *dis*utility caused by the injurer's defection from the terms of the initial contract (in Figure 2.2 this corresponded to the injurer's utility from defection). The C curve represents the victim's expected benefits from continued cooperation. The C&C line represents the liquidated damages punishment the injurer suffers when defecting from a contract enforceable by an impartial third party. Figure 3.2 illustrates the impact of weak enforceability on the victim's willingness to enter into contractual obligations. Whenever the contract contains a gap, or displays a legal loophole, it may well happen that defection against the prior understanding is imperfectly detectable, verifiable, or quantifiable. This skews the H&R curve to the left. Spurious enforceability reduces the victim's proclivity to cooperate. The scenario with insufficient enforceability results in a much less enforceable contract: for the self-enforcement case compare the darkly shaded area produced by the intersection of the dotted H&R and C curve with the lightly shaded area resulting from the intersection of H&R' and C curve. If signatories can rely on external enforcement, the cooperation space is reduced from $C^{law}$ to $C^{law'}$ through the westwards movement of the H&R curve.

---

[33] Cost and benefit curves are interchanged in comparison to Figure 2.2.

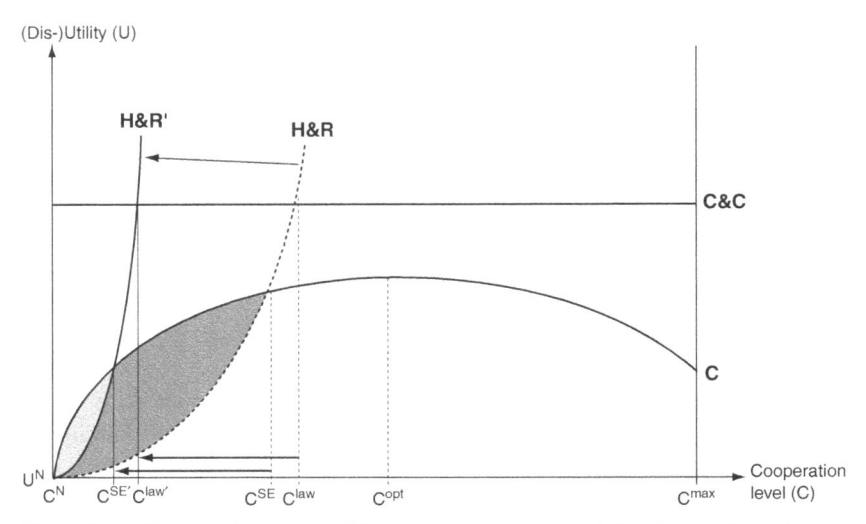

**Figure 3.2**    Impact of contractual incompleteness on the victims' commitment
Source: based on Keck and Schropp 2008, Figure 2
Note: This is a slightly modified version of Figure 2.2. The graph illustrates the impact
of weak enforceability. It represents, from a *victim's* perspective, cooperation payoffs
and disutility from defection (vertical axis), and levels of cooperation (horizontal axis).
The H&R curve represents the victim's disutility if the injurer defects from the
contract. The C curve represents the Continuation value of the game, the discounted
value from future cooperation. The C&C line represents the injurer's expected
disutility for defection if there is third party enforcement in place.

In summary: the problem with contractual loopholes created by contractual incompleteness is that too few constraints confine the injurer. He can
thus go on and engage in opportunistic breach of contract in situations where
the CCC would have deterred such behavior. Anticipating such opportunism, the victim is less inclined to engage in extensive *ex ante* commitment.

### Effect of incompleteness on injurers' willingness to cooperate

From the injurer's perspective, a serious problem of contractual incompleteness is that of overly rigid constraints, or overregulation (e.g. Goldstein
and Martin 2000; Setear 1997; Smith 2000). In a dynamic and ever-changing
environment "regret contingencies" are pre-programmed, caused by insufficient, or insufficiently clear, contract language.

Regret contingencies occur whenever performance of the actual terms of
the agreement leave gains from trade unrealized *ex post*, i.e. given the
information available to parties/courts at the time performance takes

place.[34] Regret must be taken seriously: on the one hand, parties anticipating unseized regret contingencies may decide to abstain from the contract, or to scale down their cooperative ambitions *ex ante*.[35] On the other hand, capturing regret produces welfare-enhancing gains from non-performance.[36] The problem with regret, however, is to distinguish it from flat-out opportunism: injurers may suffer a true regret contingency, yet they may also just backtrack from some contractual obligations for reasons of personal enrichment.

Rigidity is to be understood as inadequate and insufficient consideration of future external and behavioral contingencies.[37] It has a negative

---

[34] A word on the concept of "regret": a signatory experiences regret when an *ex ante* envisioned transaction value is not realized in light of the newly revealed information (see also Chapter 1, note 4). An unanticipated contingency arises which, had it been known *ex ante*, would have changed the initial content of the contract. Termed differently, regret occurs in instances where pursuit of the CCC would have excused performance, but the provisions of the real (incertitude-ridden, incomplete) contract erroneously mandate it. Regret is a function of the magnitude of the unexpected contingency, or shock (the "regret contingency"), and of the level of *ex ante* commitments. Note that the concept of "regret" is strictly different from that of *opportunism*: whereas giving in to (or "acting on") regret produces welfare gains (otherwise the CCC would not have mandated non-performance), opportunistic action by definition is welfare-depreciating (see Chapter 2, note 6).

[35] As explained at p. 78 above contractual rigidity causes injurers to reduce their *ex ante* cooperation zeal.

[36] A simple example may illustrate the significance of regret contingencies and the Pareto-superiority of *ex post* non-performance in an incomplete contract setting (adapted from Shavell 1980, p. 467). Suppose (i) a buyer enters into a contract with a seller to produce and deliver a machine, and pays at the outset; (ii) the value of owning the machine is worth US $200 to the buyer; and (iii) the relevant contingencies concern the production cost, which will become apparent to the seller *before* he actually begins the production process. Assume that the cost of production will be US $100 with probability 0.99 and US $1,000 with probability 0.01. Consider first a contract that requires the seller to perform regardless of production cost (a rule of inalienability), and that the price paid at the outset is, say, US $150. Then the expected value of the contract to the seller is $150 − [0.99($100) + 0.01($1000)] = $150 − $109 = $41. The value to the buyer is $200 − $150 = $50. Consider now the alternative contract that allows for regret contingencies and requires the seller to perform only if the production cost is US $100, and that the contract price is lowered to, say, US $145. Then, the expected value of the contract to the seller is $145 − 0.99($100) = $46, and its expected value to the buyer is 0.99($200) − $145 = $53. The second contract is Pareto-superior to the first: both seller and buyer strictly prefer the second contract that allows for non-performance in the case of regret (cf. also Sykes 1991, Appendix A for a similar example).

[37] A contract that simply states "John sells me a bushel of wheat at the price of US $5 tomorrow" displays rigidity, and is therewith incomplete in the sense that it does not consider events like John falling into a coma, or a thunderstorm devastating John's field, in which case it would be better for John not to perform, given he pays me adequate compensation.

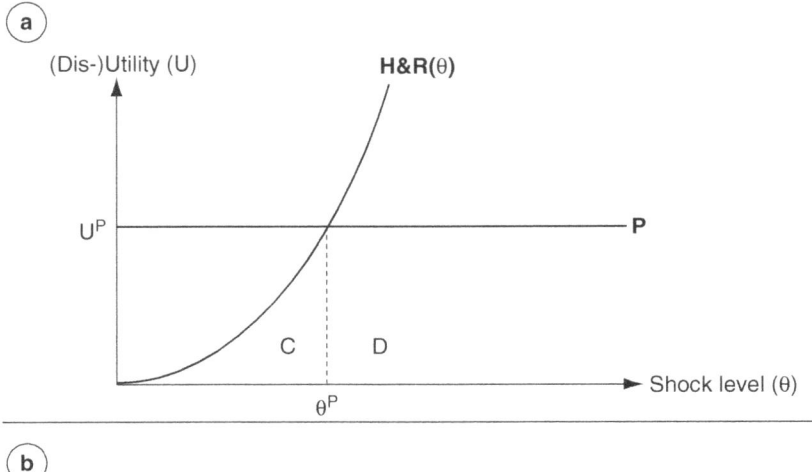

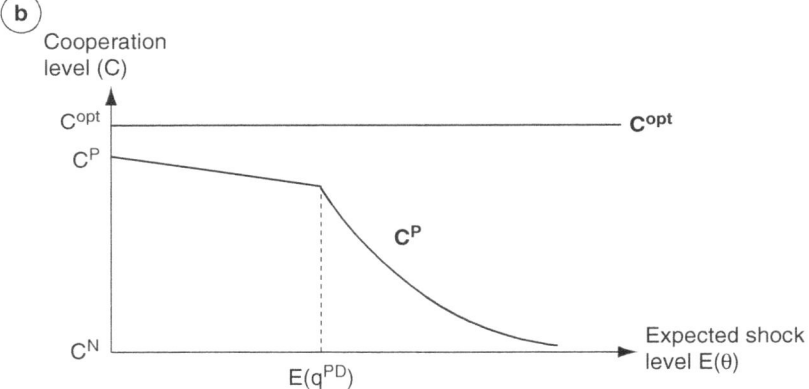

**Figure 3.3**    Impact of contractual rigidity on injurers' commitment

Source: Panel (a) based on Rosendorff 2005 Figure 1

Note: This chart is seen from the *injurer's* perspective. Panel (a) plots the magnitude of some unanticipated, exogenous shock ($\theta$) on the horizontal, and foregone utility from cooperation and utility from defection on the vertical axis. P stands for the disutility from being punished for defections. Panel (a) shows the threshold shock level above which the injurer prefers to defect (D) instead of cooperating (C). Panel (b) plots the expected shock level [$E(\theta)$] against the injurer's cooperation level. It illustrates how the injurer's willingness to cooperate is a function of the victim's enforcement capability and the magnitude of exogenous shocks (yielding $C^{opt}$ and $C^P$, respectively).

impact on injurers' *ex ante* willingness to cooperate. Consider Panel (a) of Figure 3.3: it captures a self-enforcement situation from the perspective of the injurer. An unexpected, previously unspecified state of nature occurs in the form of a negative shock ($\theta$).

Imagine a simple repeated-interaction contract. The contract is sustained by the victim's enforcement threat. The injurer can be expected to cooperate as long as his hit-and-run advantage of doing so (the H&R($\theta$) curve in Panel (a))[38] does not exceed the punishment (the discounted opportunity costs of defection, depicted by the P line).[39] The rational injurer will defect as soon as the regret contingency exceeds some threshold-value ($\theta^P$), where the hit-and-run benefit exceeds the costs of defecting and prompting punishment by the victim. Depending on the probability of occurrence and of its expected magnitude, the presence of regret (here in the form of environmental shocks) can significantly decrease the stability of a contract.

More to the point, the injurer's willingness to enter into a rigid contract and (if so) his level of cooperation, is likely to be a function of the victim's enforcement capacity and the expected shock level he anticipates to be exposed to. To see this, see panel (b) of Figure 3.3: if the victim is not able to enforce the rigid contract at all, i.e. is either lacking enforcement capacity or enforceability, or both (not pictured), the injurer's commitment level does not depend on it either. The injurer will be willing to commit to what he perceives to be his optimal level of commitment, $C^{opt}$, no matter how high future shocks will be.

However, things change if the victim possesses sufficient capacity (or can appeal to a court) to enforce her claims under the (overly rigid) letter of the contract: under full (self-)enforcement power on the part of the victim, and in anticipation of shocks, the injurer commits to the co-operation level $C^P$.[40] Whenever the injurer expects future regret contingencies to be sizeable (points further to the right of panel (b)), but knows that contractual rigidity disallows him to respond accordingly, the injurer's cooperative zeal is less pronounced. If the expected magnitude of shocks is higher than a threshold level $E(\theta^P)$, the injurer's inclination to cooperate is likely to decrease substantially, since he will not be able to seize regret contingencies under a rigid contract that prohibits any escape *ex post*.[41]

---

[38] The size of the hit-and-run payoff is dependent on the magnitude of the negative shock.

[39] Rosendorff (2005, p. 393) provides some intuition of the curvature of the H&R($\theta$) curve of Figure 3.3. The P line, notably, is flat, since the punishment is independent of today's revelation of the shock $\theta$.

[40] Note that $C^{opt}$ in Figure 3.3 is always higher than $C^P$.

[41] The concave curvature of the cooperation line is drawn for demonstration purposes. However, it is intuitive that the injurer's willingness to cooperate shrinks at a decreasing rate past some threshold level $E(\theta^P)$.

If the injurer can foresee neither the probability of occurrence nor the magnitude of future exogenous shocks (shocks hence come as a surprise), it can safely be argued that the injurer will be cautious to concede to high levels of *ex ante* concessions in the face of a rigid contract. Injurers will not engage in "risky," but instead only in "safe" (read: less shock-ridden) transactions, which brings down the scale and scope of *ex ante* promises, i.e. the level of commitments.

To conclude this section on the impact of incompleteness on signatories: if not addressed properly, contractual incompleteness is bound to bring down signatories' *ex ante* willingness to cooperate, and therewith the level of gains to be had from cooperation. In a contract where both (or all) parties know with certainty whether they will be victims or injurers, each signatory will conduct a private calculation of expected costs and benefits in making contractual *ex ante* concessions. The resulting deal is then likely to be decided by the most reluctant cooperator, i.e. by the party least willing to give concessions (see the text accompanying Chapter 2, note 25). The most reluctant transactor (victim or injurer) effectively decides on the common level of exchange.[42]

### 3.2    How to deal with contractual incompleteness: strategies of gap-filling

The presence of various types of contractual uncertainty precludes the existence of Pareto-optimal complete contingent contracts in real life. Every contract is incomplete; it contains gaps, usually to the detriment (in the expected sense) of all signatories. Any reasonably rational signatory (see note 30) is aware of the fact that it cannot contract flawlessly: try as it may, some contingencies will be omitted (either accidentally or for efficiency reasons), some mis-specified, and others imperfectly observable/verifiable. Hence, reasonably rational contracting parties know with certainty that their initial substantive agreement is mute to a range of contingencies that may occur in the contract performance phase. Those gaps (insofar as they are not pure "information gaps" produced by asymmetrical information) give way to the sensation of regret.[43]

---

[42]   If, at the conclusion of the contract, parties are uncertain about their future roles, or the frequency of becoming victim or injurer, they must assess *ex ante* the probability of assuming the role of victim or injurer. The result, however, is likely to stay the same: either the contract is never entered into or the most reluctant liberalizer will set the level of commitment for all signatories.

[43]   For the definition of the concept of "regret," see note 34 above.

The prospect that contracts (as written) may leave gains from trade unrealized, leads to the issue of how parties are to respond to opportunities of mutually advantageous *ex post* adjustment. In other words, contracting parties *ex ante* have to concern themselves with the question of how to deal with contractual gaps that will unfold *ex post*. Albeit unachievable, the Pareto-efficient complete contingent contract remains the normative benchmark that contracting parties aspire to. Achievable or not, the CCC constitutes the first-best outcome. Thus, when entering the design phase of the contract, reasonably rational contracting parties are faced with the challenge to find the most efficient, yet achievable, substitute for the CCC in the face of contractual incompleteness.

Four basic strategic trajectories of dealing with contractual incompleteness lend themselves to signatories:

(i) minimizing the number of gaps through comprehensive contracting;
(ii) seizing regret through drafting flexibility mechanisms;
(iii) minimizing the room for dispute by means of additional contract language and relational contracting;
(iv) delegating gap-filling responsibility to a third party.

As we shall show below, comprehensive contracting (strategy (i)) is geared towards replicating the original, namely the CCC itself. Seizing regret (strategy (ii)) aims at mimicking the outcome of the CCC by means of designing contractual rules of flexibility (contingency measures and rules of default). Minimizing room for regret (strategy (iii)) basically builds on the precautionary principle, and on endogenously strengthening trust in and cooperation of the relationship. Strategy (iv) finally consists of commissioning a neutral third party with gap-filling responsibility. We discuss the applicability and merit of each of these strategies of contractual governance.

### 3.2.1 Circumnavigating incompleteness: comprehensive contracting

Comprehensive (quasi-complete) contracting is the strategy of choice between negotiating parties, when the incompleteness of the contract is "bridgeable" (Cohen 1999). This means that the level of incompleteness is not too high and the costs of writing the detailed contract not so extensive such that they would outweigh the gains of doing so. Typically, comprehensive contracting can tackle situations of strategic incompleteness, featuring extremely simple contracting situations beset by asymmetrical information.

Alternatively, *risky* contingencies (see Figure 3.1) giving rise to type A (efficient) incompleteness can also be bridged, although this strategy is not always a practical option due to the high costs involved in doing so.

Under strategic incompleteness, i.e. with observability or verifiability imperfections as the only sources of incompleteness, contracting parties can fully anticipate each others' future behavior. To prevent information-induced opportunism (moral hazard, adverse selection, hold-out) from happening, parties *ex ante* agree to circumvent the information gap. As we explained in section 3.1.2, they either do so by "pegging" the contractual exchange to some related observable information (e.g. a worker's observable performance outcome instead of his unobservable effort), or by devising incentive compatible (payment or transaction) schedules that force the better informed party to reveal its information edge (higher insurance franchises for higher risk types).

In the presence of efficient incompleteness (symmetrical revelation of previously unanticipated contingencies of a known outcome probability), parties can also try to complete the contract. To this end, actors must make efforts to nail down *every* environmental and/or behavioral contingency by specifying exactly its outcome, by assigning the according probabilities and by prescribing detailed behavioral responses to be taken by all signatories (Horn, Maggi, and Staiger 2005). This is a costly endeavor that requires a lot of up-front research and bargaining (see our discussion in section 3.1.2). Hence, efficient incompleteness can only be overcome if the set of relevant environmental contingencies is small, that is, if there is a manageable number of high-probability, high-impact contingencies.

Comprehensive contracting strategies aim at replicating the CCC or, at least, relevant aspects thereof. Just like the CCC, this strategy of overcoming incompleteness assigns a *course of action to every possible contingency.*[44] Complete contracts leave no room for discretion *ex post*; they are by definition renegotiation-proof.[45] They mandate a

---

[44] The term "comprehensive contract" originates from Hart (1995, p. 22), who aptly notes that under a comprehensive contract "there will never be a need for the parties to revise or renegotiate the contract as the future unfolds." Just like the CCC, the comprehensive contract lays out a full plan of action *ex ante*, exhaustively specifying substantive entitlements, and spelling out in complete detail the corresponding protection belt of auxiliary entitlements.

[45] "Although contracts designed to elicit voluntary performance of unverifiable actions depart from the Arrow-Debreu ideal in leaving gains from trade potentially unrealized relative to the cooperative (nonstrategic) outcome, economists generally regard contracts optimally designed to deal with information asymmetries as complete in the sense that such agreements (i) still fully specify each party's performance obligations for every

compulsory specific performance of contracting parties at any point in time, which is another way of saying that (just like a CCC) they are protected by an enforcement rule of inalienability (cf. at p. 46 above).

Being able to engage in comprehensive contracting presupposes particularly simple contractual situations, or a significant abstraction from reality on the part of the researcher. Given the limited application scope of comprehensive contracting, it is quite surprising how much attention contract theorists in the economic disciplines of microeconomics and IO have expended on it. It is probably fair to say that the nature of most real-life contracts is too complex to be "bridged" by some state-contingent incentive schedule or sharing rule.[46]

### 3.2.2   Seizing regret: drafting flexibility mechanisms

Contractual flexibility mechanisms are designed with the aim of efficiently seizing the gains that *ex post* regret contingencies pose. As we mentioned in the introductory Chapter 1, flexibility mechanisms are intra-contractual, that is, legal provisions of *ex post* discretion which legitimize a departure from original performance as promised.

The strategic difference between comprehensive contracting and the design of flexibility mechanisms becomes apparent: whereas comprehensive contracting dictates a complete plan of action and thereby exhaustively specifies the transaction terms, flexibility provisions lay down general contracting goals that do not specify the contractual exchange in all its detail, but rather outline the basic rules of the game. Whenever contracting parties craft flexibility mechanisms, they usually leave the substantive entitlements rather unspecified and instead focus on the design of auxiliary entitlements, or rules of entitlement protection. Contractual flexibility instruments aim at reproducing the CCC's

possible contingency, and (ii) yield the best possible outcome given the information available to the courts at the time the agreement is carried out and thus 'never need to be revised or complemented'" (Masten 1999, p. 28, citing Holmström and Tirole 1989, p. 68, at the end of the quotation).

[46] Indeed, as Masten (1999, p. 28) points out, comprehensive contracting has been disappointing as a positive theory: "Aside from the broad prediction that efficient sharing rules will balance incentives for one party against inefficient risk bearing by that party or the incentives of trading partners, asymmetric information models yield few testable hypotheses. One reason for this is the 'extreme sensitivity' of optimal incentive schemes to slight changes in the relation between actual performance and verifiable information ... Complete contract theory also fails to account for the observed simplicity of sharing rules in most real world contracts ... [A]ctual contracts incorporate few if any explicit contingencies and generally use simple, typically linear pricing schemes."

outcome, but not its content. Their role is not to achieve completeness, but to "heal" the contract without remedying incompleteness itself.

There are two sorts of flexibility mechanisms: contingency measures intend to circumscribe *ex ante* contingency outcomes which allow for non-performance on the part of injurers. Contingency measures are additional auxiliary entitlements. Default rules, on the other hand, are general fallback rules of entitlement protection. By assigning rights of *ex post* discretion to victims and injurers, signatories attempt to trigger efficient *ex post* behavior by spelling out general rules of conduct. Default rules do not distinguish between welfare-improving and depreciating situations in explicit language, but set in place a general incentive structure that fosters appropriate post-contractual behavior.

## Contingency measures

Whereas comprehensive contracting was described as a strategy geared towards the specification of substantive entitlements (by comprehensively defining each contingency, anticipating its outcomes and probability of incidence, and by assigning the exact plan of response action taken by signatories), contingency measures are a less ambitious way of remedying incompleteness. They are driven by the desire to circumscribe the outcome of certain groups of (previously unspecified) contingencies or events, and to prescribe in exact terms the permissible action to be taken in response by signatories. Contingency measures are fine-tuned "dependent auxiliary entitlements" that are integrated into the contract (see discussion at p. 43 above). Each contingency instrument is pegged to a single substantive entitlement, has a unique level of conditionality (preconditions) and application scope, as well as an entitlement protection rule.[47] The aim is to specify in as much detail as possible (but without having to specify contingencies themselves) instances where the use of contractual non-performance is welfare-enhancing. In short, contingency measures lay out the broad contours of regret.

The use of contingency measures is encumbered by a number of potential problems.

---

[47] GATT Art. XX is a good example of a contingency measure: it lays out the circumstances under which general exceptions to tariff liberalization can be enacted, what must be considered when doing so, and how *ex post* discretion can be exercised by the injuring party.

First, contingency provisions are often difficult to operationalize. In many instances, it is not clear whether an alleged contingency has occurred at all, and whether reacting to the event falls under the ambit of the contingent escape clause, or constitutes a violation of the terms of the agreement.[48]

Secondly, contingency measures only apply to certain types of contractual incompleteness, namely those with signatories able to define *and* observe the effect of a future state of nature: the property of circumscribing clusters of regret contingencies, and of prescribing a unique course of action, makes contingency measures unfit for dealing with inadvertent incompleteness (the cluster consisting of accidental incompleteness and ignorance; see Figure 3.1), since for these types contingency outcomes are not readily predictable.

In addition, whenever the contingency provoking a certain outcome cannot be *symmetrically* observed, the legitimate source of regret cannot unambiguously be distinguished from illegitimate and opportunistic behavior. Disputes are a natural result. This rules out instances of necessary or inexorable incompleteness of type B. Hence, contingency measures only seem applicable to type A (efficient) incompleteness and to inexorable incompleteness of type A.

Thirdly, writing down contingency measures is a costly enterprise for signatories, with decreasing marginal returns at that. A lot of up-front research and legal drafting has to be devoted to codifying contingency measures. Only with this can parties find exactly those clusters of regret contingencies that warrant the effort. After the auxiliary entitlement is crafted, rules of entitlement protection and enforcement have to be supplied. Contingency measures are suitable for high-probability-high-impact groups of contingencies. However, probability of occurrence is known *ex ante* only in situations giving rise to efficient incompleteness. Not so in contracts displaying incompleteness of the inexorable type A sort, where contracting parties cannot know in advance which clusters of regret contingency to focus on. Writing contingency measures of flexibility must often be seen as "a shot in the dark."

Fourthly, contingency measures are not only costly to write, but also costly to enact for the injurer. It is usually the injurer who has to prove that some regret contingency occurred and that this eventuality actually falls under the purview of a certain contingency measure. Doing so may

---

[48] Disputes between signatories occur precisely because the nature of the gaps cannot be put into words *ex ante*. The circumstances under which unforeseen contingencies may occur, and the desired responses, can only be sketched.

often entail some serious up-front, or signaling costs, which do not entail any efficiency-enhancing added value (they are sunk costs). Thus, the presence of high enactment costs may have a "chilling effect" on injurers: although they experience regret and know that non-performance at face value would be efficiency-enhancing, they refrain from doing so, just because the fixed costs of enacting the respective contingency instrument are prohibitively high.

Fifthly, contingency measures will not cover the entire scope of regret, simply because of the considerable costs involved in researching, drafting, and writing them. Some outcomes provoked by regret contingencies are never captured, especially those of low probability and low impact (if the probability is initially known to the actors). This sort of regret is either lost, or a second line of more general flexibility mechanisms is in place to seize previously unspecified types of regret.

Finally, in addition to an insufficient application scope, contingency measures are also prone to human contracting error. Adding contractual language is always a hazard. The more explicit and elaborate a contractual clause gets, the more it is prone to contracting errors. Box 3.1 explains the general vices and virtues of express contract language.

## Default rules

A possibly complementary way of providing *ex post* flexibility for signatories of an incomplete contract is the design of default rules of flexibility. Default rules (DR) are imperatives "that define the parties' obligation in the absence of any explicit agreement to the contrary" (Craswell 1999, p. 1).[49] They are also known as "backstop, enabling, fallback, gap-filling, off-the-rack, opt-in, opt-out, pre-formulated, preset, presumptive, standby, standard-form, and supplementary rules" (Ayres and Gertner 1989, p. 91).

DR are unspecified provisions of entitlement protection, i.e. non-specific rules of *ex post* adjustment, apt to resolve *any* issues that have not been explicitly addressed in the contract before.[50] Signatories assign

---

[49] The term "default" is somewhat unfortunate, since it has nothing to do with "defaulting" from (i.e. violating) the terms of the agreement. The concept of default rather originates from IT-programming, where default rules are rules that a program follows in "default" of an explicit choice by the user to have some other principle apply (Ayres and Gertner 1989, note 24).

[50] An interesting twist here is that a contract which includes a set of DR (one DR for each traded entitlement) is *comprehensive* in the sense that no matter what happens, it prescribes a course of action. However, it is *incomplete* in that some of these actions involve *ex post* discretion by the contracting parties.

---

BOX 3.1 THE DOUBLE-EDGED SWORD OF EXPRESS
LANGUAGE IN INCOMPLETE CONTRACTS

Contracting parties often try to fight contractual incompleteness by striving to make their contract ever more complete: they attempt to anticipate and assess future contingencies and/or outcomes by devising complicated contract schemes that involve refined substantive and additional auxiliary entitlements, mixed entitlements, mixed entitlement protection regimes, and other behavioral prerogatives. Negotiating and writing up contingencies is costly and time-consuming. Verifying the realization of contractually included contingencies is also costly for uninvolved third parties. Moreover, a drive towards contractual completeness via express language is prone to severe pitfalls (see also section 3.1.3):

- **Ambivalent catch-all phrases**. The more explicit wording signatories chisel out, the more they risk interspersing textual ambivalence and ambiguities. This poses a dilemma for the framers of a trade agreement: efforts to fill gaps contractually by adding treaty language will prove counterproductive if they introduce further ambiguities. Cohen (1999, p. 80) points out that parties striving to complete an incomplete contract often resort to catch-all phrases that may sound stringent and are seemingly broad enough to achieve completeness, but often result in the exact opposite. Clauses like "best effort," "gross inequity," "serious injury," "unforeseen developments," "like products," or "appropriate countermeasures" bear the inherent need for interpretation. They entail incompleteness rather than completeness, and create gaps rather than closing them.[a]

- **Risk of "reverse hold-up."** Quite often, parties think they have anticipated and forestalled all relevant future contingencies that may give rise to opportunistic behavior. Elaborate and detailed contract schemes protect the potential victim party. However, unanticipated regret contingencies may occur which make adherence to these elaborate contractual terms generally suboptimal. The very party protected by the contract terms as a potential victim now uses contractual rigidity to blackmail her partner: the victim threatens to insist on the – overly rigid – terms of the original contract. Klein (1996) calls this opportunistic victim behavior a "reverse hold-up".[b]

- **Risk of "petty litigation."** Excessive contract language may be prone to Type-I errors (see note 32). Explicit substantive language creates the presumption of completeness. In case of a dispute, haphazard gaps may not be recognized by the courts for what they are. This may then allow "trigger-happy" signatories to initiate disputes that are formally correct, but foil the spirit of the agreement (WTO 2007, section II.D.3.b). The result of this overreliance on the letter of the agreement, some observers maintain, is a violation of the initial spirit of the contract and the loss of a shared sense of cooperation (Charnovitz 2002c). It is argued that a fully legalized, overregulated system could lead to excessive litigation, a hostile atmosphere, vengeful parties, and growing mistrust. Issues of "legal" and "illegal" threaten to replace considerations of "fair," "sensible," and "feasible" (Setear 1997).

- **Neglecting default rules.** In general, parties that focus on drafting a "watertight" complete contract risk overlooking the need for including default rules of entitlement protection (cf. at p. 90 below). This is an unfortunate situation since disputes arising from the revelation of unanticipated gaps will have to be settled by courts. Courts will need to interpret language and to supply gap-filling clauses and are likely to be overwhelmed by the task. Notably, if contingencies are revealed in a manner not verifiable by the court, judges will not be able to sensibly fill the gap, even if they have the best intentions (Schwartz 1992).

As a general conclusion to these pitfalls of express language, we submit that explicitness at times risks replacing rigidity for flexibility: if contractual contingencies are molded into express language they are usually inflexible against environmental changes and prone to prompt inefficient party behavior and costly disputes. Flexible adaptation to a dynamic world becomes much more difficult in these situations (Downs, Rocke, and Barsoom 1996; Goldstein and Martin 2000; Koremenos, Lipson, and Snidal 2001; Rosendorff 2005; Rosendorff and Milner 2001). Rational contracting parties can be expected to anticipate problems of inefficient *ex post* adjustment that excessive explicitness entails: intuitively, if a party will have to assume that pseudo-completeness will forestall flexible *ex post* adjustment to regret contingencies, and instead lead to a reverse hold-up or petty disputes, it will either refrain from entering into such a contract or at least scale back its contractual obligations and engage in less-than-full *ex ante* commitments (cf. at p. 80 above).

Various L&E scholars have recognized the pitfalls of overzealous contracting and of designing ever more fine-grained contractual entitlements. They suggest that explicit language should not attempt to eradicate contractual incompleteness, but to give structure to it by formulating general rules and entitlements.[b] Hviid (1999, p. 55) suggests that parties should focus on two topics: that of defining in broad terms the proposed outcome of cooperation, namely the object and purpose of the transaction (*substantive* rules of entitlement in our nomenclature), and that of designing the punishment strategies (i.e. the *default* rules of entitlement protection). The more complex a contract, the more contractual emphasis should shift from devising "a detailed specification of the terms of the agreement to a more general statement of the process of adjusting the terms of the agreement over time – the establishment, in effect, of a 'constitution' governing the ongoing relationship" (Goldberg 1976, p. 428).

[a] Masten (1999, p. 34) submits: "contracts that use terms such as 'best efforts,' 'gross inequity,' or 'substantial performance' to describe contractual obligations leave the parameters of acceptable performance ultimately to the courts."

[b] "[W]riting something down to be enforced by the court creates rigidity. Since contract terms are necessarily imperfect, once something is written down transactors can engage in a hold-up by rigidly enforcing these imperfect contract terms, even if the literal terms are

> contrary to the intent of the contracting parties. This is what occurred in the Fisher Bodies-General Motors case, the classic example of reverse hold-up, where the written contract terms that were meant to prevent General Motors from holding up Fisher were actually used by Fisher to create a much greater hold-up of General Motors" (Klein 1996, p. 467).
>
> c Shavell (1980, p. 488) warns against the use of express language and suggests that more specified contract terms should be contemplated only if "the use of an incomplete contract together with a damage measure [i.e. an unconditional default rule] would lead to significant inefficiency – when it would induce parties to act in a way that departs substantially from how they would act under a Pareto efficient complete contingent contract." This can, for example, be the case when the (personal, subjective) value of a good to the victim is very large compared to the costs of breach to the victim.

rights of *ex post* discretion by specifying general rules of entitlement protection *ex ante*. This allows parties to seize regret contingencies by engaging in mutually advantageous *ex post* contract modification after the revelation of any previously unanticipated contingency.

The major advantage of unspecific or unconditional default rules is that they can be applied to various types of incompleteness. The only precondition for drafting a workable DR is thereby that the outcome be definable *ex ante*. Hence, default rules of flexibility can be utilized to overcome all types of uncertainty that give rise to what we clustered in the term "foreseeable incompleteness", strategic, efficient, necessary, and inexorable type A and B variants of contractual incompleteness; see Figure 3.1). DR may even work for the ignorance type of incompleteness, as long as parties agree that they are really dealing with a contingency that they previously did not fathom.[51] Accidental incompleteness (caused by uncertainty types of ambiguity and ambivalence), however, can hardly be tackled properly with a DR, if only because signatories will be in disagreement as to the nature of the contingency. If *ex post facto* parties cannot agree on the occurrence, nature, and magnitude of the contingency at hand, they will have trouble assigning the proper DR.

As contractual rules of flexibility, default rules are very versatile in dealing with contractual incompleteness. Theories on default rules and on the choice of efficient DR have attracted considerable academic attention (see Ayres and Gertner 1989; Craswell 1999; and Dunoff and Trachtman 1999, section III.D, for literature overviews). DR theories basically examine the contractual and contextual circumstances under

---

[51] Where parties disagree on the occurrence or the nature of the contingency, default rules may not work. Note that once the contingency has occurred, it presents a *fait accompli* that one (or more) party/parties may benefit from. This party/these parties may have little desire to change this outcome through the application of an *ex post* DR (if they expect to lose out from doing so).

which intra-contractual non-performance should be permissible, and at what price this option should come for the party engaging in the "breach", i.e. legitimate *ex post* adjustment.[52] We will dedicate section 3.3 to this salient question.

### 3.2.3   *Minimizing room for disputes: the principle of precaution*

The use of flexibility mechanisms was described as a strategy to seize the regret potential of an incomplete contract by designing efficient rules of *ex post* discretion. A different strategy is pursued by signatories whenever they engage in precaution.[53] Cognizant of the inevitable incompleteness of the contract, and to prevent possible acts of opportunism from happening, signatories engaging in precautionary strategies aim at minimizing the room for tension and dispute, should contractual gaps nevertheless occur. Opportunism can be curbed by endogenously strengthening trust and cooperation of the relationship. To achieve these twin goals, two contracting options are at hand: diligence and preamble language.

*Diligence* as a strategy of remedying contractual incompleteness basically consists of contracting parties' efforts to write the best contract they can. Issues connected to the use of this strategy have been discussed at length above (*comprehensive contracting* in section 3.2.1). Writing "good," thorough, contracts is substantially more difficult than writing extensive contracts. Up-front research, information gathering, benchmarking, bargaining, and drafting are key – and ultimately costly endeavors. Yet the incurred benefits from performing diligence are unknown and undiscovered to transactors due to the difficulty of constructing a counterfactual: How can parties assess the payoffs of having spared themselves disputes arising from, say, ambiguity and ambivalence?

Another precautionary strategy is a carefully drafted *preamble language*, which lays out the general spirit of the contract, and common intentions of the parties.[54] Just as with the drafting of default rules,

---

[52] While most of the academic discussion on DR circles around what DR impartial courts should apply where parties have failed to specify contractual contingencies, it is clear that sophisticated contracting parties will devise strategies that lay out what to do in case a gap occurs during the performance of their contract. This goes even more for the international realm, where courts are notoriously weak (Pauwelyn 2006).

[53] On the use of the precautionary principle in science and technology, see Stirling (1999).

[54] Instead of, or in addition to, preamble language, some contracting parties may even prefer to conclude so-called framework agreements and protocols appendant to the original accord. Both these strategies will be subsumed under what we call preamble language.

signatories use general, non-contingent, language. Although preambles are usually at a level of generality that make them uninformative when it comes to using them concretely to interpret the various legal provisions committed (Mavroidis 2007, p. 10), they can nevertheless be helpful in two ways: first, they can serve neutral third parties (courts) as a point of reference when interpreting the contractual gap at hand, and secondly, just like commandments, they may prevent signatories from engaging in opportunistic behavior in the first place – a merit that is again difficult to assess due to the impossibility of constructing a counterfactual.

Although the precautionary principle may help address all types of contractual incompleteness, it seems particularly apt in situations of inadvertent incompleteness (see Figure 3.1), i.e. in contracts fraught with uncertainty of the types of ignorance, ambivalence, and ambiguity.[55]

### 3.2.4  Delegating responsibility: using courts as gap-fillers

A final strategy for remedying contractual incompleteness that has been suggested in the literature is to deliberately delegate gap-filling authority to previously uninvolved, impartial third parties (which we call "courts" for shorthand).

Court judges presume that rational parties expect them to engage in constructive gap-filling by concocting a clause (or giving an interpretation of an existing clause) in a way that signatories would have consented to *ex ante*, had they foreseen the existence of the contingency at hand. This "would-have-wanted" guideline that courts often apply is called the "default rule of hypothetical consent" by Ayres and Gertner (1989, p. 93). Since by contractual logic parties would have had an interest in maximizing their utility (by virtue of the normative benchmark of the CCC), courts should thus see it as their task to come up with the *ex post* welfare-maximizing solution at hand. More specifically, courts ought to fill the contractual gap in a way the Pareto-efficient CCC would have prescribed it (Craswell 1999; Goetz and Scott 1981; Scott 1990).

Outsourcing gap-filling responsibility to courts is an appropriate governance strategy in cases of inadvertent incompleteness (the collective term that we assigned to accidental incompleteness and to ignorance).

---

[55] This is so, because precautionary measures are relatively unspecific, or undirected, in nature. They help improve the general climate of contracting. Under contractual situations of foreseeable incompleteness, however, parties can actually anticipate outcomes, and thus can apply more targeted schemes in the form of pinpointed contingency measures, for example.

But will transactors freely choose delegation with respect to those categories that we bundled under the name foreseeable incompleteness (see Figure 3.1)? In other words, will signatories *ex ante* take the conscious decision to refrain from writing preambles, devising payoff schedules, drafting contingency measures, and designing default rules in contracting situations where they can actually foresee uncertainty looming on the horizon? At face value, delegating gap-filling responsibility to courts seems a smart idea: it absolves parties from having to think about future regret contingencies before they actually happen. Time and costs are seemingly saved for the contracting parties. However, this argument is ultimately a straw man.

First, the idea of contracting parties deliberately yielding constructive gap-filling to courts in situations where it is not absolutely necessary collides with the reasonable rationality assumption of actors that we maintain: when courts are charged with the task of completing a contract, they will do so by first interpreting the rules and norms *intrinsic* to the parties' relationship.[56] Thereafter, in a second step, they will consult norms *external* to the contract at hand.[57] But as a matter of methodological principle, we fail to see how it can be in the interest of contracting parties to knowingly have the court revert to external standards of gap-filling. The primary logical frame of reference for parties thus consists of intrinsic (endogenous) norms, rules, and regulations, not some exogenous legal or normative codex. Self-interested contracting parties should be expected to prefer making their own rules and regulations which are in accordance with each participating member's short-, medium-, and long-term interests.[58]

---

[56] Contract-intrinsic gap-filling can refer to parties' intent, current or prior conduct, or to the terms of the written agreement.

[57] When referring to external norms, courts presume that parties intended to contract with references to some (possibly non-economic) standard external to the written contract. Courts assume that it is the parties' desire to resort to external (socially accepted) default rules of flexibility. The US Uniform Commercial Code (UCC) has been said to be a collection of external default rules that parties wish to resort to, in the absence of any indication to the contrary (Ayres and Gertner 1989, p. 95). In public international law, the Vienna Convention on the Law of Treaties (VCLT) and the ILC Draft on State Responsibility may be seen as collections of external DR of transnational contracting conduct (Dunoff and Trachtman 1999, p. 35).

[58] This is not to say that signatories never resort to external norms. Parties *do* regularly give effect to an external set of default rules (such as the UCC or a standard tenancy agreement). Yet they can be expected to mention precisely *which* set of norms they want to be referred to, and *when* exactly it is to apply. In addition, not every contracting situation lends itself to the application of easy-to-use standard codices of default that contractors can resort to.

Secondly, courts need guidance in form of default rules when filling contractual gaps. When applying the dogma of "hypothetical consent," courts are effectively charged with concocting a default rule that parties could have crafted themselves (and probably even better): when courts want to elicit contract-intrinsic joint maximizing terms (that would have been agreed to by perfectly informed rational parties in a complete contract situation), they necessarily have to engage in contextual interpretation (Cohen 1999, p. 83). Interpreting an incomplete contract is conceptually identical with clarifying which party owns which entitlement, and establishing how that entitlement is to be protected (Craswell 1999, p. 15). But how can a court clarify the contractual entitlement regime sensibly without detailed guidance from the contracting parties? Parties must tell the court how it is to interpret their intentions. They do so by writing down *ex ante* the traded entitlements (primary rules of contracting), and the rules of protecting them (secondary rules of contracting). This is a task not to be ceded to a third party. Ultimately, there is no benefit for parties in ceding primary and secondary rules of rulemaking to uninvolved third parties.

Thirdly, courts operate not necessarily with perfection,[59] and are expensive to establish and to maintain. In addition, it is costly to provide court members with the information necessary to come up with a balanced judgment.

Finally, we note that in situations that we referred to as necessary incompleteness, even flawlessly operating judges cannot fill contractual gaps – try as they may. If a court cannot verify the facts of the case (such as the allegation that an employee "shirked" his contractual duties), it cannot complete the contract in any meaningful manner (see Schwartz 1992).[60]

In sum, courts are an indispensable instance in contracts, whenever inadvertent contractual gaps need to be filled and ambiguous contract language needs to be interpreted. However, when it comes to situations of what we termed foreseeable incompleteness, contracting parties must give courts detailed directions in the form of entitlement protection rules, or rules of default. Reasonably rational actors should be less willing to deliberately cede responsibility for gap-filling to a third party litigator.

---

[59] The existence of judicial imperfection opens the door to opportunistic conduct designed to contrive cancellation, evade performance, or otherwise force a back-tracking from existing commitments (Masten 1999, p. 33).

[60] Shavell (1980, note 6) notes: "Reliance on [courts] … can act to fill in gaps in contracts only with respect to those readily observable contingencies for which the agreement that parties would have come to can be fairly confidently imputed."

### 3.2.5  *Summary: dealing with contractual incompleteness and the significance of contractual rules of default*

So far this section has presented and assessed strategies of gap-filling in situations beset by various types of incompleteness: comprehensive contracting tries to overcome (or bridge) incompleteness by replicating the contracting ideal of the CCC; flexibility provisions (contingency measures or default rules) seek to mimic the outcome of the CCC by efficiently capturing regret contingencies; precaution is geared towards minimizing the incidence of regret and disputes; and delegating gap-filling to courts is the strategy of addressing issues only after they occurred by ordering an impartial third party to deal with them.

Figure 3.4 summarizes these different gap-filling strategies. Our analysis has shown that there are in fact only two strategic trajectories that signatories may choose when addressing instances of contractual incompleteness: the first route is that of striving for completeness and fighting incompleteness; the second route is that of accepting incompleteness and

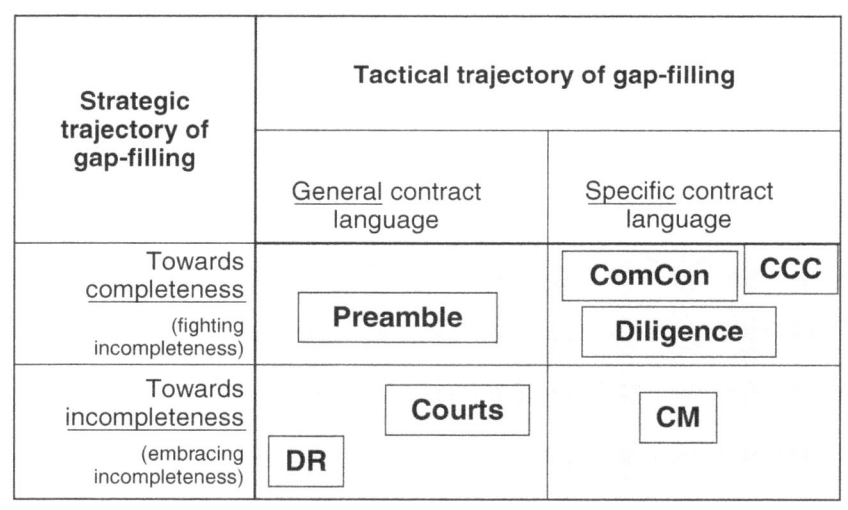

**Figure 3.4**  Overview of gap-filling strategies in incomplete contract situations
Note: The chart spans two dimensions: strategy of gap-filling (vertical continuum), and gap-filling tactics (horizontal continuum). Within this matrix space, six gap-filling strategies are plotted: preamble language (Preamble), comprehensive contracting (ComCon), default rules (DR), delegating gap-filling to courts (Courts), contingency measures (CM), Pareto-efficient complete contingent contract (CCC).

embracing the opportunities it offers. Signatories may make tactical choices along each of these two strategic trajectories: Will they give the incomplete contract additional structure by supplying detailed and explicit contract language, or by laying down general and unspecific rules of conduct? The strategic and tactical choices now span a 2 × 2 matrix.

The CCC as the contracting ideal is placed in the top right corner, next to the strategy of comprehensive contracting. Emulating the CCC, comprehensive contracting is geared towards prescribing a complete plan of action and leaves no room for *ex post* discretion. Diligence, i.e. trying to be as precise and elaborate as possible when drafting a contract, is placed in the same quadrant. Preamble language, in the top left panel, aims at lending the contract more substance and structure, yet does so by adding general, unspecific language. Parties are reminded to use their *ex post* discretion in a cooperative and non-opportunistic fashion. Opposite, in the bottom right quadrant, is the strategy of drafting contingency measures. Signatories add specific auxiliary entitlements that elaborate the conditions under which and to what extent contracting parties may engage in *ex post* discretion. Assigning gap-filling to courts is placed in the bottom left quadrant. It is a generalist incomplete-contracting approach to deal with incompleteness. However, as we discussed above, assigning gap-filling competence to courts is a strategy that logically applies to only a subset of the various types of contractual incompleteness, namely to those constituting the group we labeled inadvertent incompleteness. Also, courts need guidelines of operation, especially default rules. This is why ordering courts to fill gaps is placed above that of designing DR. Writing default rules, finally, implies embracing the possibilities that incompleteness entails by prescribing general entitlement protection rules.

This examination of strategies of gap-filling is highly schematic and abstract. In real life, signatories do not necessarily apply one strategy of gap-filling or another. Rather, they compile their contracts with a mix of gap-filling techniques, depending on the nature and number of exchanged entitlements. In other words, contracting parties design an institutional frame or governance structure to best deal with the incompleteness of their contract. Ideally, signatories assess every single entitlement they traded, try to anticipate their exposition to various types of uncertainty and incompleteness, and shape the most efficient set of gap-filling provisions possible. Depending on the nature of the contractual exchange (number of original entitlements, number of issue areas covered, depth of commitment level), as well as the complexity of the original contracting situation (number of signatories, duration of the contract, magnitude of contractual interaction, etc.), the resulting governance structure will be more or less complicated. We believe there to be a whole range from comprehensive contracts that meticulously specify all substantive rules of transaction, to complex multi-entitlement contracts, and to simple "optimally indefinite contracts".[61]

For the remainder of this chapter we will be focusing on the analysis of default rules. We do so for various reasons.

First, the research interest of this study is geared towards the study of trade policy flexibility mechanisms. As we have shown above, contingency measures, the alternative flexibility instruments to DR, are actually subsets of default rules (at p. 90 above). Contingency measures, like default rules, are entitlement protection provisions (secondary rules of contracting), but contingency measures display an added layer of conditionality, i.e. special enactment thresholds and application scope limitations. Much of the discussion on default rules can also be applied to contingency measures. However, as shown above, the contingency measures as a gap-filling strategy are far less versatile, and prone to serious stumbling blocks.

Secondly, when it comes to instances of foreseeable incompleteness, the use of default rules is vastly superior to any other measure of gap-filling. Crafting DR is the most comprehensive gap-filling strategy, since it successfully applies to four of five types of incompleteness that we bundled into the term foreseeable incompleteness.[62] Instances of efficient, necessary, and inexorable (incompleteness of type A and B) are probably the most interesting forms of contractual incompleteness, since outcomes and effects are measurable.

In summary: when the contractual context is such that incompleteness is to be rationally anticipated (i.e. in instances of foreseeable incompleteness), contracting parties regularly craft DR as a fallback rule of flexibility

---

[61] Incomplete contracting taken to an extreme leads to the concept of an "optimally indefinite contract" (Charny 1991; Cohen 1999). An optimally indefinite contract is the exact opposite of a comprehensive contract and need not be any less efficient a substitute for a CCC ("In a world in which contract formation is costly and adjudication costless, a perfectly indefinite agreement, rather than comprehensive Arrow-Debreu bargains becomes the ideal contract," Masten 1999, p. 33). Contracts of this type consist of only one substantive clause (a rule of entitlement specifying the objective of the contract and the transaction or exchange involved), one DR of entitlement protection, and one rule of enforcement. Optimally indefinite contracts exist in situations of flaw- and costless arbitration procedures, or if the instituted DR leaves no room for opportunism.

[62] DR may be of additional use in situations of ignorance (see note 51 above and accompanying text).

*ex ante.*[63] As will be shown in Part II of the study, those situations feature prominently in the WTO contract. In focusing on the study of DR, we must leave aside a closer examination of inadvertent incompleteness. Interesting as the field of inadvertent contractual gaps and strategies for remedying them may be, we will not pursue this issue any further. At this point in time, no feasible theory is emerging in that area.[64]

### 3.3 Crafting rules of flexibility: inalienability, specific performance, or liability?

Default rules of flexibility lay down whether and how parties can react to changing circumstances that have not been considered explicitly at the time of the contract formation. In this section, we will examine more closely the intricacies of default rule design for incomplete contracts. For reasons that will become clear in the course of our engagement with the WTO, we are especially interested in situations where:

(i) a contract exists between parties;
(ii) parties are reasonably rational (in the sense explained in note 30);
(iii) the *ex ante* commitment (level of concessions) is non-trivial and discrete;[65]
(iv) contracting parties live in a non-stationary (read: dynamic) world, and are faced with a situation of unforeseen contingencies;[66]

---

[63] Default rules are less relevant when we study cases of strategic incompleteness. However, we will not consider instances of strategic incompleteness any further. As said above, situations giving rise to this category of incompleteness can be expected to be quite rare (simple, one-shot, single-entitlement contracts in an environment of low volatility) and are thus of little use to the study of the WTO contract. In addition, scholars of IO have already extensively dealt with these issues and introduced ingenious schemes of comprehensive contracting.

[64] Incertitude categories that we referred to as ambiguity, ambivalence, and unforeseeability (see Figure 3.1) are admittedly difficult to study: there is no methodology in place that could predict when and how signatories conduct contracting errors and lapses. We hope that contract theory will make progress in this area. However, we submit that inadvertent and foreseeable incompleteness are complementary fields of study. The insights that we gather in future sections of this study hence come without a loss of generality, even though we will not consider instances of inadvertent incompleteness.

[65] The exchanged "good" (better: promise) is not binary, but a matter of degrees; see Chapter 2, notes 11, 35 and accompanying text.

[66] This is to say that for simplicity (but without loss of generality) we assume away all other types of contractual incertitude and focus on unforeseen contingencies. The presence of unforeseen contingencies gives rise to efficient, necessary, and inexorable incompleteness of type A and B (see Figure 3.1). Think of contingencies as some kind of negative exogenous

(v)  enforcement as promised is possible;[67]
(vi)  for simplicity, only a single entitlement is exchanged.[68]

Although this may look like a string of six rather confining assumptions, the majority of real-life contracts can be mapped by this set of assumptions.

When designing efficient default rules, the objective of signatories is to mimic the outcome of the unattainable CCC, but not its substance (replicating its substance would be the prerogative of comprehensive contracting). This naturally means having the same contractual goals as the CCC.[69] Contractual flexibility is designed to exhaust all gains from trade by inducing optimal *ex post* escape (i.e. non-performance in cases where the CCC would also mandate excuse) and by deterring inefficient, opportunistic *ex post* behavior. Safeguarding efficient "breach" will provide for full assurance to contracting parties who are thus willing to maximize their up-front commitments, namely the scale and scope of their *ex ante* concessions (including *ex ante* reliance investment in the relationship).[70]

Essentially, the objective of a flexibility rule is (i) to seize the potential presented by possible regret contingencies in a way the CCC would mandate it; (ii) to forestall opportunism; and (iii) to safeguard the maximal *ex ante* commitment level.[71] So far, so good. The difficulty consists in finding a rule of entitlement protection *ex ante* which is

environmental or behavioral shock which is either revealed symmetrically or privately to one contracting party. The (previously unanticipated) shock might hit one or all parties, and will create regret in at least one signatory (whether succumbing to the contingency is welfare-enhancing or welfare-depreciating is a different question).

[67]  This assumption essentially implies that parties do not commit to contractual concessions that cannot be enforced, either by themselves or by a neutral third party enforcer. We are not concerned with issues of self-enforcement capacity, and of the stability of the contract.

[68]  As stated in section 2.2.4, every real-life multiple-entitlement contract can logically be unbundled into a series of independent substantive entitlements. So, examining only one substantive entitlement can be understood as analyzing a very simple contract, or one aspect of a wider and more complex agreement.

[69]  The fact that environmental or behavioral contingencies are unanticipated and the contract therefore is incomplete does not mean that parties' *intentions* are uncertain: the Paretian logic, namely joint welfare maximization, common to all contracts is and stays the contractual objective. The CCC stays the welfarist benchmark.

[70]  To recapitulate: reliance investments are pre-contractual relationship-specific investments, which are (i) partly sunk, and (ii) enhance the efficiency of the contractual exchange.

[71]  Mahoney (1999, p. 118) rightly contends that the importance of default rules for non-performance is not to be under-estimated, since the choice of a DR alters "the incentives facing the breaching party, which will directly affect the probability of performance and indirectly affect the number and type of contracts people make, the level of detail with

able to set the optimal *ex post* incentives for both victim and injurer. In other words, a DR must separate situations where non-performance is mutually welfare-enhancing from those contingencies where non-performance is opportunistic and thus results in welfare-depreciation.[72]

At p. 43 above, we introduced the basic stages of contract design. It was shown that signatories must lay down their primary rules (definition of entitlement), secondary rules (rules of intra-contractual entitlement protection), and tertiary rules (entitlement-enforcement provisions). It is now easy to see that the process for designing contractual flexibility mechanisms is indispensable for defining rules of efficient entitlements protection (Dunoff and Trachtman 1999, p. 32).[73] Figure 3.5 illustrates that crafting contractual rules of flexibility is a key ingredient of the contract design process.

Figure 3.5 recapitulates the process of contract design in general as consisting of:

  (i)  fixing a substantive entitlement and the level of mutual cooperation concessions (primary rule of entitlement);
 (ii)  finding a viable entitlement protection rule (flexibility rules, especially an efficient default rule), and agreeing on enforcement rules that safeguard intra-contractual behavior; and
(iii)  deter extra-contractual behavior by all signatories (tertiary rules).

As stated at p. 46 above, the literature usually distinguishes three pure types of entitlement protection, and consequently of default rules: if one party is allowed to opt out of the agreement unilaterally (a liability or pay-or-perform rule), the discretion and most likely all the ensuing gains

---

which they identify their mutual obligations, the allocation of risks between the parties, the amount they invest in anticipation of performance once a contract is made, the precautions they take against the possibility of breach, and the precautions they take against the possibility of a regret contingency."

[72] This objective is exactly at the heart of Ethier's (2001a) "reciprocal-conflict problem" (see Chapter 1, note 22): the injurer wants to be able to seize opportunities generated by the vision of non-performance, whereas the victim wants to rest assured that she does not suffer from that escape action. An adequate *ex ante* governance structure must be in place to set the right incentives to each contracting party.

[73] Conceptually, the question of *ex post* flexibility is the flipside of the level of legal entitlement protection. Flexibility determines the "action space" of contracting parties. In particular, flexibility mechanisms lay down whether and how parties can react to changing circumstances that have not been considered explicitly at the time of the contract formation. So, while flexibility provisions nail down the legitimate behavior of the *active* party, the entitlement question is concerned with the scope of protection granted to the *passive* party.

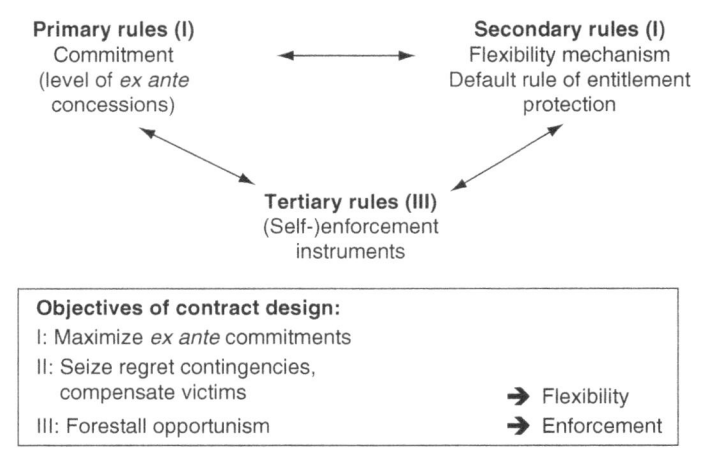

**Figure 3.5**   Designing contractual default rules

Notes: This chart is a modification of Figure 1.2, which introduced the concepts of flexibility, enforcement, and *ex ante* commitment in the trade context. The chart shows that for incomplete contracts in general the determination of an efficient rule of DR is indispensable for finding the best enforceable entitlement protection, namely one that gives the right non-performance incentives to injurers while compensating the victims such that both (or all) signatories are willing to precommit to the efficient level of contractual concessions.

from non-performance reside with the injurer. Whenever the potential injurer is under a specific performance obligation (property rule), he must engage in renegotiation in order to buy off the right of non-performance from the victim. Both *ex post* discretion and gains from non-performance are then a matter of negotiation. In case *ex post* adjustment behavior is strictly prohibited, all signatories are under an unconditional specific performance obligation (or rule of inalienability).

When searching for the most efficient substitute for the CCC in a situation of contractual incompleteness, the ultimate question that signatories have to settle effectively is: "Who owns the gap, and at what price?" The level of entitlement protection determines the *ex post* discretionary action space of contracting parties, and also fixes how *ex post* gains from non-performance are to be divided between the parties: a liability rule of protection advantages the injurer and (at best) insures the victim as a residual claimant against suffering harm. Under a property rule (PR) of entitlement protection, the victim's best alternative to no agreement is to insist on the injurer's performance as promised. Her threat to have enforced the original terms of the agreement makes her "owner" of the gap. Under the PR, victims are likely to appropriate a larger share of the *ex post* gains from contractual flexibility (cf. our discussion in Chapter 2, note 43 and accompanying text). Under an inalienability rule, no one owns the gap: the *ex ante* distribution of gains is identical to the *ex post* distribution, since contractual adjustment is prohibited.[74]

In the next three sections we will focus on four sets of questions concerning the design of default rules:

(1) In which instances of incomplete contracting is an inalienability rule of entitlement protection superior to a DR of *ex post* discretion? (section 3.3.1)
(2) What determines the rational decision between a liability and property rule of default? (section 3.3.2)
(3) What are efficient levels of intra-contractual remedies accompanying a rule of liability? (section 3.3.2)
(4) What additional modalities should be tied to a choice of a DR? (section 3.3.3)

### 3.3.1 Inalienability or efficient non-performance?

Whenever signatories decide on a rule of inalienability, they choose to prohibit any *ex post* flexibility: despite the occurrence of external or behavioral shocks, the originally established internal contractual structure is to be maintained once and for all. If the contract happens to have a gap, performance as mandated is nevertheless the only permissible action. The contract is renegotiation-proof; it must not be modified.

We saw above that a rule of inalienability is the adequate entitlement protection rule for the CCC, as well as the comprehensive contract.[75] However, inalienability can also be imperative in contracting situations featuring unforeseen contingencies, but where the exercise of *ex post*

---

[74] Dunoff and Trachtman (1999, p. 35) confirm: "Thus, default rules … are not simply neutral background rules designed to facilitate agreements; rather, they have important distributional implications."

[75] Whenever the incompleteness is bridgeable, the contract is "near-complete," for example, in instances of strategic incompleteness. In such circumstances, a rule of inalienability protects the complete set of entitlement protection rules. We showed above that complete contingent and comprehensive contracts assign a course of action to every possible contingency. There exists a comprehensive plan of action; therefore *ex post* discretion would by definition be welfare-depreciating.

discretion would be globally welfare-depreciating. A general rule of inalienability is apposite whenever *ex post* deviation from obligations is:

(1) always inefficient;
(2) contract-annihilating; or
(3) immoral, i.e. in contravention of basic external norms.

**(1) Choose inalienability whenever *ex post* escape is always inefficient**   Shavell (1980) shows that there are instances where rational welfare considerations warrant unconditional specific performance, since *ex post* non-performance of contractual obligations is always welfare-depreciating. It is welfare-optimal for signatories to tie their hands whenever two conditions hold cumulatively. First, the "breach" decision has to be less important than *ex ante* commitment. One or all of the signatories' *ex ante* commitments and/or pre-contractual relationship-specific reliance investments are fragile, and disproportionally more important (in terms of the sum of expected values) than *ex post* regret contingencies provoked by temporary shocks or long-term trends. Secondly, any *ex post* escape action by an injurer is apt to frustrate (or crowd out) the victim's *ex ante* reliance or up-front commitment.

Jolls (1997), building on the work of Fudenberg and Tirole (1990), discusses instances where contractually sanctioned *ex post* non-performance can be welfare-depreciating, even if both parties find it in their mutual interest (*ex post*) to escape or renegotiate the initial terms of the agreement. The author argues that "breach" should be unconditionally prohibited from the outset, so as to protect initial efficiency-enhancing relationship-specific investments, and to frustrate anticipatory strategic behavior in the form of under-investment. Indeed, post-contractual non-performance would lead to *ex ante* under-investment in reliance, and to a significantly lower *ex post* value of the contract.

**(2) Choose inalienability whenever *ex post* escape is contract-annihilating**   Whenever a *unique level* of commitment is indispensable for the functioning of the contract, a rule of inalienability is pertinent. This is typically the case in instances where the contract is a binary agreement,[76] or if the exercise of *ex post* discretion can be used to completely and irreversibly abrogate the terms of the accord. Consider the example of international arms control agreements, such as the Strategic Arms Limitations Treaty

---

[76]  The contract knows only two states of the world: compliance with, or deviation from, the terms of the agreement.

(SALT), or the Treaty on Anti-Ballistic Missiles (ABM): anything else than a default rule of inalienability would frustrate or annihilate the treaties' original terms, indeed the essence of these agreements (Rosendorff and Milner 2001, p. 830). No country would accede to SALT or ABM if they posited that any member may "temporarily opt out of the Agreement": "temporary" contractual escape would be tantamount to canceling the respective treaty altogether.

**(3) Choose inalienability whenever *ex post* escape is immoral**   Whenever clear, unambiguous peremptory norms of societal conduct are threatened by *ex post* discretion, an absolute protection of the initial entitlement, and the according strict prohibition to take away, or trade, the entitlement is apposite (Calabresi and Melamed 1972, p. 1111). Human rights are an example of a set of ubiquitously accepted inalienable rights that cannot be taken away or traded: a person cannot sell himself into slavery, or have his freedom of speech taken by someone in return for monetary compensation.[77] Transposed to the international realm, default rules of inalienability are pertinent whenever peremptory norms of international law (*ius cogens*) are in danger (Pauwelyn 2006). In addition to ubiquitous inalienable rights, every society or group has a set of generally accepted norms and values it perceives as untouchable.

To sum up: a rule of inalienability is in the signatories' best interest and indeed an equilibrium outcome of contractual negotiations, whenever the level or substance of the *ex ante* commitment decision is sufficiently more important than the escape decision. Whenever *ex post* back-tracking from previously made commitments frustrates contractual intent, inalienability is apposite.

### 3.3.2   Liability or property rule?

In most contractual settings, *ex post* discretion to temporarily and partially withdraw from previously made concessions is superior to "locking in" for good the initial terms of the agreement. In response to unforeseen contingencies or unanticipated party behavior, post-contractual non-performance can be mutually welfare-enhancing (in terms of expected

---

[77] Another way of arguing why peremptory rules of social conduct should be protected by inalienability is given by Calabresi and Melamed (1972, p. 1111). These rules do not lend themselves to objective and non-arbitrary measurement: "This nonmonetizability is characteristic of one category of external costs which, as a practical matter, seems frequently to lead us to rules of inalienability. Such external costs are often called moralisms."

discounted values), if the present DR implements the right set of incentives and constraints. It is a heatedly debated topic in contract theory, whether, and under which circumstances, a liability or a property rule of entitlement protection yields the better outcomes.[78]

Before we can go on to examine when and under what circumstances an LR or rather a PR makes for the more suitable default rule in an incomplete contract of the kind assumed in this section, we must find out what type of liability rule is to be pitted against a PR. As we said above, any LR of flexibility must be accompanied by an indemnity provision, or intra-contractual remedy payable to the victim (also called compensation, or damage payments).[79] We must thus examine which remedy provision signatories will rationally design so as to complement a rule of liability.

### Which remedy best complements a liability rule?

Intra-contractual remedies can be located on a continuum that ranges from zero to infinite (see Figure 2.3). Most common are the zero, the restitution, the reliance, and the expectation damage measures (Mahoney 1999, p. 121).[80]

The *expectation* damage measure aims to put the victim of contractual escape in as good a position as if the injurer had performed. It is

---

[78] In contract theory the controversy "liability vs. property rule" features prominently (see Kaplow and Shavell 1996b, note 1; Dunoff and Trachtman 1999; Krauss 1999 for literature reviews). The debate has circled around three different contexts: first, in the debate of *pre-transactional* allocation of property rights, where scholars are concerned, how (in the face of serious transaction costs) property rights should be assigned, and how to design efficient rules on the "taking of property" (injunction). In economics this literature features under the rubrics of "residual rights assignment," "comparative institutions," and "boundary of the firm" (see e.g. Coase 1937; Grossman and Hart 1986; Hart and Moore 1988; Williamson 1979). The second context of the liability vs. property debate is in the literature on rules of prescriptive jurisdiction: L&E scholars discuss the design of *court-ordered* rules of default, where parties to a contract have failed to specify their DR *ex ante* (e.g. Ayres and Gertner 1989; 1992; Craswell 1999; Johnston 1990). Thirdly, and more to the point, scholars have broached the issue of liability and property provisions as flexibility rules in contracts. Two aspects are of main concern: the effect that contractual rules of breach and remedy have on relationship-specific investments in private contracts (the hold-up issue; see note 8 above), and the ease of use and administration of flexibility rules in the face of various post-contractual transaction costs (Ayres and Talley 1995a, 1995b; Calabresi and Melamed 1972; Kaplow and Shavell 1995; 1996b).

[79] The reader is reminded that under a PR of entitlement protection, injurers and victims negotiate over the size of the damages payable to the victim.

[80] See Chapter 2, note 51. While liquidated damages are an interesting concept, it is difficult to generalize their impact and outcome, simply because their design and magnitude are unique to each contractual setting.

equivalent to the replacement value that exactly makes the victim indifferent between the injurer's performance and his default – the remedy insures her against any dynamics that unfold *ex post*.[81]

The *reliance* measure of indemnity is intended to restore the *status quo ante* the "breach" for the victim. The difference between expectation damages and reliance is that reliance damages compensate the victim for direct harm suffered, but leave aside indirect effects and foregone opportunities (such as transactional efficiency gains that would have accrued in the case of normal contractual performance).[82]

The compensation measure of restitution damages restores the *status quo ante* the contract. An injurer must re-establish the Nash-level that persisted before the contract in the non-cooperative past (this may or may not correspond to the zero cooperation level).[83] It is evident that restitution damages are smaller than reliance, whereas reliance damages are strictly smaller than remedies amounting to a victim's expectancy.

What is the appropriate amount of indemnity that reasonably rational negotiators will agree on at the outset of a contract? How can the victim best be compensated for her incurred losses? Mahoney (1999, p. 120) perceptively points out that the choice of intra-contractual remedy largely follows the *same* efficiency criteria as does the choice for an efficient rule of default. A particular damage measure can be termed efficient, if it creates an incentive for signatories to take the *identical* decisions and concessions they would have taken under the Pareto-efficient CCC. It is generally accepted that the preferred measure of damages is the expectation measure, since it induces injurers to refrain from performance only in situations where it is globally efficient to do so. At the same time, it does not make the victim any worse off after contractual default occurred.

To illustrate why expectation damages usually Pareto-dominate all other rules of remedy that can potentially accompany a liability rule of

---

[81] Expectation damages are essentially what is called "tit-for-tat" or "commensurate damages" in game theory. Mavroidis (2000, p. 800) argues that expectation damages are strictly higher than *damnum emergens* (direct harm suffered). Expectation damages must be interpreted as *lucrum cessans: all* further efficiency costs (opportunity costs or losses in value-added) caused by the partial breach of the agreement over and above direct effects must be indemnified (see also Schropp 2005, note 10 and accompanying text).

[82] It is exactly these contractual efficiency gains (transaction cost efficiency, risk transfer, transaction efficiency) that motivated transactors to conclude the contract in the first place (see Chapter 2, note 4 and accompanying text). One conceivable way of "paying" reliance damages is to seize a contested measure and return to fully cooperative behavior.

[83] Often restitution damages mandate the injurer to pay back any pre-contractual reliance investments made by the victim.

flexibility, let us consider a simple yet generalist model of a contract:[84] Suppose a single-transaction, one-shot contract between two symmetrical, risk-neutral, signatories.[85] The agreement is thereby a *perfectly indefinite contract* that contains a description of substantive entitlements to be exchanged, and a single default rule of liability. The contract notably contains no provisions for contingencies (see note 61). The possibility of renegotiation is not considered. In accordance with our above assumptions (notes 65 to 68 and accompanying text), we consider reasonably rational players, discrete commitment levels by both parties, optimal enforcement, and the presence of foreseeable incompleteness.[86]

Now define:

| | |
|---|---|
| $c$ | as level of cooperation, agreed to *ex ante* by each player. $c$ can be perceived abstractly as "willingness to cooperate." Assume a vector of some type of cooperation areas (production, trade liberalization, service, etc.). It is a non-negative set and will be endogenously determined, whereby the most reluctant transactor sets the common level of cooperation; |
| $\theta$ | as an unforeseen (previously unspecified) contingency that hits exactly one player. $\theta$ is a scalar that can be interpreted as an exogenous shock of some magnitude. The player affected by the shock will experience regret, and consequently takes the role of the injurer; |
| $B$ | as "breach" set, that is, all those revelations of $\theta$ that induce the injurer to escape his contractual obligations and to decide for intra-contractual non-performance; $\{\theta \mid$ the contract will not be performed$\}$; |
| $W^C(c, \theta)$ | as value enjoyed by the injurer if he gets hit by the exogenous shock, but performs his contractual obligations as promised (Cooperation payoff); |

---

[84] This model is used for exposition only. It is an abridged, adapted, and simplified version of the models used in Schropp (2007a) and Mahlstein and Schropp (2007), which are based on the intuition of Shavell (1980, p. 473).

[85] Stipulating a one-off contract is for expositional convenience only. Alternatively, we could assume a repeated-interaction contract, where players are uncertain if, when, and how the next interaction will take place.

[86] For the purpose at hand, it is inconsequential whether the probability density function of contingency shocks is known to players or not. Equally, it is of no consequence as to whether the contingencies are revealed symmetrically or privately to the players. It also does not matter whether or not victim and injurer know their respective roles as victim and injurer *ex ante*.

$W^D(c, \theta)$    as value enjoyed by the injurer if he gets hit by the exogenous shock and escapes from certain contract obligations (*Defection payoff*);

$V^C(c)$    as value enjoyed by the victim if the injurer performs his obligations as promised (*Cooperation payoff*);

$V^S(c)$    as value enjoyed by the victim if the injurer escapes from certain contract obligations ("Sucker's payoff" or "Scrap value" of the contract);

$V^N(c)$    as value enjoyed by the victim in the pre-contractual non-cooperative past ("Nash payoff").[87]

The game plays out as follows. Both signatories conclude a contract by fixing symmetrical *ex ante* investments/commitments and a rule of post-contractual escape, backed by a certain remedy. An unanticipated contingency occurs which hits one party that thus assumes the role of the injurer. Thereupon, the injurer decides whether to engage in legitimate non-performance ("breach"), or perform as promised. Anticipating the injurer's "breach" behavior and the damage payable to the victim, both parties shape their *ex ante* commitments accordingly.

Consider the first-best contract that signatories could possibly conclude. The Pareto-efficient complete contingent contract (CCC) is defined as the one maximizing the sum of the expected values of the contract to the injurer and the victim.[88] This implies that there will be an excuse to perform in a contingency, if, and only if, that situation will raise the sum of the values enjoyed by both injurer and victim. More precisely, the Pareto-efficient "breach" set, $B^{opt}(c)$, is given, where:

$$B^{opt}(c) = \{\theta \mid V^S + W^D \geq V^C + W^C\} \tag{1}$$

Rearranging the terms, equation (1) yields:

$$B^{opt}(c) = \{\theta \mid W^D - W^C \geq V^C - V^S\} \tag{1*}$$

---

[87] We note that $W^D(c, \theta) > W^C(c, \theta)$, and $V^C(c) > V^N(c) > V^S(c)$.

[88] To recapitulate: the CCC is the ideal contracting outcome assumed to result if players are endlessly rational, and there exist no transaction costs (see also at p. 57 above). Signatories thus anticipate any conceivable environmental (or behavioral) circumstance or contingency ($\theta$), and tailor the contract optimally to *any* conceivable realization of $\theta$.

In order to obtain the optimal "breach" set, the injurer's regret contingency (the anticipated exogenous shock) must be large enough that his regret ($W^D - W^C$) outweighs the harm done to the victim ($V^C - V^S$). The CCC strictly mandates performance, and grants non-performances, in situations where it is mutually welfare-enhancing to do so. Since the CCC is the first-best contract, it also induces both parties to concede to optimal *ex ante* commitment levels (c*).[89]

Let us now leave the contracting ideal of the CCC behind, and proceed to consider the optimally indefinite incomplete contract backed by a liability rule of flexibility. A game of complete uncertainty over the future unfolds. We define in addition to the above variables:

| | |
|---|---|
| d | as damage measure (for simplicity, a monetary compensation payable by the injurer to the victim); |
| $W^C(c, \theta)$ | as value enjoyed by the injurer, if he gets hit by the exogenous shock, but performs the contract as promised; |
| $W^D(c, \theta) - d$ | as value enjoyed by the injurer, given "breach" and subsequent damage payment; |
| $V^C(c)$ | as value enjoyed by the victim, if the injurer performs his obligations as promised; |
| $V^S(c) + d$ | as value enjoyed by the victim, given "breach" by the injurer and subsequent damage payment. |

Under an LR system of default, the injurer's *participation constraint* is:

$$W^D - d \geq W^C \qquad (2)$$

Equivalently, we can note:

$$B(c) = \{\theta \mid W^D - W^C \geq d\} \qquad (2^*)$$

The injurer's participation constraint basically states that the damage payment, or indemnity payable for non-performance, must be strictly smaller than the size of the injurer's efficiency gains from non-compliance;

---

[89] Shavell (1980, p. 475) proves this mathematically by backwards induction for the case of unilateral *ex ante* commitment (in his case, reliance investment) on the part of the victim. His results, however, carry over to the situation of double-sided investment at hand (cf. Mahlstein and Schropp 2007).

otherwise the injurer is not willing to utilize his *ex post* discretion and refrain from "breaching" his obligations.

The victim's participation constraint, next, is given by:

$$d \geq V^C - V^S \tag{3}$$

which essentially says that a reasonably rational victim must be compensated for her losses suffered from the injurer's non-performance. Otherwise the contract is a loss-making enterprise for her, whenever the injurer escapes from his contractual obligations. Consequently, the victim will not agree to sign up to the agreement if (3) does not hold.

Inserting the victim's participation constraints (3) in equation (2*) above yields:

$$B(c) = \{\theta \mid W^D - W^C \geq V^C - V^S\} = B^{opt}(c) \tag{4}$$

which is equivalent to equation (1), the optimal "breach" set. In other words, in order to satisfy both signatories' participation constraints, any feasible incomplete contract between two reasonably rational parties must feature the same (optimal) "breach" set as the CCC; otherwise the contract will be rejected *ex ante* by either one of the signatories.

Let us now compare different damage remedies (*d*) that this incomplete contract can feature:

under the expectation measure $\quad d^{exp} = V^C - V^S$
under the reliance measure $\quad d^{rel} = V^N - V^S$
under the restitution measure[90] $\quad d^{res} = V^N - V^S$
under the zero-damage measure $\quad d^0 = 0$

It is now easy to see that *only* the expectation damage measure yields a "breach" set which mimics the optimal "breach" set that the CCC provides for. Inserting the remedy variants $d^{exp}$, $d^{rel}$, $d^{res}$, and $d^0$ into equation (2*), we can see:

$$B(c)^{exp} = \{\theta \mid W^D - W^C \geq V^C - V^S\} = B^{opt}(c) \tag{5}$$

$$B(c)^{rel} = \{\theta \mid W^D - W^C \geq V^N - V^S\} \supset B^{opt}(c) \tag{5*}$$

---

[90] Reliance damages re-establish the *status quo ante* the breach, the restitution remedy re-establishes the *status quo ante* the contract. In our example of a one-shot contract without reliance investments, both damages are equivalent.

$$B(c)^{res} = \{\theta \mid W^D - W^C \geq V^N - V^S\} \supset B^{opt}(c) \qquad (5^{**})$$

$$B(c)^0 = \{\theta \mid W^D - W^C \geq 0\} \qquad \supset B^{opt}(c) \qquad (5^{***})$$

Any remedy short of expectation damages violates the victim's participation constraint, given by equation (3). In addition, equations (5\*) to (5\*\*\*) show that anything but expectation damages induces the injurer to escape more often than is optimal (the resulting "breach" sets are larger than the optimal "breach" set $B^{opt}$). Faced with reliance, restitution, or zero damages, the injurer engages in over-"*breach*" – he defaults inefficiently often, compared to the optimal "breach" set $B^{opt}(c)$.[91] This is equivalent to saying that the injurer engages in non-performance at the occurrence of shocks of a lower magnitude than the CCC would allow for default to happen. He takes the occurrence of relatively mild shocks to defect from the agreed-upon rules of the game. Hence, the injurer commits an opportunistic breach in situations where the CCC would mandate strict performance.

Absent an efficient "breach" set, the victim (as most reluctant trans-actor) will be unwilling to commit to the optimal level of *ex ante* con-cessions, $c^*$:[92] cognizant of the presence of some sort of shocks, she will anticipate over-"breach" by the injurer. Thereby, any efficiency loss from escaping the original contractual obligations will be shouldered by the victim, and she will not have a stake in any efficiency gain seized from non-performance either. Excessive escape behavior on the part of the injurer will leave her in a worse state than had he performed. Factoring into her calculation this opportunistic escape behavior will bring down her *ex ante* willingness to cooperate (her commitment level c); in fact, she will be hesitant to enter the contract at all.

Summing up the insights from these formal illustrations: only expec-tation damages possess the necessary incentive compatible characteris-tics that effectuate efficient non-performance by the injurer, on the one hand, and optimal *ex ante* commitment by all signatories on the other. Behind a veil of ignorance, commensurate remedies in the form of the victim's expectancy emerge endogenously.

---

[91] The corresponding "breach" sets $B(c)^{rel}$, $B(c)^{res}$, and $B(c)^0$ form supersets of $B(c)^{opt}$. In other words, smaller revelations of $\theta$ induce the injurer to escape his contractual obligations than the CCC would prescribe.

[92] Shavell (1980, p. 483) proves formally that any damage measure that is to induce the optimal level of *ex ante* commitment *must* safeguard an efficient "breach" set ("If there were a damage measure which always induced Pareto-efficient behavior, then in par-ticular it would have to induce Pareto-efficient breach").

To conclude, in this section we have illustrated (rather than proven formally) why "there does not exist a damage measure which is always Pareto superior to the expectation measure" (Shavell 1980, p. 483) – at least in one-shot contracts where the need for temporary and partial escape is as important as, or more important than, the preceding commitment decision. An LR of entitlement protection is best complemented by an expectation damage measure of indemnity. Most other commonly used compensation instruments short of expectation remedies encourage opportunistic over-"breach" on the part of the injurer. This not only brings down the mutual welfare level (hence constitutes Pareto-inferior behavior), but also discourages the victim(s) of such escapist behavior and induces them to engage in suboptimal *ex ante* cooperation. This decreases the value of the contract for both players.

### Property rule or liability rule? A question of transaction costs

Now that we have shown that a liability rule of default is best accompanied by the expectation damage remedy, we can proceed with our initial endeavor, namely to compare the respective suitability of LR and PR as efficient rules of default.

The choice of the efficient DR depends on post-contractual transaction costs: those TC that unfold during the contract-performance phase, after the conclusion of the contract determine whether an LR or a PR is more apt to address contractual incompleteness.[93] In section 3.1.1 we distinguished between two groups of *ex post* TC: Coasean (exogenous, or objective) TC, and endogenous (behavioral, or subjective) TC.

There are two groups of exogenous *ex post* TC: measurement costs of damages, and renegotiation costs. Each renders one of the two DR options more problematic. An LR is encumbered by calculation/measurement costs of damages, while renegotiation costs eschew a PR regime of flexibility.

A liability rule of entitlement protection backed by an expectation damage remedy requires the presence of an external arbitrator to calculate the harm done to the victim, and consequently to assess the appropriate size

---

[93] In a world absent of *ex post* imperfections, the choice of default rules is inconsequential: given that all post-contractual actions from bargaining to calculating damages are costless, the resulting resource allocation will always be Pareto-optimal (though not necessarily equitable). This is another application of the Coase Theorem (see Kaplow and Shavell 1996b). Contrarily, this means that owing to the presence of *ex post* TC the choice of flexibility DR *does* make a difference to the outcome, and consequently to signatories' choice of *ex ante* cooperation.

of remedies. This entails considerable transaction costs for all signatories. First, the injurer must engage in information gathering and processing costs in order to estimate the damage that his planned act of non-performance will cause to the victim. He must do so in order to assess whether opting out and paying expectation damages will be worth his while. Secondly, further TC are generated by the creation and maintenance of an impartial and capable legal authority which is to act as arbitrator. This is not only a costly endeavor, but also a collaborative expense prone to collective action problems. Thirdly, appealing to an arbitrator may bring about litigation costs for both injurer and victim (preparation costs, costs of using legal advice, opportunity costs of time invested in litigation, etc.). Fourthly, as a precondition for an LR to work, parties must agree that interpersonal comparison of utility is possible: the victim's subjective value should be "monetizable,"[94] and the victim must be willing to subordinate the subjective valuation of her incurred damage to the judgment of an impartial outsider (see Dunoff and Trachtman 1999, p. 31; Krauss 1999). A monetization of damages depends strongly on the underlying contractual exchange: where commitments and contractual efficiencies are easily measurable (money invested, profit made, tariff-lines decreased, etc.), posting a price tag on the damage suffered is substantially easier than in cases where commitments are multifaceted, emotional, or profoundly subjective (e.g. the value of a painting, the value of a limb). Fifthly, serious exogenous TC ensue if the arbitrator commits systematic errors: whenever arbitrators chronically under- or over-estimate the damage, injurers will either engage in opportunistic breach, or refrain from defaulting in cases where it would be welfare-enhancing to do so, respectively.[95]

Under a property rule of default, parties can do without an arbitrator. Instead, a PR of entitlement protection relies on the instrument of renegotiation of the contract. This brings with it a different set of exogenous *ex post* TC. First, although an objective interpersonal comparison of utility is less of a problem in a negotiation between an injurer

---

[94] We are not suggesting that compensation must always be paid in monetary units. Indemnity can take many forms: seizure of the measure in question, additional concessions by the injurer, an offer of consolation, etc. Our point here is simply that damage and compensation must somehow be inter-subjectively comparable in kind.

[95] Interestingly, Kaplow and Shavell (1996a) find that an independent arbitrator need not be omniscient or operate flawlessly. As long as its judgment is not systemically biased, the arbitrator's verdict will be acceptable to parties (see also Rosendorff 2005).

and victim, the parties nevertheless have to strike an implicit deal.[96] In particular, parties have to reach terms as to the size of expectation damages, since this is the victim's fallback option of negotiation, her best alternative to a negotiated agreement.[97] Hence, the injurer has to incur significant information gathering and processing costs, and costs of verifying the victim's expected harm resulting from his intended act of non-performance. Secondly, the victim also has to invest resources in identifying the potential efficiency gains from non-performance (of which she wants her share). This means that she has to assess the nature of the regret contingency, as well as its expected effect on the injurer's wellbeing. This requires serious fact-finding efforts on the part of the victim. Thirdly, in contrast to an LR, where the injurer is free to opt out and immediately seizes his regret contingencies, bargaining induces time costs in terms of opportunities foregone: whenever an injurer is hit by a significant shock, every minute lapsed without reacting to it (in the form of temporary withdrawal from previous commitments) will incur costs. If renegotiation drags on, efficiency gains from non-performance are lost. At the margin, renegotiations can persist until non-performance has become meaningless, and the prospective gains therefrom are lost (e.g. because the crisis has subsided). Fourthly, the number of signatories and the complexity of the contractual entitlements are another factor to reckon with when considering the option of renegotiation: the larger the group of victims, the more heterogeneous their preferences and the more diverse and versatile the underlying contractual deal, the more difficult, complex, long-winded, and conflicting will be the ensuing negotiations over contractual escape.

This comparison of exogenous *ex post* TC gives a first indication of when and why it is better to apply an LR or a PR of flexibility. Yet there is a second group of transaction costs which must be closely considered. Endogenous *ex post* TC are costs induced by strategic gamesmanship on the part of one or more signatories. We distinguish two kinds of situations: those in which symmetrical revelation of previously unforeseen contingencies induces parties to act strategically, and those that emerge

---

[96] Rogerson (1984, note 6) remarks: "Even though the agents can estimate the other's cost or value, it may still be impossible or very costly to specify the contingencies in objectively verifiable terms suitable for legal enforcement."

[97] As pointed out before (see text around Chapter 2, note 43), a rational victim has no interest whatsoever in a renegotiation outcome that does not at least put her in as good a position as if the injurer had performed (which exactly corresponds to the expectation damage remedy). She can threaten to cancel renegotiations and instead insist on the injurer's specific performance obligation.

from asymmetrical, or private, knowledge. Only the injurer's *regret contingency* may be private knowledge (the contingency or its effect is privately observable by the injurer). Alternatively, or additionally, the *harm* caused to the victim can be private knowledge to her.

Under symmetrical revelation of previously unforeseen contingencies,[98] three types of strategic behavior may occur.

**(1) Crowding out**    Under symmetrical information and a PR mandating renegotiation, the victim can effectively blackmail the injurer. Without any contractually fixed sharing rule or a distinct renegotiation procedure, the victim as a reasonably rational actor will try to appropriate *all* efficiency gains of non-compliance through renegotiations. She will make efforts to leave the injurer exactly indifferent between performance and default.[99] The victim thereby crowds out the injurer's regret. A PR without a structured renegotiation process can then become structurally equivalent to a variant of the game in which no *ex post* discretion is permitted. This outcome of essentially prohibiting *ex post* discretion is not intended by signatories (otherwise they would have opted for an inalienability rule from the outset, and not for a PR of flexibility).

**(2) Hold-out**    Even if there is some contractual sharing rule, or some sort of fixed renegotiation process (e.g. in the form of a timeline) in place, the victim under a PR nevertheless has an incentive to hold out on her counterpart (see note 8). Knowing that time is precious for the injurer, the victim may engage in opportunistic procrastination ("foot-dragging") with the aim of influencing the *ex post* distribution of the resulting non-performance gains in her favor (see Fearon 1998). This may result in either hold-out welfare losses and a "blackmail premium" for the victim, or even lead to an outcome in which the victim appropriates all the *ex post* gains from non-compliance.[100]

---

[98] Symmetrical revelation of previously unanticipated contingencies gives rise to efficient incompleteness and inexorable incompleteness of type A (see Figure 3.1).

[99] The victim can be expected to do so, because she sees only upside potential in engaging in blackmailing, yet virtually no downside. Under a PR she has the bargaining leverage of threatening to exit the renegotiations and to insist on the injurer's contract performance as promised at any point in time.

[100] Aghion, Dewatripont, and Rey (1990; 1994) discuss model situations, where one signatory appropriates all renegotiation surplus despite some (exogenous or contractually negotiated) renegotiation process (see also Chung 1991; Nöldeke and Schmidt 1995). Edlin and Reichelstein (1996) develop a renegotiation bargaining protocol that allows for "sharing rules."

**(3) Over-investment** Under an LR backed by expectation damages, and in a situation of symmetrically revealed information, the victim may be tempted to engage in overzealous (and hence suboptimal) *ex ante* levels of concession, or in excessive reliance investments.[101] Under the expectation damage remedy the victim has nothing to lose from the injurer's default. Yet she also has nothing to gain from contractual non-performance, since she does not enjoy any of the *ex post* gains from non-performance. Hence, the victim is not concerned by issues of non-performance altogether, and instead sees *ex ante* concessions as an investment with a contractually guaranteed rate of return (expectation damages act as "compensation floor"). This leads her to exceed the Pareto-efficient *ex ante* commitment level: the victim behaves as if her *ex ante* investment (in the form of commitment level or reliance) was not risky at all. This causes her to neglect the fact that even under the CCC *ex ante* commitment will not always produce efficiencies in instances of non-performance (Shavell 1980, p. 478).[102]

In summary, we see that both non-performance regimes show weaknesses when it comes to withering strategic gamesmanship on the part of the victim in situations of symmetrical revelation of contingencies. The general verdict in the literature is divided: whereas Rogerson (1984) and Edlin and Reichelstein (1996) see a clear superiority of the PR in situations of unilateral and bilateral reliance investments, Sykes (1991, Appendix A) and Ethier (2001a) show that an LR complemented by expectation damages will equally lead to efficient outcomes.[103]

Things change, once the contexts of asymmetrical revelation of contingencies (a situation that we previously termed necessary and inexorable incompleteness of type B) are examined. Under asymmetrical information the following strategic party behavior problems may be observed.

---

[101] Note that the concern of *under*-investment caused by the notorious hold-up behavior (see note 8 above) is *not* of issue under an expectation damage remedy. As we saw in the last section, overzealous "breach" and *under*-investment occur when victims are not sufficiently compensated for their losses. This is the case for the reliance, restitution, and zero damage measures, but not for the remedy of expectancy.

[102] "Because expectation damages 'insure' the [victim] against all breaches of the other party, [her] private return to reliance exceeds the joint return. As a consequence, levels of reliance are set excessively high" (Rogerson 1984, p. 40). Thus, over-investment is a contract-theoretical version of the "tragedy of the commons" (cf. Hardin 1968).

[103] The discrepancy in outcome between Rogerson and Edlin and Reichelstein, and Ethier and Sykes can be attributed to a difference in modeling: Ethier and Sykes assume that parties negotiate behind a veil of ignorance, that is, signatories do not know whether they will turn out to be injurers or victims later on. Rogerson and Edlin and Reichelstein, on the other hand, assume predefined, fixed roles. Note that none of these models consider the presence of any exogenous *ex post* transaction costs.

**(1) Over-investment** Under a regime of LR-cum-expectation damages, overzealous investment by the victim party may also occur in games of asymmetrical revelation of contingencies (Shavell 1980): the victim, ignorant of (and indifferent to) the nature and size of the injurer's regret contingencies, takes his *ex ante* promises as an investment with a certain rate of return. This leads to inefficient overcommitment.

**(2) Hold-out** In situations where the victim possesses private know-ledge of the damage incurred against her,[104] hold-out behavior can occur under a PR of entitlement protection. The victim has a strong incentive to overstate her incurred damage, and to drag on renegotiation talks. Ideally, she will expropriate the injurer of all the (commonly known) gains from non-compliance.

**(3) Reverse hold-out** Whenever the revelation of a previously unspe-cified contingency or its effect is private knowledge to the injurer, he has an incentive to misconstrue reality, if the flexibility regime is a PR. The gains from non-performance are thus the injurer's proprietary know-ledge. Under the specific performance requirement this induces the injurer to make believe that the exogenous shock (his regret contingency) was small and insignificant, and that the efficiency gains from non-performance are minor. The victim has all the reasons in the world to mistrust his assertions. Instead of accepting the injurer's compensation offer, she may make a counter-offer which apportions the (unknown) gains from non-performance substantially more in her favor. A sequen-tial bargaining model unfolds, in which the injurer, caught in between wasting time and losing his bargaining leverage to the victim, tries to maximize his payoffs by signaling his true intentions.[105]

**(4) War of attrition or double-sided hold-out** In situations where both the regret contingency to the injurer *and* the damage incurred by the victim are private knowledge to the respective parties, renegotiations prescribed by a PR of default are even more difficult. Both parties try to

---

[104] The victim possesses proprietary information whenever the continuation value of cooperation or her "sucker's payoff" (value of the contract after escape has occurred) is private knowledge to her.

[105] Grossman and Perry (1986) have described such a game, and found a novel solution concept called "perfect sequential equilibrium." The mathematics involved is notor-iously difficult. For our present purposes it suffices to note that signatories incur substantial opportunity costs in due course of a lengthy bargaining procedure.

misconstrue their real conditions in the renegotiation talks. Bargaining in situations of two-sided incomplete information has been termed a "war of attrition," because each party tries to hold out against its opponent. In this case, solution concepts are very difficult to come by, indeed.[106] For the purpose at hand it suffices to say that wars of attrition incur severe efficiency losses (time costs) and opportunity costs of bargaining.

Whenever asymmetrical information dominates the contractual relationship *ex post*, a property rule of default loses its appeal: entering into renegotiation triggers strategic hold-out behavior on the part of all signatories. A liability rule of default is superior in these situations. Under an LR the injurer opts out whenever he feels the gains from doing so exceed the expected compensation remedies payable to the victim. He may do so without being held up by a rent-seeking victim. *Ex post facto*, an impartial arbitration instance calculates the damage awards to the best of its knowledge and ability. Recent contributions in the realm of WTO scholarship confirm the general superiority of the LR in situations of private information (see Rosendorff and Milner 2001; Rosendorff 2005 for the case of victim's private knowledge of damage; and Herzing 2005, chapter 3; Mahlstein and Schropp 2007 for the case of private revelation of the contingency to the injurer).[107]

Some conclusions emerge: it is ultimately a question of context as to whether an LR-cum-expectation-damage or a PR of renegotiation is more appropriate to protect a certain entitlement in a situation of uncertainty. Transaction costs that occur *after* the conclusion of the contract and during the contract performance phase determine which of the two options is better suited to the circumstances at hand. We stressed the fact that not only Coasean, exogenous, TC are an issue, but notably also endogenous TC, caused by strategic party behavior. We

---

[106] See Ordover and Rubinstein 1986, Osborne 1985, or Hendricks and Wilson 1985 for overviews of the literature on wars of attrition in bargaining with asymmetrical information.

[107] In contractual situations featuring asymmetrical revelation of the contingencies *and* bilateral *ex ante* commitment, an expectation damage-backed LR neither leads to opportunistic breach (moral hazard) on part of the injurer, nor to excessive *ex ante* commitment on the part of the victim – if the damage calculation by the arbitrator is not systematically biased (Mahlstein and Schropp 2007). Opportunistic breach is ruled out, because the victim receives compensation amounting to her expectancy. Excessive over-investment on the part of the victim is ruled out, because the injurer will want to fix the mutual *ex ante* commitments on a lower level than the victim (Schropp 2007a, Appendix). Being the more reluctant liberalizer of the two, the injurer manages to set the reciprocal commitments on the *ex ante* efficient level. We shall return to this important finding in Chapter 6.

showed that in situations of asymmetrical information about contingencies and/or their effect on signatories' utility, property rules lose their competitive edge. In such circumstances, renegotiations are costly and prone to strategic brinkmanship by both the injurer and victim.

### 3.3.3   Additional modalities of default rule design

When drafting a proper gap-filling strategy, the contracting parties' decision to take one of the three DR options (LR, PR, or rule of inalienability) is only one, albeit important, question to consider. Signatories have to be mindful of additional questions on DR modalities.

First, there is the issue of enforcement: parties have to define the extra-contractual remedies that best complement the default rule at hand. It is evident that a rule of inalienability must be backed by coercive (or infinite) penalties (see Figure 2.3 and accompanying text). Signatories must be discouraged from ever deviating from the terms of the default rule. A property default rule that mandates specific (but renegotiable) performance must also be protected with very high punishments. Else, some injurers would prefer to defect from the rules of the game, and subsequently sustain the subsequent penalty.[108] How to protect a liability rule of default that is complemented by an expectation damage remedy? It is important that the extra-contractual remedy be more costly for the injurer than expectation damages. If so, a reasonably rational injurer will always prefer to adhere to the intra-contractual escape strategy instead of violation-cum-punishments.

A second issue of DR design is that of divided entitlement and level of conditionality: Should the enactment of a DR be tied to any preconditions? Is it advisable to limit the DR's scope of application? That is, should the entitlement protection be co-owned by both sides, injurer and victim in a situation of incompleteness? Probably not. The whole point of a default rule of flexibility is to act as a fallback for an unconsidered occurrence. How can signatories attach a conditionality to something they are insufficiently aware of *ex ante*? Attaching preconditions to a DR necessarily means limiting its scope. But large scope and far range are exactly the point of a DR.

In addition, a DR tied to conditionality is conceptually similar to a contingency measure. And as stated above at p. 88, contingency

---

[108] If a PR were not backed by very high extra-contractual remedies, it would turn into a de facto LR of escape and thereby thwart the default rule's initial purpose.

measures, though valuable, have a number of serious drawbacks.[109] Thus, a rule of default based on divided entitlement is predestined for disputes. An accurate rule of thumb is to keep both the underlying entitlement and the rule of default as simple and clear-cut as possible.

A third issue is that of divided entitlement protection: Does a hybrid rule between a liability-cum-expectation damage and pure property rule make sense? Should contractors *ex ante* craft remedies that are systematically lower or higher than expectation damages? The answer depends on the idiosyncrasies of the contracting context, as well as on the prevalent type(s) of incompleteness. In situations of strategic incompleteness, certain information-forcing rules of default probably make sense which systematically overcompensate the less-informed victim (see Ayres and Gertner 1989). However, under the set of assumptions used in this section (see notes 65 to 68 and accompanying text), especially in the presence of unforeseen, unspecified, and unanticipated contingencies, everything but an LR-cum-expectation-damage or a pure rule of renegotiation was shown to be an incomplete substitute for the first-best CCC.

Fourthly, do multiple rules of default make sense? Absolutely not. A DR is a fallback rule that allows for *ex post* discretion whenever an unforeseen or unspecified contingency occurs. A DR becomes effective in the absence of any explicit agreement to the contrary. Having two rival DR in place to protect the same entitlement is an arrangement that is bound to create havoc and disagreement.

The discussion in the previous two paragraphs leads us to a final consideration, namely that of the relationship and interplay between contingency measures and default rules. As explained in section 3.2.2, both measures are flexibility tools apt to remedy contractual incompleteness. Contingency measures are a special case of default rules and can be used as complementary tools of gap-filling. It may well be that a contractual entitlement is protected by several contingency measures and a single DR at the same time. However, two preconditions of an efficient system of multiple flexibility mechanisms must be heeded by transactors. First, signatories must effectively single out and unambiguously circumscribe all those bundles of outcomes they want to see protected by provisions other than the DR. Secondly, a clear hierarchy of flexibility

---

[109] A high enactment threshold always limits the application scope and brings with it the issues of sunk costs. Furthermore, contingency measures do not work properly in situations of asymmetrical revelation of contingencies. Writing contingency measures also bears the risk of provoking contracting errors due to imprecise and ambiguous language.

rules must be kept in mind: DR should trump any contingency measure, which means that unless contingency measures unambiguously apply, a DR comes into effect whenever a previously unspecified contingency occurs.

## 3.4    The efficient "breach" contract as the incomplete-contracting ideal

Chapter 2 gave a general introduction to the nature of contracts. The Pareto-efficient complete contingent contract was introduced as the undisputed first-best. Chapter 3 has so far dealt with the reasons for, and types of, contractual incompleteness; ways of addressing and remedying incompleteness were also reviewed. The objective pursued in this section is to revisit the concept of the efficient "breach" contract (EBC). We want to identify what an EBC really is, and what it is not. The EBC will be established as the contracting ideal in incomplete-contract situations: although second-best in nature, the *achievable* first-best contractual governance structure that reasonably rational parties wish to conclude in the presence of incompleteness. The EBC thus serves as the normative yardstick for *all* incomplete contracts.

Finding the contractual governance structure that best organizes various contractual flexibility mechanisms means looking for the EBC. As a matter of axiomatics: if the CCC is the unattainable Pareto-efficient complete contingent contract, then the EBC is the one – attainable – governance structure for incomplete contracts that best mimics the outcome of the CCC.

The concept of the EBC is quite often misunderstood, partly because of its ambiguous terminology, partly because the L&E literature applies the concept in a theoretical, abstract, and often a-contextual manner. In the following paragraphs and as a conclusion to our general introduction to incomplete contracting, we would like to set this record straight. In light of findings thus far we suggest putting the notion of the EBC into conceptual perspective.

**Efficient "breach" is no breach**    As mentioned before (Chapter 1, note 15), the terminology "breach" is somewhat unfortunate. This is so for at least three reasons. First, if parties *ex ante* agree on the permissibility of *ex post* non-performance under certain well-defined circumstances, this arrangement forms an integral part of the contract. Since this provision constitutes an intra-contractual arrangement, it is conceptually distinct from sanctionable defection from the contract. It is not a breach of contractual obligations. Secondly, the term "efficient breach" does not resolve the more vital question of how to organize non-performance efficiently – as a liability rule or a property rule, or a mix thereof.[110] The third reason why the terminology "breach" is misleading is slightly more subtle: an efficient "breach" clause is geared towards replicating the CCC's outcome. However, the CCC only knows *inefficient* breach. It defines an efficient set of performance and excuse obligations, which are optimal, *ex ante*, as well as *ex post*. Non-performance of the CCC provisions must by definition be inefficient. So, it is the CCC that logically defines breaching (extra-contractual) behavior, and not party behavior in an incomplete contract. Using the term "breach" is unfortunate when what is really meant is *non-performance as would be prescribed by the CCC*.[111]

We acknowledge that the term "breach" as a generic category for intra-contractual escape is problematic and may be misleading. However, it is useful shorthand.

**Efficient "breach" is not just about opting out of the agreement**  It seems that for many economists the concept of "efficient breach" is tantamount to that of a safety valve that allows for ready (uncompensated) opt-out: a party experiencing regret contingencies just withdraws from its previously made obligations; as a reaction, the victim might engage in vigilante justice and retaliate. This understanding of the concept is wrong. First, efficient "breach" can be achieved just as well under a property rule regime of renegotiation. Secondly, simple opt-out may constitute a breach, albeit not an efficient one: to constitute efficient "breach," a flexibility mechanism must necessarily be accompanied by a compensation provision. Usually (depending on the present context and constraints) an expectation damage rule of remedy achieves efficient "breach" under an LR (see at p. 109 above); alternatively, negotiated remedies under PR can achieve the same result. An *uncompensated* opt-out possibility is akin to a property rule for the injurer – logically a very different animal than a liability rule of entitlement protection (see Figure 2.3 and accompanying text).

---

[110] As was pointed out above (Chapter 2, note 44), efficient *ex post* adjustment to changing circumstances and unforeseen contingencies is possible under both a liability rule and a property rule.

[111] Terms like "efficient *ex post* default," "efficient adjustment to contingencies," or "efficient release from previously mis-specified obligations" would definitely be more correct in the message they convey, but sound more circumstantial and less catchy.

**An efficient "breach" contract is not an optimally indefinite contract** L&E literature of efficient "breach" often suggests that *ex post* discretion will naturally result in efficient outcomes (see e.g. Bello 1996; Schwartz and Sykes 2002b for the WTO contract). Saying it this way means elevating efficient "breach" (usually understood as a general liability rule of entitlement protection) to the overarching principle. In other words, the concept of an EBC is degraded to a contract, where *all* gaps that may surface in the contract performance phase are to be filled by the same liability rule granted to the injurer (Friedman 1989). This notion is of an entirely different caliber: a contract of this kind is exactly what we referred to above (note 61 and main text) as an "optimally indefinite agreement," namely one in which *all* entitlements are protected by the same unconditional liability rule of default.

This is a strong assumption, and one that we by no means wish to maintain. As we showed before, the optimal choice of gap-filling strategies depends on the nature of each traded entitlement, the contingencies affecting this entitlement, and on the *ex post* transaction costs involved. For a pure, across-the-board liability rule system of gap-filling to be effective, *ex post* transaction costs related to all possible entitlements and contingencies would have to be such that a simple LR is the negotiation equilibrium. This is quite a rigid corset, and one that is not likely to work in many contexts. Realistically, an optimally indefinite contract may only be operable in extremely simple contractual situations with a very limited number of contingencies (e.g. the sale of harvested and stored crop, the lease of a good).

A *maximally* indefinite contract is not *ipso facto* an *optimally* indefinite contract: in more complicated contractual situations that involve various volatile entitlements, a general liability rule of default may well be unworkable.[112] Some L&E scholars (implicitly) contend that the concept of an EBC equals an optimally incomplete contract. This is a dangerous oversimplification of contracting reality. An optimally indefinite contract (just like a comprehensive contract at the other end of the completeness spectrum) is but *one* governance structure for organizing contracts. It is fair to say that for most real-life contracts, the efficient

---

[112] Imagine an employment contract. Suppose the employer is granted an unmitigated liability rule of non-performance. He could breach *any* of the employees' rights by simply compensating them, including their basic human rights, their freedom of speech, their entitlement to have leisure and holidays, their entitlement to work breaks, their entitlement to form trade unions, etc. It is unlikely that an employee will *ex ante* give her consent to a contractual arrangement of this kind.

governance solution hardly lies on the extremes, but resides somewhere in the middle: most contracts are multi-entitlement accords and thus best protected by a mix of different default rules of flexibility.

**An efficient "breach" contract is not necessarily the most efficient contract** Contracting parties seek to negotiate the best possible substitute to the CCC – ideally one that is equally efficient. The epithet "efficient" thereby refers not to the quality of the "breach," but to the *nature* and *quality* of the contract in general. A contract may prompt efficient *ex post* non-performance decisions on the part of injurers, yet may well display inefficiencies compared to the CCC benchmark. It may prompt suboptimal mutual *ex ante* commitments or *ex post* welfare losses due to post-contractual transaction costs.

**An efficient "breach" contract is the ideal of an incomplete-contract governance structure** The L&E literature is cognizant of contracting parties' inability to achieve the ideal of the CCC in a non-stationary world. In situations where *ex post* discretion can be welfare-enhancing, an efficient "breach" contract is the optimal substitute for the CCC. As argued in the previous paragraphs, this is not to say that every entitlement of a specific contract should be subject to *ex post* discretion. Despite contractual incompleteness, many entitlements are best protected by an inalienability rule.

An EBC is one that strictly fulfills two criteria: first, *ex post* non-performance in every entitlement is identical to what the CCC would have mandated. Secondly (and this is a point that has received little attention in the literature of default rules), the extent to which signatories commit to *ex ante* concessions (size and number of promises) must be welfare maximal, as prescribed by the CCC. In short, an efficient contract requires efficient "breach" *ex post*, and efficient reliance (commitment) *ex ante* (Craswell 1999, p. 18).[113] Efficient non-performance (opt-out or renegotiation) is a necessary but not sufficient condition for the contract to be efficient.

In summary, the concept of efficient "breach" is an outflow of the maximization logic in a situation of contractual incompleteness. An efficient intra-contractual rule of non-performance aims at instilling

---

[113] As Rogerson (1984, p. 40) points out, Shavell (1980) was the first author to claim that the choice of default rule will affect the *ex ante* incentives to "rely," as well as the incentives to default *ex post*. Shavell was also the first author to establish that a comparison of the efficiency of various damage measures requires both factors considered.

mutually efficient *ex post* behavior irrespectively of what has (or rather: has not) been prescribed by the original contract. An efficient "breach" clause forms part of the contractual agreement. In a situation of contractual incompleteness, it constitutes a negotiated meta-rule for *ex post* discretion that supersedes previously agreed substantive commitments.

However, the efficient "breach" principle, geared towards remedying the incompleteness with respect to a single entitlement, risks being misinterpreted as a *pars pro toto*. An efficient "breach"clause is not an invitation to opt out of all legal rights and obligations. In fact, an efficient "breach" contract is one in which each entitlement is protected by that (set of) rule(s) which generates the most efficient outcome and safeguards the optimal pre-contractual commitments. It is the perfect governance structure that can be crafted in the presence of insurmountable contractual incompleteness.

## 3.5    A first step towards a general theory of disputes?

In lieu of a conclusion, this chapter closes with some deliberations on disputes in incomplete contracts and how efficient flexibility design can help minimize the number of trade disputes. Mavroidis (2006) argues that a theory of disputes is derived from the reasons for contracting, the "primary law" (entitlements) that signatories have given themselves, from the protection of entitlements that is agreed upon, and from the degree of contractual completeness. This chapter has dealt extensively with exactly those issues. We have introduced a typology of incompleteness and distinguished between the two groups of inadvertent and foreseeable incompleteness. We have also presented several strategies of bridging contractual incompleteness. The analysis led to an elaboration of the concept of the efficient "breach" contract (EBC), which is geared towards minimizing opportunism and seizing regret contingencies. To what extent can this chapter's insights contribute to a theory of disputes?

Contract disputes are a nuisance: they entail costs and create little added value. Their occurrence is an inevitable by-product of contractual incompleteness.[114] Interesting insights can be generated if we distinguish between two types of contractual disputes.

---

[114] A CCC is not expected to feature lengthy disputes. Being Pareto-efficient, any action in contravention of the letter of the contract is necessarily opportunistic and deserves uncompromising and instant punishment. No extensive litigation, interpretation, or gap-filling are required to solve the case.

(1) A contractual disagreement may occur because there is general ambiguity in the contract. Due to textual ambiguity, incoherencies, contracting lapses and omissions, or due to the emergence of contingencies of unanticipated nature, magnitude, and effect, parties feel a distinct and urgent need for clarification of contractual provisions. Parties are genuinely unsure whether the measure in question, or the occurred contingency, is within the limits of the contract, or constitutes an infringement. We shall call those instances "good-faith clashes."

(2) Disputes can, of course, also be caused by "bad-faith clashes": one contracting party, driven by self-interest, engages in opportunism, either intentionally or acting with gross negligence. This signatory deliberately "games" the system in search of private rents.

However, it is not the presence of uncertainty (and the resulting incompleteness) per se that make the distinction between good and bad faith clashes difficult, but deficiently drafted contracts, or contracting errors. As Chapter 3 showed, four types of contracting errors can be distinguished:

(i) ambiguous and ambivalent language;
(ii) insufficient language;[115]
(iii) rigidity;[116]
(iv) suboptimal remedies.

Ambiguous/ambivalent language is an outflow of accidental incompleteness resulting from poorly described contingencies and their outcomes (see Figure 3.1). As a consequence, legal loopholes may open up, or the need for clarification may become pressing. Contracts may also be flawed due to insufficient contract language, which means that the agreement fails to address gaps, either by explicit language or by flexibility rules. As a result, victims and/or injurers can engage in opportunistic behavior. Rigidity occurs whenever the contract demands performance in situations where non-performance would be welfare-enhancing. Finally, as was shown in section 3.3, suboptimal intra- and extra-contractual remedies either cause injurers to "breach" excessively often, or deny them the opportunity of doing so when it would in fact be welfare-enhancing.

Contractual disputes are a result of contracting errors. They emerge, because it is difficult to evaluate *ex post* whether a signatory's behavior results from ignorance, opportunism, or a drive to create added value. What can be learnt about contract disputes from this chapter?

---

[115] In section 3.1.3, insufficient language was labeled Type-II errors.
[116] In section 3.1.3, rigidity was called Type-I errors.

Our contribution may be considered a step towards a theory of disputes. Although we could not address issues of inadvertent incompleteness, and hence are unable to say much about disputes emerging as a consequence thereof, this chapter's findings can help assess the quality of contracting when it comes to foreseeable incompleteness. Taking the EBC as a benchmark contract against which signatory behavior can be assessed, we are able to evaluate whether or not a contract is well-prepared to deal with instances of foreseeable incompleteness.

In a world absent of inadvertent incompleteness, the EBC is free of disputes: good-faith behavior will always be channeled through intra-contractual flexibility mechanisms, while bad-faith behavior must necessarily be extra-contractual, illegitimate behavior. In an "EBC world" with inadvertent incompleteness, all disputes that arise can thus be expected to emerge from instances of ambiguity, ambivalence, and unforeseeable contingencies. Signatories must find ways of dealing with these disputes, perhaps by establishing a competent and impartial court.

Our findings are not a panacea. We have not found a way to deal with instances of inadvertent incompleteness. Yet we have come quite a way in showing how signatories to a contract can efficiently deal with situations of foreseeable incompleteness. We contend that contracting parties could free themselves from a number of disputes if they addressed their existing governance structure more seriously vis-à-vis issues of foreseeable incompleteness. Many contracting lapses caused by insufficient language, rigidity, and suboptimal remedies could be side-stepped if contracting parties tackled with rigor those types of uncertainty that cause foreseeable incompleteness. We showed in this chapter how signatories can effectively do so by crafting efficient rules of flexibility, and rules of default in particular.

# PART II

# Theorizing about the WTO as an incomplete contract

In Part I we studied the nature of incomplete contracts and way of overcoming them. Based on the insights gathered in Chapters 2 and 3, Part II will examine the World Trade Organization (as we could any multilateral trade agreement for that matter) from a contractual perspective. We will show that the WTO is best understood as a relational contract between self-interested policy-makers, characterized by complexity, longevity, repeated interaction, and by sizable incompleteness.[1] The WTO has outgrown the narrow confines of the GATT 1947, and is now a bundle of Agreements covering a wide array of issue areas, including services, intellectual property, government procurement, and technical barriers to trade.

In order to comprehend and assess trade policy flexibility in the WTO, Chapter 4 will examine the nature of the WTO as an incomplete contract. We will moot the identity and preferences of WTO signatories, and will discuss their incentive(s) to conclude a multilateral trade agreement. This will be followed by a presentation of the basic entitlements – the nature of mutual commitments exchanged in the contract. We then proceed to investigate the intricacies of contractual interaction, and the contingencies (or shocks) that might occur during the performance phase of the WTO contract. This will allow us to sketch the types of incompleteness the trade agreement is beset with. Finally, we shall assess the scope for regret caused by the inevitable incompleteness of the contract.

---

[1] Some authors go as far as to liken the WTO to a *constitution* (e.g. Jackson 2004; Petersmann 1986; 2002). Other scholars treat it as a *regime* or an *institution* (see references in WTO 2007, section II.B.3). However, as was argued in subsection 2.3.2 (Chapter 2, note 60 in particular), both constitutions and institutions are in fact contracts of sorts. They adhere to the fundamental contractual logic. It hardly matters what technical definition we give to the WTO, its essence is that of a treaty – the international equivalent of a contract.

Whereas Chapter 4 is concerned with basic entitlements (the primary rules of contracting). Chapter 5 looks at the contemporary regime of entitlement protection (the secondary rules of contracting) and of enforcement (tertiary rules of contracting). We will examine how well WTO signatories are dealing with the Agreement's incompleteness by mapping the current governance structure of the contract: its existent flexibility mechanisms, and the current rules of enforcement. We will discuss whether the existing system of non-performance makes sense, and if not, what the potential consequences on parties' *ex ante* commitments are, and what that means for the value of the entire contract. Special attendance will be given to the protection of the "market access" entitlement, which is the most important contractual commitment exchanged between WTO Members.

# 4

## Adding context: the WTO as an incomplete contract

The WTO emanated from the International Trade Organization (ITO, which never came into existence), as well as from the GATT and its subsequent extensions, which were laid down in codes.[1] The WTO was the outcome of the Uruguay Round (UR) negotiations and came into being on January 1, 1995. It is a single institutional framework organized around various pluri- and multilateral agreements, encompassing the GATT (as modified in the UR), all agreements and arrangements concluded under its auspices in the period between 1947 and 1994, and the complete results of the UR, most notably the GATS, TRIPS, TPRM ('Trade Policy Review Mechanism'), TRIMs, and DSU. The Marrakech Agreement to Establish the World Trade Organization, or "WTO Agreement" in short, is sometimes referred to as the "Charter" or "Constitution" of the treaty. It is a multilateral contract among sovereign states that establishes the WTO as an international organization and defines various committees, bodies, and councils, as well as the duties of and relationships between these groups.[2]

The WTO is a Member-driven organization with a compact Secretariat. It is mainly a negotiating forum for trade liberalization, a set of legal ground-rules of conduct in international trade, and a venue where signatories can debate and settle their trade disputes. The treaty's prescribed mission and objectives include freer trade, non-discrimination, competitive markets, rule of law, predictability and stability of international trade, and economic development.

---

[1] We take for granted that the reader is acquainted with the WTO, its origin, genesis, design, and functioning. Elementary primers are Dam 1970; Hoekman and Kostecki 1995; Hudec (1990); Jackson 1969; 1997a.

[2] As a convention, we will utilize the terminology "WTO" or "WTO contract/treaty" to encompass the WTO Charter (Marrakech Agreement), including the various agreements mentioned in Annexes 1–4 of the WTO treaty. This terminology at times also is used as shorthand for the WTO as an international organization.

In this chapter we wish to thoroughly examine the WTO in detail from a contractual angle. To that end, we will apply the insights generated in Chapters 2 and 3 to the context of the WTO. As a critical first step, the nature and the context of the contract will be assessed. Section 4.1 will single out the relevant contracting parties, their preferences and their (likely) contractual intent pursuant to negotiating a multilateral trade agreement.

WTO observers are trained to think of the WTO in terms of its multi- and plurilateral agreements that regulate the trade in goods, trade in services, trade-related aspects of intellectual property rights, government procurement, dispute settlement, antidumping, and so forth. However, in order to understand the WTO from a contract-theoretic point of view, it is important to shift from an agreement-centric view to one that distinguishes between different contractual *entitlements*, the primary rules of contracting. As shown in Chapter 2, entitlements form the essence of any contract.[3] Section 4.2 will examine what are the basic entitlements that signatories exchange in the WTO. We will show that the entitlement to reciprocal trade (the "market access entitlement"), in which countries commit to granting each other mutual market access, exceeds all other entitlements in importance.

Section 4.3 will finally assess the nature of contractual interaction and possible contingencies that may occur in a non-stationary world. We will discuss which categories of contractual uncertainty are present, acute, and relevant to the contractual relationship, and what types of incompleteness result. Comprehending the contractual incompleteness is a first and important step in understanding and criticizing the Agreement's system of non-performance – trade policy flexibility mechanisms and enforcement provisions. This task will be dealt with in Chapter 5.

## 4.1   Players, preferences, and contractual intent

It was the Appellate Body (AB) that stated in one of the early cases that the "WTO is a treaty, the international equivalent of a contract" (see Chapter 1, note 2). The nature of the WTO is that of a relational contract characterized by longevity, open-endedness, repeated interaction,

---

[3] At p. 43 above, contractual entitlements were introduced as residual rights of ownership or property that contracting parties assign to each other. A contract then is a bundle of entitlements (rights and obligations) that specifies the scale and scope of interpersonal cooperation.

complexity, and incompleteness.[4] In this section we will identify the key actors representing WTO contracting parties, their preferences and objectives. We will rely on the results of the political economy literature, a coherent theory of decision-making which has become standard in economic literature today.

### 4.1.1 Players and preferences: political economy theories of endogenous trade policy-making

The WTO is a contract between sovereign states or territories. Who really takes the decision to join a multilateral trade agreement on behalf of a country, and who decides the conditions and modalities of the contract? Is it the electoral majority (the median voter) of a democratic country, the parliamentary legislative, a "benevolent dictator" or "social planner" who wishes to maximize general welfare, or is it rather the administration or government of a state that is in charge of conducting the initial trade negotiations? We follow the tradition of the political economy school in economics, and maintain that the WTO is a mutually advantageous political contract among self-interested political officials.[5]

---

[4] We take these assertions to be uncontested: open-endedness implies a long-term setting without clear termination date, and openness to acceding Members. Repeated interaction is a characteristic of a trade agreement in which countries do not interact on a one-off basis, but routinely and permanently engage in the trade of goods and services. Complexity of the contract is a natural result: with 153 Members currently participating (July 2008), multiple issue areas (such as services, goods, investment), many thousands of tariff-lines and service commitments in four modes, and a multitude of protective rules and regulations in place, the WTO can rightly be called a complex setting. The criterion of incompleteness, finally, will be subject to a substantial discussion in this chapter.

[5] Political economy is the economistic concept of methodological individualism and rational choice applied to the realm of political decision-making. The political process is understood as a means of achieving reciprocal advantages (rents). Political economy approaches are critical of classical and neoclassical economics: they dismiss the tenet of policy being shaped by high-minded, welfare-maximizing decision-makers ("benevolent dictators" or "social planners") as naïve thinking. Applying the concept of methodological individualism more stringently, political economists contend that policy is drafted by self-interested government officials who care predominantly about maximizing their personal wellbeing, be it in the form of political support, re-election endeavors, receiving important information, or maximizing their budgetary discretion. In the realm of trade policy, political economy approaches are considered the state-of-the-art methodology (see Grossman and Helpman 2001; Rodrik 1995; Staiger 1995 for an overview of the literature). It has become widely accepted in contemporary economic trade literature that members of a trade agreement are represented by rational, self-interested trade policy-makers. In fact, it is hard to come up with any contemporary economic model of the WTO that would claim (and model) otherwise.

While we feel safely backed by contemporary trade literature in that claim, we nevertheless prefer to formulate our opinion about signatories and their preferences as what it essentially is: an assumption.

> Assumption: A negotiating party (would-be WTO Member) is represented by a single self-interested policy-maker, who is driven by a re-election/re-appointment objective. That objective manifests itself in the policy-maker's striving for political support maximization.

This assumption comprises three elements, namely concerning:

  (i)  the locus of decision-making;
 (ii)  the manner of decision-making;
(iii)  the specification of main actors' preferences and objective functions.

**(i) Locus of decision-making**    First, we reduce complexity by asserting that there exists only *one* key decision-maker per country. This individual (or homogenous group of individuals) is in charge of shaping the domestic trade policy and representing a contracting country's government in multilateral trade negotiations. This is a significant but reasonable abstraction from reality. Trade deals are usually shaped by institutions, such as DG Trade in the European Union or the USTR in the United States, under the guidance and supervision of their respective administration(s), and after having consulted the respective legislature(s). But what matters here is not how many people are involved in shaping a national trade policy, but whose decision ultimately counts. This is likely to be a small group of like-minded people ("the administration," "the government"), or even, as we assume, a single person, the "policy-maker." We will use the words policy-maker, government, and administration interchangeably.[6]

**(ii) Theory of decision-making**    The second element of the above assumption is the approach of *methodological individualism* as a guideline for decision-making: all actors, be they policy-makers, consumers, or

---

[6] The alternative to assuming the presence of a single key decision-maker lies in explaining or modeling the domestic decision-making process. This implies inserting an additional layer of strategic decision-making to the trade-policy game (e.g. between the EU Commission and the twenty-seven Member governments or between the USTR and Congress). However, doing so adds little additional insight, but complicates modeling considerably (see Grossman and Helpman 2001, chapter 9, for an attempt to give the domestic trade process additional structure). For a general discussion of the right locus of decision-making see Allison 1971.

producers, are *homines oeconomici* who behave self-interestedly, rationally (albeit not always perfectly so), and with reasonable far-sightedness when it comes to important decisions.[7]

**(iii) Actors' preferences and objective functions** The third part of the assumption specifies the preferences of trade policy-makers. Trade policy-makers officially act in their capacity of representing a state or territory. Yet we assume that they are ultimately interested in their own personal wellbeing. According to political economists there is no inherently logical reason why trade policy-makers should be any different from other individuals in their behavior. Concerning their professional life, it is assumed that what decision-makers want most is to be re-elected or re-appointed. The re-election/re-appointment assumption is broad enough to encompass various secondary preferences, such as policy-makers' drive to amass power, collect bribes, become rich, to "make a difference," to enter into history books, or to maximize a budget: without being re-elected, a policy-maker cannot achieve any of the latter goals.[8] Therefore, the assumption that policy-makers' preferences culminate in re-election/re-appointment is a solid and well-accepted proxy for their wellbeing.[9]

Re-election chances are maximized if policy-makers can rally as much political support from voters and pivotal domestic special interest groups

---

[7] There are, of course, alternatives to the assumptions of individualism and rational choice. Non-rationalist, or "constructivist," approaches to decision-making are norm-driven and collectivist in nature (see at p. 179 below).

[8] Although the policy-makers' objective of re-election or re-appointment seems to be tailored to democratic countries, we would contend that this statement is valid for *any* regime. Take a dictatorship: "A dictatorship is a democracy with a much smaller electorate" (Richard Baldwin in personal communication with the author). Under a dictatorial regime the identity of the body of voters may differ from democratic regimes, and the kind of influence they exercise on the self-interested policy-maker may be different. But ultimately, a dictator will have to be "re-elected," or continuously supported, by the dominant powers of the state. For this reason, we assume re-election and re-appointment to be equivalent concepts.

[9] There are alternatives to the re-election objective: policy-makers might exclusively act out of patriotism, a sense of duty, according to standard operating procedures or divine intervention, or out of sheer conviction that what they do is right. However, in the realm of trade policy-making, the re-election assumption is now standard in the literature. Ever since the seminal contributions by Stigler (1971) and Hillman (1982) it is readily accepted that trade policy is shaped by "incumbent politicians who make policy choices while being aware that their decisions may affect their chances for re-election" (Grossman and Helpman 1994, p. 834).

(SIGs) as possible.[10] SIGs are important in domestic politics, since they have successfully overcome collective action problems, are usually well-organized, and, importantly, are ready to invest time, effort, and money into influencing the ongoing political processes. Geared by their objective to maximize the welfare of their respective membership,[11] SIGs can influence and shape domestic policies, especially if policy-makers become reliant on their political support. Political support can take the form of financial contributions, ballot-box power, information provision, or coercive power (Grossman and Helpman 2001, chapter 1.1).

The policy-makers' aim of maximizing political support is reflected in the concept of "politically realistic objective functions" (PROF) (Baldwin 1987): governments are assumed to maximize some weighted average of general welfare (a measure that presumably safeguards votes) and SIG-welfare (which upholds political support by special interests). The relative weight that general welfare and SIG welfare assume in each policy-maker's calculation eventually depends on the personality of the respective policy-maker, the specific context, and, not least, on the micro-foundations (modeling specifications) of each model.[12] Some models exogenously assume the source of policy-makers' political support ("social democrats are supported by the unions"), others assume that SIGs competitively vie for domestic influence in the form of "government auctions" (on that account, see Grossman and Helpman 1994). These assumptions are for modeling convenience only, however. It is certain that the channels of influence are *never* clear-cut and stable, and that policy-makers' utility functions are likely to be in a dynamic flux, depending on the policy situation, the context, the current political strength of different SIGs, and on the personality of the politician in charge.

Turning to the trade realm, the relevant players are trade policy-makers (who are also trade negotiators), consumers/voters, and trade SIGs. Trade SIGs may be import-using (downstream) industries, exporters, import-competing sectors (e.g. farmers), foreign exporters, or labor unions, and

---

[10] SIGs can be industry associations, labor unions, NGOs, single-issue lobbies (such as the National Rifle Association, or the Royal Society for the Prevention of Cruelty to Animals), or important organized societal groups such as retirees, guerillas, religious factions, or gays and lesbians.

[11] This statement, of course, is another simplifying assumption.

[12] A policy-maker is not necessarily "auctioning" herself off to the highest bidder. Politicians' personal convictions, intentions, and standpoints can be reflected in the respective objective functions. They enter according to the weight a policy-maker attaches to general welfare, specific groups, or by the choice of SIGs that she strives to be supported by.

occasionally also environmental or civil liberty SIGs. Special interest groups are interested in changing the domestic relative prices so as to maximize the (economic) welfare of their constituents. In order to do so, they are contesting for political access to the trade policy-makers.

Trade policy-makers are primarily interested in maximizing their own political welfare. They are driven by a trade-specific PROF, a weighted average of general consumer and particular SIG welfare. Political entrepreneurs are assumed to exchange trade policy decisions (concerning issues of trade liberalization, subsidization, protectionism) in return for special interest group support. They devise trade policies that may redistribute revenues among domestic groups by crafting trade rules which are apt to change the domestic relative prices in favor of SIG sponsors. Every trade policy decision then has an effect on domestic general *welfare*, but also on the wellbeing of influential SIGs, and therewith on the decision-maker's political support.[13]

For our purposes, it is fully satisfactory to demand a *generic* politically realistic government objective function in trade affairs which is geared towards a redistribution of funds. In order to maintain the highest level of generality, we are not concerned with microfoundations of trade policy-making. We are agnostic when it comes to the specifics of governments' PROF, and would like to avoid the pitfalls that "endogenous trade models" have grappled with.[14]

---

[13] Baldwin (1987) was the first to show that a model in which SIGs lobby for protection (or trade liberalization) can equivalently be obtained from a model in which governments give more weight to producers' than to consumers' interests. The author demonstrates that policy-makers care about the domestic income distribution more than the maximization of total domestic income. They achieve their preferred domestic income distribution by means of tampering with the domestic trade structure.

[14] Formal political-economic models of endogenous trade policy-making and the structure of protection supply microfoundations of the domestic trade-making process. To that end, they specify in more detail governments' PROF, and SIGs' channels of influence-taking. This requires researchers to open the "black box" of domestic decision-making, and to supply the necessary formal specifications of trade policy-making. In that respect Grossman and Helpman's 1994 *American Economic Review* article "Protection for Sale" must be lauded for presenting the first model to give the lobbying game of trade policy-making a convincing microeconomic foundation. Their model is generally acknowledged as the standard workhorse of endogenous tariff policy-making (Rodrik 1995). In their model, Grossman and Helpman assume that trade policy-makers maximize a weighted sum of general social welfare and special interest group income (securing political support in the form of financial campaign contributions). SIGs welfare thereby enters policy-makers' PROF with a larger specific weight, signaling their higher importance relative to the general electorate (consumers). Policy-makers auction off their

Taking self-interested individuals/governments as the principal actor of national trade policy-making brings with it a string of important implications, formulated below as corollaries to the above assumption.

**Corollary 1: the state is not a unitary actor**   A political economy view on trade-making is basically a rejection of "statist" perceptions that assume nations are unitary actors with a fixed utility or set of norms and values. Domestic interaction shapes the preferences and norms of policy-makers in charge of formulating national trade policy and of negotiating international trade agreements. Assessing trade policy on the substate level opens up the "black box" of domestic decision-making, and gives an important role to various non-signatory actors, such as consumers, lobby groups, or NGOs.

**Corollary 2: self-interest is the driving force behind trade policy-making**   An important implication is that trade agreements are not concluded for the sake of the general welfare. This is a direct rejection of classical economic thinking which conjectures that welfare-oriented social planners, or benevolent dictators, conclude trade agreements to avoid negative economic externalities, or to tie the hands of future generations of policy-makers. General welfare considerations *may* play an important role in trade policy-makers' trade policy considerations – these considerations just enter the equation *indirectly* via policy-makers' own utility function.

Much in the same vein, the assumption that self-interested policy-makers represent countries in trade negotiations and consequently draft contracts to their liking, is in contrast to some lawyers' view that the WTO was created first and foremost so as to protect the needs, expectations, and rights of *non-contracting* parties such as consumers, farmers in least developed countries (LDCs), exporters, or NGOs.[15] From the viewpoint of methodological individualism these commentators' notion of the WTO is noble, but eventually a myopic conception of reality: following political-economic methodology, trade negotiators *a priori* have no interest in ameliorating the situation of substate factions (as long as they

---

domestic trade policy (a vector of trade protection of all industries) to special interest groups. SIGs simultaneously and competitively bid for their preferred trade policy vector. The policy-maker maximizes over the competitive bid and directs a unique trade policy accordingly.

[15]  The latter view seems to prevail in various contributions (e.g. Charnovitz 2001; Jackson 2004; Pauwelyn 2001; Petersmann 2002; 2003; Vazquez and Jackson 2002).

are not powerful) if that comes at the cost of depriving themselves of political discretion. If governments decide to do so, it happens out of ("selfish") re-election reasons and not out of altruism vis-à-vis these uninvolved third parties.

Of course, non-contracting parties *are* (or at least can be) influential in shaping trade policy decisions, but they just do so *indirectly* via the political support function of trade policy-makers. As stated above, SIGs can influence domestic trade policy outcomes by "purchasing" acts of trade intervention (be it protection, subsidization, market liberalization, or some other kind of market intervention) in return for political support.[16]

**Corollary 3: trade agreements are member-made legal orders** WTO Members[17] make their own law. Although the GATT/WTO "does not exist in a vacuum, but [is] an integral part of the wider structure of international law,"[18] WTO Members will contract freely, as long as basic tenets and peremptory norms of international law are not violated by the treaty.

This is consequential, since it means that the frame of reference for the analysis is explicitly *endogenous*. Self-made rules of the game are in strict accordance with policy-makers' short-, medium-, and long-term interests. The frame of reference for WTO Members thus consists of the norms, rules, and regulations *intrinsic* to the contractual relationship itself – it is not some exogenous legal or normative codex.[19]

**Corollary 4: trade agreements pursue political, not economic, goals** The above political economy assumption makes any type of agreement between self-interested policy-makers an inherently *political* contract. The rhetoric of trade agreements notwithstanding, the utility function of

---

[16] Political economy quite accurately presents trade policy as a "two-level game" in which trade decision-makers have to accommodate domestic constituents when cooperating internationally (Ethier 2006; Grossman and Helpman 1995b; Milner 1997; Milner and Rosendorff 1997; Putnam 1988; Ruggie 1982): in the first-level game, domestic special interest groups lobby for a policy-maker's support, and thereby significantly shape the second-level game outcome, in which two or more policy-makers carve out the details of an international trade agreement amongst each other.

[17] The term "WTO Members" is shorthand for "trade decision-makers representing a WTO Member in international trade negotiations."

[18] Stated in the GATT panel *US – Nicaraguan Trade* case (Report by the Panel L/6053 at para. 4.5).

[19] On this account, see our discussion at p. 96 above, where doubt is cast on theories of external relational contracting.

policy-makers in charge of trade negotiations is such that it does not directly maximize general economic welfare, but instead (partly) pursues redistributional objectives.[20] Thus, *a priori* trade agreements are not concluded for purely economic efficiency reasons. The relevant metric is political wellbeing, not general economic welfare.[21]

**Corollary 5: the natural state of affairs is protection not free trade**    Ever since the writings of David Ricardo and John Stuart Mill, the welfare-enhancing qualities of international trade have been among economists' most cherished beliefs (Irwin 1996). If it were up to economists, free trade should be the natural state of affairs in the world, since in the absence of trade barriers global consumption, production, and resource allocation are optimal. Reality, however, paints a different picture: countries are customarily reluctant to open up their borders to foreign products, and are often unwilling to liberalize trade unilaterally. What Krugman (1991; 1997) termed the "GATT-think"[22] may seem like economic illiteracy, but is absolutely logical, once the paradigmatic self-interested policy-maker enters the scene of trade decisions. Under a set of political economy assumptions, mercantilism – but not free trade – becomes the dominant explanation for the domestic structure of protection in practically all countries: obviously, there exist *some* domestic interest groups that benefit from trade protectionism in *some* sectors, and which can somehow convince domestic policy-makers to discriminate against foreign exports.[23] Free trade as a domestic equilibrium of the trade-setting game can be expected to be a result of the domestic tariff-setting game in the rarest circumstances only.[24]

---

[20] One could argue that trade politicians are profoundly hypocritical, because they never reveal their real motivations for concluding trade agreements. Instead, they constantly seem to emphasize the positive welfare implications of having achieved further market access for exporters and cheaper prices for consumers (Bagwell, Mavroidis and Staiger 2003). The long and the short of it is that both are true: trade agreements serve the selfish interests of policy-makers and render general welfare benefits.

[21] Although both SIGs and policy-makers individually strive for wellbeing and hence wish for the most efficient agreement to be concluded, the resulting contract does not necessarily lead to an outcome that is globally efficient in terms of general welfare.

[22] "1. Exports are good. 2. Imports are bad. 3. Other things equal, an equal increase in imports and exports is good" (Krugman 1991, p. 5).

[23] An alternative but essentially congruous argument is that policy-makers have a preferred domestic distribution of production and consumption rents, and that they choose border measures (tariffs, red-tape measures, quotas) to achieve this goal.

[24] Indeed, the situation in which a government only cares about social welfare is treated as an improbable "special case" in contemporary models of trade agreements: either the head of a government in an economically insignificant country is motivated by an

If we assume that policy-makers have a preferred domestic distribution of rents, the question is effectively why they do not content themselves with pursuing these mercantilist aims, but instead may wish to conclude a trade agreement with other states or territories. The short answer is that trade liberalization – just like technical progress and technological innovation – produces consumption and production efficiencies.[25] Gains from trade enhance welfare and foster economic growth, which in turn may boost policy-makers' political support, and thus their re-election chances. Yet this answer is too simplistic: it sketches a drive towards free trade, but neglects opposition thereto. In addition, the explanation is apt to describe why governments may unilaterally liberalize, but insufficient for elucidating why countries demand trade cooperation to be a mutual commitment. Lastly, it does not explain what motivates sovereign states to organize their cooperation in the form of a formal written contract.

As a matter of logic, international trade agreements must help trade policy-makers achieve their self-interested political economy aims better, faster, and more effectively; otherwise they would not conclude them in the first place, and prefer non-cooperative Nash-settings. Finding convincing explanations for why policy-makers want to conclude a binding trade contract is the topic of the next section.

### 4.1.2 Contractual intent: what is the rationale for trade cooperation?

Why do sovereign countries cooperate in trade affairs? Starting with the seminal work of Harry Johnson (1953), economists have strived to formally address this question. In this section we will review the contemporary literature on rationales for trade policy cooperation. We will start by discussing economic explanations (at p. 144 below). This will be followed by a short critique of these approaches: where they fail to convince and what aspects they neglect (at p. 155 below). Consequently, we point to the rich field of non-economic literature on trade cooperation: IR scholars and legal scholars were able to open new explanatory avenues previously untapped by economic scholarship (at p. 162 below). A summary of rationales (at p. 177

---

autonomous ideological concern (is a "free-trader," see Baldwin 1989), or no special interest groups exist in a country. As a final alternative, rival special interest groups' efforts to exercise political influence on the government exactly cancel each other out (Grossman and Helpman 1995b, note 11).

[25] In fact, conceptually, the presence of cross-country trade and international division of labor is little more than in-sourcing technological progress from abroad.

below) then presents communalities and differences between the different disciplines when it comes to rationales for trade agreements.

### An overview of economic approaches to trade agreements

Figures 4.1(a) and (b) provide an overview of the existing economic explanations for why countries conclude trade contracts.

International economics has come up with two generic answers as to why countries cooperate in trade. One strand of the literature, the so-called commitment school, alleges a strictly internal, domestic problem that a trade agreement can overcome. Another, by far more widely accepted, branch of the literature contends that it is international spillovers and policy-makers' preference for market access that motivate countries to engage in mutual trade cooperation.

As Figure 4.1(a) shows, the commitment approach subdivides into three branches of literature, namely into the time-inconsistency, the hand-tying, and the constitutional approach (numbers 1–3). The market access branch breaks down into two broad categories: the terms-of-trade school (which separates into the optimal tariff and the politically enhanced terms-of-trade perspectives, numbers 4 and 5), and the political externalities view (number 6). As we will show below, the terms-of-trade (TOT) and the political externality variants differ vastly in their assessment of the nature of the international externality that causes countries to cooperate. Some authors have set out to combine two rationales for contracting: Ethier (2004c; 2006) and Grossman and Helpman (1995b) assume the presence of terms-of-trade *and* political externalities (number 7), while Maggi and Rodriguez-Clare (2005), and Bagwell and Staiger (2005b) combine a domestic commitment with a terms-of-trade argument (number 8).

Figure 4.1(b) puts the information from Figure 4.1(a) in a matrix along two axes: the horizontal axis plots the *rationale for contracting*, according to the underlying problem that the conclusion of a contract can solve. It distinguishes between a purely domestic and an international problem. The vertical axis depicts the *nature of objective* pursued, or the function that is to be maximized. This can either be general welfare or self-interest of the policy-makers.[26]

---

[26] The rationale for contracting, and the nature of objective pursued are two quite distinct issues. The former is about the contractual *intent*: "What problem can a contract solve?" The latter is about the *objective* that guides actors' decisions: "What is to be achieved by cooperating?"

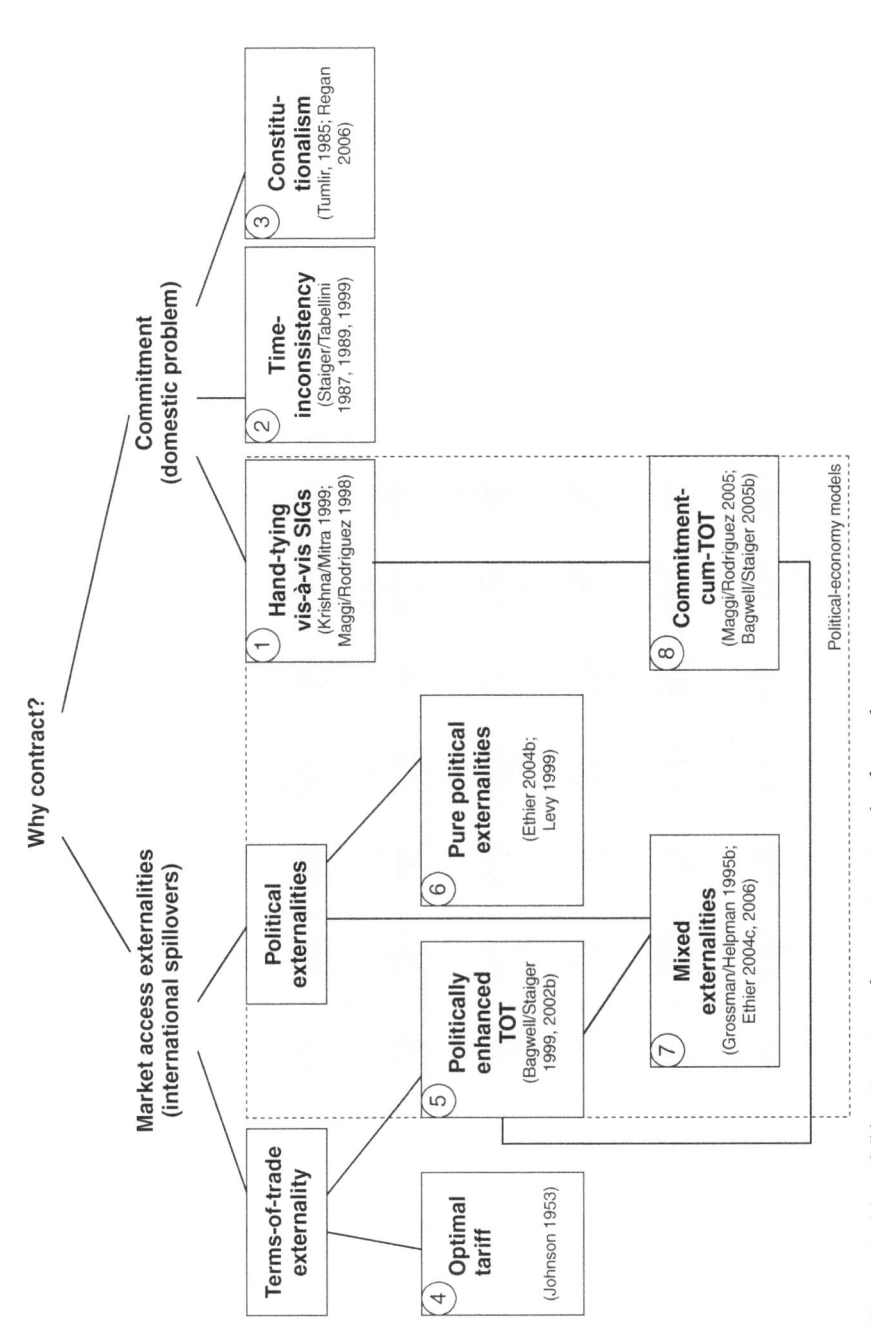

**Why contract?**

**Market access externalities** (international spillovers)

**Commitment** (domestic problem)

**Terms-of-trade externality**

**Political externalities**

① **Hand-tying vis-à-vis SIGs** (Krishna/Mitra 1999; Maggi/Rodriguez 1998)

② **Time-inconsistency** (Staiger/Tabellini 1987, 1989, 1999)

③ **Constitu-tionalism** (Tumlir, 1985; Regan 2006)

④ **Optimal tariff** (Johnson 1953)

⑤ **Politically enhanced TOT** (Bagwell/Staiger 1999, 2002b)

⑥ **Pure political externalities** (Ethier 2004b; Levy 1999)

⑦ **Mixed externalities** (Grossman/Helpman 1995b; Ethier 2004c, 2006)

⑧ **Commitment-cum-TOT** (Maggi/Rodriguez 2005; Bagwell/Staiger 2005b)

Political-economy models

**Figures 4.1(a) and (b)** Overview of economic rationales for trade agreements

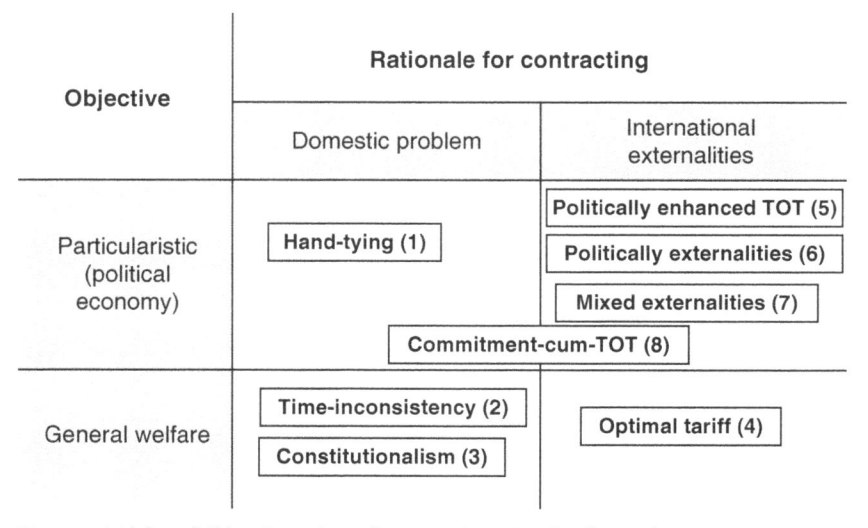

**Figures 4.1(a) and (b)**    Overview of economic rationales for trade agreements
Note: Figures 4.1(a) and (b) offer a categorization of different economic rationales for
trade agreements that can be found in international economics literature. Eight distinct
approaches can be distinguished (numbered 1–8). Panel (a) shows that economics has
come up with two generic reasons for the existence of trade contracts: the commitment
literature alleges a purely domestic problem that an international contact can help
overcome, while the market access externalities approach contends that international
spillovers are at the source of the trade contract. Two distinct market access strands
differ in their assessment of the nature of international externalities. Some hybrid
approaches exist which seek to combine two literature strands. The shaded area shows
approaches that are based on political economy assumptions which we subscribe to.
TOT is "terms-of-trade." Panel (b) is another way of categorizing the existing
economic literature: the horizontal axis plots the rationale for contracting, while the
vertical axis marks the maximand (objective), which can be general welfare, or
particularistic welfare of the self-interested policy-maker in charge.

Without going into great detail, we briefly characterize the existing
economic rationales for trade agreements.[27]

---

[27] Extensive reviews of the economic literature of trade agreements can be found in Bagwell
and Staiger 2002a; Hauser and Roitinger 2004; WTO 2007, chapter II.B. Economic
rationales of the GATT can be found in Mavroidis 2007, chapter 1 and Irwin,
Mavroidis, and Sykes 2008, chapter 3.

## Commitment approach to trade agreements

The commitment approach to trade agreements alleges a distinct inward-oriented domestic problem that can be solved by international trade covenants. Proponents of this approach argue that policy-makers merely utilize external pressure generated by the binding conclusion of an international contract to overcome a domestic inefficiency resulting from the strategic interaction between government and the private sector. A trade agreement is concluded so as to deliberately restrict the future discretion of governments over trade policy. By exposing themselves to sanctions in case of contractual defection (protectionist back-tracking from previously made trade liberalization concessions), domestic trade policy-makers can credibly commit to welfare-superior trade liberalization (lock-in effect). Hence, the commitment to an international agreement is used as a signal against domestic actors that the government cannot afford to renege on its initial contractual commitment, and that *ex post* back-tracking is not an option. This external threat makes the policy announcement *ex ante* credible vis-à-vis domestic agents. The commitment argument comes in three flavors (denoted by numbers 1–3 in Figures 4.1(a) and (b)).

The first variant is an adaptation of the well-known time-inconsistency literature in macroeconomics.[28] Domestic problems between a benevolent-dictator-type government and the private sector can arise when the government's decision to implement a domestic trade liberalization policy at some future time is no longer optimal when that time arrives. Certain domestic groups, unhappy with the proposed policy, engage in strategic actions, knowing that doing so will make the promised policy enactment impossible, or at least very costly for the implementing government. Consequently, the announcement that a certain policy will be implemented at a later time is not credible *ex ante*.[29] As a solution to this conundrum, the benevolent policy-maker deliberately "tie[s her]

---

[28] The problem of time-inconsistency was first highlighted with regard to monetary policy. Kydland and Prescott (1977) show that the discretion of central banks to revisit certain monetary policies after initial announcements to the contrary can create a time-inconsistency problem which makes the entire economy worse off. For a general and non-technical introduction into time-inconsistency theories, see Bernhardt, Broz, and Leblang 2002.

[29] One example of time-inconsistency in trade policy is offered by Matsuyama (1990): suppose that country A protects a large yet inefficient industrial sector behind high tariff barriers. A's government realizes that at present the costs of maintaining this sector are too high. It therefore announces that at a future date it will open up the sector to international competition. If the announcement is credible, the industry will decide to

hands to the mast of freer trade" (McGinnis and Movsesian 2000, p. 515) in order to maximize long-term general welfare. She hopes that an international trade agreement will help her make credible policy commitments affecting the private sector that she would not be able to maintain without the agreement.[30]

The second variant of the commitment school will be called the hand-tying approach. Literature on hand-tying adds a political economy element to the domestic trade-making story: trade agreements offer a way for a weak government to foreclose political pressure in the face of powerful domestic special interest groups which are lobbying for trade protection.[31] At first sight, this argument may appear contradictory to political economy models that stress the role of lobbies in maximizing a government's political support. After all, why would a government want to commit to a trade agreement that isolates itself from powerful lobby groups if it receives electoral contributions from them? Maggi and Rodriguez-Clare (1998) describe situations in which short-term benefits in the form of SIGs' political support are outweighed by long-term costs of protection.[32] By escaping a dominant SIG and concluding an external

restructure and invest in cost-saving technologies. The problem of time-inconsistency arises if the industry foresees that the government will not liberalize, should the sector prove to be not yet ready for international competition. Acting strategically, the industry will not undertake the required restructuring after the announcement of trade liberalization. At the stage of policy implementation, the government has no choice but to postpone (or refrain from) liberalization, because if it did push reforms through it would face the costs of a crisis in the sector. The government is trapped in a situation in which it cannot credibly liberalize.

[30] Proponents of this time-inconsistency view in the field of international trade include Grossman and Maggi 1998; Gruenspecht 1988; Lapan 1988; Maskin and Newberry 1990; Mayer 1994; McLaren 1997; 2002; Staiger and Tabellini 1987; 1989; 1999; Tornell 1991.

[31] The case of hand-tying is different from the time-inconsistency story. The government does not lack credibility, and there is no time-inconsistency problem present. Nevertheless, a government may wish to lock in its policy to diminish the likelihood that its current policies are reversed in the future.

[32] Think of a situation, where a government is subject to lobbying pressure by a well-organized, powerful, but eventually uneconomical import-competing sector. If the country does not have (nor may develop over time) a comparative advantage in that industry, protection will distort investment and lead to an oversized sector. Although letting the SIG have its way may be better for the self-interested policy-maker in the short run, the costs of these distortions may prove to be too large in the long run. The government may thus seek to enter into a predefined (possibly sectoral) international trade liberalization agreement in order to minimize these distortions from the outset. The authors mention another example where hand-tying may prove beneficial: an inefficient firm with a strong lobbying power is engaging in over-investments in order to secure future protection from the government. By committing to a trade agreement, a government will seek to avoid such long-term distortionary investments.

trade contract, governments seek to minimize unwanted distortions in the present that may arise in the future.[33]

The third variant of the commitment approach to trade agreements is an extension of the economic literature of constitutionalism.[34] It is rooted in the belief that citizens are able to write a social contract to overcome all sorts of collective action problems, to avert government failure and to curb rent-seeking behavior by particularistic groups of society. In the presence of overwhelming SIG pressure for trade protectionism, a trade agreement with another country acts as an additional constitutional constraint, a "second line of constitutional entrenchment of personal rights" (Tumlir 1985, p. 87). The conclusion of a trade agreement may hence be seen as a logical extension of the national (economic) constitution, aimed at safeguarding the latter's functioning. For the citizenry of a country an international trade contract operates as an international peg (or anchor) against government misdemeanor and lobby influence.[35] We will have more to say about the ideology of constitutionalism at p. 173 below.

### Market access externalities approach to trade agreements

Most economists tend to prefer another explanation for the existence of international trade agreements, namely that of market access-related externalities.[36] The argument of this branch of trade cooperation literature runs like this.

Governments want to gain market access to foreign countries for their export sectors. At the same time, they have a preference for high tariff barriers at home (which reduces other countries' market access to the home market). Unilateral trade protection of one country affects the

---

[33] For variants of this political-economic hand-tying argument, see Krishna and Mitra 1999; Maggi and Rodriguez-Clare 2005; and Mitra 1999.

[34] Early proponents of the literature of "constitutionalism," such as James Buchanan, Gordon Tullock, Anthony Downs, and Mancur Olsen, have shown how citizens, by writing a national constitution, overcome collective action problems, tie down policymakers' discretion, and curb the influence of government and private actors on fundamental freedoms and civil liberties.

[35] Contributions to trade scholarship in the constitutionalist vein include McGinnis and Movsesian 2000; Petersmann 1986; 2002; 2003; Regan 2006; and Tumlir 1985. Hauser and Roitinger (2004, p. 642) provide for an explanation and overview of the constitutional approach to the WTO.

[36] "[A] cross-country externality, such as the terms-of-trade externality, lies at the heart of all of the major theoretical approaches to the study of trade agreements" (Bagwell and Staiger 2002b, chapter 1, note 4).

welfare of trade partners negatively; it provokes harmful market access externalities, or negative spillovers. The strategic set-up of a prisoners' dilemma (PD) emerges.[37] Excessive trade protection, albeit inefficient, becomes the dominant strategy for importing countries. International trade agreements can help overcome these inefficient economic and political market access-related externalities. A trade contract is apt to constrain unilateral "beggar-thy-neighbor" policies by eliminating those inefficient restrictions in trade volumes which arise when policies are set unilaterally. Thus, trade agreements offer governments an opportunity to escape a PD.

Theories for trade agreements based on market access externalities come in two general categories. The first variation is the TOT school which further subdivides into the optimal tariff approach (number 4 in Figures 4.1(a) and (b)) and the politically enhanced TOT approach (number 5). The second variation is the political externalities school (number 6). A mixed externalities school tries to combine both categories (number 7).

**Optimal tariff approach**    The oldest theory of trade cooperation alleges a TOT-driven PD between two benevolent welfare-maximizing governments. The dilemma can be overcome by means of concluding an international trade accord. The literature on optimal tariff policy has a long history dating back to John Stuart Mill, and was formalized by Harry Johnson in 1953. Its basic insights remain influential through the work of Bagwell and Staiger and their politically enhanced TOT theory (below). In brief, the optimal tariff approach recognizes that large, economically powerful countries can shift some of the costs of a domestic protectionist measure (the erection of an import tariff) on foreign trade partners through the depression of world prices for that import good. Trade protection can improve the TOT of large countries, and therewith enhance the general welfare of its citizenship, at the expense of trade partners' welfare: beggar-thy-neighbor behavior depresses world prices for foreign export goods.

According to proponents of the optimal tariff view, large countries realize that a reciprocal selection of import tariffs produces significant

---

[37] A state's government sets its import barriers in order to maximize its welfare. It recognizes that some of the cost of this measure will fall upon foreign exporters whose products sell less. This externality leads all rational governments to set unilateral trade barriers that are higher than would be efficient.

global inefficiencies.[38] These inefficiencies can be avoided by mutual trade cooperation in the form of a trade agreement which fixes worldwide terms of trade, and thereby locks in world prices.

So far, so good. But what is the intellectual link between the rather abstract concept of TOT consequences of trade policy choices and trade policy-makers' proven appreciation for market access? After all, trade negotiators are always eager to point out the additional market access commitments they have secured over the course of trade talks. Yet they rarely mention the TOT implications of their negotiations. Bagwell and Staiger (2002b, p. 28) claim to have found a surprisingly simple answer. "The terms-of-trade consequences of trade policy choices can be expressed equivalently in the language of market access, and so the terms-of-trade consequences and the market-access implications of trade policy choices are different ways of expressing the same thing" (2002b, p. 5). According to the authors, any price effect (say, a TOT deterioration for country A through B's imposition of a trade impediment) necessarily has a corresponding volume effect (country A's reduction of access to B's markets).[39] Countries have a (TOT-induced) appreciation for unequal, imbalanced market access, and are wary of granting unilateral liberalization for that same reason. The conclusion of a reciprocal free trade deal contractually fixes mutual market access via common, undistorted world prices for all goods and services.

**Politically enhanced TOT approach** Influenced by the advances of political economy models in international economics, Bagwell and Staiger have enhanced the neoclassical optimal tariff approach by giving it a political-economic twist (see approach 5 in Figures 4.1(a) and (b)).[40]

---

[38] By taxing its imports, a large country has the means to inflict TOT inefficiencies on its trade partner(s). In return, however, each country is prone to TOT deteriorations inflicted upon its own export sectors through large countries' erection of import tariffs.

[39] Bagwell and Staiger (2002b, p. 29) contend: "[W]e may interpret 'cost shifting,' 'terms-of-trade gain,' and 'market-access restriction' as three phrases that describe the single economic experience that occurs when the domestic government raises its import tariff and restricts foreign access to its market … We may now say that a government *secures additional market access* from its trading partner through negotiations if there exists a world price such that the trading partner's negotiated policy changes provide additional access to the trading partner's market". See also Bagwell and Staiger 1999; 2002a, and Bagwell, Mavroidis, and Staiger 2002.

[40] The politically enhanced TOT school is championed by Kyle Bagwell and Robert Staiger, but was taken up by a multitude of WTO scholars (Bagwell and Staiger 1990; 1997; 1999; 2002a; 2002b; Bagwell, Mavroidis, and Staiger 2002; Bown 2002a; 2004; Ethier 2001a; 2004a; Grossman and Helpman 1995b).

The distinguishing feature between the traditional optimal tariff school and the politically enhanced approach is that governments, in addition to caring about economic efficiency consequences of local-price movements implied by their tariff selections, may also be motivated by political (i.e. distributional) objectives.[41]

The outcome of the politically enhanced economic externality school à la Bagwell and Staiger is that eliminating the TOT externality is still the sole rationale for trade agreements, even under a political-economic perspective. Abandoning the assumption of benevolent policy-makers does not decrease the significance of purely economic TOT externalities as the core motivation for the conclusion of international trade agreements.[42] The only outcome that is truly different from the optimal tariff approach is that the resulting reciprocal trade accord does not necessarily prescribe free trade, but displays positive, politically optimal reciprocal tariffs in the equilibrium.

**Political externality school of thought** The political externalities strand of the trade literature (number 6 in Figures 4.1(a) and (b)) gained prominence through Ethier (2004b; 2004c). It is critical of the terms-of-trade approach, alleging that "a trade agreement serves governments to get credit for the reduction in foreign trade barriers. International cooperation is not about the elimination of economic (world-price) externalities, but about political externalities. The latter arise when politicians in one country believe that their political status is directly affected by actions of politicians of another country" (Hauser and Roitinger 2004, p. 652; see also Levy 1997; 1999).

In a model of two small countries (where the established TOT theory would postulate reciprocal free trade as a Nash solution, and therefore an absence of a trade contract), Ethier (2004b) detects a motivation for trade

---

[41] Self-interested policy-makers are concerned primarily with a number of internal (political-economic) objectives that relate to the domestic relative price of imports in terms of exports. Bagwell and Staiger (2002b, p. 19) formally model this concern by assuming the most general government objective function possible: the only structure placed on policy-makers' PROF is that, holding its local price fixed, a government is assumed to achieve higher welfare when its TOT improves.

[42] "While the inclusion of political concerns enhances the realism of the model, we show that does not offer any separate purpose for trade agreements. Whether or not governments have political motivations, it is their ability to shift the costs of protection onto one another through terms-of-trade movements that create an inefficiency when tariffs are selected unilaterally ... the purpose of a trade agreement is to offer a means of escape from a terms-of-trade-driven prisoners' dilemma" (Bagwell and Staiger 2002b, p. 3).

agreements based on international political spillovers. The model features self-interested policy-makers,[43] unsophisticated factor owners, and multiple sectors. Factor owners (import-competing and exporting interests) care about trade volumes independently of factor rewards, and give trade decision-makers extra (mis-)credit for the direct market access effects of government actions.[44]

The same mercantilist logic as is held by the traditional models applies: governments benefit from being granted market access by other states, but dislike ceding market access. Unilateral liberalization is thus out of the question for self-interested policy-makers.[45] Hence, even in the absence of any TOT effects some level of mutual market access cooperation will occur between the policy-makers of the two small trading nations. Governments need direct market-opening achievements vis-à-vis their exporters in order to counterbalance the ire of import-competing sectors over direct losses in domestic sales. A trade agreement can remedy this situation. Governments exchange market access commitments in the form of tariff cuts, since each signatory party is dependent on the goodwill of the other. This is the nature of political externalities. Any trade agreement must be based on reciprocity. This results in additional market access (and therewith extra profits for exports), but also in a neutralized direct market access balance (which could be called a policy-maker's *balance of blame*). A balanced market access score brings about sufficient political support from exporters so as to outweigh protectionist pressure from import-competing industries.[46]

Ethier's model yields results that are quite distinct from the classical TOT-induced rationale for trade agreements. In contrast to Bagwell and Staiger's politically enhanced TOT approach (international market

---

[43] Ethier's underlying government PROF follows the tradition of earlier political economy contributions which have stressed the importance of political motives behind reciprocal market access exchange (such as Finger 1991; Hauser 1986; Hillman and Moser 1996; Hillman, van Long, and Moser 1995; Hillman and Ursprung 1988; 1994; Moser 1990).

[44] Exporters appreciate direct market access gains from trade cooperation, while import-competing interests feel hurt by lower domestic trade barriers (see Axioms 1 and 2 in Ethier 2004b). Technically, factor owners are bounded rational in that they are ignorant of the "Lerner Symmetry," which postulates balanced trade volumes. This does not seem an unrealistic hypothesis in a world with more than two sectors (let alone more than two countries), yet must be seen as an additional confining assumption.

[45] Also, since export subsidies are assumed away, a government is not able to simply tax imports and use the tariff revenue to subsidize exports.

[46] Due to their comparative advantage, exporters are assumed to have greater clout with domestic policy-makers.

access is appreciated for purely general welfare reasons), political market access externalities are part and parcel of the government's domestic objective function. The international market access balance directly influences the domestic political support balance, since the support of governments by specific factor owners is directly linked to market access considerations. Without the trade agreements that secure market access cooperation, policy-makers would not be able to achieve their goal of maximizing their political support function. In other words, political externalities are political-support reverberations of the unilateral market-closing behavior of trade partners.

**Mixed externality school of thought**  In Grossman and Helpman (1995b), and Ethier (2004c; 2006), trade scholars link an endogenous trade policy model of domestic tariff-setting with a mixed model of trade agreements based on political and economic externalities (see number 7 in Figures 4.1(a) and (b)). These contributions must be lauded for opening the "black box" of the domestic trade policy structure: the models in question present explicit microeconomic foundations for the interaction between self-interested policy-makers and domestic SIGs.[47] The authors use an extended version of Grossman and Helpman's 1994 "Protection for Sale" model (see note 14). The domestic trade-setting game is hereby supplemented with an additional stage of international trade cooperation: self-interested policy-makers in two large countries are assumed to maximize a weighted sum of consumers' and industry-SIGs' welfare. Again, governments' desire to contract is driven by market access considerations. Parties enjoy additional access, avoid unilateral market opening, and are happy with a reciprocal market access balance that is evened out. In contrast to models of the two previous approaches to trade agreements described above, both political support and TOT externalities emerge from the structure of the domestic lobbying game. Notably, their presence is not assumed *ex ante*. Grossman and Helpman's (1995b) article confirms findings of the politically-enhanced TOT approach, namely that the only relevant externalities travel through TOT movements. Applying a slight modification of the Grossman and Helpman

---

[47] The mixed externality approach does not only present solid microfoundations for the domestic lobbying game. It is also free from the arbitrary assumptions that were criticized in the original political externality-approach (Bagwell and Staiger 2002b, p. 31): SIGs are *not* assumed to be ignorant of the Lerner Symmetry (cf. note 44 above), and export subsidies are allowed as feasible domestic trade policy (they are not assumed away).

(1995b) framework, Ethier (2004c; 2006) reaches a different conclusion: if self-interested policy-makers only care about political externalities and not at all about TOT, the resulting trade agreement will look like the GATT/WTO, viz. a cross-sectoral, multilateral agreement that ousts export subsidies.

### A brief evaluation of economic rationales for trade contracts

Why do sovereign countries conclude trade liberalization contracts? Above we have reviewed eight answers from the discipline of international economics. In this section, we would like to set out a short evaluation of these theories. This will be followed by a more encompassing critique of economic approaches in general.[48]

**Commitment approach**  It is often argued that the commitment approach to trade agreements is still in its infancy (Bagwell and Staiger 2002b, p. 35; Hauser and Roitinger 2004, p. 649). We concur with this point of view. Although we do not deny that international trade agreements may indeed help governments *justify* awkward trade liberalization policies to domestic constituencies (cf. Staiger and Tabellini 1999),[49] it is hard to accept the commitment approach as a full-scale motivation for policy-makers to conclude a trade agreement. We summarize briefly what we take to be the most pressing counter-arguments against the commitment approach.[50]

*No historical evidence.* Irwin, Mavroidis, and Sykes (2008) engage in an extensive historical analysis of the international negotiations in the run-up to the GATT/ITO. Examining historical records (Agreement drafts, minutes, cables, diary entries, newspaper articles, bibliographies, etc.), the authors find hardly any historical evidence that would substantiate a commitment rationale for the WTO (2008, chapter 3).

*A "commitment contract" does not solve a problem.* Commitment scholars suggest that international trade agreements are concluded for

---

[48] We do not engage in a full-blown evaluation of all economic approaches here, but rather choose to highlight certain criticism that strikes us as most relevant. The inclined reader is referred to the reviews in Bagwell and Staiger 2002b, section 2.1.5; Hauser and Roitinger 2004, sections 1.2 and 1.3; and WTO 2007, section II.B.2–6.

[49] Commitment- and externality-based theories are argued to be "possibly complementary" (Bagwell and Staiger 2002b, p. 14). Various commitment-cum-TOT (number 8 in Figures 4.1(a) and (b)) approaches seem to support this contention (e.g. Bagwell and Staiger 2005b; Maggi and Rodriguez-Clare 2005).

[50] On this note, see Mavroidis 2007, chapter 1, and Srinivasan 2005 in addition to the sources mentioned in note 48 above.

entirely (or largely) domestic reasons. The trade contract is therewith merely a *means to an end*. All contracting parties subscribe to the same end of trade liberalization, employing the means of punishment threats. This reduces trade negotiation dynamics from a PD-type collaboration game to a simple coordination game. A synergetic coordination agreement, where every party has congruent objectives, does not solve a problem, since one does not exist – the risk of opportunism is notably absent (see our discussion at p. 54 above). This begs the question of why parties would feel the need to sit down, negotiate, and put into writing a substantial body of rights and obligations at all. A simple handshake and the common accord to apply infinite (coercive) punishments for defections would suffice to achieve policy-makers' objective of tying their hands.

*A trade contract solely based on the commitment rationale has a counterfactual institutional design.* A hypothetical "commitment contract" (i.e. one that follows the strict logic that commitment theorists allege) would have characteristics quite distinct from *any* trade agreement observed in the real world. If policy-makers really needed the trade agreement as a mere commitment device for binding their future discretion, any sort of *ex post* discretion should consequently be completely prohibited. Contractual flexibility mechanisms, as well as non-coercive enforcement remedies, clash with this commitment logic (Irwin, Mavroidis, and Sykes 2008).[51] Yet escape and less-than-prohibitive punishment for contractual deviation are a key feature of virtually every trade agreement in existence today.

Another counterfactual of a hypothetical trade agreement based on commitment problems is that we should see a very low level of trade concessions: intuitively, a high level of rigidity (bindingness of trade obligations) in a trade agreement significantly reduces a country's readiness to commit to extensive liberalization.[52] Hence, the depth and breadth of liberalization should be expected to be relatively modest and commitments rather static in nature. This, however, collides with the

---

[51] If we were to explain the role of trade policy flexibility mechanisms in a "commitment world," we would need convincing explanations as to how non-performance clauses and policy-makers' commitments can co-exist. One way could be along the lines of Ethier (1998; 2002), who models trade negotiators as individuals *different* from those deciding on subsequent protectionist policy.

[52] Fierce interest group battles in the run-up to the conclusion of such a rigid agreement can be expected. These turf wars should prevent governments from making far-reaching commitments (see Ethier 2001b; 2004b for economic underpinnings of this assertion).

successful trade liberalization efforts the world trading system has witnessed over the last sixty years.

*Why would governments choose an external agreement to lock in their commitments vis-à-vis influential special interest groups?* The commitment approach posits a domestic problem, but proposes an international hand-tying solution. A trade agreement is probably not the most intuitive and definitely not the most straightforward solution to a domestic commitment problem. Isolating trade policy-makers from the domestic political process, or delegating authority to politically less exposed actors (such as the executive or a national trade board) may be an equally efficient national means to achieve this commitment end. Giving a domestic trade decision-maker an independent third party status akin to a Supreme Court judge or a central bank could yield better outcomes.

*Why would self-centered policy-makers forestall their future policy discretion?* The political economy approach to international trade replaces the maximization of social welfare by a PROF that reflects the self-interest of the incumbent. Under this notion, can hand-tying really be a viable long-term strategy for trade negotiators, and if so, under what circumstances? Intuitively, it is hard to see why trade policy-makers would give away their most important policy tool – trade policy flexibility – once and for all in return for the straitjacket of a trade agreement.[53]

**Politically enhanced terms-of-trade approach**   Turning to the politically enhanced terms-of-trade approach to trade agreements, it seems important to note that this is the only research program that formally integrates an explanation of *why* countries cooperate, with an explanation of *how* they can do this. So far, it is the only available economic approach to explain both the existence of multilateral trade agreements and important aspects of their architecture, such as national treatment and non-discrimination (Keck and Schropp 2008, p. 5).

---

[53] Maggi and Rodriguez-Clare (1998) examine the conditions under which the commitment approach would lead self-interested policy-makers to sign a trade agreement. The counter-intuitive results of their model are that countries with strong import-competing special interest groups and weak government are more likely to enter an international trade agreement. In addition, only if policy-makers care significantly about *both* social welfare *and* campaign contributions will they engage in trade negotiations. Notably, too much responsiveness of policy-makers to political contributions, as well as too much benevolence (low responsiveness to special interests) will render efforts to engage in multilateral trade negotiations futile.

However, there is some conceptual criticism to be brought against the Bagwell and Staiger school. First, their approach can neither explain why small countries join trade agreements, nor why large countries would allow small countries to accede.[54] Secondly, the politically enhanced TOT school fails to elicit why export tariffs (which are apt to influence world prices just as well as import taxes do) are not banned in most trade agreements, and why export subsidies on the other hand are prohibited (but see Irwin, Mavroidis, and Sykes 2008). Thirdly, this theory does not explain why governments would use a relatively inefficient policy tool, such as import tariffs, to manipulate domestic prices in order to max-imize their political support (Rodrik 1995, p. 1476). Fourthly, the pol-itically enhanced TOT theory assumes a neoclassical world characterized by perfect competition, constant returns to scale, and constant demand elasticities. These are consequential and indeed confining assumptions. For example, in a Bagwell and Staiger world, producers always operate along their production-possibility frontier and can always sell all their goods and services. Under this notion, policy-makers cherish additional market access *not* because of additional export sales, but solely for its TOT impact on world prices. But reality paints a different picture in this respect. Exporters cherish additional market access precisely for herald-ing additional sales and larger capacity utilization. This raises some doubt as to the general applicability of the Bagwell and Staiger world.

As a final criticism, the politically enhanced TOT approach fails to explain the persistent antitrade bias which permeates real-life domestic trade policy (Ethier 2004c, p. 3). Why is TOT-induced protectionism more valuable to large-country governments than political pressure for free markets on the part of export SIGs, of foreign SIGs, and of down-stream industries' lobbies, or than consumer welfare? (See Ethier 2004b, 2004c; Hauser and Roitinger 2004; Levy 2003; Rodrik 1995; Roitinger 2004 reviews these points of criticism in more depth.)

**Political externalities approach** Ethier's (2004b) small-country approach to trade agreements, featuring pure political externalities, must be reproached for deploying a fairly unusual and arguably "hand-waving" government PROF. Many of the author's findings are a direct consequence of his Axioms 1 and 2 (2004b, p. 306), which present a rather rigid corset of assumptions. As Bagwell and Staiger (2002b, p. 30)

---

[54] See WTO 2007, chapter II.B.5 on the issue of asymmetrical trade cooperation between countries of different economic sizes.

contend, Ethier's argumentation is driven by the external restrictions of (i) bounded SIG rationality, and (ii) the prohibition of export subsidies. Also, Ethier is notoriously ambiguous about the real nature of his alleged political externalities.

**Mixed externalities approach**    This approach to trade agreements is a promising path, but still in working paper stage. Ethier's (2004c; 2006) contributions in particular are extremely difficult to follow, and it is almost impossible to present a sensible economic interpretation of his outcomes. Also, the author bases his analysis on a modified Grossman and Helpman (1994) model of domestic trade protection, which itself uses quite special and rigid assumptions.[55] On the whole, Ethier's mixed externality model is good in terms of its general intuition, but far from a full-blown theory of political market-access externalities.

**A general critique of economic models**    As a more general critique that concerns economic theories of trade agreements in general, we would like to point out three shortcomings. First, we take issue with those approaches based on the assumption that trade policy-makers try to maximize a general welfare objective function (this goes for the optimal tariff, the time-inconsistency, and the constitutionalism theories, as Figures 4.1(a) and (b) illustrate). Not only does general welfare max-imization collide with our political economy assumption of politically realistic, government objective functions; the assumption of benevolent dictators also defies realism. Governments, no matter whether democrat-ically elected or dictatorial, always have domestic distributional goals that they address by means of trade instruments. Practically no small country in the world (except perhaps Singapore) applies anything remo-tely close to a zero tariff-level on imports.

Secondly, another important shortcoming of all eight reviewed approaches is that they are mainly theories of trade in goods. Little consideration is given to trade in services, intellectual property rights, investment measures, issues of competition or government procure-ment, etc.

Thirdly, even theories about trade agreements based on goods are in effect models of tariff protection, but not ones of trade protection in general. They explain trade cooperation only in terms of import taxes;

---

[55] See note 14 above.

non-tariff barriers are usually completely omitted from these models.[56] Non-tariff barriers can be expected to alter results, just because they involve issues of observability, verifiability, and quantifiability.

### An overlooked economic rationale for trade agreements

The commitment school alleges a distinct domestic problem that a trade agreement is able to solve. Theories based on market externalities suppose the presence of an international prisoners' dilemma that can be overcome by a trade accord. However, there is a third rationale for contracting that has largely been unexplored by trade economists. It concerns the nature of strategic international interaction.

The theories of trade agreements based on market externalities reviewed above assume the presence of an international PD at work, which affects the interaction between countries.[57] Hence, it is assumed that international trade is akin to a collaboration game. The commitment approach, on the other hand, sketches a simple coordination game that hardly solves an international problem and therefore does not warrant the time and effort to negotiate and write a legal compact. However, as we stated in at p. 54 above, contracts are also regularly concluded with the aim of solving complicated coordination problems between individuals and countries.[58]

In a complex cooperative context, heterogeneous preferences of signatories will inevitably lead to disagreement over the distribution of gains from cooperation. Although parties know that cooperation is generally welfare-improving for all signatories, each participating party has a unique preferred outcome (game theorists speak of multiple

---

[56] Notable exceptions include Copeland 1990; Horn 2006; Hungerford 1991; and Levy 2003.

[57] "Different as the two rationales for trade agreements [i.e. the TOT and the political externalities approach] may be in substance ... their basic intuition is identical: both schools allege a simple game set-up where two or more rational players are faced with a PD situation. A trade contract can help overcome the inherent inefficiencies – given that two fundamental conditions hold: infinite repetition and the self-enforcement property. Infinite repetition avoids an immediate breakdown of the trade game, and self-enforcement means that any punishment (or rather: threat thereof) can successfully be enacted by the membership of the agreement itself" (Keck and Schropp 2008, p. 6).

[58] To recapitulate (see Chapter 2, note 28): in coordination games signatories join forces so as to reap mutual transaction efficiencies (synergies). All contracting parties know that conceding to some level of regulation is mutually efficiency-enhancing. However, doing so requires them to contractually fix the mutual level of cooperation *ex ante*. Disagreement may arise among the signatories over finding, and maintaining, the optimal level and composition of cooperation.

equilibria). Disagreement is likely to increase with the complexity of the contract (the number of parties, issue areas under negotiation, agents' action spaces) and not least with the uncertainty over future contingencies.[59] In order to avoid endless bargaining *ex ante* and opportunism *ex post*, negotiating parties settle for and put into writing a specific combination of welfare-improving coordination equilibria (or standards). The contract essentially functions as a focal coordination equilibrium whose outcome (the resulting cooperation level) is in the collective interest and mutually acceptable to every party. Signatories promise to adhere to the contractual standards of cooperation and not to defect from certain standards, even if doing so may yield some short-term gains. Various WTO commitments built on minimum standards of cooperation can be perceived as accords aimed at solving coordination problems (see WTO 2007, chapter II.B.3.b), and we will have more to say on this below.[60]

For an illustration of how contracts can ease the tensions of complex coordination problems, consider Figure 4.2. The utility of two countries/governments (X and Y) is plotted on the axes ($U_X$ and $U_Y$). Both countries are cognizant of the fact that the non-cooperative *status quo* (point SQ) is inefficient, and believe that they can improve on their welfare by cooperating. Suppose the parties understand the details of the contract possibility curve UU′ (the locus of all efficient contracts). Every point on the PP′ segment corresponds to a unique cooperation level (a bundle of cooperative commitments or minimum standards along several issue areas). Points along PP′ are mutually welfare-improving and in principle acceptable to both parties. Yet party X prefers cooperation levels as far to the right of P as possible (preferably point P′), while party Y's welfare increases, the higher the agreement point is (point P, if possible).

In the presence of multiple cooperative equilibria, the two parties are in disagreement over which specific commitment level should be chosen (schematically represented by points A, B, C, and D). Bargaining over this distributional conflict might drag on forever, which frustrates the gains from cooperation and binds other resources (e.g. Fearon 1998). To

---

[59] A complicated coordination game extends the strategic set-up from the $2 \times 2$-matrix of a battle-of-the-sexes game (see Chapter 2, note 55) to a $Q \times R \times R \times S$-matrix, where $Q$ is the number of players and $R$ is the number of agent strategies (levels of cooperation and defection), with $S$ as the number of issue areas of cooperation.

[60] As we will argue at p. 187 below, trade agreements based on "minimum standards" or "positive integration," such as the WTO Agreements on intellectual property rights or import licensing, may be properly conceptualized as collaboration games.

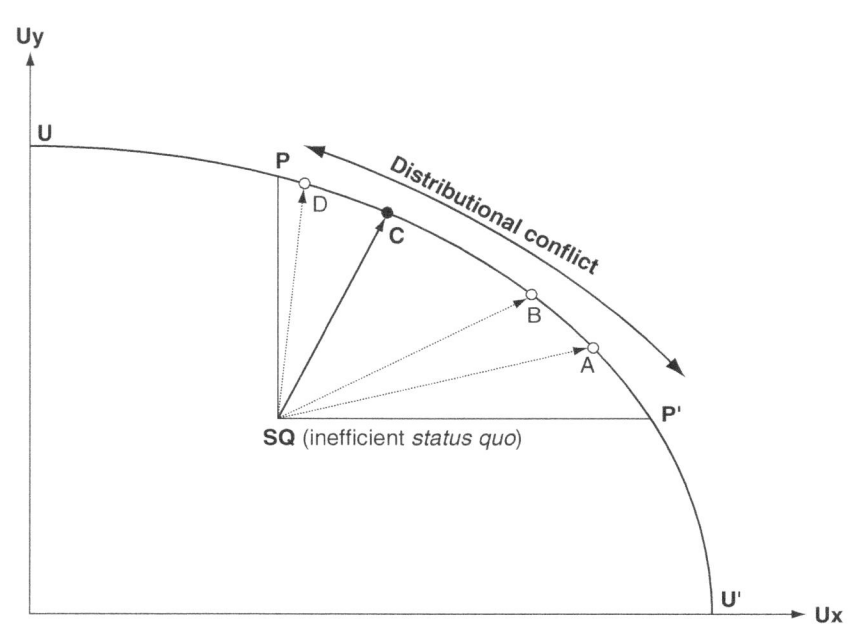

**Figure 4.2**   Coordination issues as rationale for trade agreements
Source: based on WTO 2007, chart II.C.1(c)
Note: This chart schematically represents the coordination problems that contracts
may help overcome. Signatories X and Y know that a contract will be more beneficial to
welfare ($U_X$ and $U_Y$, respectively) than the *status quo ante* (SQ). Yet they are in conflict
about the level of cooperation (illustrated by different points on the contract curve
PP'). A contract fixes one level of cooperation and therewith creates a focal and
permanent equilibrium.

put an end to discussions (and to discourage later instances of defection),
negotiating parties decide to pinpoint once and for all a single equilibrium level (in Figure 4.2 the cooperation level corresponding to point C)
that is then accepted as the binding outcome and incorporated into the
letter of the contract.

### Non-economic rationales for trade contracts I: lessons from the international relations literature

So far, we have limited ourselves to the discussion of economic and
political-economy approaches to trade cooperation. International cooperation in trade matters, and the factors that promote or inhibit such

cooperation have also been discussed from a range of different theoretical perspectives in the international relations (IR) literature.[61] In this section we summarize the discipline's most important theories of international cooperation and highlight additional insights that IR literature can offer over and above the purely economic and political-economy explanations analyzed so far.[62]

We propose to categorize different IR theories of international trade cooperation in the following manner (Figure 4.3):

This chart, adapted from the World Trade Report 2007 (WTO 2007) plots the leading IR theories of international (trade) cooperation along two axes. The vertical axis distinguishes between different underlying assumptions of decision-making. Two grand approaches to decision-making can be differentiated in IR literature: rationalist and constructivist approaches.

*Rationalist* theories assume that actors – the presence of informational constraints and market imperfections notwithstanding – take decisions with the strict aim of maximizing some utility function. States as the principal actors in the international system act "as self-interested, goal seeking actors whose behavior can be accounted for in terms of the maximization of individual utility" (Hasenclever, Mayer, and Rittberger 1997, p. 23).[63] One rationalist strand of literature assumes that all negotiating parties are driven by *mutual efficiency concerns* (first row of the matrix). Each cooperating party is believed to bargain for that solution which maximizes the "size of the pie" that cooperation generates.[64] Another theme of the rationalist conception in IR assumes that players try to maximize their *power position* relative to their competitors. To proponents of this view (middle row), international cooperation is akin to a zero-sum game, where gains to one party necessarily come at a loss to another one (the "size of the pie" hence is thought to be fixed).[65]

---

[61] For general overviews of IR theories on international cooperation and institutionalization see, e.g., Haggard and Simmons 1987; Hasenclever, Mayer, and Rittberger 1997; 2000; Krasner 1999, pp. 43–72; Kratochwil and Ruggie 1986; Martin and Simmons 1998; Simmons and Martin 2002; and Snidal 1997.

[62] The reader interested in a deeper discussion is referred to WTO 2007, section II.B.3 and the references mentioned therein.

[63] On the use of rational choice-based theories in IR theory see, e.g., Snidal 2002.

[64] These theories contend that signatories to an international contract strive for Pareto efficiency, which maximizes the absolute gains of interaction.

[65] This strand of rationalist thinking advocates a maximization of distributive efficiency ("Kaldor-Hicks" efficiency). Under this rationalist conception, parties worry about relative gains, and largely ignore (or take for granted) absolute gains of cooperation.

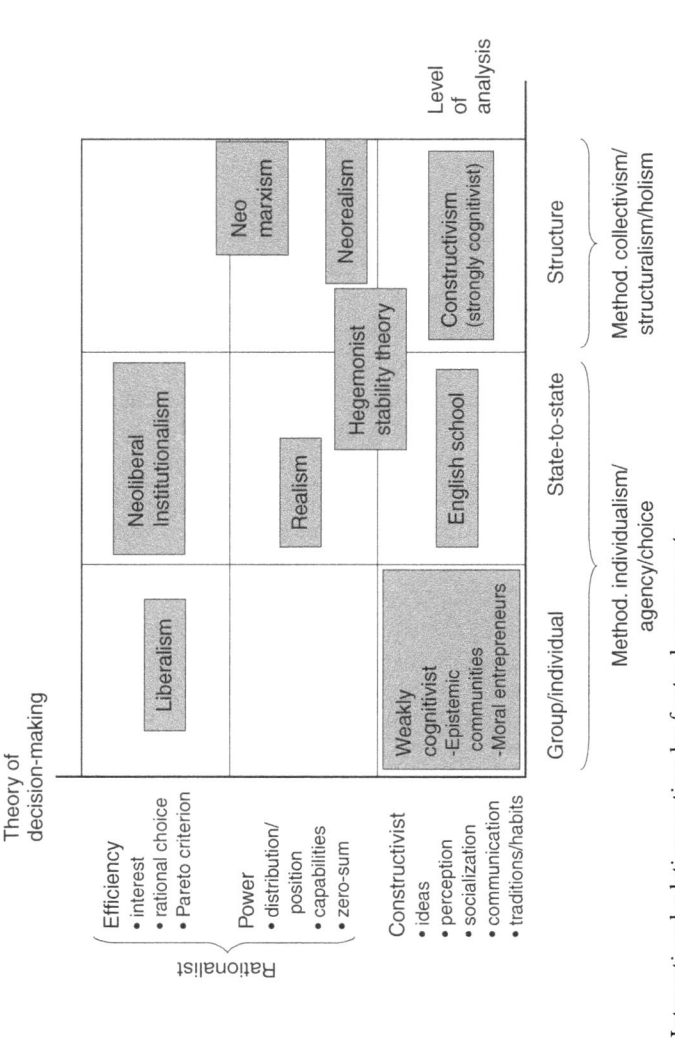

**Figure 4.3** International relations rationales for trade agreements

Source: based on WTO 2007, chart II.B.3(a)

Note: This chart maps the most important IR theories of trade cooperation along two axes: the vertical axis distinguishes underlying theories of decision-making (rationalist/constructivist), while the horizontal axis plots the level of analysis (group/state-to-state/systems approach).

Heeding the zero-sum nature of gains and losses in the international system, cooperating parties anxiously watch over their power rank within the international system.

In contrast to rationalist theories of decision-making, *non-rationalist*, constructivist, or cognitivist, approaches to decision-making adopt a more sociological view of the international system (bottom row). They reject the assumption that agents are "rational computers," driven only by a narrow pursuit of selfish wellbeing and rigid cost-benefit considerations. Instead, constructivists subscribe to the power of fundamental norms, shared ideas, inter-subjective beliefs, traditions, and habits as drivers of all human interaction. Perception, interpersonal communication, learning and socialization to a large degree shape these common and fundamental norms and ideas in the international system.[66]

The horizontal axis of Figure 4.3 can be labeled *level of analysis*. The distinguishing criterion is the object of examination, therewith the locus of decision-making (and utility-maximization). Two grand approaches are contesting in IR literature.

Theories pertaining to *methodological individualism* or "agency" hold that agents (individuals, groups, or countries) can actively and consciously shape the consequences of their interaction. Agents' choice is thought to determine the outcome, i.e. the system.

A number of schools in IR take a *statist* perspective on international trade cooperation (center column in Figure 4.3). Their subjects of examination are sovereign nation states that are assumed to be main actors in the international system staffed with a fixed utility or set of norms and values. How these national objective functions emerge and evolve usually is of no interest to this strand of the IR literature.

Various IR scholars reject the statist assumption that nations are monolithic actors. These *non-statist* approaches are concerned with investigating how domestic interaction shapes preferences and norms of policy-makers in charge of formulating national trade policies and of negotiating international trade agreements (left column in Figure 4.3). Assessing trade policy on the substate level, these theories examine how the interests of various domestic government entities, "political entrepreneurs," and non-state actors (lobby groups, NGOs, corporations, consumer protection groups) influence the (endogenous!) design of domestic trade policy.

---

[66] On constructivism in IR theory, see Adler 2002; Checkel 1998; Finnemore 1996; Guzzini 2002; Kratochwil 1989; Reus-Smit 1997; Ruggie 1998; and Wendt 1999b.

In contrast to theories of methodological individualism, theories adhering to the school of *methodological collectivism*, structuralism, or holism, contend that it is the system that shapes the agents, not vice versa. The system, according to structuralists, is more than the sum of its constituent parts, and therefore assumes "a life of its own." It determines what actors want, how they think, and how they act and interrelate. The international context, or the nature of the system, impels agents to act cooperatively in trade affairs, or to refrain from cooperating.

Along those two dimensions the various schools of IR can be plotted.[67]

**Neoliberal institutionalism**     The school of neoliberal institutionalism is a rational and statist approach to international cooperation, and therefore is quite similar to the optimal-tariff argument set forth by economists (see text accompanying note 38). According to institutionalists, countries cooperate with the substantive aim of increasing efficiency for every concerned party.[68]

The fundamental insight of this theory is that collective action dilemmas, transaction costs, and information asymmetries may create situations in which behavior that is rational from the perspective of individual countries may prevent them from reaping mutual benefits. In such situations, international regimes (or "institutions") enable states to cooperate by providing information, reducing uncertainty, and lowering transaction costs.[69] Regimes facilitate cooperation in that they influence cost-benefit calculations of alternative courses of action by states. In its original formulation by Keohane (1984) a central feature of neoliberal institutionalism was that cooperation between states does not require a formal international organization with centralized enforcement capacity.

---

[67] Ikenberry, Lake, and Mastanduno 1989 classify IR approaches in a similar fashion along the following two dimensions: level of analysis (system-centered, society-centered, state-centered) and driving forces (power, interest, norms/ideas).

[68] Efficiency gains may be achieved by reducing uncertainty, increasing mutual information levels, producing collective goods (such as forums for bargaining and dispute settlement), centralizing certain tasks so as to reduce transaction costs, raising the costs of opportunistic actions (e.g. through repetition of the game or through pooling of enforcement capabilities), and so forth.

[69] See Keohane 1984. Keohane (2005, p. xi) says: "International regime – clusters of principles, norms, rules, and decision-making procedures reduce transaction costs for states – alleviate problems of asymmetrical information, and limit the degree of uncertainty that members of the regime face in evaluating each others' policies ... [I]nternational regimes can be explained in terms of self-interest. Furthermore, they exert an impact on state policies largely by changing the costs and benefits of various alternatives. They do not override self-interest but rather affect calculations of self-interest."

Rather, regimes are self-enforcing agreements, and compliance with a regime's rules can be explained by reciprocity and the role of reputation (see Abbott and Snidal 1998). Keohane's theory was significantly influenced by the experience of the GATT trade regime in the 1970s and 1980s. Keohane (2005, p. xi) observes that "indeed, it could be argued that my theory generalizes the experience of GATT."

**Liberalism** Rationalist approaches to domestic trade policy generation are labeled "liberalist," and examine the role of individuals and interest groups as the fundamental actors in world politics. Scholars of liberalism part with the somewhat arbitrary idea that states are unitary actors with steady utility functions. In order to explain what motivates governments to cooperate in the international realm, liberalists firmly base their research on domestic politics and on substate interaction between rational stakeholders. Rational rent-seeking behavior on the part of special interest groups and elites influences or even determines the actions of elected officials and bureaucrats. According to liberalists, trade agreements are concluded if the decision to collaborate is the equilibrium outflow of some rational deliberation process among salient domestic groups in two or more countries (e.g. Grossman and Helpman 1995b; Milner 1997; Milner and Rosendorff 1997; Ruggie 1982). Liberalist approaches to trade cooperation thereby share many properties with political-economy approaches to domestic trade policy formulation (endogenous trade theories; see note 14). On the level of methodology and research design, liberalists often use the same modeling techniques as contemporary economics, such as game theory, principal-agent models, or utility maximization concepts.

**Neomarxism** Neomarxism or "world systems analysis" is a structural approach to international cooperation giving primacy to economic power relations. World systems analysis is usually grounded in the Marxist conception of social reality.[70] The central argument is that the world economy contains two types of countries: a dominant *Core* and a dependent *Periphery*. Core and Periphery trade and interact and thereby function as an integrated whole. In a unified global capitalist system the hierarchy of states is held together by economic dependency. The Periphery is the source of the wealth of the Core; the latter extracts and

---

[70] Early formulations of world system analysis include Baran 1967; Frank 1969; and Wallerstein 1974. For more contemporary approaches, see e.g. Chase-Dunn 1998.

siphons off the resources of the former. This produces underdevelopment throughout the dependent Periphery.[71] Core countries (industrialized nations) create alliances with each other so as to choreograph the "development of underdevelopment" (Frank 1969, p. 9). Trade cooperation agreements between Core and Periphery are more akin to adhesion or dependency contracts than to contracts of mutual consent and benefit.

**Realism**    Realism is a state-centric, power-oriented approach to international relations. It is the longest-standing paradigm in IR, and was dominant from at least the 1930s to the 1970s (Simmons and Martin 2002).[72] Realists contend that countries in the international system nearly exclusively strive for power maximization. Countries candidly act in ways that satisfy their power interests. Although realist scholars are mainly preoccupied by issues of military security, the issue of international trade is sometimes broached. Where trade is mentioned by realists, its proponents see the hand of power exerting the true influence behind the façade of international agreements (Morgenthau 1948). Generally, treaties and international law are "epiphenomenal" to state power and interests (Carr 1939).

**Neorealism**    The neorealist school is usually seen as the successor of realist thought. Neorealism, however, is less preoccupied with state-to-state power politics, but is an inherently *structuralist* approach to international affairs. The international system (a concept that logically transcends the collective of countries) is characterized by anarchy. In a state of anarchy, any country is exclusively occupied with its own survival (Waltz 1954). Interaction among rational cost-benefit-conscious countries is assumed to be a zero-sum game. Thus, each nation must watch its power position in the international system by propping up its military capabilities and by actively influencing the distribution of coercive power within the system. To maintain (or improve) their power rank, countries

---

[71] According to world systems theorists, there exists an inherently unfair international division of labor, where modern high-profit industries are located in the Core and traditional labor-intensive industries and natural resource extraction originates in the Periphery. This division of labor produces capital accumulation and development in the core, and yields economic and political underdevelopment in the periphery. The more the world economy progresses, the more difficult it is for the periphery to develop, and the greater is the revolutionary effort required to escape global market forces.

[72] The earliest available works of realism, Thucydides and Sun Tzu, date back further than 400 BC.

utilize their own resources or form (spontaneous) short-term international alliances or blocs ("balancing" and "bandwagoning"). Alliances can temporarily mitigate anarchy, but never overcome it.

Whereas neoliberal institutionalists focus on the efficiency-enhancing qualities of trade agreements (see above), neorealist theories stress the importance of the power aspect and distributional conflict as key factors determining the prospects and extent of international trade cooperation. Countries, cognizant of the fact that economic profits can eventually be transferred into military capability, are hesitant trade liberalizers. Although acutely aware of the efficiency-enhancing role of trade cooperation, countries fear the relative gains this may bring to rival nations.[73]

Gruber (2000) argues that the fact that states enter into trade arrangements on a voluntary basis does not at all mean that such contracts are necessarily efficient in the absolute sense, i.e. welfare-improving for all participants. Powerful states regularly coerce weaker players into trade agreements, and try to "squeeze out" as many concessions from other players, in order to be propelled onto a higher power rank. If powerful countries, through the exercise of "go it alone power" can alter the rules of the game in the world trading system, and thus remove the *status quo* from the choice set of weaker players, weaker countries have the choice between a rock and a hard place: either they accept a trade agreement that is worse than the *status quo ante*, or they accept to be left behind in conditions that are even more disadvantageous to them. At any rate, entering into cooperative arrangements will leave them in a worse position than before.

Trade agreements thus may not be concluded because countries want them, but because they are coerced to do so by powerful countries whose aim is to create dependency or to exploit weaker countries. The concept of "go it alone power" and the concomitant idea that states are forced to enter into welfare-depreciating international agreements have recently also been used by some authors in the analysis of GATT/WTO negotiations.[74]

---

[73] According to neorealist authors (e.g. Grieco 1988; 1990; Grieco and Ikenberry 2003; Mearsheimer 1995) countries refrain from concluding trade agreements when they suspect that rival states will enjoy higher relative gains from trade cooperation. Grieco (1990, pp. 168–215) has argued that an analysis of the implementation of some of the GATT's Tokyo Round Agreements on non-tariff barriers supports his theory on the importance of security-related relative gains.

[74] For this post-colonial perception of trade cooperation, see Barton *et al.* 2006, p. 206; Jawara and Kwa 2004; and Steinberg 2002, p. 341.

**Hegemonic stability theory**   Hegemonic stability theory is another variant of realism. It takes a more nuanced stance on international cooperation: an incumbent hegemon (such as the United Kingdom in the nineteenth and early twentieth centuries or the United States after World War II) aims at fortifying its predominance in the international system through cooperation.[75] At the same time, the hegemonic country wants to forge a global community of values, and aims to instill some of its cherished norms and ideals into the system. In addition, only the hegemon as the most powerful state in the system is in a position to address international collective action problems so as efficiently to fight global externalities, such as environmental pollution or opportunistic beggar-thy-neighbor trade policies.

Yet a hegemonic power faces the problem of having to assure other countries that its policies are genuine and not (only) opportunistic. In this regard, it has been suggested that the United States encouraged the formation of the post-war international trade regime partly to make its commitment to free trade credible.[76]

**Constructivist approaches**   Constructivist approaches in IR reject the methodology of rational choice and agent-centric views of decision-making. They claim that rationalist theories of choice fail on two accounts. First, they neglect the formative influence of ideas, norms, and values on behavior. To them, decision-making is much better explained by resorting to fundamental norms, shared ideas, inter-subjective beliefs, traditions, and habits. Perception, interpersonal communication, learning, and socialization to a large degree shape these norms and ideas. Secondly, rational choice theories allegedly fail to acknowledge the influence that the system has on the actors. The power of inter-subjective beliefs, shared understanding, culture, and socialization, according to constructivists, is completely overlooked by agent-centric theories of rational choice. Hence, for proponents of constructivism, the dictum "actors' preferences shape the outcome" is false.

---

[75] See e.g. Gilpin 1987; Kindleberger 1973; Krasner 1976.

[76] This may also explain the interest of the United States in multilateralism in the 1990s: while the Cold War resulted in a commitment to a stable and prosperous Western Europe and thus decreased "the need for a trade-specific signal of the United States' willingness to adhere to free trade" (Goldstein and Gowa 2002, p. 154), the end of the Cold War again confronted the United States with the problem of how to assure other countries of the credibility of its commitment to free trade, given its reputation for unilateralism.

Instead, system and agents are strongly interdependent: the structure shapes actors' perceptions, perception shapes agents' preferences and consequently their behavior. Collective behavior can then have a "feedback" impact on the system (see e.g. Checkel 1998; Finnemore and Sikkink 2001; Wendt 1999a, 1999b).

Constructivist theories come in three (possibly complementary) variations.

*(i) Structural*, or *strongly cognitivist* theories maintain that the behavior of states is rule-driven and that international cooperation and institutionalization cannot be understood without reference to generally accepted normative superstructures that shape the identities of states (Hasenclever, Mayer, and Rittberger 1997, pp. 167–168). For example, Reus-Smit (1997) argues that neither neorealism nor neoliberal institutionalism can explain the historical development of multilateralism in the twentieth century. According to strongly cognitivist literature, multilateralism as a fundamental institution of modern international society reflects a global constitutional structure consisting of dominant beliefs about the moral purpose of the state, a norm of procedural justice, and an organizing principle of sovereignty (see also various contributions in Ruggie 1993).

An early example of the use of social constructivist theory in the analysis of the international trade regime is Ruggie's seminal article on "embedded liberalism" (Ruggie 1982). It analyses the multilateral trading system as an "inter-subjective framework of meaning" (1982, p. 196). According to Ruggie, the formation of the GATT is a manifestation of "the internationalization of political authority."

*(ii)* A variation of structural constructivism (and arguably its forerunner) is the *English school of IR*. This theory is less concerned with how the system shapes countries' norms, but rather with the transnational *diffusion* of certain international norms and values. Its proponents have emphasized the importance of the "international society" in maintaining global order. The concept of collective security is a good example, showing how like-minded countries form a coalition to inject their defensive aims into the international system.

In the trade realm, the establishment of a like-minded international society and the fundamental belief in the peace-promoting quality of trade are said to be important norm-drivers for the conclusion of trade pacts and of the GATT in general. The idea that multilateral, non-discriminatory trade would contribute significantly to global peace was reportedly a central motive for English and US policy-makers designing the post-World War II trading system (see Meade 1942; Penrose 1953). The genuine belief that trade "dovetailed with peace" (Hull 1948, p. 81) seemed to have driven Western allies towards a new world trade order (see Irwin 1996; 2005; Irwin, Mavroidis, and Sykes 2008). The historical record clearly shows that the ITO/GATT was envisioned by the allied powers to be part of a bigger cooperation scheme that included the establishment of the United Nations, the World Bank, and the International Monetary Fund (see e.g. Dam 1970; Gardner 1980; Jackson 1969).

*(iii) Weakly cognitivist* approaches, finally, examine how guiding norms and principles emerge, are being disseminated, and consequently influence the cooperative choice of domestic decision-makers (Finnemore and Sikkink 1998; Hasenclever, Mayer, and Rittberger 1997). The roles of eminent individuals ("moral entrepreneurs"), elites, and epistemic communities are paramount in this process.

Weakly cognitivist IR theories have highlighted the role of epistemic communities in the formation and evolution of international regimes.[77] One example of the application of this concept to the GATT/WTO is a study by Drake and Nicolaïdis (1992) on the emergence of an epistemic community in trade in services during the Uruguay Round negotiations on the GATS. The authors argue that "by framing the issues and establishing the policy options, the community provided governments with the bases on which to define or redefine their national interests and pursue multilateral cooperation" (1992, p. 92).[78]

The role of moral entrepreneurs is also an important feature in weakly cognitivist scholarship. Eminent individuals influence important norms and values needed for international cooperation, and/or crucially shape the content and structure of treaties (e.g. Checkel 1998; Finnemore 1996). For the case of the GATT, the salience of certain spearhead figures of liberal trade is well-documented. Various authors (Dam 1970;

---

[77] The term epistemic community has been defined in this context as "a network of professionals with recognized expertise and competence in a particular domain and an authoritative claim to policy-relevant knowledge within that domain or issue-area" (Haas 1992, p. 3).

[78] See also Lang 2006. More generally, Goldstein (1998, p. 146) argues that: "there exists an epistemic community of economists, policy-makers, and lawyers who share a common vision about economic growth ... This community acts as a transnational interest group, advocating trade liberalization and villainizing protectionism in their home countries. There are multiple reasons why members of a free trade epistemic community advocate trade openness ... Whatever the origin of their beliefs, these advocates monitor government action and provide authoritative advice on the workings of the economy."

Gardner 1980; Irwin 1996; Irwin, Mavroidis, and Sykes 2008; Jackson 1969; Miller 2000; Penrose 1953) have emphasized the prominent role that individuals such as John Maynard Keynes, James Meade, Lionel Robbins, and Cordell Hull have played in establishing common ground for trade cooperation and for formulating the treaty text.

## Non-economic rationales for trade agreements II: lessons from legal scholarship

After having looked at how economic and IR scholarship have explained countries' rationale for contracting in trade matters, this section will review legal theories of trade agreements, or rather, what additional insights legal scholars have added to the discussion.[79] All legal theories of trade agreements that we are aware of represent variations of the basic idea of constitutionalism (see at p. 149 above). They are based on two fundamental insights (or assumptions), namely that the individual citizen is the legitimate principal in all domestic and world affairs (including trade policy), and that government failure and rent-seeking behavior of public officials are rampant and need to be curbed by means of an adequate legal framework – namely a "constitution" of sorts. Based on these central tenets, four legal rationales for trade agreements can be distinguished.[80]

**Internal constitutional view**    The internal, or inward-looking, constitutional approach to trade agreements focuses predominantly on *domestic* problems within the country which yields to particularistic special interests and consequently undertakes protectionist measures. The conclusion of a trade agreement can be seen as a logical extension of the national constitution to safeguard the latter's functioning. In the presence of overwhelming special interest group pressure for protectionism, a trade agreement acts as an additional constitutional constraint, a second line of constitutional defense against policy failure (Tumlir 1985).

---

[79] The term "legal theory" is not quite correct, since the theories described in this section are not particularly legalistic. Rather, the introduced theories are lawyer's interpretations of social interaction. Legal scholarship rarely examines the rationale for concluding international agreements and establishing international organizations, such as the WTO. As Schermers and Blokker (1995, p. 8) argue, "in the land of legal science there is no strongly established tradition of developing theories on [treaty regimes]." Rather, legal science offers descriptive accounts of the history and institutional architecture of treaties, as well as doctrinal analysis of norms and texts, especially the normative output of organizations such as GATT/WTO panel decisions (Abbott and Snidal 1998).

[80] This section draws on WTO 2007, section II.B.4.

Proponents of this internal approach to trade agreements (e.g. McGinnis and Movsesian 2000; Petersmann 1986; Regan 2006) contend that by "tying its hands to the mast of liberal trade" both protectionist endeavors on the part of special interest groups and opportunistic rent-seeking behavior by trade officials can be successfully kept in check, without risking domestic democratic values or a loss of sovereignty.[81]

**External constitutional view**   The external, or transnational, constitutional view perceives trade agreements to be contracts aimed at reciprocally granting countries transnational representation and participation in the trade policy-making of the partner countries. This rationale for contracting shifts the perspective from a domestic to a transnational (cross-border) problem: whereas the internal constitutional view is concerned with the harm a country, by taking protectionist measures, causes to its own citizens, the external view on constitutionalism focuses on the harmful actions that other nations inflict upon the home country.

At the core of the external view is the argument that the risks of government failure and rent-seeking are not a domestic problem. Citizens are well able to contain their own domestic officials (by means of a home-grown economic constitution). Yet protectionist trade barriers *abroad* are the real issue: domestic exporters have no leverage over trade policy-making abroad, yet foreign actions have significant effects on their wellbeing. By raising protectionist barriers, foreign countries de facto "expropriate" domestic exporters of basic economic rights and market freedoms. This reciprocal "taxation without representation" conundrum (Gerhart 2003, p. 22) can successfully be overcome if citizens authorize their governments to engage in trade negotiations. An international trade contract thus allows citizens to participate in the making of foreign countries' trade policies.[82]

---

[81] Notice the similarity in the argumentation of the internal constitutionalist vision and that of the economic commitment approach (discussed at p. 147 above). Both schools of thought allege that trade agreements are motivated by a domestic dilemma that is solved by curbing decision-makers' protectionist discretion through international commitments. However, while the economic literature seems to assume an exogenous liberal trade stance of policy-makers, legal explanations give a more thorough rationale for the hand-tying motivation: citizens (through an unspecified mechanism) coerce policy-makers to contract with other countries, because it is in the majority's interest to do so.

[82] "The external, participatory vision of the WTO therefore sees the WTO as a complex, multiparty forum for barter between nations that allows each nation to represent the interests of its constituents to other nations, and facilitates agreements that reduce the

According to external constitutionalists the significance of trade contracts transcends the purely economic realm. Important representational, participatory, and democratic implications are connected to the conclusion of trade agreements: trade accords effectively give rights and voice to previously disenfranchised groups of economic actors. With an agreement in place, all those agents who are adversely affected by a protectionist trade policy abroad can comment on, and influence, the policies of other countries (via their home governments). In the age of globalization and transnational exchange, trade contracts are thus a novel means of democratic representation across borders. In addition, cross-border participation in trade policy-making promotes freedom: economic agents are granted the freedom to produce and sell where and what they want, knowing that this freedom cannot be taken away from them without their voices being heard.

**Internal-external constitutional view**   A third constitutionalist rationale for trade agreements cherished by lawyers can be called the internal-external view. In essence, this view combines a clear internal problem (domestic policy failure) with an external contracting motivation (fear of retaliation and welfare-depreciating dynamics). As a matter of self-restraint, a political elite (the legislature) delegates authority to a third party (namely to the executive) in the hope that the latter will make better and more balanced trade policy decisions. The administration, whose interests are presumably more aligned to overall national welfare, concludes an international contract, a deed which is in line with the long-term interest of the legislature. Legislators thus choose "agency" over direct action. A trade agreement is thus the natural outflow of the legislators' decision to remove themselves from the trade policy-making process.

The internal-external view is motivated by the experience of the 1930 Smoot-Hawley Tariff Act, and the disastrous consequences it triggered. As is well known, the fervent tariff hikes by the United States resulted in trade war dynamics that set off a sharp contraction of world trade and contributed to the length and depth of the Great Depression of the 1930s. After the experience with the Smoot-Hawley Act, the US Congress passed

harmful external effects of national policy" (Gerhart 2003, p. 25). Notice the similarity in argumentation between this external constitutionalist approach and economic theories based on market access externalities discussed at p. 149 above. Note also that the focus on overcoming external spillover effects is also at the core of neoliberal institutionalism (previous section). Common to all views is the contention that international spillovers (of some nature) are what motivates the conclusion of trade agreements.

legislation that authorized the administration to negotiate tariff reductions with other governments. As Hudec (1993, p. 314) argues, members of Congress were persuaded of their own ineptitude in dealing with tariff matters. Congressmen realized their inability to counter domestic interests, and feared the international repercussions of future instances of excessive protectionism. To that end, legislators thought it better to remove themselves from tariff-setting and to delegate trade policy to the executive, which they thought was further removed from special interest group pressures and more aligned with general-welfare gains.[83]

**Global constitutional view**     A final approach to trade agreements put forth by international lawyers is the global constitutional view. This theory alleges that citizens in an interdependent world enact an international multilevel trade constitution, since narrow national constitutional solutions and state-centric international law necessarily fail to curb transnational policy failures.

The global constitutional view of international law applies the same basic constitutional logic, but just assumes the world to be akin to one big nation of "world citizens" that gives itself a multilevel trade constitution, with the same goals of non-discriminatory competition and prevention of protectionism.[84] Global trade constitutions depoliticize and decentralize state-to-state trade conflicts and replace them by constitutional rules of a higher legal rank, which can be directly applied and enforced in domestic courts.

This view is harshly critical of both the internal and external constitutional view on trade agreements, especially because of their emphasis on state sovereignty. Proponents of the global perspective (most prominently Petersmann 1995; 1998; 2005; 2006) argue that the "Westphalian" notion of international law is outdated, because state-centric "Memberdrivenness" is hostile to the vital interests of citizens. On the one hand, national trade laws are necessarily "partial constitutions" that cannot tackle global problems involving transnational spillovers. Also, national

---

[83] Goldstein's (1996) analysis of the United States-Canada Free Trade Agreement indeed suggests that actors who have the most to gain from a pursuit of general welfare – such as executives elected by a national constituency – tend to show the most interest in turning to international agreements (see also Simmons and Martin 2002).

[84] The term "multilevel" means that non-state actors have legal access to domestic *and* international courts so as to keep rent-seeking governments in check, and to defend their constitutional guarantees of freedom, non-discrimination, the rule of law, and social safeguard measures in case of rampant government failure (Petersmann 2006, p. 6).

constitutions have frequently failed to control domestic protectionism.[85] On the other hand, international trade agreements between governments fail to eradicate the risk of (inter)national government failure, for the simple reason that it is exactly self-interested, rent-seeking governments who negotiate and sign the deal. Having opportunistic governments interconnected as brokers between citizens of different countries is likely to produce unwanted outcomes.

As argued by Petersmann in his numerous contributions, world citizens, by giving themselves global multilevel constitutions, manage to remove domestic policy-makers from the trade-game and to produce truly global public goods (the European Union being a prominent example). Allegedly, this paradigm shift from the historically state-centered, power-oriented Westphalian system to a modern citizen-oriented system of international law has finally reached the realm of world trade. In the trade realm, the global public bypasses national governments and manages to establish a worldwide, multilevel economic constitution (for a critical view, see Cass 2005; Howse and Nicolaïdis 2001; Tarullo 2002; WTO 2007, chapter II.B.4(a)).

## Summary of rationales for trade contracts

At p. 155 above, we have contended that none of the reviewed economic rationales for trade cooperation is flawless in its argumentation. Further, as argued at p. 160 above, it seems that economic scholarship has overlooked an additional economic motivation based on collective-action games different from that of the prisoners' dilemma. As we discussed, chances are that trade agreements may also be concluded with the aim of solving a complex multilateral coordination problem and of establishing and safeguarding minimum trading standards. Discussing IR and legal theories of trade cooperation, the previous two sections showed that economists have excluded from consideration various important non-economic objectives of cooperating in trade affairs, such as ideational, power-oriented, and constitutionalist explanations for trade compacts. Figure 4.4 summarizes the landscape of contracting rationales in trade scholarship.

---

[85] "[M]ost constitutions provide for only few procedural constraints on discretionary foreign policy powers to tax, restrict, and regulate the transnational relations of citizens across frontiers. Thus, national constitutions turn out to be incomplete partial solutions. They don't constrain discretionary foreign policy powers and fail to provide the collective supply of 'global public goods'" (Petersmann 2006, p. 8).

**Nature of objective**

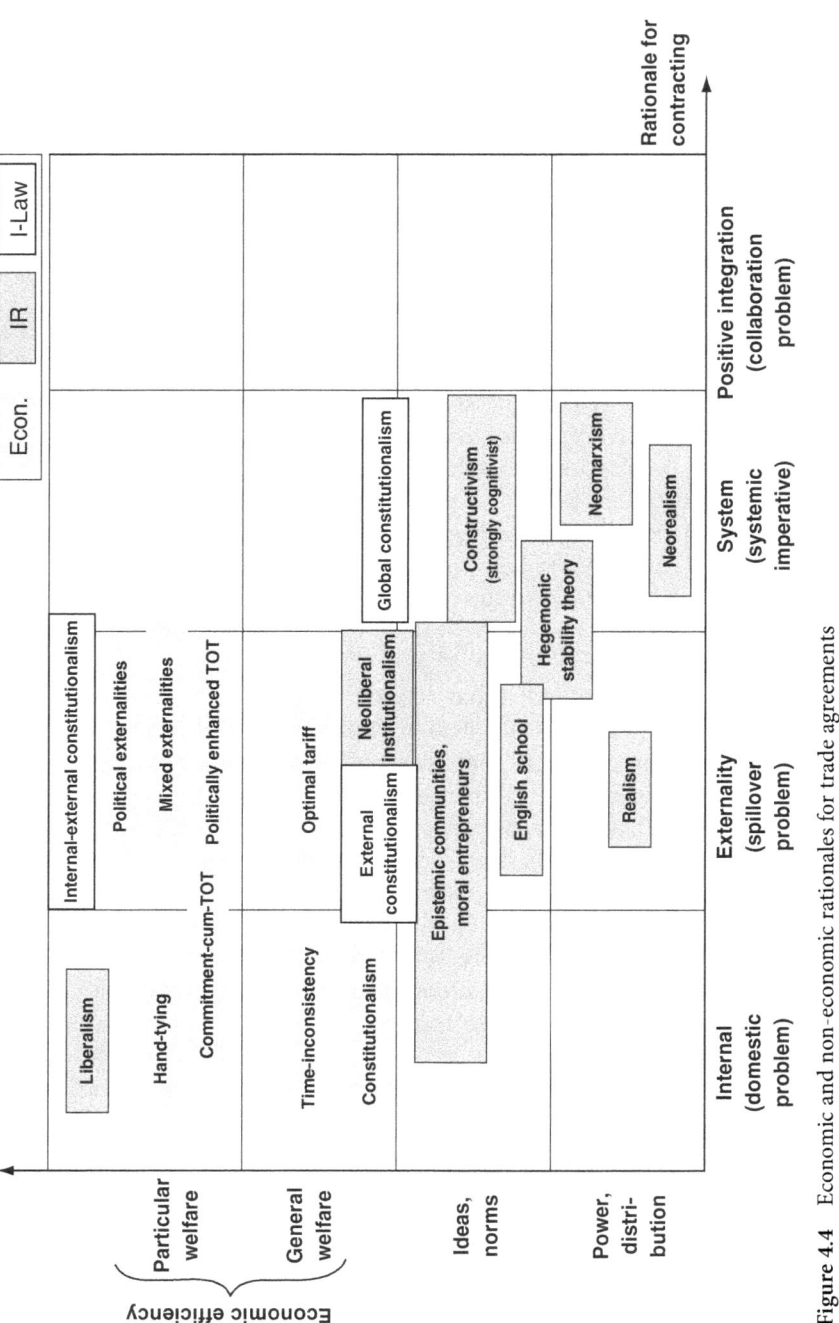

**Figure 4.4**   Economic and non-economic rationales for trade agreements

Source: based on WTO 2007, chart II.B.6.1

Note: This chart, just like Figure 4.1(b), is drawn along two axes: the vertical axis represents the nature of policy-makers' objective functions, while the horizontal axis plots the underlying rationale for contracting. The chart maps rationales for trade agreements originating in the disciplines of economics (Econ.), international relations (IR), and international law (I law), theories emanating from these three disciplines are marked in different shades of gray.

Figure 4.4 is an extension of Figure 4.1(b), and is plotted along the same two axes (see text accompanying note 26): the vertical axis plots the *nature of objective* (the "maximand" of social interaction), while the horizontal axis distinguishes between different *rationales for contracting* (or problems to be overcome by the conclusion of a trade contract). The boxes of the matrix are filled with the various rationales for trade agreements emanating from the disciplines of economics, IR, and international law that were reviewed above.

The first two rows plot rationalist theories of trade agreements that place economic efficiency at center stage. Economic models of trade cooperation assume that agents cooperate if it serves their rational interest: governments may wish to maximize the general welfare of their citizenship; alternatively, self-interested policy-makers maximize their own PROF. By combining forces, signatories seek to "maximize the size of the pie" by inducing efficiency.

(Political) economic utility maximization and absolute efficiency objectives may not be the only motives that drive countries into trade cooperation. Players may try to maximize their relative power position vis-à-vis other countries (see the bottom row of Figure 4.3). To proponents of this view (mostly IR scholars), international trade cooperation is about rivalry rather than cooperation. Cooperating parties carefully watch over their power rank within the international system, constantly aiming to maximize their "slice of the pie."

In the third row are non-rationalist approaches that reject the assumption that all social interaction is driven by egoistic or particularistic cost-benefit considerations. To them, it is cultural patterns, shared norms and ideas, inter-subjective beliefs, social objectives, traditions, and habits that define and shape cooperative behavior between human beings. Just as economic or power rationales simply cannot satisfactorily explain why child, slave, or prison labor, human trafficking, or trade in narcotics are repugnant concepts, economic thinking is seen as incapable of fully explaining why trade agreements are concluded. Basic civilizing norms and values, age-old traditions, a collective sense of history, and a duty towards humanity are assumed to inspire influential individuals, pivotal groups, and states as a whole to conclude trade agreements.

On the horizontal axis, the distinguishing criterion is "rationale for contracting," or the kind of problem that the conclusion of a trade agreement can help overcome. As was shown in Figure 4.1(b), economic trade theorists allege that trade contracts can either solve a distinctly domestic commitment issue (left-most column) or problems connected to international market access externalities (second column from the left). As our explanations of IR and legal theories showed, however, trade contracts may be concluded for alternative (or at least additional) reasons. First, theories adhering to *methodological collectivism* contend that it is the system that shapes the actors and not vice versa. As discussed, some theorists from the disciplines of IR and international law thus allege some form of super-ordinate systemic imperative for concluding trade accords (second row from the right). Secondly, as suggested at p. 160 above, it may also be a profound concern of signatories to trade agreements to establish minimum standards as focal equilibria, and to lay down positive integration norms with the aim of overcoming multilateral coordination problems.

What is the picture emerging from the summarizing Figure 4.4? Three key observations suggest themselves.

First, the eight economic explanations for trade agreements discussed above are scrambled into four cells in the upper left-hand corner of the matrix. This may be indicative of the limited or lopsided explanatory scope of economic theories; it may also be a token of the compactness of economic methodology.

Secondly, the issues as to in what respects trade agreements can be conceptualized as solutions to coordination problems and what impact this would have on the design of trade agreements have been little studied in WTO scholarship. There is no literature filling the far-right column. Political economists should start thinking beyond the prisoners' dilemma set-up when trying to explain trade cooperation and ought to dedicate more energy into alternative collective-action games of strategy.

Thirdly, the various theories for trade agreements can be grouped into four (partially overlapping) clusters of explanations for why countries may wish to cooperate in trade affairs. A first cluster along the left-most column of Figure 4.3 posits a purely domestic problem that an international contract can help to overcome.[86] A second cluster of explanations along the second column from the left views some kind of international eco-nomic spillovers as the key problem that a contract can remedy. An international contract can successfully mitigate an (economic, social, or political) beggar-thy-neighbor problem.[87] A third cluster of trade

---

[86] The IR school of liberalism, the legal internal constitutionalist view, and political economy and commitment approaches originating in economics are all variations of this theme.

[87] This basic insight is at the core (with some variations and extensions) of the external and internal-external constitutionalist legal approaches, the IR school of neoliberalist insti-tutionalism, and the terms-of-trade and political externalities theories in the field of economics.

agreement motivations can be termed "ideational contracting" (second row from the bottom). According to scholars who can be associated to this cluster,[88] it is non-economic, normative objectives that guide the actions of trade policy decision-makers. A final cluster along the bottom row of Figure 4.3 can be termed the "realpolitik" rationale for trade agreements. Countries cooperate in trade affairs, or refrain from doing so, for reasons of power and subsistence (i.e. distributive efficiency).[89]

### 4.1.3 A tentative conclusion: trade agreements based on market access externalities and minimum standards

The above section was concerned with finding explanations for the contractual intent behind the WTO. Why did we spend so much effort on assessing different possible motivations for contracting in trade matters? As we have shown in Chapter 2, treaty design (the design of contractual rules, provisions, procedures, and organizational features) is fundamentally shaped by the underlying goal(s) pursued by the contracting parties. Hence, possessing a coherent understanding of the rationale for contracting is an indispensable prerequisite for engaging in any argument about the quality of outcomes engendered by that agreement. The rationale of a trade agreement is the logical yardstick against which to measure its success.[90]

What can be learned from this literature review of trade cooperation theories? We draw two conclusions.

First, a sobering remark: whilst current economic, political, and legal approaches seem able to elucidate facets of the cooperative drive, each one is unable to capture the whole picture. Trade scholarship is still far from establishing a convincing answer as to why sovereign countries engage in trade cooperation. More work needs to be done to produce *testable results* as to which of the discussed theories (or which combination thereof) best

---

[88] In the realm of IR literature, ideational elements can be found in neoliberal institutionalism, hegemonic stability theory, and idealism, but especially in weakly and strongly cognitivist schools of constructivism. Non-economic objectives for contracting parties also play a crucial role in the legal approaches termed external and global constitutionalism.

[89] This concern for power and distribution is most notably at the core of the IR school of neorealism, but also of realism, neomarxism, and hegemonic stability theory.

[90] Any scholar criticizing efficiency or effectiveness of a trade agreement and/or laying out an agenda for reform should reveal his or her understanding of the treaty's central objectives. Failure to do so may mean that the agreement is discussed in a logical vacuum.

manages to explain countries' cooperation motivations. Cross-disciplinary work seems a fruitful and promising avenue for future research.

Secondly, a speculation: trade agreements are probably best character-ized as "mixed-motive games," where every signatory country is likely to possess an idiosyncratic and uniquely weighted set of cooperation motives (see Mavroidis 2007, sections 1.2.4 and 1.2.5; WTO 2007, section II.B.6). There are two aspects to the mixed-motive issue: *internally*, any country is likely to be motivated by an array of (possibly conflicting) economic and non-economic objectives that are pursued by signing up to a trade agreement. The government of a country may wish to promote peace and stability in its region, propel its power rank in the international system, attract foreign direct investment, fight unemployment, mitigate the influence of special interest groups, or stop trade partners from enga-ging in excessive beggar-thy-neighbor policies – all at the same time. It is very likely that more than one soul is housed within the breasts of trade policy-makers, when they decide to negotiate a trade agreement.

An *external* aspect of trade agreements as a mixed-motive game is that different WTO Members can be expected to be motivated by quite heterogeneous contracting goals, when signing on to the WTO Agreement. Different countries are likely to possess idiosyncratic sets, or bundles, of trade cooperation objectives. By concluding (or acceding to) a trade agreement, small, dictatorial, developing countries can be expected to pursue sets of core objectives differently from large, demo-cratic, developed regimes. In other words, each country probably pos-sesses a unique set/bundle of trade cooperation objectives.

Where does that leave us in our quest to identify the contractual intent of the WTO? More research by sharper minds will have to settle the issue, which (combination) of the various possible rationales really drives countries into contracting. In lieu of a conclusion we offer a conjecture: we believe that economic theories of trade agreements offer the largest "traction," i.e. the biggest explanatory scope. We therefore largely side with Mavroidis (2007, chapter 1.2.5) who contends that the GATT, albeit a mixed-motive game, was probably *mainly* concluded so as to constrain excessive unilateralism.[91] In other words, countries (for whichever deep-er underlying reason) are driven by the objective of gaining access for domestic goods and services to foreign markets. Trade contracts are thus

---

[91] "The various GATT instruments are there to guarantee that the multiple negotiation effects stemming from unilateral definition of trade policies will be addressed" (Mavroidis 2007, p. 26).

concluded with the predominant aim of achieving and safeguarding a mutually acceptable *reciprocal market access balance*. We defend this conjecture below and characterize our notion of trade agreements based on market access externalities at p. 184 below. At p. 187 below we present in detail what we believe to be a second, subordinate, rationale for contracting, namely the provision of general minimum standards in important trade areas such as intellectual property, import licensing, or health-related aspects.

### Primacy of market access externalities

Our argument in favor of the primacy of the market access motivation is nurtured by the following deliberations.

First, it is probably fair to say that *economic* rationale is at the core of the WTO.[92] After all, trade is about exchange of goods and services, a profoundly economic enterprise. Had peace, security, development, and social philanthropy been the central objectives for contracting, parties could have concluded treaties with exactly these aims. In fact, countries, by establishing the United Nations with all its adjunct organizations, have proven to be willing to contract for these reasons. This contention rules out non-economic rationales as the main drivers of cooperation in trade. It is sufficient to require trade not to interfere with concerns of global peace and stability.

Secondly, we argued above that trade policy is likely to be shaped by self-interested policy-makers who are directly influenced by domestic stakeholder groups. This political economy tenet leaves little room for orthodox state-centric approaches to trade cooperation, which assume that governments are monolithic entities that strictly pursue general welfare objectives. In the same vein, constructivism and all other theories adhering to methodological collectivism are largely excluded from the explanatory ambit that we cherish.

Thirdly, we adhere to a Paretian logic of contracting: policy-makers are inclined to conclude trade contracts that are good for themselves. This is a rejection of those IR approaches that assume trade agreements to be merely a continuation of war by other means (to paraphrase von Clausewitz's famous dictum), geared towards forcing other countries

---

[92] The actual content of the contracts, preparatory work of the ITO/GATT, recollections of contemporaries (e.g. Hull 1948; Meade 1942; Penrose 1953), and findings by economic historians (e.g. Irwin 1996; 2005; Miller 2000) may count as arguments in favor of the profoundly *economic* nature of ITO, GATT, and WTO.

into submission, and securing the nation's power rank in the international system. Although the issue of "trade as a geopolitical instrument" may constitute an interesting topic, we do not consider it in this study (see discussion in Chapter 2, note 3).

Fourthly, we deem the theories based on a purely domestic commitment rationale unconvincing. As discussed at p. 155 above, we take the three variants of the commitment approach to trade cooperation to be weak rationales for contracting, not least because they construct counterfactual outcomes.

Finally, we note that trade negotiators emphasize the market access implications and opportunities of trade agreements in their communication with the public (see Bagwell and Staiger 2002b, p. 182, Irwin, Mavroidis, and Sykes 2008, chapter 3).

In summary, we regard externality-based theories of trade agreements most fitting to explain why sovereign countries may want to conclude multilateral trade contracts: a trade contract based on market access externalities solves a problem and thereby displays all the ingredients of a contract. It displays a clear motivation for a trade agreement – market access potential to foreign markets. It also assigns an assurance function to the contract, i.e. the goal of constraining excessive unilateral behavior by repetition of the prisoners' dilemmatic trade game.[93]

### Trade contracts based on market access externalities

This section summarizes our conjecture of trade agreements as contracts based on the market access externality motivation and as concluded by self-interested policy-makers.

We are agnostic as to the microfoundations, character, shape, and composition of the PROF of trade policy-makers (see note 14 and accompanying text). The aim of policy-makers is to be re-elected. In pursuit of this goal, they strive to maximize their political support. Depending on its degree of responsiveness to lobby influence, each government's objective function is biased more or less in favor of organized interests.

Domestic special interest groups are keen on maximizing the well-being (income) of their members, and hence have a profound stake in the structure of domestic trade policy. SIGs mainly fall into two groups: pro-protection (import-competing) and pro-export interests. Exporters have

---

[93] As stated at p. 30 above, motivation and assurance are the two most decisive components of every contract.

a genuine interest in export subsidies as well as in open international markets, since those measures promise them additional access to foreign markets and cheaper sourcing, respectively. Import-competing interest groups, of course, also cherish subsidies, but favor trade protection (at least in their respective sectors) over open markets. The general electorate (consumers) prefers cheaper products, more efficient resource allocation, employment opportunities, and higher wage levels.

Accordingly, the self-interested policy-maker has at least four (partially countervailing) interests to consider when defining national trade policy. The components of her domestic political support balance are (i) consumer, (ii) export, (iii) import-competing, and (iv) TOT interests.[94] Any trade policy decision may produce complex domestic reverberations in the form of *direct* (political) and *indirect* (economic) implications for the initiating government, namely in the form of TOT and political support effects.[95]

Domestic decisions aside, it is certain that protectionist trade measures taken by a trade partner will affect general welfare (through TOT deterioration and reduced gains from trade) as well as local lobbies' income. The political status of policy-makers is thus damaged by opportunistic market-closing policies by foreign countries. Yet in the same vein, the home government's political status increases if it manages to "snatch" unilateral market access from its trading partner(s). The familiar prisoners' dilemmatic situation is the result: anticipating the risk of excessive unilateral action by trade partners, both (or all) countries will revert to non-cooperative Nash behavior, in which trade barriers are high, trade in goods and services inefficiently low, and political support suboptimal – voters, exporters, and consuming industries punish the government for the high trade barriers and promise more support if international trade is promoted. A mutual trade agreement can help trade policy-makers reap higher political support levels from the general electorate and domestic SIGs: countries agree to cut down on their trade barriers with each other, be they tariffs, quotas, red-tape measures, or

---

[94] Consumer and exporter interests presumably work at cross-purposes with import-competing interests and TOT motives.

[95] For example, fixing world prices with the aim of neutralizing TOT externalities may not go down well with import-competing industries which had hoped for extra protection, but is popular with consumers, importers, consuming industries, and exporters. Depending on the political or financial clout that import-competing lobbies bring to bear, a trade decision-maker may refrain from liberalizing that sector, which in turn may upset the TOT balance and enrage export interests and consumers.

other market-closing policies. As long as the political loss of doing so (in terms of foregone TOT gains and political support losses of import-competing lobbies) is outweighed by positive externalities (political support gain and general trade efficiencies), a trade agreement is mutually beneficial to self-interested policy-makers.

Two aspects are important for our characterization of trade agreements based on market access externalities. First, the resulting market access deal between signatories is profoundly political (as per policy-makers' utility functions), and it must be reciprocal. Reciprocity is an imperative of the Paretian logic of contracting. Two signatory countries engage in market access negotiations until the first party (the most reluctant liberalizer) hits its political optimum, i.e. its preferred domestic political support balance. That country (rather: its political representative) has then successfully optimized its preferred bundle, consisting of sector-specific market access commitments received and commitments granted. It has successfully exchanged the biggest possible set of concessions for the politically lowest price.[96] Once at its optimum, the government is no longer willing to change the terms of the deal. Any further liberalization would lead to a deterioration of the trade negotiator's domestic political support balance. Free trade, notably, is rarely the outcome of these reciprocal market access negotiations.[97]

The second point we wish to emphasize is that multilateral trade contracts are essentially webs of bilateral trade deals. The existence of non-discrimination provisions notwithstanding, every signatory engages in bilateral and reciprocal promises of market access.[98] Trade liberalization

---

[96] Ideally, a trade negotiator would trade off the access to her domestic market as "cheaply" as possible: she would like to liberalize those domestic sectors that are economically unimportant, where consumer and/or downstream industry interests are powerful, or sectors which are weakly represented by special interests (e.g. truck drivers, who in many countries are notorious for failing to organize their interests). Naturally, each policy-maker urges trade partners to liberalize as many important markets as freely as possible (especially those where domestic export interests are strong).

[97] Policy-makers consent to tariff levels, GATS concessions levels, or other commitments in various sectors so as to maximize their selfish, subjective utility functions in the respective arguments. Since liberalization in each sector inevitably pits exporter and using-industry welfare against that of import-competing interests, the optimal level of liberalization varies depending on the private-sector power balance in each industry. That the politically optimal depth of this liberalization would be free trade is highly unlikely, and if so, of a purely coincidental nature (cf. note 24 above).

[98] Non-discrimination provisions are transaction cost-efficiency enhancing tools, but they do not change the inherently bilateral logic behind market access concessions.

commitments are owed on a country-to-country basis, not towards the membership as a whole.[99]

## Minimum standards as a second(ary) rationale for trade agreements

Above, we criticized mainstream economics for having rooted the rationale for trade agreements exclusively in the prisoners' dilemma *problématique*. Theories of trade agreements based solely on market access externalities fail to explain why and how the trade community integrated (or attempted to integrate) relatively novel issues, such as intellectual property rights or competition policy, into the world trade regime. Consider for example the TRIPS or the Agreement on Import Licensing Procedures (ILP): the nature of these new agreements has probably less to do with granting and maintaining reciprocal market access than with the motivation to set universally binding standards.

While GATT and GATS are bilateral market access deals, these new Agreements and various components in existing Agreements should rather be characterized as *positive integration accords* geared towards enhancing interaction efficiency of the world trading system.[100] Positive integration contracts (as well as numerous positive integration provisions in market access Agreements) aim at creating new markets, or at enhancing the general efficiency of the existing ones. The TRIPS Agreement, for example, contains several minimum standard obligations that mandate the quasi-ubiquitous introduction of certain institutional features and procedures, independent of the state of implementation in other countries.[101] Other "new WTO issues," such as competition, trade

---

[99] Trade concessions are exchanged, and therefore owed, on a bilateral basis. This is a consequential finding, which warrants a bit of elaboration: it is in the self-interest of every policy-maker to extract the most extensive trade concessions possible from other contracting parties. She therefore only cares about how many concessions she has to "give away" in return. This logic is inherently bilateral. Whether or not a party B frustrates previous market access commitments of another third party C is inconsequential to the policy-maker who represents party A, as long as this measure does not infringe on her own utility. The right to trade is not owed to the collective membership, but *directly* to every signatory party. The market access obligation is consequently organized in a web of bilateral deals.

[100] Positive integration norms are based on a "thou shalt" (prescriptive) logic, whereas negative integration norms are based on a "thou shalt not" (prohibitive) logic. Positive norms mandate the establishment of a certain result or effect, while negative norms prohibit certain behavior or outcomes.

[101] The WTO Secretariat summarized the ambit of the TRIPS Agreement as follows: "The Agreement recognises that widely varying standards in the protection and enforcement

facilitation, labor and environment, belong to the same category of positive integration rules. Though these new issues have not yet been cast into WTO Agreements, they have been on the bargaining table for some time.[102]

Trade agreements motivated by minimum standards differ from a market access explanation of the WTO in three important aspects, namely in:

   (i)  the contractual motivation;
  (ii)  the underlying problem; and
 (iii)  the nature of commitments.

(i) **Different contractual motivation**   Whereas under the market-access-externalities rationale trade contracts are concluded so as to achieve transaction efficiency (*ex post* efficiencies from exchanging goods or services, cf. at p. 31 above), minimum standards in the WTO may well be traced back to a desire to ameliorate the general trading environment. "Law-harmonizing" efforts by Members (Petersmann 2002, p. 51) in the areas of intellectual property rights, labor standards, competition policy, or licensing procedures are geared towards setting universal core standards for international trade. Ubiquitous trade standards are apt to ameliorate the underlying conditions in which world trade takes place, and to raise the general efficiency of the world trading system.[103] Thus, minimum standard agreements and provisions are

of intellectual property rights and the lack of a multilateral framework of principles, rules and disciplines dealing with international trade in counterfeit goods have been a growing source of tension in international economic relations. Rules and disciplines were needed to cope with these tensions. To that end, the agreement addresses the applicability of basic GATT principles and those of relevant international intellectual property agreements; the provision of adequate intellectual property rights; the provision of effective enforcement measures for those rights; multilateral dispute settlement; and transitional arrangements" (source: www.wto.org).

[102] For in-depth introduction into new trade policy issues, see Hoekman and Kostecki 1995; Jackson 1997a, pp. 305–318; Trebilcock and Howse 2006.

[103] By concluding trade contracts based on minimum standards or by integrating minimum-standard norms into existing trade agreements, policy-makers are far from acting altruistically. Rather, self-interested trade decision-makers can be assumed to act under duress from important special interest groups. According to some authors (e.g. Harms, Mattoo, and Schuknecht 2003; Odell and Sell 2006) this is exactly the dynamic that led to the conclusion of some multilateral trade agreements, such as GATS, TRIPS, and TRIMs: self-interested private firms or lobby groups formed cross-country coalitions, negotiated with self-interested public entities in affected countries, and so pushed the formation of these accords.

geared towards achieving transaction cost efficiencies in a repeated-interaction setting.[104]

**(ii) Different underlying problem**   The basic *problématique* which minimum standards are able to solve may not be found in a PD, or any other collaboration game, but effectively in a coordination game. As discussed at p. 160 above, signatories understand that some sorts of legal harmonization and some minimum level of policy coordination is beneficial to every party involved. Every government thus has an inherent interest in a binding agreement on general efficiency-enhancing measures. The contentious issue, however, over which parties are in disagreement, is the optimal level of positive integration, i.e. the contractual level of common standards. The contract thus fixes this negotiated level.[105]

**(iii) Different nature of commitments**   Finally, the nature of commitments in trade agreements based on market access externalities is different from the kinds of commitments following a minimum-standard logic. These promises are based on prescriptive norms that mandate WTO Members to prepare the legal institutional grounds for frictionless and orderly interaction in the fields of intellectual property, import licensing, government procurement, etc. As will be argued in more detail below, minimum standard promises are not bilateral, but multilateral, because if one country fails to live up to its promises, the efficiency of the entire system suffers.

---

[104]   As shown at p. 31 above, transaction cost efficiency can be achieved in repeated-interaction settings, where parties save themselves from having to rebargain the terms of a contractual exchange over and over again. The contract sets binding standard operating procedures, which reduce the costs of interaction.

[105]   This contention that trade contracts are partially motivated by the objective of solving complex coordination problems may be contested. Consider the case of IP protection: it may be argued that some countries profit from IP infringements (e.g. China's repeated copyright encroachments), and that TRIPS was concluded precisely to forestall those kinds of opportunistic behavior. Critics may then prefer the prisoners' dilemma or "stag hunt" (see Chapter 2, note 54) metaphors to the "battle-of-the-sexes" set-up to explain the rationale for TRIPS. We do not contest that the TRIPS Agreement may also partially be concluded with the aim of forestalling temporary opportunistic IP infringements (indeed, in Chapter 2, note 57 and accompanying text, we reviewed the argument made by Fearon 1998 that contracts frequently involve both a coordination and a collaboration component, a contention that we subscribe to). However, our point is that the core rationale for concluding TRIPS in the first place may be better explained by the idea that every WTO Member has an interest in *some* common level of IP protection. That China's optimal level is potentially lower than that of the United States is another, separate, story.

Positive multilateral integration is probably more difficult to achieve than the negative integration used in GATT and GATS: negative integration in the trade liberalization agreements of GATT and GATS proceeds via the removal of trade barriers in bilateral deals that are then applied in a non-discriminatory way to all other Member states. Bargaining is not constrained by the decision rule of unanimity, since no Member is under an explicit obligation to lower its tariffs. Positive integration agreements, by contrast, can only be achieved with the formal approval of all WTO Member states (de Bièvre 2004, p. 4).

## 4.2 Primary rules of contracting: basic entitlements in the WTO

Contractual commitments define the gains to be had from cooperation. Commitment in trade agreements is determined by the composition and level of concessions in international trade. In this section, we want to assess more closely how contracting parties in the WTO have defined trade cooperation, what the basic commitments of the contract are, and how parties have molded these commitments into contractual entitlements.[106]

In the last section it was argued that the WTO, as we know it today, is best understood as a multiple-objective, political agreement among self-interested policy-makers. The two main motivations for contracting were argued to be:

(i) market access externalities; and
(ii) minimum standards in international trade.

WTO Members have converted this pair of cooperative objectives for entering into a trade agreement into treaty language by putting in place entitlements or primary rules of contracting. The contract's paramount entitlement, which we call the "market access," or "trade" entitlement, is exchanged bilaterally between contracting party dyads. As we will explain below, the market access entitlement consists of a mixture of substantive trade liberalization entitlements and dependent auxiliary entitlements.

However, as Pauwelyn (2006, notes 91 and 93) aptly states, the WTO contains various non-market access-related entitlements in the WTO,

---

[106] Following Calabresi and Melamed 1972, section 2.2 above defined contractual entitlements as mutual commitments (rights and obligations) that allocate ownership rights between signatories within a specific area of contractual exchange.

which are not easily explainable by the logic of reciprocal market access concessions but rather by the need to coordinate policies and to establish minimum standards of protection in international trade. As we will discuss in section 4.2.2, there is a second group of substantive entitlements which we shall call "minimum standard," or "positive integration" entitlements. This group of entitlements takes account of the secondary rationale we established at p. 187 above.

The rationale for contracting aside, most contracts need auxiliary entitlements (see at p. 48 above) that back up the substantive ones. The WTO Agreement accommodates a third group of entitlements. As will be shown in section 4.2.3, a number of multilateral "basic auxiliary entitlements" render international trade more efficient without, however, carrying any substantive contracting motivation.

For reasons that will become clear later on in section 4.2.4, we will group minimum standard and basic auxiliary entitlements together into the umbrella term "multilateral," or "coordination entitlements."

### 4.2.1   Bilateral market access entitlement

The market access entitlement puts into effect what we consider to be countries' key rationale for contracting. It is a *reciprocal* commitment by signatories to grant each other market access, in order to overcome detrimental externality effects. The entitlement is a combination of each Member's right to compete in other markets and its obligation to grant other countries access to its own market.[107] We shall use the terms "market access" and "trade entitlement" interchangeably.[108]

The entitlement is composed of substantive and contracting obligations. Substantive obligations define the reciprocal trade liberalization commitments in the form of tariff cuts and service concessions in the four GATS service modes of supply. These substantive elements are accompanied by contracting provisions (auxiliary norms) which are

---

[107] Each WTO Member is presented with the right to compete fairly in its trade partners' markets up to the degree granted by each of those countries. In return, the respective signatory agrees to be bound by its obligation to grant its trade partner(s) market access up to the level of market opening it consented to in the initial trade liberalization negotiations (or subsequent trade rounds).

[108] The nomenclature "trade entitlement" is chosen because the market access entitlement is each Member's right to trade, i.e. to supply goods and services without being discriminated against, within the limits of previously negotiated market access commitments. This is, of course, not to say that other entitlements have no trade-relatedness.

aimed at maintaining and safeguarding the agreed-upon level of bilateral cooperation.[109]

Substantive trade liberalization concessions are the currency of any trade contract. It lies in the contractual nature of the WTO that the trade entitlement is reciprocally owed. Each contracting party enters into a bilateral trade liberalization deal with every other WTO Member, and fixes the level of market access it is willing to grant in return for access to the foreign market.[110] The level of market access is equivalent to the size of the promise – the number of sectors signatories are willing to liberalize, and the degree of market-opening they agree to be bound to. Trade liberalization concessions are constituted by the compulsory tariff bindings (the "schedules of commitments" regulated in GATT Arts. II and XXVIII*bis*) and by positive GATS concessions in the four service modes.[111]

However, the market access entitlement would be incomplete (and arguably meaningless) without mechanisms that safeguard the initial balance of concessions. Hence, the trade entitlement is more than just the substantive commitment to open up various sectors. It also covers every modality that may negatively influence the mutually agreed initial trade balance. Integrated into the trade entitlement are auxiliary or dependent entitlements in the form of:

(i) non-discrimination stipulations (e.g. GATT Arts. I and III);
(ii) a prohibition of quantitative restrictions (GATT Art. XI);
(iii) codes of conduct detailing how to deal with non-tariff barriers (e.g. GATT Art. III, but also some aspects of other multilateral Agreements, such as Part I of the TRIPS, the SCM, TBT, SPS, GPA, TRIMS, or ROO);[112]

---

[109] Some WTO scholars, particularly those engaged in formal modeling, regularly portray the WTO/GATT as a tariff-exchange contract. This is inaccurate. The market access entitlement is not just an entitlement to a bilateral exchange of tariffs, but one to offer – and maintain – reciprocal market access in general. This includes provisions about non-tariff barriers, quotas, and other protectionist practices.

[110] See our discussion in note 99 above.

[111] Concessions in the four basic GATS modes determine how international trade in services is supplied and consumed: mode (1) regulates cross-border supply, mode (2) consumption abroad, mode (3) foreign commercial presence, and mode (4) the movement of natural persons (see Hoekman and Kostecki 1995, chapter 7).

[112] I.e. the Agreement on Subsidies and Countervailing Measures, the Agreement on Technical Barriers to Trade, the Agreement on Sanitary and Phytosanitary Measures, the Agreement on Government Procurement, and the Agreement on Rules of Origin, respectively.

(iv) explicit exceptions to the right to compete in foreign markets also form part of the trade entitlement: examples of exceptions include GATT Arts. IV (on cinematography), XVII (on state trading), XXIV (on preferential trade agreements), XXI (on national security), the "Enabling Clause" (based on GATT Arts. XXXVI to XXXVIII), and waivers (WTO Agreement Art. IX).

### 4.2.2 Minimum standard entitlements

The bilaterally owed trade entitlement is crucial, simply because reciprocal market access is the overwhelming motivation for concluding a trade agreement. However, just as much as reciprocal market access is not the sole rationale for contracting, the market access entitlement is not the only entitlement exchanged in the WTO contract. Positive integration or minimum standard entitlements in the WTO are contractual concessions that prescribe every participating Member to adhere to an agreed set of legal standards. Positive integration rules mandate the introduction of certain institutional features and procedures, independently from the state of implementation in other countries. Examples of minimum standard entitlements can be found most poignantly in the multilateral TRIPS and ILP Agreements, whose conclusion is probably best explained by the logic of a coordination game (as discussed at p. 189 above).[113] However, note that other Agreements, such as the SPS, GPA, or the ROO also contain numerous positive integration norms.[114]

What is the nature of minimum standard entitlements, and what sets them apart from the bilaterally owed market access-based trade entitlements that form the backbone of GATT and GATS? Minimum standard entitlements are owed to the contracting community as a whole, that is, they have a multilateral ambit. Their *erga omnes partes* scope is distinct from a bilateral logic:[115] with reciprocal entitlements, the *rights* of one contracting party constitute the *obligations* of the other. Signatories

---

[113] Take the TRIPS Agreement: Part II (Arts. 9–40) is entitled *Standards Concerning the Availability, Scope and Use of Intellectual Property Rights*. These articles lay down for each intellectual property right in succession, what the applicable minimum standards for protection are, and to what extent – and how – Member countries are required to comply with them.

[114] See e.g. SPS Art. 8 and Annex C (both entitled *Control, Inspection and Approval Procedures*), ROO Art. 2 and Part IV on the so-called "harmonization program," or GPA Art. XII (*Tender Documentation*).

[115] Multilateral obligations are sometimes called *obligations erga omnes partes* (see Pauwelyn 2001), since they are owed to all Members alike. This nomenclature is, however, slightly

exchange entitlements by securing commitments in return for the ones given. A multilateral entitlement mandates every contracting party to behave in a certain manner (for example, that every WTO Member establish a national patent office): the entitlement is not exchanged, it is owned by the entire community of signatories, as well as owed to the entire WTO community. Multilateral entitlements oblige every signatory to abide by the same "rules of the game." If a country violates its multilateral entitlement to, say, supply patent protection by refusing to establish a patent office, that country impairs the competitive opportunities of all other Members. It brings down the general level of cooperation and harms the system as a whole.

### 4.2.3    Basic auxiliary rules of entitlement

Basic, or multilateral, auxiliary rules of entitlements are phrased in the form of positive norms, i.e. as contractual prescriptions that rarely leave any degrees of freedom or discretion to transactors. They, too, are multilateral by nature in that they oblige all contracting parties to the same degree. Multilateral auxiliary entitlements are social ordering devices that supply the trade agreement with a fundamental structure necessary to facilitate the underlying exchange that the substantive entitlements ensure.

Yet in contrast to substantive entitlements, basic auxiliary entitlements carry no proper transactional motivation or contracting rationale. They do not change the net balance of contractual obligations laid down by substantive commitments. Basic auxiliary entitlements are merely guided by a desire to ameliorate the general trading environment, the basic conditions in which world trade takes place. We propose to distinguish four types of basic auxiliary entitlements in the WTO.

(i) **Procedural rules**    The purpose of procedural rules is to organize and structure a contractual relationship in a sensible manner. The WTO

---

inaccurate and misleading, because as a matter of positive law (by virtue of DSU Art. 3.4), all WTO rights and obligations are de iure applicable to the whole membership. Based on this insight, some scholars have argued that reciprocity and bilateral market access-related rights and obligations are a thing of the past, and that all contemporary WTO legal obligations have a multilateral ambit (Charnovitz 2001; 2002a; Jackson 1997b; 2004; Pauwelyn 2000). We disagree. As we have shown, the logic of the market access entitlement is essentially bilateral (see note 99 above), even though it is de iure owed to the entire membership. As a convention, we will use the term *erga omnes partes* only for those entitlements whose contractual and systemic logic is inherently multilateral in nature, i.e. that are de facto owed to all Members at the same time.

contains a whole range of rules that delineate organizational issues, such as timelines (for example, those laid down in DSU Arts. 4, 8, 16, 17, 20, and 22), rules of decision-making (WTO Agreement Art. IX), voting and selection procedures (e.g. DSU Art. 8.4 on dispute panel composition), special procedures (e.g. on interpretations laid down in WTO Agreement Art. IX.2), disclosure requirements (such as those in GATT Art. XXIV.7, or DSU Arts. 3, 4, 10, 25), or general provisions of *modus operandi* (such as GATT Art. XXVIII*bis* on initial tariff negotiations, WTO Agreement Arts. XXII, XIV and XV on "accession," "acceptance, entry into force and deposit," and "withdrawal," respectively).

**(ii) Transparency entitlements**    Transparency entitlements are obligations spread across the range of WTO Agreements. They safeguard the observation of basic rules of the game, and are aimed at reducing unnecessary search and error costs in connection with economic exchange.[116] We find Wolfe's (2003) classification helpful, which groups transparency provisions into: (i) tariff and services schedules which codify Members' commitments (e.g. GATT Art. II or GATS Art. XX); (ii) the Trade Policy Review Mechanism; (iii) publication and notification (e.g. GATT Art. X on "publication and administration of trade regulation"); (iv) internal transparency which ascertains transparency of the institution to its Members; and (v) external transparency to civil society.

**(iii) Obligations owed to the institution**    Another kind of basic auxiliary entitlements are Member obligations owed to the institution itself. Yearly financial contributions by Members to the WTO may count as an example, as well as the obligation to assign trade experts to serve on dispute panels.

**(iv) "External" entitlements**    International trade has crucial ties to many other activities of international concern (Pauwelyn 2003). Public international law is the relevant "playground," or domain, within which WTO Members are free to contract. Multilateral external entitlements constitute and delineate the limits of contract freedom in international trade law. External entitlements may be especially important as rules of default,

---

[116] While a transparency provision in a particular WTO Agreement may be concerned only with the narrow range of measures covered under that Agreement, such as subsidies or SPS regulations, the cumulative effect of these provisions is to diminish the opaqueness of a Member's trade regime and trade policy-making process.

| Nature of entitlements | Bilateral ("Market access entitlement" or "Trade entitlement") | Multilateral ("Multilateral entitlements" "Coordination entitlements") |
|---|---|---|
| Substantive | **Mutual trade liberalization concessions** <br> – Tariff schedules <br> – Service concessions in 4 GATS service modes of supply | **Minimum standard entitlements (positive integration norms)** <br> – Intellectual property <br> – Investment <br> – Import licensing <br> – … |
| Auxiliary | Specify/maintain/safeguard market access <br> – GATT, Arts. III, XI, e.g. <br> – TBT, SPS, ROO, e.g. <br> – Exceptions | **Basic (or multilateral) auxiliary entitlements** <br> – Rules owed to organization <br> – Procedural rules <br> – Transparency rules <br> – External rules |

**Figure 4.5**    Overview of primary entitlements in the WTO
Note: This chart gives an overview of the three basic entitlement types exchanged in the WTO. Minimum standard and basic auxiliary entitlements are formed into a group termed "multilateral" or "coordination entitlements."

in situations where the WTO contract is mute as to a certain issue (Dunoff and Trachtman 1999, p. 35).

Of special importance are peremptory norms of international law (*ius cogens*). Peremptory norms are fundamental principles of public international law. They have acceptance among the international community of states as a whole, not only for WTO Members. Unlike norms of customary international law that can be modified/changed by mutual consent, WTO Members must not "contract around" *ius cogens* norms. Under the Vienna Convention on the Law of Treaties, any treaty in violation of a peremptory norm is null and void (VCLT Art. 53).[117]

### 4.2.4    Prominent role of the market access entitlement

By means of a summary, Figure 4.5 categorizes the nature of WTO entitlements along the bilateral/multilateral dichotomy and along the substantive/auxiliary divide. Above, we distinguished three types of WTO entitlements: first, the market access, or trade entitlement,

---

[117] Generally accepted *ius cogens* norms include prohibitions on waging aggressive war, crimes against humanity, war crimes, piracy, genocide, slavery, and torture (Malanczuk 1997, p. 375).

consisting of substantive reciprocal tariff liberalization commitments, and dependent auxiliary entitlements that specify, safeguard, and maintain the mutual level of market access; secondly, various substantive minimum standard entitlements, which are multilateral in nature and apply to areas like intellectual property protection or wherever common standards help signatories to achieve higher efficiency levels; thirdly, numerous basic auxiliary entitlements, which are multilateral and auxiliary primary rules of contracting. Owing to the fact that they are both multilateral in nature and written with the aim of setting common levels of cooperation, minimum standard and basic auxiliary entitlements together will be termed multilateral, or coordination entitlements.[118]

An important conceptual issue seems worth reiterating. We stated in the introduction of this chapter that, in order to understand the WTO contract, it is important to shift from an agreement-centric to an entitlement-centric view. Doing so, we find that distinguishing between various WTO entitlements is less clear-cut an exercise than distinguishing between different WTO Agreements: most multilateral or plurilateral Agreements in the WTO contain more than one entitlement. There are minimum-standard entitlements in the SPS Agreement, an accord which primarily deals with specifying the market access entitlement. Likewise, the TRIPS, albeit arguably conceptualized as a positive-integration agreement, does contain certain market access provisions, and the GATT contains many basic auxiliary entitlements. Hence, the three groups of entitlements horizontally transcend the entire WTO contract, and anyone interested in studying WTO entitlements must check each individual article and assess its nature. Yet we believe that a specific contractual provision cannot be a market access and a minimum-standard entitlement, or a minimum-standard and a basic auxiliary entitlement at the same time.

Of the three types of WTO entitlements, the reciprocal market access entitlement bears the greatest significance for contracting parties – and as an object of research. The following reasons motivate this assertion.

*The trade entitlement is "self-standing": it fully justifies a contract.* Every contract has a motivation and is concluded to solve a problem (fulfills a *motivational* and an *assurance* function). The trade entitlement is a direct consequence of the most important rationale for entering into

---

[118] The nomenclature "coordination entitlement" is chosen because of the contracting rationale of those entitlements. As explained at p. 187 above, coordination efficiencies are at the core of multilateral positive-integration entitlements.

international trade agreements, namely that of constraining market access externalities (see also at p. 183 above). Multilateral auxiliary entitlements, however, neither represent an objective to contract, nor do they solve a problem that would warrant the conclusion of a trade accord. No transactor concludes an agreement just to prescribe some procedure or other. Minimum standard entitlements, like those mandated by TRIPS, contain a contracting motivation, and may even solve a collective action problem (at p. 187 above). Yet minimum standards are hardly "stand-alone" reasons for concluding a multilateral trade agreement. The TRIPS Agreement is not easily fathomable without a prior market access contract like GATT or GATS.

*The trade entitlement is an extensive commitment.* While, say, a procedural entitlement to obey a certain notification requirement is relatively limited in significance and scope, the trade entitlement is extensive and far-reaching. It is equivalent to the promise to grant trade partners a certain level of market access, across a wide range of sectors and industries. A market access commitment affects thousands of tariff-lines (or service concessions), and it pertains to a great number of domestic non-tariff measures that are prone to partially undo the market access level (such as subsidization, health and safety requirements, technical standards, rules of origin). It is fair to say that keeping up the level of market access for one's trade partners significantly reduces the policy discretion of domestic policy-makers. Therefore, market access entitlements are profound, across-the-board concessions by signatories.

*Trade entitlement violations are easily enforceable.* As was shown at p. 31 above, an integral part of a contract is credible enforcement. Self-enforcement lies in the nature of the WTO as a treaty.[119] Currently, the WTO has no other ultimate enforcement provisions in place than the "suspension of concessions or other obligations." Therefore, a violation of multilateral entitlements traded in the WTO must be avenged through partial withdrawal of market access vis-à-vis a culprit Member (but note retaliation under TRIPS). This is yet another sign that the trade entitlement is at the core of the WTO treaty.

---

[119] There is unanimity in the literature that the WTO is a self-enforcing contract among sovereign nations (cf. Keck and Schropp 2008, note 10). In absence of a supra-national authority, any contract among sovereign nations must necessarily rely on self-enforcement. "The WTO has no jailhouse, no bail bondsmen, no blue helmets, no truncheons or tear gas" (Bello 1996, p. 417).

Let us summarize where we stand so far in our contract-theoretical analysis of the WTO. If we are to understand the WTO from a contractual perspective, we have to understand the fundamentals of the contract formation phase, viz. the locus of decision-making, the general objectives of agents, the rationale for the conclusion of a contract, and the primary contractual entitlements exchanged. Sections 4.1 and 4.2 discussed the motivation of self-interested policy-makers for cooperating and why they prefer doing so in the form of an explicit international trade agreement. Examining the three fundamental entitlements that contracting parties are likely to exchange in pursuit of their contracting objectives, it was shown that some contractual obligations follow a transaction-oriented, bilateral logic, while others follow an *erga omnes partes*, multilateral logic. Reciprocal market access is the dominant (but not the sole) rationale for entering into a trade agreement. Consequently, the reciprocal contractual obligation to grant market access is the most important promise that WTO Members exchange. Positive integration norms enhance the contracting efficiency of the global exchange of goods and services and basic auxiliary norms contribute to the effectiveness of the contract.

### 4.3 Establishing the WTO as an incomplete contract

The fact that the WTO is an incomplete contract is not new, and has been suggested by various WTO scholars.[120] Yet few authors have really laid out the sources of the Agreement's incompleteness, and how it affects the making and shaping of the WTO treaty.[121] Based on the theoretical

---

[120] See sources in Chapter 1, note 3.

[121] The WTO literature usually exogenously assumes the presence of some type of previously defined "uncertainty," and therewith presupposes the existence of contractual incompleteness. Compare four examples of uncertainty from the GATT/WTO literature: Bown (2002a, p. 295) defines uncertainty over the future loosely as "unanticipated preference shocks" to the political-economy parameter of governments. Ethier (2001a, p. 10) gives the concept of uncertainty slightly more structure: "I am especially concerned with three types of uncertainty to which [signatories] would be subject *ex ante*: 1 Uncertainty about what actual policy situation (environmental issues, health or safety concerns, etc., etc.) might give rise to [a contractual escape] action. 2 Uncertainty about the identity of the country in which the situation might emerge. 3 Uncertainty about the extent to which the potential action might be trade-related." Kovenock and Thursby (1992, p. 159) poetically explain random deviations in signatories' protection structure as "demons" that "temporarily possess countries." Finally, Milner and Rosendorff take uncertainty to be "ignorance of the configuration of political pressure to policymakers in future periods" (Rosendorff 2005; Rosendorff and Milner 2001), or as "ambiguity regarding preferences of key domestic players" (Milner and Rosendorff 1997).

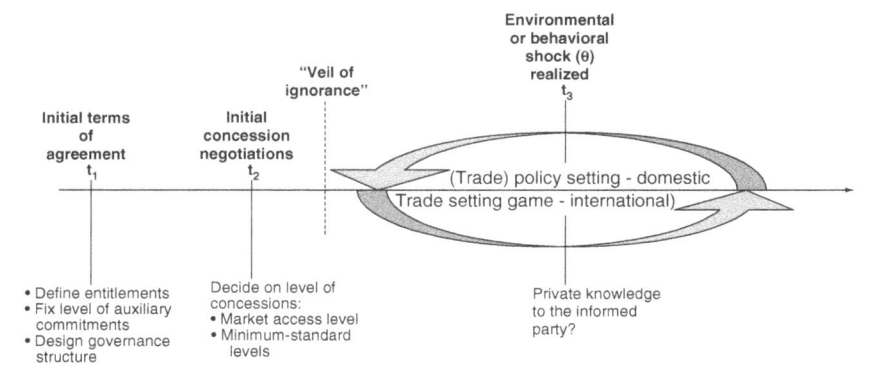

**Figure 4.6**    Nature of interaction in the WTO
Note: This chart illustrates the interaction between countries that conclude a trade contract based on market access externalities and common minimum standards. $t_1$, $t_2$, and $t_3$ mark consecutive points in time.

findings collected in Chapter 3, we want to examine thoroughly what types of uncertainty are present, acute, and relevant for the WTO Agreement. We locate the source of the contractual incompleteness with which the WTO is fraught and which signatories need to anticipate at the point of ratification. These insights will be useful later on for verifying whether the GATT and WTO framers have chosen the best governance structure to address and overcome these imperfections (Chapter 5). They will also come in handy when we assess the best strategy for dealing with the Agreement's incompleteness (Chapter 6).

When trying to understand what type(s) of incompleteness the WTO is burdened with, we must take a closer look at the contractual interaction in the performance phase of the contract, i.e. in the game that unfolds after the contract is concluded. By characterizing and assessing the nature of contingencies occurring during contract performance, we can extract the prevalent types of uncertainty that reasonably rational trade negotiators had to anticipate (or should have anticipated) when they sat down to conceptualize the WTO.

The nature of interaction in a trade agreement concluded for reasons of market access externalities and minimum standards is fairly simple. Consider Figure 4.6.

At some time $t_1$, self-interested trade negotiators convene to elaborate and write down the basic terms of their trade agreement. They lay out the mutual substantive entitlements and the institutional design supporting the trade deal (auxiliary entitlements and flexibility rules). Shortly thereafter (at $t_2$), or concomitantly,[122] the signatory Members decide on their level of cooperation, i.e. the level of reciprocal market access concessions and the generally applicable level of minimum standards. After the conclusion of the contract, the "trade setting game" plays out: contracting parties continuously exchange goods and services under the improved conditions and according to the rules of the trade agreement. Domestically, each Member government is constantly engaged in all sorts of policy-setting. Domestic policies may have (unintended) trade-related international spillovers on other countries (more on that below). Both the trade game and domestic policy-making are infinitely repeated, since the WTO is an open-ended, long-term contract.

At a time $t_3$, a political economy contingency occurs (the nature of which will be explained below). Policy-makers are reasonably rational actors.[123] An important facet of the assumption that policy-makers may not be perfectly rational shows in the presence of a Rawlsian "veil of ignorance."[124] Behind this proverbial veil, parties negotiate the terms of the contract without full knowledge of the identity of acceding countries, of their economic significance in the distant future, of their role as injurers or victims, and generally of how future states of the world will impact their wellbeing.

We can now proceed to examine the nature of contingencies, uncertainty, and incompleteness in the WTO contract. We do so separately for the market access entitlement (section 4.3.1) and multilateral obligations (minimum standard and basic auxiliary entitlements; section 4.3.2).

---

[122] Stages 1 and 2 take place concomitantly (but not simultaneously) in real life. However, it is conceptually apposite to treat the negotiation of basic institutional design and the negotiation over depth and breadth of commitments as temporally separated instants: parties must agree on fundamental contracting principles (such as the MFN principle, non-discrimination, or enforcement instruments) *before* being able to decide on their mutual reduction of trade barriers and collective minimum standards.

[123] In Chapter 3, note 30, reasonably rational players were characterized as considerate (or rationalist) utility maximizers, who seek to take into consideration all accessible information, and carefully weigh the costs and benefits of their actions. Yet they are no rational supercomputers, and sometimes have trouble processing all existing information, or running through complicated scenarios or sensitivity analyses. This makes them prone to human contracting lapses and errors in reasoning. However, reasonably rational players are not irrational: they would never deliberately act against their self-interest.

[124] The concept of the "veil of ignorance" is important in long-term, repeated-interaction contracts. It implies that players do not know the future distribution of gains and losses from the initial agreement with certainty (Rawls 1971).

### 4.3.1   Contingencies and uncertainty affecting the market access entitlement

The reciprocal market access entitlement is the single most important primary rule of the WTO (section 4.2.4). Parties bilaterally exchange market access concessions. They negotiate the liberalization of sectors and industries up to a political cooperation-equilibrium which is reached once the first government hits its optimal domestic political support level. The reciprocal balance of market access concessions between governments is not stable, but highly dynamic and volatile. In the following sections we examine the nature of contingencies, and how they affect the initial negotiated international market access balance between countries.

### The nature of market access contingencies: political support shocks with spillover potential

We saw at p. 184 above that trade policy-makers, in an effort to maximize their re-election chances, must constantly balance domestic pro-export and pro-protectionism interests. As self-interested utility maximizers they strive for an optimal domestic political support balance at any point in time. However, a domestic political support balance is a fragile affair prone to considerable volatility: the future course of all those variables that directly and indirectly enter the PROF of governments determines the domestic support balance of policy-makers.[125] Since none of these variables is stationary, any change in relevant conditions bears the risk of unhinging the fragile domestic political support equilibrium.[126] Hence, in a dynamic environment, policy-makers' objective functions are constantly exposed to a wide range of temporary or permanent, direct and indirect shocks.

---

[125] As stated above (note 94 and accompanying text), four (partially countervailing) interests may enter into the PROF of trade policy-makers: (i) consumer, (ii) export, (iii) import-competing; and (iv) TOT interests. Any state of nature that has an impact on those four interests potentially has an effect on the domestic political support balance of the policy-maker.

[126] The domestic reverberations of any new situation, or event, on a policy-maker's political support balance are likely to be complex in nature: they crucially depend on the politician's personal preferences, the composition of special interests, as well as the political and financial clout of affected SIGs. It is almost impossible to predict with certainty how, for example, a decrease in the world price of sugar will affect a Swiss policy-maker's political support balance: Will the agri-lobby push for heightened protection? Will consumers care? Will sugar-using industries make efforts to keep the domestic price low?

A *direct* shock to a policy-maker is any variation of those variables that are an integral part of a policy-maker's selfish welfare function. A direct shock can be *any exogenous* contingency or event that affects general social welfare, because consumer welfare is assumed to enter directly into the policy-makers' utility function. An example of a direct exogenous shock is vast unemployment following a technological revolution. Direct shocks can, however, also have endogenous (or behavioral) causes. Contracting parties may, without any noticeable external change, feel differently about certain issues: a policy-maker may feel more altruistic, care less for the general welfare, be more responsive towards campaign contributions and backhanders, etc.[127]

An *indirect* shock to the domestic support balance is constituted by any exogenous change in the state of the world that affects domestic SIGs' demand for, or ability to, lobby for special policy favors. Any external occurrence that has an impact on SIGs' organization, composition, concentration, economic wellbeing, political clout, or willingness to "bribe"/influence politicians will affect a policy-maker *only* if it is prone to upset (improve or deteriorate) the initial domestic political support balance. Examples of indirect political support shocks are price or supply changes that intensify international competition (and may consequently stir lobbying efforts by affected domestic firms); technological breakthroughs that reduce employment in a sector or trigger an export boom; unemployment (which brings workers' interests to the fore); macroeconomic instability; constitutional changes in the country's political institutions (e.g. a successful campaign finance reform that alters the political pressure that firms can apply); or changes in political cleavages or alignments which might make a previously pivotal sector less influential in domestic politics (e.g. due to changes in political majorities).[128]

Yet (in)direct domestic political support shocks of the kind explained above are not quite the contingencies that affect market access entitlements. A contractually relevant contingency is present only if, subsequent to the revelation of a state of nature, one or more policy-makers are

---

[127] A policy-maker may consider asbestos a health hazard, while feeling all right about tobacco – and change her mind next month. People may reconsider issues due to a change in perception, to successful learning, to sudden enlightenment, or because new information is processed differently. But these underlying factors are secondary here. What counts is the result: a novel political-support situation.

[128] On the nature of political shocks, see e.g. Bown 2002a, p. 295; Ethier 2001a, p. 10; Hauser and Roitinger 2004, p. 654; Rosendorff 2005, p. 392; and Rosendorff and Milner 2001, p. 832.

impelled to react (in the form of a trade-related policy instrument). Many political support shocks are absorbed domestically and do not create new international market access externalities. If however, upon the incidence of a domestic political support shock, a decision-maker is willing to undertake actions that are apt to upset the initially negotiated balance of market access concessions, it will give rise to a proper "market access contingency." Market access contingencies are thus a subset of domestic political support contingencies; they are political support shocks with spillover potential.

Some remarks are appropriate here to clarify our understanding of the concept of market access contingencies.

*Market access contingencies can be exogenous or endogenous.* Just as political support contingencies can have an external or internal origin, market access contingencies can also be exogenous or endogenous. Parties may react in a trade-related manner to some external shock, or act due to some psychological, emotional, or behavioral contingency.

*An event is more than a contingency.* A specific incident or event (say, a technology-related demand shock in country A causing an externality in country B) is more than a state of nature, or contingency. Events are composed of a bundle of concurring contingencies. We may think of an event as a vector of contingencies, where time, duration, location, identity of affected parties, etc. are all decisive.[129]

*Regret contingencies and opportunistic contingencies.*[130] Opportunistic contingencies are those that, if acted upon, will lead to inefficient redistribution. If a signatory seizes an exogenous or strategic contingency of this kind, it enriches itself at the expense of its trading partners. Regret

---

[129] This may explain why the occurrence of a seemingly equivalent event, e.g. a technological demand shock, in a different context (at a different time, in a different country, under a different political support constellation), often does not at all have equivalent consequences: the event "technology shock" really consists of a completely different set of contingencies. Sensitivity to contingencies becomes more intricate the more complex the underlying contractual situation (number of actors involved, longevity, depth and breadth of promises, etc.).

[130] See our related discussion in Chapter 3, note 34. As an example from WTO practice consider the following scenario: country A notifies that it will withdraw from previously made GATT concessions for reasons of a balance-of-payment (BoP) crisis. If the state of nature is such that A really experiences a BoP crisis, this can properly be called a *regret* contingency. If, however, country A only claims to be under macroeconomic distress just to opt out of its commitment to grant market access, it is under the influence of a (possibly endogenous) opportunistic contingency.

contingencies are those that, if considered and acted upon, may lead to general welfare-improving behavior.

*Market access contingencies are policy situations of a certain degree of trade-relatedness.* Ethier (2001a, p. 7) refers to market access contingencies as "policy situations of a certain trade-relatedness." This statement contains two messages: (i) the political nature of contingencies, and (ii) the concept of trade-relatedness. Trade deals are inherently political in nature, since economic concerns enter but indirectly into decision-makers' personal objective functions via the wellbeing of influential stakeholder groups. Thus, even if a market-access-relevant state of nature has an economic, technological, societal, or natural origin, only its effect on the policy-maker's political support function matters to her.

The impact of a domestic policy measure on a foreign country depends on the level of trade-relatedness of a contingency: actions by one country might mainly be intended to address domestic (non-trade) issues, but happen to slightly affect the international trade balance. The relevant market access contingency thus displays a low trade impact. Other shocks entail a strong trade impact, such as a protectionist policy reaction to an economic depression (think of the dynamics unfolding after the Great Depression and the Smoot-Hawley tariff in 1929 and 1931).

*Unintentional spillovers are possible.* The few economic models of the WTO that consider a non-stationary world usually model market access contingencies as protectionist "preference shocks" (Bown 2002a, p. 295). Contingencies are assumed to be such that they provoke a direct, unambiguous, political pressure for protection at home, or for more open markets abroad (e.g. Bagwell and Staiger 2005b; Bown 2002b; Copeland 1990; Furusawa 1999; Herzing 2005; Hungerford 1991; Kovenock and Thursby 1992). In short, it is assumed that external shocks are direct pro-protection market access contingencies. It should be noted, however, that governments, in pursuing their objective of achieving the best possible domestic political support balance, do not exclusively try to craft *trade* policies, but in fact shape any kind of domestic policy measures with the objective of maximizing political support.[131] In fact the majority of a country's policies are primarily geared towards domestic objectives. Yet some of these policies have unintentional trade impacts. Various domestic sanitary, health, environmental, or

---

[131] Political economy literature on endogenous trade policy-making (see note 14 above) assumes any government policy to be trade-related solely for the purpose of convenience.

consumer-safety policies may be geared towards domestic non-trade objectives, but are somehow trade-related. As Ethier (2001a) rightly contends, any redistributive domestic policy may provoke international spillovers.[132]

The incidence of market access contingencies shows that an initially negotiated market access balance is far from stable. In fact, in a non-stationary world the mutually agreed balance of market access entitlements between two self-interested policy-makers is in constant flux. Many efforts undertaken by a trade policy-maker to bring into balance her domestic political support structure may – intentionally, inadvertently, or due to negligence – entail spillover effects on the international market access balance.

### How contingencies affect the entitlement to trade: the nature of uncertainty and the resulting type of incompleteness

Intuitively, in a complex contract such as the WTO, featuring many players and repeated interactions, complex domestic settings, many issue areas, and a dazzling number of liberalized sectors, it is impossible for signatories to consider in advance every possible state of the world in the contract. Based on our previously developed typology of contractual uncertainty (see Figure 3.1), we are now prepared to lend that intuition a bit more structure and scientific rigor.

The following paragraphs elucidate the types of incompleteness that the market access entitlement is encumbered with. To that end, we detect the underlying categories of uncertainty that burden the WTO contract. We follow the structure illustrated in Figure 3.1, searching for answers to the suite of questions: (i) Can contingencies be defined/specified in advance? (ii) Can their outcome be defined? (iii) Is the probability density function known? (iv) Is the contingency symmetrically revealed?

**(i) Can market access contingencies be forecast?** If WTO signatories could anticipate and specify all the exogenous and endogenous contingencies that might lead to a disruption of the mutual market access balance, they could write a complete contingent contract. To achieve that end, contracting parties would need to foresee and consider all those myriads of contingency-bundles that have a potential bearing on the

---

[132] Applied to the context of market access contingencies, this means that inadvertent spillovers make the transnational market access balance even more volatile, since more domestic actions are apt to inadvertently provoke international spillovers.

market access balance, even if they occur with the slightest of probabil-ities.[133] Not only would parties have to foresee the origin, nature, and domestic impact of an endogenous/exogenous market access contin-gency, but also anticipate the domestic reverberations on the injuring governments' domestic support balances, policy-makers' likely reac-tions, and the trade-relatedness that these will cause. In addition, signa-tories would need to devise and prescribe the optimal response to be taken by every affected party.

We have to conclude that WTO signatories are not able to forecast all possible market access contingencies. Horn, Maggi, and Staiger (2005; 2006) have convincingly shown that even fully rational and perfectly capable transactors prefer living with uncertainty over future events to having to negotiate a completely state-contingent contract. The transac-tion costs of adding a contingency to the WTO can easily outweigh its benefits.

### (ii) Can parties predict the outcome of a market access contingency?
Following the lead of section 3.1.2 above (see Figure 3.1), the next question to tackle is whether possible outcomes can be foreseen by signatories or not. The answer is yes, because the effect can be detected. The outcome of a market access contingency is the partial closure (or opening) of trade flows. Although affected parties may not understand exactly what caused one Member to enact a market-closing (or opening) trade policy instrument, they will be quite aware of the consequences, especially if they are negative, i.e. market-closing. Affected SIGs in victim countries, in particular, will do their best to bring a loss of their compe-titive position in export markets to the attention of domestic trade policy-makers.

### (iii) Can signatories define the probability of occurrence?   Here, the
answer is "maybe, but not likely." We saw domestic political support contingencies become market access externalities only if a signatory "acts out" on the shock, that is, enacts a trade-related policy instrument. We submit that it should be quite hard for signatories to predict the probability with which certain market-opening, or rather, protectionist

---

[133] As shown above, there is a myriad of political, technological, economic, and environ-mental contingencies in a non-stationary world, all of which may have an impact on the welfare of consumers and of special interest groups, and therewith on the international political support balance.

outcomes will occur in the future. Contracting parties may *assume* that market access contingencies take place along some probability distribution (e.g. normal distribution), but to actually *know* the probability density function of outcomes should be extremely difficult for signatories, given that they cannot foresee contingencies properly.

**(iv)  Is the information symmetrically observable?**   The last question to address is whether contingencies are revealed symmetrically or asymmetrically. This question is especially important in relation to the opportunistic/regret dichotomy. Whenever market access contingencies are comprised of generally accessible information, the party affected by the domestic political support shock has little opportunity to strategically misrepresent the truth. Yet market access contingencies, it is safe to say, are privately revealed to the party affected by a shock. This party reacts to some domestic political support shock with a protectionist policy measure, and the victim of that measure has little means of knowing (or finding out) what caused the injurer to act: an opportunistic contingency or true regret.[134]

What kinds of uncertainty is the market access entitlement burdened with? Figure 4.7 summarizes our findings by revisiting Figure 3.1 and highlighting the relevant paths. We see that WTO Members must deal with "unforeseen contingencies," since it is impossible to anticipate, define, agree on, and write down all possible market access contingencies. Contracting parties prefer to leave certain contingencies unmentioned and certain policy measures unconsidered, due to cost-induced inefficiencies connected with considering all relevant contingencies and

---

[134] To see why this is so, consider the BoP contingency measures in the WTO. GATT Arts. XII and XVIII allow for the enactment of trade restrictions for BoP purposes. The regret contingency "BoP crisis" (actually an event) is private knowledge to the domestic administration; it is not symmetrically known to every WTO Member. How can any outsider know with certainty if there is a threat of "serious decline in monetary reserves" (as GATT Art. XII.2(a) mandates)? No WTO Member, except for the government affected, is likely to know whether a BoP crisis really takes place, and if so what caused it, and what domestic social, political, and economic reverberations entail as a result. The affected country may appeal to the BoP clause for legitimate reasons; it may well, however, invoke it for selfish, protectionist reasons. Given this asymmetrical revelation of information, the party wishing to deviate from the Agreement is likely to use its informational edge in order to engage in opportunistic behavior (but see panel and AB reports of the *India – Quantitative Restrictions* case, WT/DS 90). India, for example, has a long history of making ample and long-term use of the BoP clause of GATT Art. XVIII. In 1997, the country justified quantitative restrictions on 2,700 agricultural and tariff-lines with recourse to GATT Art. XVIII.B (cf. Mavroidis 2007, chapter 4.3).

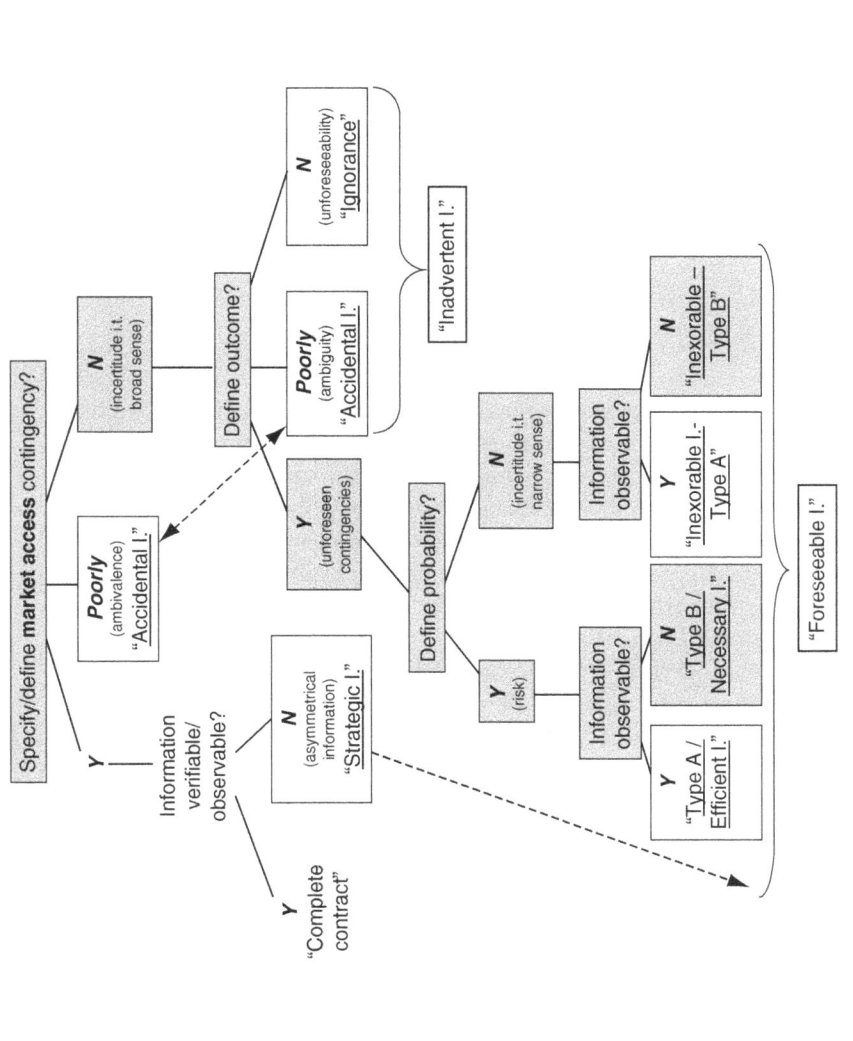

**Figure 4.7** Nature of incompleteness affecting the market access entitlement

Note: This chart is a modified version of Figure 3.1 applied to the market access entitlement of the WTO contract. It illustrates the uncertainty that WTO signatories face in connection with their reciprocal commitment to trade. The resulting types of incompleteness (highlighted) are either the necessary or the inexorable type B categories of incompleteness.

having to prescribe the adequate policy responses (or due to constraints on rationality, for that matter). Signatories may or may not take up the effort to work out the probability of some contingency outcomes. Due to transaction costs, however, they will have to leave contingency outcome space uncovered. Despite this, any market access contingency is most certainly private knowledge to the party affected by a political support shock. Therefore, the market access entitlement is beset with one of two kinds of incompleteness: necessary (or type B), or inexorable incompleteness of type B, depending on whether parties are willing to research the probability density function of contingencies and write a contractual provision accordingly.

### 4.3.2   Contingencies, uncertainty, and incompleteness affecting minimum standard entitlements and other multilateral entitlements

As with market access contingencies, those states of nature that affect previously agreed minimum standards and other basic multilateral entitlements are a subset of policy-makers' political support contingencies: domestic political support shocks may prompt policy-makers to retract from previously agreed minimum standards or other basic entitlements, such as transparency obligations or timelines. Self-interested policy-makers thus wish they had contracted for a different level of concessions, or more/less rigid regulation.

There are, however, two noticeable differences between market access and multilateral contingencies. One lies in the opportunistic/regret contingency dichotomy: due to the multilateral nature of said entitlements, practically every back-tracking behavior taken in response to a domestic political support crisis must be assumed to be opportunistic, unless there is unanimous consent by all contracting parties about its practicability (cf. de Bièvre 2004, p. 4).[135] The second difference between market access and multilateral contingencies resides in the urgency and immediacy of response: shock situations requiring emergency relief action are less likely to occur with respect to multilateral contingencies. It is difficult to come up with examples of surprise contingencies that would require immediate remedial action with respect to minimum standard obligations, such as the establishment of a patent office. Since multilateral obligations are usually written with a longer-term objective, temporary

---

[135] See discussion in note 105 above.

and short-term shocks will less often warrant immediate relief action that must not be delayed by the injurer.

How do multilateral contingencies affect the minimum standard and other multilateral entitlements? Following the same suit of questions applied to the case of market access contingencies, we find that multilateral contingencies are (i) not predictable, but (ii) their effect or outcome is well recognizable and therefore predictable: it is easy to observe whether minimum standards and other regulation norms have been infringed upon. (iii) The probability of contingency-induced outcomes may or may not be known in advance by signatories, but (iv) contingencies are certainly revealed privately to affected parties only. Hence, minimum standard and other basic multilateral entitlements, just like the market access entitlement, are beset by either necessary or inexorable incompleteness of type B, depending on whether parties can or cannot foresee the probability density function of contingencies. Figure 4.7 thus may equally be applied to incompleteness affecting all non-market access entitlements.

## 4.4 Conclusion: the WTO – an incomplete contract based on market access externalities and minimum standards

Writing a complete contingent trade agreement is not in the realm of possibility for WTO signatories. Even if signatories were fully rational and willing, they could not anticipate all the bundles of political support contingencies that may have an impact on policy-makers' market access and minimum standard entitlements – not least, since unanticipated contingencies are privately revealed to affected parties. Private revelation of previously unforeseen contingencies makes incompleteness of the contract an inevitable consequence. The WTO is fraught with incompleteness of either the necessary type B type or with inexorable incompleteness of type B.[136] Staffed with an information edge, shock-affected parties (injurers) have the option to sham a domestic crisis and (allegedly as a reaction to the crisis) enact a trade-related policy measure that does more harm to the other parties than good to the injurer. Thus, the nature of a trade agreement based on market access externalities and minimum standards is such that it is uncompleteable.

---

[136] Refer to our discussion of necessary and inexorable incompleteness of type B at p. 71 above.

When we state that the nature of the WTO is that of a incomplete contract type of necessary or inexorable incompleteness of type B, we do not mean to imply that the WTO Agreement is free from the other types of uncertainty discussed in section 3.1.2 above: for by trying to overcome and master the original contractual uncertainty, WTO Members have introduced other types of incompleteness "through the contractual backdoor."

How did this happen? We saw at p. 84 above that contracting parties, when designing the contractual governance structure, can make use of one or more of the following strategies: (i) minimize the number of gaps through comprehensive contracting; (ii) draft flexibility mechanisms; (iii) exercise precaution; and (iv) delegate responsibility to a third party. As we will demonstrate, the WTO Agreement makes use of all of these strategies. In an effort to overcome "natural" uncertainty in the form of necessary and/or inexorable incompleteness of type B, Members added supplementary contract language: over and above substantive and basic auxiliary entitlements, the WTO framers introduced dependent auxiliary entitlements in the form of additional contract language on contingencies and policy measures, trade policy flexibility provisions, and enforcement mechanisms.[137] Yet doing so came at the cost of additional uncertainty and therefore new types of incompleteness: whenever explicit contract language is inserted, room for haphazard gaps, ambiguities, ambivalence, and rigidity is created.[138] What is more, the incorporation of additional auxiliary entitlements is likely to create room for unforeseen and even unforeseeable contingencies. Thus, fighting incompleteness may have proven to be akin to "robbing Peter to pay Paul": one type of incompleteness being addressed by introducing another. The next chapter proceeds to evaluate the WTO framers' success in dealing with the treaty's contractual incompleteness.

---

[137] The merits of this endeavor and the actual quality of the Agreement's governance structure are elaborated in the following chapter.

[138] See Box 3.1 in Chapter 3 for an explanation of the downside of excessive contractual language. GATT Art. III is a good example of a contractual clause that utilizes very broad and unspecific language and therewith introduces additional incertitude. This article is aimed at curbing discriminatory domestic practices. Yet the instruments affected are neither mentioned nor specified. Ambiguity and opposing interpretations are the natural consequence (Mavroidis 2006, note 17; WTO 2007, section II.C.1.b).

# 5

## Analyzing the system of non-performance in the WTO

Substantive entitlements are the commitments that form the essence of contracts. Any contract that does not consider every possible contingency is by definition incomplete and must have in place a governance structure that protects its substantive entitlements from uncoordinated and, in particular, uncompensated *ex post* escape. At the same time, the institutional design should leave room for welfare-enhancing *ex post* flexibility. Safeguarding efficient post-contractual discretion is the role of a contract's *system of non-performance*. To that end, signatories shape secondary and tertiary rules of contracting.[1]

The benchmark for an incomplete contract is given by the achievable first-best, the efficient "breach" contract (EBC) (section 3.4 above). The EBC mimics the outcome of the hypothetical complete contingent contract. It strikes the optimal balance between flexibility and entitlement protection: every contractual entitlement is protected in a way that prohibits opportunistic opt-out. This is equivalent to saying that injurers may engage in flexibility so as to seize welfare-enhancing *ex post* non-performance opportunities without harming the victims of contractual escape. Whenever one of these two conditions fails to hold, the contractual system of non-performance is out of balance. If signatories to a contract provide for provisions that are unsuccessful in safeguarding the initially traded level of commitment, a signatory expecting to assume the role of a victim is likely to commit to less cooperation up-front. Unseized flexibility opportunities, on the other hand, discourage future injurers from engaging in contractual exchange in light of unforeseen or unanticipated contingencies.

This chapter will examine the current structure of trade policy flexibility and entitlement protection in the WTO. We will review how the

---

[1] Secondary entitlement rules lay out the scope and limits of intra-contractual *ex post* behavior; tertiary rules of enforcement outline how extra-contractual behavior (if discovered) will be punished (see at pp. 46 and 49 above, respectively).

market access entitlement, the minimum standard entitlements, and all other basic auxiliary entitlements are protected both de iure and de facto (sections 5.1 to 5.3). Based on the insights gathered in Chapter 3 which discussed signatories' strategies of overcoming contractual incompleteness, section 5.4 will examine whether the GATT and WTO framers have chosen the best governance structure to address and overcome the unavoidable incompleteness of the WTO contract. Assessing flaws and problems in the WTO system of non-performance, we shall conjecture about the consequences of the international trading system's malfunctioning.

The verdict is not complimentary. The WTO as it stands today is rather far from being an EBC. It will be argued that the current functioning of contractual escape in the WTO does not address the Members' needs adequately, and consequently crowds out cooperative zeal. The WTO system of non-performance is dearly in need of reform.

## 5.1   Trade policy flexibility and protection of the market access entitlement

The GATT/WTO framers at the time had realized that the market access entitlement must be protected against undesired *ex post* back-tracking. Technically, trade liberalization commitments (positive tariff commitments and GATS concessions) can easily be undone by all sorts of tariff and non-tariff measures, such as quotas, voluntary export restraints, export subsidies, regulatory red-tape measures, or the erection of technical impediments. *Ex post* trade barriers have the potential to completely vanquish the initial promise.

Yet the trade entitlement is not protected by an inalienability rule that would mandate unconditional, obligatory specific performance. Signatories were well aware that the WTO Agreements must leave injurers with some "breathing space" in case unforeseen market access contingencies occur that would justify temporary or permanent, partial or total, *ex post* non-performance.[2] To that end, positive market access concessions are supplemented by a protection belt of auxiliary,

---

[2] This was indeed a wise decision of the WTO founding fathers. Many WTO scholars have convincingly shown that a market access agreement beset by unforeseen contingencies which permits trade policy flexibility Pareto-dominates one which rigidly demands mandatory specific performance (Dixit 1987; Downs and Rocke 1995; Herzing 2005; Mahlstein and Schropp 2007; Rosendorff 2005; Rosendorff and Milner 2001; see also our discussion at p. 266 below).

non-substantive, contracting rules. These contracting rules lay out how and to what extent the mutual market access entitlement is shielded from *ex post* discretion. These secondary rules of entitlement dictate who "owns" the contractual gap (should one exist), and under what circumstances and at what price. This section will review the existing governance structure which protects the market access entitlement and authorizes trade policy flexibility.[3]

### 5.1.1 De iure protection of the market access entitlement[4]

The WTO has various auxiliary entitlements that protect the trade entitlement so as to ensure that each party's expectations are not frustrated in the performance phase of the trade contract. De iure, the contractually agreed level of market access is safeguarded by a defense line consisting of four kinds of contracting rules: (i) negative integration provisions, (ii) non-violation complaints, (iii) contingency measures, and (iv) a default rule.

### Negative integration provisions

Instead of specifying detailed market access contingencies, signatories to incomplete contracts can engage in restricting or encouraging certain policy behavior by injuring parties, if four preconditions hold. First, transactors must concentrate on regulating relevant policy instruments which are apt to cause the largest market access impact. To that end, signatories must anticipate the probability of the occurrence of those domestic political support contingencies that prompt injuring parties to enact certain policy measures. Secondly, the benefits of negotiating and writing down the acceptable policy instruments must outweigh the costs.

---

[3] We re-emphasize that, conceptually, the question of trade policy flexibility is largely the flipside of the issue of legal entitlement protection (see Dunoff and Trachtman 1999, p. 32): the level of entitlement protection determines the action space of contracting parties. It sets out whether and how parties are allowed to react to changing circumstances that have not been considered explicitly at the time of the contract formation. Analogously, the choice of trade policy flexibility mechanisms lays down what behavior is permissible in case of a contractual gap, i.e. in case of an unforeseen/unspecified contingency. So, while flexibility provisions nail down the legitimate (intra-contractual) behavior of the *active* party, the entitlement issue is concerned with the scope of protection granted to the *passive* party (see our discussion in Chapter 3, note 73).

[4] The discussion of trade entitlement protection in this chapter will be reduced to trade in goods covered by the GATT (and appending Agreements). Similar instruments for trade in services are provided for in the GATS.

Thirdly, signatories must make sure that the defined (trade-)policy measures are effective in separating opportunistic policies from those policies that are driven by real regret.[5] Fourthly, by writing down permissible and prohibited policy instruments, signatories must be careful not to restrict the sovereign policy-making discretion of policy-makers. Domestic policies may be enacted for non-contractual reasons (in the trade realm: health, public morals, standards, etc.), yet display significant spillover potential. National decision-makers, however, cannot be expected to forgo their duty to regulate domestic affairs.

WTO signatories have gone down that route of contracting. They have integrated explicit contract language in the WTO Agreements that strives to regulate those policy instruments that are prone to cause market access externalities. These so-called *negative integration provisions* are not flexibility rules. Quite the contrary, for they demonstrate an effort towards contractual completeness. Aimed at preventing injurers from *ex post* escape in certain situations, negative integration rules prohibit those trade-restrictive measures, or policy instruments, that are decidedly enacted with an opportunistic intent.[6] Examples of negative integration provisions are:

  (i) rules of non-discrimination (e.g. GATT Arts. I and III);
 (ii) rules dealing with specific clusters of non-tariff barriers (e.g. regulated in the TBT, SPS, GPA, or ROO);
(iii) the prohibition of quantitative restrictions, voluntary export restrictions and orderly marketing agreements (VERs and OMAs; GATT Art. XI);
 (iv) the prohibition of export subsidies (GATT Art. XVI and parts of the SCM);
  (v) the prohibition of unfair trade practices (GATT Art. VI and the ADA);
 (vi) directives on customs valuations (GATT Art. VII and the Agreement on Customs Valuation).

---

[5] If some policy measure can be used in response to both regret *and* opportunistic contingencies alike, its regulation is useless and needs additional definition so that it better separates permissible from opportunistic behavior.

[6] At p. 94 above we called this gap-filling strategy "diligence." Diligence basically means that transactors make efforts to write the best contract they can. Horn, Maggi, and Staiger (2005; 2006) call these efforts "discretion" (prohibiting policy instruments). According to the authors, discretion stands in contrast to *rigidity* which represents an effort towards anticipating environmental contingencies.

Aside from the apparent problems of ambiguity, ambivalence, and rigidity that the inclusion of negative integration rules create (see Box 3.1 in Chapter 3), these WTO provisions cannot possibly regulate in advance all those policy instruments that are apt to partially renege on the contract: it lies in the nature of market access contingencies that unforeseen eventualities are bound to happen during the performance phase of the trade contract. In the same vein, WTO Members are able to engage in unanticipated trade-related policy behavior.[7] Therefore, the market access entitlement is not protected in an absolute way. Signatories possess the discretion to temporarily renege on previously made trade liberalization commitments.

## Non-violation complaints

We saw at p. 202 above that market access contingencies can arise in the form of inadvertent spillovers of domestic policy instruments. A purely domestic policy measure may have trade-related consequences of sorts. Non-violation complaints (NVC), now, protect victims from such unintentional, haphazard spillovers. NVC are described in GATT Art. XXIII.1b and DSU Art. 26.[8] The injurer is not under an international legal obligation to withdraw the measure in question. A mutually agreed solution is encouraged. If parties fail to achieve agreement over compensation, the WTO arbitrator under the mandate of DSU Art. 22.6 issues a non-binding damage measure (Mavroidis 2007, section 4.5.6.2; Petersmann 1991).

---

[7] *Ex ante*, signatories are likely to be ignorant of the underlying probability of outcomes provoked by potential market access contingencies. They cannot decide which instruments and states of nature to focus on. Even if they could foresee the probability of the occurrence of certain outcomes, laying down an exhaustive list of prohibited instruments would be prohibitively expensive: Horn, Maggi, and Staiger (2006) show that *discretion* costs of tailoring instruments can be expected to be extremely high. A thorough assessment has to be conducted as to whether a policy instrument can have trade-related effects, what its cross-country impact will be, and how harmful this is going to be for affected parties. This process is certainly research-intensive and tedious to negotiate. It is therefore completely rational to leave some, or many, policy measures unnamed.

[8] "The idea underlying [GATT Art. XXIII.1(b)] is that the improved competitive opportunities that can legitimately be expected from a tariff concession can be frustrated not only by measures proscribed by the General Agreement but also by measures consistent with that Agreement. In order to encourage contracting parties to make tariff concessions, they must therefore be given a right of redress when a reciprocal concession is impaired by another contracting party as a result of the application of any measure, whether or not it conflicts with the General Agreement" (GATT Panel Report on *EEC – Oilseeds*, L/6627 – 37S/86, at para. 144).

## Contingency measures

Turning from dedicated rules of entitlement protection to explicit provisions of trade policy flexibility, contingency measures were defined at p. 88 above as rules of *ex post* flexibility geared towards seizing the potential of *ex post* regret contingencies. Contingency measures are additional auxiliary entitlements driven by the desire to circumscribe the outcome of certain groups of (previously unspecified) contingencies or events, and to impose in exact terms the permissible action to be taken by signatories in response. Contingency measures lay out the broad contours of regret, without tackling the impossible task of specifying the underlying contingencies themselves.

WTO signatories crafted the following contingency provisions of flexibility for trade in goods.[9]

GATT Art. XIX allows WTO Members to take *safeguard action* (by means of the erection of protectionist barriers) so as to react to a sudden, unforeseen surge in imports. The nature and origin of the principal contingencies notwithstanding, GATT Art. XIX allows for adjustment in the event of serious economic pressure. The multilateral Agreement on Safeguards (SGA), which adds detail to GATT Art. XIX, was concluded during the Uruguay Round. At face value, the safeguards clause is a liability-type rule of opt-out: the injurer can decide whether and when to enact them so as to receive temporary relief in case of domestic distress.

In order to be able to perform escape via the safeguards clause, the potential injurer is faced with a substantial threshold of application.[10] An enacting country must show that "i) as a *result* of *unforeseen development;* ii) imports in *increased quantities;* iii) have *caused* or threatened to cause; iv) *serious injury* to the domestic industry producing the v) *like product.*"[11] Except for "critical circumstances" (SGA Art. 6), GATT Art. XIX.2, SGA Arts. 3 and 8 oblige the injuring party to give a public notice,

---

[9] Similar contingency measures exist for the trade in services, regulated by GATS (see note 4 above).

[10] To recall: the enactment threshold puts down the legal conditions imposed on the injuring signatory. It is usually determined in the form of a series of prerequisites that have to be fulfilled before the contracting parties may engage in *ex post* discretion.

[11] Howse and Mavroidis (2003, p. 686). For specifics of the legal test, and additional restrictions on the enactment of GATT Art. XIX by case law, see also Mavroidis (2007, chapter 4.7.4), or Roitinger (2004, p. 102). For example, according to the AB ruling in *US – Wheat Gluten*, WT/DS 166/AB/R, para. 55, the injurer, when claiming "serious injury," must take into consideration all relevant factors that determine injury.

engage in consultations with the potential victims (of at most thirty days' duration), and to offer the victim adequate trade compensation for the partial withdrawal from its market access obligations. If a mutually agreed solution is not found, the victim is free to suspend substantially equivalent concessions and other obligations.

The application scope of GATT Art. XIX is relatively restricted:[12] Safeguard measures can be invoked exclusively in times of economic distress and applied only once. Tariffs and quantitative restrictions are the only permissible trade instruments. The duration of safeguard measures is for a period of four years, although this can be extended up to eight years, subject to the findings of a mandated review panel (SGA Art. 7.1). In principle, safeguards cannot be directed at the country or set of countries that are the source of the injury (by virtue of SGA Art. 2.2). Instead, they have to be applied on a non-discriminatory basis.[13] The remedy rule accompanying the opt-out clause is probably most accurately described by the reliance damage measure, which mandates a re-establishment of the victim's *status quo ante* the breach.[14]

At a high level of generality GATT Arts. XX and XXI can be seen as contingency measures written with the intention of allowing for flexibility in the event of threats to public order and national security. Both provisions are also liability rules, but they alleviate the injurer from paying any remedies to the victim.[15] Using these contingency measures as tools of market access flexibility, however, is constrained by a high level of preconditions, and a restricted application scope. First of all,

---

[12] The application scope specifies the contractual strings attached to the use or application of a trade policy flexibility mechanism.

[13] In other words, safeguard measures are a non-selective, or non-discriminatory, flexibility tool. They must be "MFN'-ed," in WTO parlance. Whenever safeguards are applied in the form of quantitative restrictions, however, SGA Art. 5.2 on tariff modulation may leave room for selectivity.

[14] If no agreement on compensatory action is reached, GATT Art. XIX.3(a) allows the affected Member (the victim) to "suspend ... substantially equivalent concessions or other obligations." This demand for commensurate damages has been interpreted by WTO arbitrators to include only prospective, direct trade damages, a situation that roughly re-establishes the *status quo ante* the breach (more on that below). A special provision of GATT Art. XIX, however, is the "grace period" of SGA Art. 8.3 which mandates that "the right of suspension ... shall not be exercised for the first three years that [the] safeguard measure is in effect."

[15] Instead of contingency measures, GATT Arts. XX and XXI can be seen as exceptions to the obligations under the GATT (see discussion at p. 193 above; cf. also Mavroidis 2007, chapter 4.1.2). In this case, the provision would not be a liability rule backed by a zero-rule of remedy, but a property rule granted to the injurer.

injurers have to prove that their reason for opting out falls under the exclusive scope of Art. XX (a) to (j), or Art. XXI (a) to (c), respectively. Secondly, discrimination by intent is foreclosed by the requirement laid down in the chapeau of Art. XX. This is consequential, since it does not allow a policy-maker to accord less favorable treatment to imports than to domestic producers when resorting to the "general exceptions" clause. Such unequal treatment, however, is part and parcel of trade policy flexibility (Roitinger 2004, p. 21). Although this does not mean that GATT Art. XX cannot be abused (by enacting protectionist measures under the guise of non-discrimination), this caveat makes the contingency measure of GATT Art. XX a difficult tool for *ex post* discretion.

GATT Arts. XII, XV, and XVIII on balance-of-payment crises, exchange arrangements, and infant industries, are also liability-type opt-outs, albeit accompanied by a high threshold of enactment, as well as a narrow scope of application. The purpose of these contingency measures is to protect Members from financial crises and to maintain financial stability (GATT Arts. XII, XV, and XVIII.B). GATT Art. XVIII, sections A, C, and D protect nascent industries in developing countries from international competition and let them establish a comparative advantage in the production of skill-intensive goods. Just like GATT Arts. XX and XXI, these contingency measures largely avail injurers of remedy payments. However, the use of these flexibility tools is crippled by a rather high level of precondition.[16]

## Default rule

In the realm of trade in goods, GATT Art. XXVIII on modification of schedules is the de iure default rule of the market access entitlement. Art. XXVIII can be invoked independently of any contractually agreed contingency. Political expediency by the injurer, or "requesting country," suffices to initiate tariff renegotiations at any time.[17] The renegotiations

---

[16]  See Roitinger 2004, p. 20. When a country enacts a policy measure due to a BoP problem, for example, it must notify all Members, must confer with the WTO BoP committee, and remains under the periodic review and constant monitoring of that committee (for details, see Mavroidis 2007, chapter 4.3 and 4.4). Whenever a country wants to engage in infant industry protection, it has to consult with Members concerned and offer adequate compensation. If those consultations fail, the entire WTO membership presides over the issue.

[17]  Although it is nowhere stated *expressis verbis* that GATT Art. XXVIII on tariff renegotiations is the market access default rule, we infer that this is the case: whenever none of the contingency measures of flexibility apply, a country wishing to alter its previously negotiated market access balance is left with the possibility of tariff renegotiations as the sole flexibility solution.

requirement shows that GATT Art. XXVIII is a property-rule-type flexibility mechanism accompanied by a negotiated remedy of at least commensurate damages.[18] The injurer is asked to engage in tariff renegotiations with the "primarily concerned Members," i.e. with those WTO Members holding "initial negotiation rights," those that qualify as "principle supplying interests," and those that have "substantial interests."[19]

The enactment of a protectionist measure is burdened by a substantial threshold, as well as by a limited scope of application. First, GATT Art. XXVIII allows market-closing measures in the form of tariffs only. No other trade protection instruments are granted.[20] Secondly, should the renegotiation request not coincidentally fall into a triennial renegotiation period of three months' length (laid out in Art. XXVIII.1), the injuring Member must secure the prior authorization of the entire membership in order to enact its right to renegotiate (Art. XXVIII.4). Thirdly, given the elaborate and extensive procedure entailed in tariff renegotiations, this instrument is evidently not designed for temporary, but for permanent deviations. Therefore, GATT Art. XXVIII is not well-suited to dealing with emergency situations or transient shocks.[21] Finally, there is the issue of selectivity: tariff renegotiations are an untargeted, non-discriminatory measure. Tariff concessions offered as compensation have to be offered on an MFN-basis. This essentially turns the bilateral nature of market access entitlement and market access contingencies into a *multilateral* obligation.

Who owns the gap of the market access entitlement according to the letter of the WTO contract? We see that the market access entitlement is not protected in an absolute sense. Instead, *ex post* trade policy flexibility is possible. The market access entitlement is guarded by a divided

---

[18] GATT Art. XXVIII.2 mandates that the WTO Members participating in the renegotiation of the concession "shall endeavour to maintain a general level of reciprocal and mutually advantageous concessions not less favorable to trade than that provided for in this Agreement prior to such negotiations." Although this adds a nice touch to the article, the stipulation of commensurate damages is somewhat superfluous: as was demonstrated in Chapter 2, note 43, no reasonably rational victim country is going to settle for anything less than commensurate damages anyway, since specific performance is its best alternative to a mutually agreed solution.

[19] See *Interpretative note ad Article XXVIII* at para. 1, as well as the detailed discussion in Mavroidis 2007, chapter 2.3.6.3.

[20] Yet by virtue of the equivalence propositions (e.g. Krugman and Obstfeld 1994, chapter 9), the imposition of an additional tariff can achieve the same market-closing outcome as any other trade measure could.

[21] Messerlin (2000, p. 162) contends that renegotiation under GATT Art. XXVIII is a disproportionate instrument for the aim of temporary protection.

entitlement protection rule (see our discussion at p. 52 above). Some gaps are owned by the victim and are protected by (well-described) negative integration rules. Other gaps are owned by the injurer, who can engage in trade policy flexibility by resorting to contingency measures. If a contingency occurs that does not fall under the ambit of negative integration and contingency measures but causes regret in injurers, the Member concerned is obliged to resort to GATT Art. XXVIII. By virtue of the PR of default, most unforeseen gaps are thus owned by victim Members, who are free to sell off parts of their entitlements to the injurer. Any other behavior must be considered a violation of WTO law. Whenever the injurer engages in behavior that is not deemed illegal, but nevertheless impairs the victim's level of market access, the resort to NVC protects that affected party.

### 5.1.2   De facto protection of the market access entitlement

The de iure system of entitlement protection and non-performance is not the end of the story. In the contemporary WTO contract there are various informal, de facto escape tools available to WTO Members. Although they are in contravention of the letter of the law, or at least of the spirit of the Agreement, injurers make regular use of the following trade policy flexibility tools: (i) VERs and OMAs, (ii) subsidies, (iii) non-discriminatory domestic policies, (iv) antidumping (AD) and counter-vailing duty (CvD) measures, and (v) violation of the Agreement.[22]

As will be shown in the next four sections, these trade policy instruments are (to varying degrees) suitable protectionist escapes from previously made trade liberalization commitments. Injuring Members appreciate and choose these instruments for their ease of use, low

---

[22] The practice of "binding overhang" is sometimes included in the list of informal contingent devices of trade policy flexibility (see Roitinger 2004, p. 16). Indeed, some WTO Members are using the margin between bound and applied tariff rates as a temporary tariff flexibility tool. The applied tariffs are increased to shelter domestic industries from imports but not to the extent that they move above the bound rate, so that no WTO commitment is breached (see e.g. Bagwell and Staiger 2005b; Horn, Maggi, and Staiger 2006). However, we note here that binding overhangs, although technically a tool of *ex post* discretion, should not be included in the list of market access flexibility instruments, since applied tariffs do not form part of the initially agreed mutual market access balance. Consequently, a deviation from something that is not factored into the initial balance of concessions does not constitute a partial back-tracking from *ex ante* made trade liberalization commitments.

enactment costs, a far-reaching scope of application, and damage requirements that are strictly lower than those of official flexibility instruments.

## Voluntary export restraints (and orderly marketing agreements)[23]

A VER is a mutually agreed reduction of exports between an importing and an exporting country. It lies in the nature of the quantitative restriction instrument that the exporter thereby collects the quota rents (e.g. Smith and Venables 1991). VERs, thus, are property rules of flexibility featuring negotiated remedies.[24] The use of VERs as trade barriers was common in the 1970s and 1980s (Baldwin 1989; Bhagwati 1988), but was prohibited in the course of the Urugvay Round negotiations (by virtue of SGA Art. 11.2) for three reasons. First, although VERs were never formally tested by a GATT panel, they probably violate GATT Art. I (because they are discriminatory), Art. XI (because they are quantitative restrictions) and Art. XIX (because they are targeted against single export nations). Secondly, VERs undermine the spirit of the multilateral trading system: they impose externalities on third parties. Thirdly, the origin of VERs is notoriously difficult to prove (but see the GATT panel on *Japan – Semiconductors*).

The prohibition of VERs by the WTO contract, however, does not mean that the incentives to conclude such arrangements have been abolished. Actually, VERs are probably still in full practice as protectionist tools. First, the proverb "no plaintiff, no judge" applies. How can an outsider find out whether exporters reduce their output due to, say, bottlenecks in production or due to a secret bilateral agreement? Rosendorff (1996), for example, points out that even today many VERs are the outcome of negotiations which originated as AD investigations or actions.[25] Bown (2002b, p. 53) suggests that AD actions themselves offer a loophole for signatories to engage in managed trade and VER-like price undertakings. Secondly, VERs are even *legally* possible through a

---

[23] For our purposes, OMAs and VERs are substantially equivalent trade protection instruments. We will only discuss VERs in detail.

[24] But note that no extra-contractual remedies (enforcement instruments) are available, since these arrangements take place in the shadow of WTO law.

[25] Rosendorff (1996) shows that a VER is preferred to the erection of AD duties by self-interested governments of both the exporting and the importing Members. Hence, a VER is an equilibrium outcome.

loophole created by the application of GATT Art. XIX in connection with the footnote to SGA Art. 11.2 and Art. 5.2.[26]

VERs are easy to enact, and relatively cheap for the injuring country (the price for the victim's consent is that of forgone tariff revenues). Importantly, VERs are far-reaching in their application scope: they are free from official restraints, such as timeframes, sunset reviews, or enactment preconditions; the underlying market access contingency can be technical, political, social, or economic. Also, in contrast to Art. XXVIII GATT, VERs are a selective measure, which can be targeted at a specific exporter of concern.

## Subsidies

Export subsidies are sometimes added to the list of informal trade flexibility mechanisms (e.g. Kleen 1989). However, the economics of subsidies as a strategic tool of trade protection are rather shaky: it is difficult to construe cases where a production subsidy is actually advantageous to the policy-makers of the subsidizing country (Roitinger 2004, p. 128). Consider the following reasons. First, not every subsidy is apt to raise the export volume of a country at the expense of production in other countries. Secondly, export subsidies are prohibited by virtue of SCM Art. 3. Countries have to concoct alternative production subsidies which are apt to circumvent the purview of Art. 3. Thirdly, export subsidies can function as trade policy flexibility tools as long as a unique game set-up is given, as used in Brander and Spencer's famous model of strategic trade (Brander 1987; 1995; Brander and Spencer 1985): only in the presence of a *Cournot* duopoly or oligopoly, and if countries have a predatory intent,[27] can the subsidization of exporters be used to gain world market shares at the expense of foreign rivals. Under less clinical circumstances, this outcome does not hold anymore.[28] In general,

---

[26] See Mavroidis (2007, chapter 4.7.5): SGA Art. 5.2 allows for the discriminatory application of safeguard measures, whereas the footnote to SGA Art. 11.2 permits import quotas as safeguard measures to be administered by the exporter. This is little more than having VERs enter through the backdoor.

[27] Predation occurs if three cumulative conditions hold: first, thanks to subsidies foreign exporters can afford to out-price domestic competitors. Secondly, exporters have the motivation and means to drive competitors out of the market and to obtain monopoly power. Thirdly, once the domestic competitors have exited, the remaining monopolist raises the prices so as to maximize its welfare.

[28] For example, if countries engage in a *Bertrand* competition (over prices), instead of a *Cournot* competition (over volumes), the Brander and Spencer outcome of monopolistic competition breaks down (see Eaton and Grossman 1986; for a general critique of theories of strategic trade see Grossman 1987 or Krugman 1993).

subsidies tend to lead to *more* competitive industries and *lower* world prices, so "victim" countries should actually "write a note of thank you" to the subsidizing country (Bhagwati 2002).

To conclude, subsidies are liability-type rules of flexibility. They are not accompanied by an official remedy to the victim (an indirect compensation in the form of cheaper inputs for victim countries, however, can occur). Yet as rules of trade flexibility, subsidies are inapt: they are costly to enact, and indirect and uncertain in their outcome.

### Non-discriminatory domestic policies

Opportunistic beggar-thy-neighbor policies can result from the use of domestic trade-related instruments. In the absence of exhaustive contractual regulation of all instruments, domestic policy measures may be used as *ex post* flexibility tools (Mavroidis 2007, chapter 3.1, p. 270). Domestic policies, be they related to the environment, health, competition or human rights, may be defined unilaterally by each WTO Member government. The effect of such measures can be market-closing, since they may depress world prices (improve TOT), or produce political support disadvantages to policy-makers abroad.[29] Hence, non-discriminatory trade-related policies are liability-type opt-outs without any remedy payments to victims. Remedies are only payable if the victim sues for non-violation, and if the dispute panel/AB concurs.

The letter of GATT Art. III and standing case law make clear that Members are free to choose their policies as long as they are not applied in a manner that confers an advantage on domestic over foreign production. Yet it has to be noted that opportunistic trade politicians can circumvent the non-discrimination stipulation of Art. III by crafting targeted policy instruments *in the guise* of a non-discriminatory measure. Especially if the enacting country itself does not produce any "like" or "directly substitutable" products, a measure can be crafted that pinpoints exactly a certain export good from a certain country.[30]

---

[29] This informal trade policy flexibility instrument is much like GATT Art. XX without the conditionality of titles (a) to (j), but also without the opportunity to renege upon explicit negative integration provisions.

[30] For example, country A, itself not a cheese producer, enacts a sanitary measure that prohibits the purchase and sale of "white, soft cheese made from buffalo milk and pickled in brine." This policy measure would pretty much exclusively target original Italian buffalo mozzarella.

## Antidumping and countervailing duties

It is no secret that AD and CvD measures are quite frequently abused as protectionist tools of flexibility. Officially, both these tools only can be invoked to counter "unfair" trade practices by foreign exporters, subject to the occurrence of material injury caused by the allegedly unfair imports. AD duties address private practice, whereas CvD action addresses government practice (in the form of subsidization). Unofficially, these two measures are highly fungible mechanisms which are easily turned into protectionist instruments.[31] Since they are very similar tools (Mavroidis 2007, chapter 4.6; Roitinger 2004, p. 135), we will discuss AD and CvD together.

The level of precondition for the enactment of AD and CvD actions is reportedly very low. Domestic investigating authorities have to (i) prove the existence of dumping, or the use of a subsidy; (ii) demonstrate material injury; and (iii) establish a causal relationship between the two. Investigating national authorities have ample leeway to initiate and investigate dumping allegations, and in so doing are largely unchecked by the WTO or any other multilateral organization. They profit from a striking lack of basic contract language, common methodology, and calculation standards for dumping margins, injury, and antidumping tariffs.[32] Thanks to the extremely strong deferential standard of review mandated by ADA Art. 17.6, national AD authorities have additional latitude in their investigation.[33]

---

[31] Trade scholars have called AD and CvD actions "ordinary protection with a good public relations program" (Finger and Zlate 2003), or "a poor man's escape clause" (Hoekman and Leidy in Rosendorff and Milner 2001, p. 830), because they are easily enacted without requiring compensation of the victim(s). The protectionist abuse of these trade remedy measures is the dominant perception in the trade literature (examples include Barfield 2005; Bown 2001; Finger, Hall, and Nelson 1982; Finger, Ng, and Wangchuck 2001; Messerlin 2000; Neufeld 2001; Palmeter 1991a; 1991b; 1996; Prusa and Skeath 2002; Schuknecht 1992; Sykes 1989; Tharakan 1995; Tharakan and Waelbroeck 1994; Trebilcock and Howse 2006).

[32] Special interest groups reportedly bring to bear a significant influence on national bureaucracies in the process of AD/CvD investigations (Finger, Hall, and Nelson 1982). Empirical research substantiates the role played by political influence in affecting the decisions taken by domestic investigation authorities (e.g. Schuknecht 1992; Tharakan and Waelbroeck 1994).

[33] ADA Art. 17.6 comes very close to a *carte blanche* for domestic AD authorities. It reads in pertinent parts: "If the establishment of the facts [of the investigation] was proper and the evaluation was *unbiased* and *objective*, *even though the panel might have reached a different conclusion, the evaluation shall not be overturned*" (emphasis added). The ADA thus hands the AD process (conduct injury tests, evaluate causality, calculate dumping

Coupled with a lax level of precondition, AD and CvD actions are also staffed with a comfortable scope of application for injuring countries. The instruments can be used in versatile fashion: AD and CvD punishments can take the form of cash deposits or bonds (SCM Art. 17/ADA Art. 7.2), "voluntary undertakings" by the "culprit" (SCM Art. 18/ADA Art. 8), or of non-most-favored-nation (MFN)'ed countervailing/antidumping duties (SCM Art. 19/ADA Art. 9). Next, because "unfair" trade practices may be supplier or country specific, AD and CvD measures can be pinpointed at exporters down to the firm level; they are imposed only on those suppliers found to be dumping or receiving subsidies. Since AD/CvD actions are applied in response to "unfair" trade, there is no requirement to offer compensation to the affected trade partner. There is no possibility of retaliation by the country found guilty of dumping or subsidizing, either.[34] Finally, neither countervailing nor antidumping duties have a specific timeframe by which they must be terminated. Both are, however, subject to sunset reviews at maximum intervals of five years (SCM Art. 21/ADA Art. 11).

## Violation of the WTO Agreement

A violation of the WTO Agreement is a final informal trade policy flexibility mechanism that allows for partial defection from agreed-upon market access concessions. Violations constitute illegal, extra-contractual behavior.

Engaging in contract violation is a liability-rule-type opt-out, free from prerequisites, limitations of application, and without compensation requirements. If violations are discovered and condemned, however, the official enforcement procedure of the WTO sets in (more on enforcement and extra-contractual remedies below). In addition to the official punishment, convicted WTO Members may suffer reputation losses for their uncooperative behavior.[35]

---

margin) down to the national authorities of WTO Members, which consequently have substantial discretion in all stages of their investigations (see Barfield 2005; Lindsey 2000; Lindsey *et al.* 1999; Lindsey and Ikenson 2002; 2003; Mavroidis 2007, chapter 4.5; Roitinger 2004, sections 5.2 and 5.3).

[34] The victim Member can, however, bring a nullification and impairment claim against the injurer (GATT Art. XXIII.1.a). In fact, many GATT and WTO disputes are challenges of illegitimate AD and CvD action: as the WTO Secretariat (WTO 2007, section II.D.3.b, Table 19) finds, roughly 16 percent (or 79 out of 505 dyadic disputes) that have been initiated between January 1, 1995 and February 28, 2006 challenge "measures taken to offset 'unfair' trade practices," viz. protectionist abuses of AD and CvD actions.

[35] The reputation loss, or "name-and-shame" factor, resulting from a violation of the WTO Agreement has been stressed by various authors (such as Bütler and Hauser 2002;

To conclude this section on the de iure and de facto protection of the market access entitlement: although the de iure protection of the market access entitlement is rather strong in protecting the market access rights of victims, the de facto situation of trade policy flexibility paints a different picture. Since countries can readily resort to informal instruments of *ex post* discretion, the market access entitlement is protected less rigidly than the letter of the Agreement makes believe. The contractual gaps are comfortably owned by the injuring WTO Members.

## 5.2    De iure and de facto protection of the coordination entitlements

As was shown at p. 193 above, multilateral or "coordination entitlements," consisting of the WTO's various minimum standard and basic auxiliary entitlements, are of a quite different nature as compared to the bilateral market access entitlement. These latter entitlements also are prone to significant uncertainty but, as we shall demonstrate, their protection is more straightforward and less complicated than that of the bilateral trade entitlement. By virtue of their multilateral nature, the protection of coordination entitlements is more absolute, i.e. there is less room for regret contingencies that would justify formal *ex post* flexibility.

### 5.2.1    De iure protection of multilateral entitlements

Multilateral entitlements are written with an eye to reaping transaction cost efficiency. They streamline the channels of international trade. This is made possible by obliging every signatory party to adhere to a commonly applicable code of rules or standards. As discussed previously (Chapter 4, note 135 and accompanying text), it lies in the nature of *erga omnes partes* entitlements that unilateral escape by an injuring Member affects all other contracting parties negatively. Injuring behavior brings down the general level of operations in the system, and harms the competitive opportunities of *all other* signatories. Hence, chances are

Charnovitz 2002b; 2002c; Chayes and Chayes 1993b; Dam 1970; Guzman 2002a; 2002b; Hauser 2000; Hudec 2002; Kovenock and Thursby 1992; Schwartz and Sykes 2002b). There is mistrust of the reputation-loss hypothesis for conceptual reasons (Schropp 2005, section 3.3). Also, reputation gains and losses are notoriously difficult to formalize, let alone measure. We do not consider reputation losses in connection with WTO violation any further in this study.

that this back-tracking behavior is driven by opportunistic intent or is welfare-depreciating at least.

But how to assess or calculate damages incurred by victims of *ex post* back-tracking from multilateral obligations? It is notoriously difficult to put a "price tag" on the defection from multilateral entitlements. The harm caused lies in having negatively affected the entire trading system, and hence is very diffuse and hardly palpable. How can the community of Members assess the disutility caused by one Member infringing upon its obligation to notify a policy instrument, to pay its membership fees, or to have in place a functioning patent office?[36]

WTO framers have addressed this conundrum, by legally protecting coordination entitlements very strictly. Compared to the reciprocal market access entitlement, fewer official trade policy flexibility tools are available. Unless unforeseen contingencies fall under the restrictive ambit of a general or security exception (e.g. TRIPS Art. 73, or GATT Arts. XX/XXI), multilateral coordination entitlements are protected quite strongly. No de iure contingency measures of *ex post* flexibilty can be detected when it comes to multilateral entitlements.

It is difficult to identify a default rule for multilateral entitlements, since nowhere in WTO Agreements is there explicit mention of how to proceed in case something previously unforeseen happens. WTO Agreement Art. X could be seen as some sort of a default rule: it explains the specific procedure to be followed whenever a Member tables a proposal to *amend* the WTO Agreement or any Agreement mentioned in Annex 1. If consensus is not reached, a qualified two-thirds majority of the Ministerial Conference is required for an amendment proposal to be submitted by the Ministerial Conference to WTO Members for their approval.[37] WTO Agreement Art. X could thus be seen as a property-rule-type DR of flexibility.

---

[36] To see the logical and practical difficulties connected with the defection from a multilateral entitlement, take as an example the *Norway – Trondheim Toll Ring* case from 1991 (a GATT dispute). Norway failed to respect its transparency obligations under the Agreement on Government Procurement (GPA). The Trondheim municipal authorities assigned unnotified public works to a Norwegian company. This infringement of GPA transparency provisions may have led to damage. Yet who was harmed by the measure and how could such damages be quantified? Note that in principle any company operating in the relevant field and originating from a GPA signatory country could have won the contract bid. Hence, any supplier could have successfully litigated against Norway (see Mavroidis 1993).

[37] Amendments to five imperative provisions set forth in WTO Charter Art. X(2) require unanimous acceptance by the WTO membership (negative consensus). So far, only one

### 5.2.2   De facto protection of multilateral entitlements

Most coordination entitlements are phrased as positive, not negative, obligations. They lay out what WTO Members are to do, instead of trying to specify and circumscribe which measures and instruments they are prohibited from undertaking. Provisions written in positive language are more easily protected from illegal and opportunistic *ex post* defection.[38] Whereas the trade entitlement is plagued by many informal opt-outs, there are fewer de facto flexibility loopholes when it comes to coordination entitlements.

However, one significant caveat should be noted: as was the case with the trade entitlement, multilateral coordination entitlements can also be reneged upon through the backdoor by violating the Agreement: Members can simply breach the Agreement, risk being sued, and sustain the punishment that they may have to incur. We shall proceed to show that the punishment for injuring countries is generally quite low.

## 5.3   Rules of enforcement[39]

As discussed in detail in Chapter 2 (at p. 32 above), contract enforcement is a fundamental aspect of contracting in general. The quality of enforcement crucially determines the willingness of contracting parties to cooperate in the first place. Signatories design tertiary rules of contracting that lay down how the exchanged entitlements, that is, of the primary and secondary rules of contracting, are to be protected from extra-contractual, defective, behavior. The DSU is the principal legal text governing enforcement issues within the WTO contract.[40] In the DSU, dispute and litigation procedures are laid down, as are enforcement provisions for the violation of substantive and auxiliary rules.

---

amendment has ever passed the WTO General Council (see WTO Doc. WT/L/641, December 8, 2005).

[38] For example, the obligation to grant fifteen years of patent protection for pharmaceuticals leaves little room for legal loopholes: signatories do not care why or by which instruments an injuring country defected from its obligations. What matters is that it did so. So, in writing down positive norms, signatories save themselves from having to foresee and integrate into the contract future contingencies and scenarios.

[39] This section draws in parts on Schropp 2005, section 2.1.

[40] By virtue of DSU Art. 23, the WTO subjects all Members to the exclusive jurisdiction of the dispute settlement mechanism (DSM). Accordingly, the DSM is "the only game in town", precluding both unilateral actions and the use of other fora for the resolution of a WTO-related dispute. The DSU applies to all covered agreements (by virtue of WTO Agreement Art. II.2 and DSU Art. 1).

Whenever signatories are in conflict about some contested measures, they are obliged to first engage in mutual settlement negotiations (DSU Arts. 4 and 5). If these consultations prove futile, the dispute settlement body (DSB) issues a report or ruling.[41] After the lapse of the "reasonable period of time" (RPT) granted by DSU Art. 21.3, and after the compliance panel has established that possible novel measures taken by the defendant (read: the injurer) are inadequate (DSU Art. 21.5), DSU Art. 22 comes into play. It lays down the enforcement procedures. De facto, the defendant now has two options:[42] it can either re-enter into negotiations with the injured state in order to negotiate "a mutually acceptable compensation," as DSU Art. 22.2 stipulates; alternatively, the violating party can decide to stay recalcitrant and endure retaliation. The remedy of retaliation provides the complainant (victim) with "the possibility of suspending the application of concessions or other obligations under the covered agreements on a discriminatory basis vis-à-vis the other Member, subject to authorization by the DSB of such measures" (DSU Art. 3.7). A winning complainant can engage in presanctioned unilateral tariff increases (or other barriers to trade) against some of the non-compliant Member's export sectors.[43]

Compensation and retaliation ("countermeasures" in WTO parlance) are temporary solutions only, and are (arguably) "merely instruments to 'restore the balance of concessions' with compliance as the ultimate objective" (Bronckers and van den Broek 2005, p. 102). Both remedy

---

[41] The DSB is composed of all WTO Member countries, and passes recommendations by dispute panels or the AB by virtue of a negative consensus rule (see e.g. Pauwelyn 2000, p. 336). Therewith, panel or AB recommendations become DSB rulings quasi-automatically. The two terms "recommendations" and "rulings" can thus be used interchangeably.

[42] The qualification de facto is appropriate here because WTO scholarship is in dispute about the legal nature of panel recommendations. It is subject to debate whether or not a condemned defendant is under an international-law obligation to comply with the panel or AB recommendation, which usually advises the defendant to withdraw the illegal measure in place. The widely cited "rebalancing-vs.-compliance" debate in WTO scholarship deals with exactly this issue (see Schropp 2007b for history and origins of the compliance/rebalancing debate).

[43] Before an injured complainant can bring into place its unilateral tariff hikes, however, it has to notify an "authorization request" to the DSB. This retaliation schedule has to be in accord with basic principles and procedures of retaliation (DSU Art. 22.3). If challenged by the defendant country (which is most often the case), an arbitration panel (DSU Arts. 22.6 and 22.7) will review the victim's request for countermeasures and set the quantitative amount of "suspension of concessions or other obligations," and the mix of Agreements, in which concessions can be suspended.

instruments must match the damages suffered by the injured party.[44] Compensation offers, however, in contrast to being exposed to retaliation, are voluntary (DSU Art. 22.2), and consequently not an automatic obligation on the part of the injuring Member.

De facto, the size of remedies for extra-contractual behavior is less than the reliance measure of damages. DSU Art. 22.4 demands that the "level of the suspension of concessions or other obligations authorized by the DSB shall be equivalent to the level of the nullification or impairment." This condition of commensurate damages has consistently been interpreted by arbitration panels and the AB as prospective direct trade damages apt to re-establish the *status quo ante* the breach. To illustrate this, consider the four quantification issues authoritatively established by WTO panels and AB case law (Mavroidis 2007, section 5.4.6): (i) remedies are calculated prospectively; (ii) indirect benefits are not recouped; (iii) only added value matters; (iv) legal fees are not reimbursed.

*(i) Prospective remedies.* Remedy awards have largely been future-oriented (see e.g. Bronckers and van den Broek 2005; Grané 2001; Pauwelyn 2000; Spamann 2006). Injury is calculated not from the time when an illegality was committed, but from the end of the RPT.[45] The prospective nature of WTO remedies is not put down *expressis verbis* in any WTO provision, but so far only manifested in coherent WTO jurisprudence.[46]

---

[44] Throughout the WTO Agreement, the fallback alternative to offering compensation is the remedy of retaliation. Retaliation is mandated to be commensurate to the harm suffered by the injured party by virtue of GATT Arts. XIX.3(a), XXVIII.3(a),(b), or DSU 22.4. Given the retaliation prospect as the best alternative to a breakdown of negotiations, no complainant (victim) will accept a compensation offer that is substantially less than what it expects to gain from retaliation.

[45] In total there were five panels that departed from the standard of prospective remedies, all of them dealing with AD/CvD duties or subsidies. Panels recommended revocation and reimbursement of illegally imposed duties (Mavroidis 2000, p. 775; Lawrence 2003, chapter 3). Disputes in subsidy and CvD matters are not regulated by the DSU, but by special procedures in the SCM (SCM Arts. 4 and 7). Crucially, SCM Art. 4.10 has a different standard for remedies. It allows victims to enact "appropriate," rather than "substantially equivalent" countermeasures. Panels and the AB have interpreted the language of SCM Art. 4.10 to bear a more extensive meaning than DSU Art. 22.4. Panels in *Brazil – Aircraft, Canada – Aircraft*, and *US – FSC*, WT/DS 46, 70, 108 (all subsidy cases) applied retroactive damages.

[46] Bronckers and van den Broek (2005, p. 103) and Grané (2001, p. 768) claim that the prospective nature of WTO remedies is justified by virtue of DSU Art. 19.1. Mavroidis (2000, p. 789; 2007, p. 584), however, does not detect any constraint on retroactive remedies as a matter of positive DSU law, and sides with the *Australia – Automotive Leather II* panel report (para. 6.26).

*(ii) Indirect benefits and added value.* DSB arbitrators have interpreted the "level of nullification and impairment" to be tantamount to direct trade damages, i.e. equivalent to the effective trade losses (Charnovitz 2002c, p. 418; Hudec 2002, p. 86; Lawrence 2003, p. 37; Mavroidis 2000, p. 774; WTO 2004, para. 243).[47] The arbitrators in *EC – Bananas III (Ecuador) (Article 22.6 – EC)* denied the United States indemnity for lost profits resulting from the EC banana importing regime which, *inter alia*, harmed the Mexican banana industry, a major consumer of US fertilizer (WT/DS 27 at paras. 6.12–14). A direct outcome of the discussion on indirect benefits is the decision by the arbitrators in the same case to compute only value added when calculating the level of nullification and impairment (at para. 6.18).[48]

WTO case law has ruled out any consideration of compensation for efficiency losses and other second-order effects resulting from illegal interruption in trade. Hence, these losses always come at the expense and to the detriment of the complaining party.[49]

*(iii) Legal fees.* The arbitrators in their report on *US –1916 Act (EC) (Article 22.6 – US)* made it clear that legal fees paid cannot form part of the calculation of nullification and impairment (WT/DS 136, para. 5.76).

In conclusion, DSU Art. 22.4 mandates commensurate damages for victims who saw their benefits under the Agreement nullified or impaired. By granting prospective remedies amounting to direct trade damages, WTO arbitrators have interpreted the term "commensurate damages" to imply the re-establishment of the *status quo ante* the breach. Actual WTO damage awards under DSU Art. 22.6 are roughly apt to restore the trade level that would exist, had the injurer brought its contravening measure into conformity. Therefore, the current system

---

[47] See also Anderson 2002; Breuss 2004; Grané 2001; Schropp 2005; Schwartz and Sykes 2002b; Spamann 2006; Trachtman 2006. Direct trade damages are estimated as price increase (or decrease) due to the tariff measure, multiplied by import (or export) losses, multiplied by import (or export) substitution elasticity (WTO 2005, section III.A).

[48] As to the concept of value added, see Mavroidis 2007, p. 423.

[49] Efficiency losses are opportunity costs or losses in domestic value-added (see Lawrence 2003, p. 36; Mavroidis 2000, p. 800) caused by the partial breach of the Agreement over and above direct trade effects. Those efficiency losses include the present (discounted) values of profits forgone, lost economies of scale and scope, costs of finding new markets/partners, switching-costs in production, production downsizing costs, etc. Second-order effects are costs created by the application of the countermeasure of retaliation: suspension of concessions depreciates the initially agreed-upon mutual balance of market access and leads to two-way trade on a lower, hence suboptimal, level (Charnovitz 2002c, p. 418; Schropp 2005, note 10).

of extra-contractual remedies is probably best characterized as a remedy short of the reliance damage measure.[50]

## 5.4 Does the current system of trade policy flexibility and entitlement protection make sense?

We now proceed with putting the WTO system of non-performance into perspective and submitting it to a test. How well does the current WTO framework deal with the contractual incompleteness of the Agreement? Does the current regime of entitlement protection in the WTO make sense? There is evidently a need for improvement. In fact, the WTO trade policy flexibility regime as it stands today pretty much defies what contract theory has to say about flexibility instruments and efficient entitlement protection in incomplete contracts. Essentially, violation-cum-retaliation is the ultimate default rule for all entitlements traded in the WTO contract. Violation-cum-retaliation is a de facto liability rule accompanied by remedies which are systemically undercompensatory. Since contract-conforming and extra-contractual behavior are sanctioned in the same way, enforcement of violations is deficient as well. Thus, the WTO misses the benchmark of the EBC by far, as we will demonstrate below. We proceed by discussing the flaws in the protection of the market access entitlement first (5.4.1), and will continue with the assessment of coordination entitlements (5.4.2). Section 5.4.3 discusses the dynamic effects of the defective system of non-performance for the international trading community.

### 5.4.1 Flawed protection of the market access entitlement

What is wrong with the WTO's protection of the reciprocal market access entitlement? We find that both the de iure and the de facto entitlement protection regime show remarkable weaknesses. Coupled with ineffective enforcement, the system of non-performance protecting the market access entitlement is in trouble and could benefit from a healthy reform.

---

[50] We say "roughly" and "short of" the reliance damage measure, because the prospective nature of the arbitration award renders impossible the exact re-establishment of the *status quo* of the market access balance as it existed before the breach. The remedy applied by WTO arbitrators fails to compensate the victim for direct trade damages incurred between the enactment of the measure in question and the lapse of the RPT.

### Examining flaws in the de iure system of entitlement protection

We take note of six concerns in connection with the de iure system of flexibility and entitlement protection of the market access entitlement.

**GATT Art. XXVIII is a questionable rule of default**   The renegotiation provision of GATT Art. XXVIII is a weak and inept default rule of flexibility. First, as was mentioned previously (note 21 and accompanying text), the scope of Art. XXVIII is limited to permanent, not temporary, tariff modifications. The procedural build-up connected to tariff renegotiations renders emergency and temporary protection impossible.[51] Secondly, the renegotiation provision of GATT Art. XXVIII is foiled by a weak remedy accompanying the entitlement protection rule. Contract theory tells us that a property rule of renegotiation must be complemented by remedies in excess of the expectation damage rule in order to be operable.[52] Anything less reduces a property rule to a liability rule, because the injurer will practically always choose to pay the remedy instead of engaging in renegotiations. This is exactly the case with Art. XXVIII: although at first sight it looks like a property rule of flexibility backed by negotiated compensation, the tariff renegotiation clause is effectively a liability-rule-type opt-out accompanied by WTO arbitrators' interpretation of commensurate damages. Paragraph 3 of Art. XXVIII states that an injuring Member may proceed to unilaterally withdraw concessions in cases where negotiations over MFN compensation break down. Adversely affected trading partners may then bilaterally

---

[51]  If the renegotiation request does not happen to fall into an official triennial renegotiation period of three months (laid out in GATT Art. XXVIII.1), the injuring Member has to secure the prior authorization of all Members in order to enact its right to renegotiate (GATT Art. XXVIII.4). As per *Interpretative Note ad Art. XXVIII GATT*, paras. 4.1, 4.4, the injurer must submit a written request to the Council of Trade in Goods, the relevant organ to decide. The requesting Member must supply comprehensive statistical and other information justifying its appeal and listing the effects of the envisaged measure. The Council will then give notice of its consensus decision within thirty days. *Interpretative Note ad Art. XXVIII GATT*, para. 4.5 states that later on in the process the same Council determines (i.e. all WTO Members decide unanimously) whether the compensation offered by the injurer is sufficient. This sort of conditionality is certainly apt to slow down the process of reacting promptly to unforeseen contingencies and unanticipated shocks.

[52]  As was demonstrated above (see text accompanying Chapter 2, note 43 and Chapter 3, note 97), negotiated remedies usually safeguard this outcome, since the victim country's best alternative to a mutually agreed solution is to insist on contract performance.

retaliate by withdrawing substantially equivalent concessions or other obligations.[53]

**What is the substantial difference between GATT Arts. XIX and XXVIII?** The finding that tariff modification is actually a liability-type escape provision then begs the question of whether there is a substantial difference between GATT Arts. XIX and XXVIII. It is somewhat elusive as to why the trade entitlement is protected by two flexibility mechanisms, both of which feature a liability rule and the same remedy ("substantially equivalent" damages, see note 44). Both articles allow injurers to opt out at their discretion for the price of offering compensation or enduring suspension of concessions or other obligations. Only the set of enactment preconditions, as well as the scope of application, differ. These differences notwithstanding, it is incomprehensible from a contract-theoretical point of view why a contingency measure and a default rule should be so similar in nature and design.

**Insufficient scope of de iure escape mechanisms**    Another concern is the insufficient scope of existent de iure escape clauses. As stated before, we believe that the WTO is best characterized as a political contract. It is somewhat odd that the drafters of the WTO/GATT have not provided for any *political* escape mechanism, and in addition have given such a strong conditionality to GATT Art. XIX (Roitinger 2004).[54]

The *EC – Hormones* cases[55] demonstrated that the European Communities, for political or health reasons, wished to withdraw from a previously made market access commitment it had undergone under

---

[53] Pertinent parts of GATT Art. XXVIII.3 read (emphasis added): "If *agreement* between the Members primarily concerned *cannot be reached* ..., the Member which proposes to modify or withdraw the concession shall, nevertheless, be *free to do so* and if such action is taken, any Member with which such concession was initially negotiated, any Member [having] a principal supplying interest and any Member [having] a substantial interest shall then be free not later than six months after such action is taken, to *withdraw ... substantially equivalent concessions* initially negotiated with the applicant contracting party." This paragraph does no more than put into effect a liability-type escape possibility for injurers. It arguably renders the previous renegotiation clause futile.

[54] Sykes (1991, p. 289) concurs that high requirements undercut the political utility of the escape clause.

[55] EC – *Measures affecting Livestock and Meat (Hormones)*, WT/DS 26 and 48, and *US – Continued Suspension of Obligations in the EC – Hormones Dispute*, WT/DS 320 and 321.

the SPS.[56] This endeavor was not backed by any formal WTO escape clause: given GATT Art. XIX's narrow application scope of reacting to economic shocks, and heeding the apparent inadequacy of Art. XXVIII renegotiations as a safety valve, the European Communities felt obliged to keep on violating the GATT Agreement.[57] Lacking any formal means to spontaneously and temporarily withdraw from existing concessions is a serious issue, because it effectively blurs the line between good-faith and bad-faith (opportunistic) behavior.

**Application scope of non-violation complaints is limited**    WTO signatories are heedful of domestic policy measures that may display external trade effects. A victims' right to balanced market access is protected from inadvertent back-tracking by way of the non-violation complaint (NVC) in GATT Art. XXIII.1.b. Technically, NVC can be applied whenever a victim government feels that its previously made trade liberalization concessions have been nullified and impaired by a legal (or rather: not illegal) policy measure of another signatory.[58] De facto, however, WTO dispute panels have been extremely reluctant to admit NVC in situations other than regulatory subsidies.[59] WTO practice has thereby burdened victims with a relatively high enactment threshold for invoking an NVC.[60]

---

[56] In fact, the *Hormones* story actually predated the WTO. Banning hormone-treated beef was a legal measure (under the GATT 1947), and became illegal after the conclusion of the SPS. Be that as it may, the EC, after having concluded the SPS, wished to partially withdraw from its obligations under the SPS. Why the EC did not invoke SPS Art. 5.7 is a different story.

[57] This is, of course, only one interpretation. Other observers may come to different conclusions, arguing that the EC acted genuinely malevolently, or was "putting to a test" the infant dispute settlement system of the WTO.

[58] This reading of GATT Art. XXIII.1.b is confirmed in *EC – Asbestos* (at para. 188). The case law in *EC – Asbestos* "did not limit the realm of possible applications of a non-violation complaint. [NVC are] based on the open-ended language employed in Art. XXIII.1.b GATT. Following this jurisprudence, it seems plausible to argue that non-violation complaints can be raised against practically each and every government measure that might have an impact on the value of negotiated concessions" (Mavroidis 2007, p. 571).

[59] Bagwell (2007) and Bagwell and Staiger (2002b) take the view that non-violation complaints are an attractive yet starkly under-utilized means of ensuring that reciprocal commitments will be observed.

[60] Standing GATT/WTO case law (e.g. in *Kodak – Fuji, Spain – Unroasted Coffee*, or *EC – Asbestos*) has ruled that for a WTO Member to successfully launch a non-violation complaint, the victim must demonstrate that four conditions are cumulatively met: (i) the complaint must be as a result of some action taken by a WTO Member, the

**WTO framers picked the wrong battlefield: negative integration clauses are over-engineered whereas default rules are neglected** By putting too much effort into the drafting of negative integration norms, the framers of the WTO not only created the questionable impression of contractual completeness, but also neglected the much more salient issue of drafting solid default rules. The WTO founding fathers shoved the square peg of explicit treaty language into the round hole of inevitable contractual incompleteness. Consider the following arguments:

First, concentrating on negative integration rules is a problematic endeavor. The trade liberalization negotiations of the Uruguay Round witnessed a boom in negative integration provisions protecting the market access entitlement (e.g. in the TBT, SPS, GPA, ROO, etc.). Some authors interpreted this impulse as a general drive towards a rule of law over the last decade.[61] To us, however, this evolution does not mark a paradigmatic shift in the world trading community, let alone in the contractual logic (as sources claim). Rather, we interpret this evolution as an attempt to ameliorate the general contracting environment. WTO signatories tried to mend legal loopholes that had become apparent through the GATT years by adding explicit (and quite often complicated) language that anticipates possible contingencies and prohibits certain types of policy behavior.[62]

We are critical of these efforts in the contracting strategy of diligence: the uncertainty connected with the market access entitlement in the WTO is insurmountable (at p. 208 above). Trying to overcome incompleteness by writing down ever more explicit obligations must necessarily remain a patchwork endeavor. Next to creating additional room for ambivalence and ambiguity (see text accompanying note 7), more

---

consistency of which with the WTO Agreement is not in dispute; (ii) such action occurred subsequently to the conclusion of a tariff concession; (iii) such action could not have been reasonably anticipated by the complainant; (iv) the action at hand impaired benefits accruing to the victim, i.e. reduced the value of the concession negotiated between the complainant and the defendant (Mavroidis 2007, p. 571; Petersmann 1991).

[61] Charnovitz (2001; 2002a; 2002c), among others, alleges a gradual move from a diplomatic bargaining forum under the GATT (1947–94) towards an international rule-of-law system with proper norms and common values in the WTO. The drive towards a stronger rule of law has also been termed "rule-orientation" (as opposed to "power-orientation": Bagwell and Staiger 2002b, pp. 5 and 36; Jackson 1997a, p. 109; Roitinger 2004, p. 143).

[62] This drive towards completeness seems to be an organic development in relational contracts (Cohen 1999, p. 82). It seems debatable, however, whether this evolution is beneficial to the international trading system.

contract language brings with it the illusion of completeness. Parties think they have "nailed down" all eventualities. On the one hand, this creates unnecessary rigidity, deterring injurers from reacting to regret contingencies. On the other hand, only when they are actually involved in lengthy and costly disputes do signatories realize that they did not nail down all eventualities at all.

The second aspect of the argument is the striking imbalance between "complete" and "incomplete" contracting in the WTO: as shown, market access contingencies are of such a nature that they render a completion of the contract impossible. This calls for the design of flexibility rules, more precisely, of an efficient rule of default. We demonstrated at p. 90 above that DR are important provisions in incomplete contracts, because they enter into effect whenever a previously undescribed contingency occurs. In order to fit many different contexts, DR should be easy to enact, have the broadest possible application scope, and be accompanied by the appropriate rule of remedy. GATT Art. XXVIII as the DR for the market access entitlement, however, is evidently at fault. Its enactment is slack and cumbersome; it is protected by an inadequate intra-contractual remedy rule; its application scope is porous.[63] Instead of shaping a more efficient rule of default, WTO framers put the emphasis on crafting ever more elaborate negative integration rules.

**Retaliation is a questionable mechanism of remediation**   Most de iure flexibility mechanisms couple the injurer's *ex post* escape with a compulsory remedy, which is the offer of tariff compensation. If compensation negotiations break down, the victim is authorized to engage in suspension of concessions or other obligations. As we will lay out in our discussion of DSU enforcement below, the countermeasure of retaliation as a mechanism of remediation is questionable and certainly inferior to compensation offers.

To sum up our reservations with the de iure system of market access entitlement protection: any incomplete but efficient contract must protect its substantive entitlements against *ex post* opportunism, but nevertheless allow for Pareto-superior post-contractual flexibility. On the one

---

[63] The application scope of GATT Art. XXVIII is quite obviously porous. It is deficient from the point of view of injurers, as shown above. It is also insufficient from a victim's point of view: if it were an efficient rule of entitlement protection, victims would not need to resort to non-violation claims. But since the available contractual rule of default patently fails to kick in whenever an unforeseen contingency occurs, the design of non-violation claims seemed apposite to the framers of the WTO.

hand, the WTO features entitlement protection instruments that are imperfect and porous: negative integration norms neither cover all possible market access contingencies, nor prohibit all sorts of opportunistic behavior, as the presence of NVC attests. The provision of NVC, in and of itself a valuable tool of entitlement protection, is crippled by WTO practice. On the other hand, the de iure configuration of trade policy flexibility is also less than satisfactory: a country that wants to opt out for non-opportunistic reasons cannot easily do so in the face of rigid flexibility mechanisms that are difficult to enact and narrow in their application scope. The default rule that eventually protects the market access entitlement is thwarted against potential injurers.

### Examining flaws in the de facto system of entitlement protection

So much for the systemic flaws of the *de iure* system of non-performance. Things get more irritating, once the *de facto* situation of trade policy flexibility enters our assessment: the de facto system of flexibility is apt to annihilate many a market access provision written down in the WTO contract. For injurers, informal flexibility tools (especially domestic policy measures, AD and CvD action, and violation of the Agreement) supersede de iure trade policy flexibility tools, simply because they are (i) easier to enact, (ii) possess a broader scope of application, (iii) are cheaper in terms of political currency, and (iv) are inexpensive in terms of remedies payable to the victim.

**(i) Informal flexibility instruments have lower enactment thresholds** As was indicated in section 5.1.2, informal instruments of *ex post* flexibility have lower enactment thresholds precisely because they are enacted in the shadow of the law: AD and CvD, for example, were written to counter unfair trading, not to be abused as tools of protectionism. Violation of the Agreement and trade-related domestic policy measures can be enacted by injurers at any time and without any precondition.

**(ii) Informal flexibility mechanisms possess a broader scope of application** Informal escape tools are either illegal or at least counter to the spirit of the Agreement. Hence, they are less impeded by contractual language geared towards restricting their application scope. Market-closing domestic policy instruments, for example, can be enacted for all sorts of reasons, not just because of unforeseen economic shocks (as prescribed by GATT Art. XIX). An important factor is the issue of selectivity: many informal escape mechanisms, most notably VERs, AD, CvD, and violation of the Agreement, can be pinpointed against those exporting countries, industries, or firms that are of special concern to an importing WTO Member. Instead of having to treat all countries in the same way, injurers can better address their protectionist needs.

(iii) Informal trade policy flexibility tools are politically more convenient to policy-makers   Numerous authors have examined the political economy of flexibility mechanisms.[64] They find various reasons why informal escape mechanisms (in particular AD, CvD, and violation-cum-retaliation) are politically more opportune to protectionist policy-makers than formal flexibility tools.[65] There is a rather intuitive explanation for the reluctance of countries to utilize de iure escapes. First, policy-makers are averse to overtly legitimizing a protectionist measure applied against fairly traded goods: this would be tantamount to an official admission of guilt and incompetence. Informal opt-outs such as AD/CvD action or VERs circumvent problems of this kind. Secondly, the direct nature of the de iure measures does not allow for "blame-shifting" or "scapegoating" of allegedly unfair foreign trade practices. Thirdly, formal flexibility tools display a lack of selectivity.[66] Finally, the requirement that compensation be offered immediately, and not after a lengthy litigation, undermines the engagement in formal escape.

(iv) De facto flexibility tools are accompanied by lower remedies   An additional and indeed compelling feature of informal escape mechanisms for injurers is that damage remedies payable to the victim pursuant to an unofficial escape are unequivocally lower than those looming in the aftermath of a formal act of non-performance. Depending on which de facto flexibility tool is chosen, remedies range from zero to damages that

---

[64] See Schropp 2005, section 3 for details and literature references.

[65] It is well-documented in the WTO literature that for purely political-economic reasons protectionist Members prefer enacting informal trade policy flexibility tools to utilizing de iure escapes (see e.g. Anderson 2002; Barfield 2001; Barton et al. 2006; Blonigen and Bown 2003; Bown 2001; 2002a; 2002b; 2004; Finger 1991; 1998; Finger, Ng, and Wangchuck 2001; Jones 2004; Lawrence 2003; Palmeter 1991b; Roitinger 2004; Rosendorff 1996; Schropp 2005; Sykes 1991; Tharakan 1995; Tharakan and Waelbroeck 1994).

[66] The non-discriminatory feature of formal safeguard measures has been cited as one reason why it is infrequently used: governments may prefer a more targeted instrument which can be directed at the country or set of countries that are the source of the injury (e.g. Barton et al. 2006).

are strictly less than those "substantially equivalent to the level of nulli-fication or impairment" – which WTO jurisdiction has interpreted to be roughly equivalent to the reliance damages. This is so because damages are payable only if the victim sues and the injurer is subsequently found guilty of the violation. Due to the probability that the victim may not go to court at all, to the possibility that the injurer may actually win the case, and to the probability that the victim country may refrain from enacting its awarded retaliation rights, the de facto remedy expected by the injurer is strictly smaller than the reliance damages payable under the formal opt-out mechanisms.[67] We omit considerations of potential reputation losses on the part of the injurer (see note 35).

### Examining flaws in the system of enforcement

This discussion of remedies regarding informal, and largely extra-contractual, flexibility measures immediately leads to an examination of problems connected with the WTO system of enforcement (the tertiary rules of contracting). The contract's extra-contractual remedies, which signatories have shaped in order to safeguard the abidance to intra-contractual rules of flexibility, have three serious drawbacks.

**Intra- and extra-contractual behavior are sanctioned in the same way**   Throughout the GATT and the DSU, the same remedy of with-drawal of "substantially equivalent concession" appears as a counter-measure to legal *and* illegal nullification or impairment of previously agreed market access concessions.[68] It is hard to think of reasons why the framers of the GATT/WTO could have felt that intra- and extra-contractual behavior should be sanctioned identically.[69] Contract theory

---

[67] An exception here is the instrument of VER, where, due to a mutual side-agreement, the victim does not file a complaint with the DSB. Instead, the remedy is bilaterally negotiated. However, given that the injuring Member's best alternative to a negotiated solution (its "reservation utility") is the outcome of a trade litigation, it will not settle for a higher remedy than what it would have to pay if it lost a trade dispute.

[68] See DSU Art. 22.4, GATT Arts. XVIII.7.b, XIX.3.a, and XXVIII.3.a/4.d. An exception is the remedy against non-violation complaints, which are regulated in DSU Art. 26.

[69] Our hypothesis for why the current punishment for violation of the WTO Agreement is lax ("toothless") is that the WTO framers were cognizant of their insufficient handling of the contractual incompleteness. The founding fathers of the WTO may have realized that the current governance structure was insufficiently selective between good-faith and bad-faith clashes. Afraid to enrage well-intentioned injurers by punishing them over and above the trade damage they caused, the drafters opted for the stopgap solution of commensurate punishment for extra-contractual behavior. To substantiate this

would postulate the opposite: illegal *ex post* behavior should be punished by high extra-contractual remedies. Yet by sanctioning extra-contractual defection as lightly as contract-conform default, the WTO reduces the distinction between illegal and legal behavior to a legalistic formality.

The bottom line is that deliberately violating the Agreement de facto is indeed penalized *less* than if a Member resorts to the de jure, intra-contractual flexibility mechanisms (see above). Thus, the WTO contract effectively establishes violation-cum-retaliation as the de facto default rule. The lax punishment of DSU Art. 22.4 turns violation-cum-retaliation into the fallback option for any injurer, since this fallback strategy is at the same time one of the most attractive escape tools (Mavroidis 2000). This is consequential: for the potential injurer, the fallback option sets the benchmark for all other (formal and informal) escape remedies the WTO knows today. Moreover, it determines the power relationship in all settlement negotiations between injurers and victims: when bartering over voluntary compensation, no injurer will be willing to settle above its reservation utility, i.e. the expected cost of enduring retaliation.

**Extra-contractual remedies are systematically undercompensatory**   DSU Art. 22.4 mandates that extra-contractual remedies are to be "substantially equivalent" to the damage done. As just demonstrated, the WTO's interpretation of commensurate damages is effectively standard-setting for all flexibility mechanisms of the WTO. However, arbitration panels have shown a somewhat inadequate understanding of commensurate damages. So far, WTO arbitrators have awarded retaliation roughly equivalent to reliance remedies – at best. The currently applied countermeasure of retaliation amounting to direct (prospective) trade damages is insufficient. These trade damages may roughly re-establish the *status quo ante* the breach, but do not even satisfy the benchmark of expectation damages needed to meet the proportionality principle usually demanded by intra-contractual remedies.

Many authors have criticized the way in which equivalent damages have been calculated pursuant to DSU Art. 22.4. They have argued that official retaliation awards failed the benchmark of rebalancing the mutual market access balance (Anderson 2002; Breuss 2004; Mavroidis

conjecture, more historical research would have to be conducted. However, if it were true, the framers' strategy is a distant second-best strategy of fighting contractual incompleteness compared to the achievable first-best of the efficient "breach" contract (as our analysis in Chapter 6 will show).

2000; Spamann 2006; Trachtman 2006; as well as various contributions in Horn and Mavroidis 2004; 2005; for an in-depth discussion see Keck 2004). Two main criticisms have been set forth.

First, a systematic undercompensation is said to result from the absence of *retroactive* damage awards (cf. Bronckers and van den Broek 2005; Pauwelyn 2000). Prospective damages fail to compensate the victim for losses incurred between the enactment of the violating measure and the end of the RPT.[70]

A second point of concern is dispute panels' interpretation of "substantially equivalent damages" as the *reliance* measure of remedy. Apart from the fact that WTO panels have not been fully transparent in the methodology they applied for calculating retaliation awards,[71] the reliance damage measure misses the minimum target of the *expectation* damage measure (see the related discussion at p. 108 above).[72] Reliance remedies simply do not make up for the actual welfare loss which the injurer caused by the offending measure, because these damages are strictly less than the replacement value which includes efficiency losses that the victim requires to be properly compensated.[73]

**Retaliation is a suboptimal countermeasure**    Although bilaterally negotiated compensation is the preferred countermeasure in the WTO (by virtue of DSU Art. 3.7), "compensation is a rare event" (Pauwelyn 2000, p. 337).[74] Retaliation is the more frequently applied remedy. The

---

[70] In addition, prospective damages coupled with weak procedural rules invite opportunistic "foot-dragging" tactics by offending Members. The most powerful procrastination strategy is to swap one non-compliant measure with another one (Lawrence 2003; Schropp 2005). Also, countries can enact any illegal measure for the time period until a report is adopted which determines its illegality (Bronckers and van den Broek 2005; Pauwelyn 2000; Trachtman 2006). The United States in *US – Steel*, WT/DS 248, 249, 251–254, 258, 259, tellingly revealed that foot-dragging indeed is a workable strategy (Hufbauer and Goodrich 2003a; 2003b).

[71] See related discussion in WTO 2007, section II.D.3.c.(iii).

[72] Expectation damages comprise direct trade damages and all efficiency costs from the moment the measure in question was enacted. As to the nature of efficiency losses in the trade context, see note 49 above.

[73] The Sutherland Report (WTO 2004, para. 243) notes: "Valuation [i.e. the monetized calculative basis for trade damages] would have to consider not only effective losses, but also potential gains that are nullified and impaired."

[74] There is only one official dispute in which compensation was agreed. Following arbitration in *US – Section 110(5) of the US Copyright Act*, WT/DS 160, the United States paid financial damages to the European music industry until the offending law was repealed (see Grossman and Mavroidis 2004).

basic idea of retaliation is that sectors not directly involved in the dispute are punished, and consequently exert pressure on the non-compliant government to bring its measure into conformity.[75] Besides the deterrent effect on the offending party, protection of its own import-competing sectors constitutes at least a partial indemnification for the complaining party (the victim).[76] The significant advantage of retaliation over compensation is its self-enforcement quality; retaliation can be executed by the complainant without prior consent by, or accommodation of, the defendant.

Yet retaliation as a mechanism of remediation poses grave disadvantages for WTO signatories.[77]

First, retaliation is economic nonsense. Higher levels of protection introduce additional economic inefficiencies on both sides. This brings down the general level of the previously negotiated (presumably politically optimal) market access commitments.[78] Hence, as long as self-interested policy-makers care about the general welfare (which they should if they are to be re-elected, see text accompanying Chapter 4, notes 13, 14), the welfare-depreciating effect of retaliation should be of concern. Secondly, some authors contend that the instrument of suspension of concessions violates human rights by barring uninvolved individuals from economic activity (Bronckers and van den Broek 2005; Charnovitz 2001; Petersmann 2002; 2003). Retaliation harms "innocent bystanders," such as consumers and competitive industries. Thirdly, retaliation is likely to lead to trade diversion, and thus has economic spillovers on uninvolved third countries. Fourthly, the complaining Member itself may have no interest in implementing retaliatory measures, when the costs of raising tariffs on much needed imports are considered too high, both economically and politically. Even large WTO Members may face strong resistance from domestic consumers and importers of intermediate products, who suffer from higher prices or

---

[75] Retaliation leads affected exporters to lobby with their government to keep foreign markets open and to act as a counterweight to the influence of import-competing industries.

[76] This is so owing to either political economy considerations or to a positive terms-of-trade effect, if the retaliating country is large enough to affect world prices.

[77] See also Schropp 2005, section 2.2, and WTO 2007, section II.D.3.c.

[78] Many scholars have noted that retaliation restricts (rather than promotes) economically beneficial trade. It harms consumers and competitive industries worldwide, while protecting declining sectors that vie for protectionism (Brainard and Verdier 1994; Bronckers and van den Broek 2005, p. 107; Charnovitz 2001, p. 811; 2002c, p. 419; Mavroidis 2000, p. 800; Pauwelyn 2000).

disturbed relations with regular suppliers (Anderson 2002). Fifthly, many WTO scholars allege that the instrument of tariff retaliation is severely biased against small countries, and hence inherently unfair (Anderson 2002; Bronckers and van den Broek 2005; Charnovitz 2001; 2002c; Diego-Fernandez 2004; Hudec 2002; Pauwelyn 2000). Small countries, in view of their limited market size, may well be unable to exert sufficient pressure on larger Members to alter their behavior (e.g. Hudec 2002). Retaliation threats of small countries thus fail to deter economically powerful Members from committing a violation (Mavroidis 2000; Pauwelyn 2000). Large countries may either remain non-compliant, or offer the complaining small country settlements on unfavorable conditions.[79] The futility of retaliation gives rise to the suspicion of "missing cases" due to a significant "chilling effect" (Bown and Hoekman 2005): small-country complainants may not bother to bring up disputes, because the costs of dispute settlement are incurred without any hope of obtaining reparation (Bronckers and van den Broek 2005).[80] Sixthly, and summarizing all previous drawbacks, the counter-measure of retaliation completely frustrates the spirit and purpose of the WTO as a whole. Raising protectionist barriers in response to market access defections runs counter to the liberalizing spirit of the WTO, and its objective to secure predictable business opportunities.[81]

Self-interested policy-makers must trade off all these disadvantages against the advantages of enacting retaliation, such as the deterring effect of retaliation threats and possible (political support) improvements that trade retaliation may entail (see Schropp 2005, section 3.3 for advantages of trade sanctions).

---

[79] Latin American trade diplomats are quoted with the remark that "trade sanctions are a huge club in the hands of industrial giants and a splinter in the hands of developing countries" (quoted from Charnovitz 2001, note 211; see also Palmeter 2000, p. 472). Indeed, developing countries have never suspended concessions so far. In at least nine pertinent instances small countries won trade disputes, but no action followed – neither compliance by large Members, nor a mutually agreed solution, nor retaliation. These cases are DS 27, 122, 217, 241, 267, whereby co-complaints are counted as separate instances (see Horn and Mavroidis 2006a, 2006b).

[80] Bown (2004) shows that the retaliatory capacity of complainants is the crucial determinant affecting injuring governments' policy decision to comply with panel rulings, or to stay recalcitrant in the face of the adopted panel/AB report. Retaliation capacity is thereby understood as the complainant's market power vis-à-vis the defendant: the more dependent the defendant's exports are on the market of the complaining party, the more credible and deterring are the latter party's self-enforcement threats.

[81] On that account, see the Sutherland Report (WTO 2004, para. 240), or Hudec 2002, p. 88.

To conclude our discussion of de iure and de facto flexibility mechanisms and the accompanying extra-contractual remedies with regard to the market access entitlement: intra- and extra- contractual behavior are sanctioned in the same way. This opens the floodgates to unchecked use of informal trade policy flexibility instruments in the WTO. As a consequence, the contemporary trade flexibility regime practically obliterates any de iure rule. To a considerable extent, it defies what contract theory has to say about efficient entitlement protection.

While the de iure system of trade protection privileges victims and exacerbates *ex post* discretion of potential injurers, the de facto system of non-performance seriously disadvantages victims of *ex post* discretion: no matter what the various WTO Agreements may say, with regard to the market access entitlement the current flexibility regime is tantamount to a pure liability rule with varying substandard remedies. This sets strong incentives for injurers to simply disregard the rules of the game.

It is not too difficult to see that in a given situation a reasonably rational injurer will always go for the very escape instrument which promises "most mileage," i.e. the fewest enactment costs, the lowest compensation, and the largest scope of application.[82] With the informal flexibility tools, VERs/OMAs, subsidies, domestic trade-related policies, AD or CvD actions at its discretion, the injuring country can renege on the trade entitlement practically for free. Alternatively, the injurer can simply infringe upon the contract at the price of losing a trade dispute and having to pay prospective reliance damages, which (in expected terms) are strictly less than the harm done to the victim(s). Violation-cum-retaliation is the ultimate de facto default rule for the market access entitlement, whereby the court-ordered retaliation sets the standard for all intra- and extra-contractual remedies.

### 5.4.2 Flawed protection of multilateral coordination entitlements

Turning to the protection of multilateral obligations traded in the WTO (minimum standard and basic auxiliary entitlements), our biggest criticism of the de iure situation concerns the absence of a clear and

---

[82] For example, between 1994 and 2007 there were twenty times more antidumping initiations (2,851) than there were safeguard initiations (142), and nearly twenty-six times more (1,804 compared to 70) AD than safeguard measures applied (source: WTO 2007, section II.C.4).

unambiguous default rule: *quid* in case a situation occurs that is not anticipated in the letter of the contract? The WTO Agreement is largely mute on that issue. Earlier, in section 5.2.1, we mentioned WTO Charter Art. X on treaty amendments. However, as Mavroidis (2007, p. 547) notes, the WTO (in contrast to the Vienna Convention on the Law of Treaties) does not distinguish between *amendments* and *modifications*. Amendments are once-and-for-all changes of the treaty language, whereas modifications bear a more temporary, intermittent, and discretionary connotation.

In the absence of any explicit treaty language concerning a DR of flexibility, we are forced to conjecture as to how the WTO framers intended to deal with unforeseen non-market-access contingencies. We can see three possibilities on the nature of default rules of multilateral WTO entitlements:

(i) Alternative 1 is that Members chose to make *ex post* changes in multilateral obligations difficult, yet not impossible. Therefore, WTO Agreement Art. X (a property rule of renegotiation) is actually the only way for signatories to react to unforeseen contingencies.[83]

(ii) Alternative 2 would assume that, when drafting the Agreement, WTO Members desired that there should be no possibility to temporarily escape from previously agreed multilateral concessions. To that effect, signatories deliberately omitted any language on emergency actions or temporary modifications. Post-contractual non-performance would automatically be interdicted by virtue of a general rule of inalienability. This, however, would have been extremely poor drafting on the part of the founding fathers: the WTO as an international treaty is not concluded in a vacuum, but is part of the grander structure of public international law. That means that wherever the WTO contract is mute on a certain issue, external norms of international public law automatically take effect.[84]

---

[83] There are some problems connected with this interpretation. For example: Does WTO Chapter Art. X protect all multilateral entitlements in the same fashion? This would mean that peremptory norms of international law are protected in the same way as, say, procedural notification requirements. Also, the strict enactment requirements of rule renegotiations under Art. X (see note 37 above and accompanying text) make temporary emergency escape notoriously difficult. Is it really sensible to request a qualified three-quarter majority of the entire membership to nod through temporary relief from a deadline or transparency obligation?

[84] Dunoff and Trachtman (1999, p. 35) opine that the Vienna Convention on the Law of Treaties (VCLT) and the ILC Draft on State Responsibility may be seen as collections of

(iii) Alternative 3 is that the WTO framers deliberately did not "contract around" customary rules of international law, so that the VCLT takes effect as the adequate rule of default for multilateral entitlements whenever an unforeseen regret contingency occurs (Pauwelyn 2006).

All three alternatives are unsatisfactory, because they lump together all multilateral entitlements, and do not give consideration to the idiosyncrasies of each entitlement type. Is it sensible to protect procedural rules or transparency provisions in the same way as a *ius cogens* norm or minimum standard entitlements? There is no logical or economic reason for that.

Considerations of de jure default rules notwithstanding, the de facto DR of multilateral entitlements is violation-cum-retaliation, just as is the case for the market access entitlement. Violating the Agreement and then enduring retaliation is a liability rule granted to the injurer, backed by less-than-reliance damages by virtue of DSU Art. 22.4. Consequently, WTO Members have an incentive to over-"breach" WTO Agreements: injured parties may or may not challenge that measure, and may or may not succeed. Arbitrators will face the immensely difficult task of putting a price tag on the challenged measure (see note 36 and accompanying text), and the successful victim may or may not actually engage in retaliation. This de facto result should, by any reckoning, be the exact opposite of what the framers must have had in mind when they were contemplating the nature of entitlement protection of the various multilateral entitlements.

### 5.4.3  Conclusion and consequences

To conclude this section on the assessment of the current WTO system of entitlement protection, trade policy flexibility, and enforcement, let us offer a short summary of our findings and discuss the dynamic implications that a flawed system of non-performance in international trade entails.

external DR of international contracting conduct between sovereign states (see also Grané 2001; Mavroidis 2000; Pauwelyn 2003). On the relevance of public international law in the WTO legal order, see the comprehensive studies by Pauwelyn (2003) and Trachtman (1999).

## Summary of the main flaws of the current WTO system of non-performance

It is well-established that contractual escape mechanisms are an indispensable feature of incomplete trade contracts. Yet the contemporary system of trade policy flexibility and entitlement protection in the WTO is remarkably flawed.

The efficient "breach" contract – the first-best achievable contract – mandates equivalence between rules of *ex post* flexibility and entitlement protection: a system of non-performance must prohibit opportunistic *ex post* market-closing behavior, yet reap the opportunities looming by unforeseen regret contingencies. It must also compensate victims of post-contractual discretion so that their *ex ante* commitments do not get frustrated by *ex post* escape. Finally, the system must be able to protect signatories from illegal extra-contractual behavior.

The current WTO system of non-performance misses that mark. It is plagued by striking imbalances: its governance structure fails to find a balance between the market access entitlement and coordination entitlements,[85] between its approaches to incomplete contracting and complete contracting,[86] between the de iure and de facto organization of trade policy flexibility, and the way injurers and victims are treated. Our critical analysis of the current WTO system of non-performance revealed a series of grave shortcomings.

First, the WTO's system of entitlement protection fails to draw the line between welfare-enhancing regret contingencies and opportunistic behavior. On the one hand, injurers acting in good faith and striving to react to regret contingencies cannot easily do so legally. The scope for good-faith escape from previously made concessions is too narrow to suit signatories' trade policy flexibility needs, especially concerning market access obligations. Injurers are much better off resorting to illegal means of opt-out.[87] On

---

[85] The imbalance between market access and coordination entitlements is striking. As shown above, entitlement protection and flexibility rules abound when it comes to the market access entitlement. Eliciting the protection of multilateral coordination entitlements on the other side is a bit like reading tea-leaves; one has to go hunting for clues about how the WTO framers *might* have wanted to protect multilateral entitlements.

[86] See the discussion at note 61 above and accompanying text.

[87] Some WTO scholars argue that de facto breaches of WTO obligations often occur because of the rigidity with which formal escape mechanisms are written and have been interpreted so far. The current WTO safeguards regime allegedly does not sufficiently address Members' needs for policy flexibility. Barred from the necessary breathing space, WTO Members instead turn their attention to informal means of flexibility (see e.g. Bagwell and Staiger 2002b; Finger 1993; Horn and Mavroidis 2003; Mavroidis 2006; Sykes 2003).

the other hand, bad-faith injurers are highly advantaged by the de facto system of escape which offers many convenient ways of unencumbered defection.

Secondly, even if the system could neatly separate acts of good-faith from bad-faith *ex post* non-performance, the remedies for legal escape payable to victims would still be chronically undercompensatory. Prospective reliance damages do not put the victim in as good a position as if the injurer had performed. The effects of any market-closing *ex post* behavior will be partly shouldered by the victim(s) of that measure – a classical externality that the WTO was founded to overcome in the first place. This is not only somewhat unfair, but has repercussions on the cooperative behavior of all those signatories that must expect to become victims at any point in time during the existence of the contract (on that note, see below).

Finally, the tertiary rules of contracting (the system's extra-contractual remedies) are too weak to deter illegal behavior. Insufficient punishment converts legal and illegal flexibility mechanisms into substitutes. This propels violation-cum-retaliation as the de facto rule of default: the one trade policy flexibility mechanism that is always available and applicable is to violate the Agreement and to endure the bearable consequences in the form of substandard countermeasures. Furthermore, extra-contractual remedies in connection with violation-cum-retaliation establish a benchmark for all contractual remedies available in the WTO: reasonably rational injurers will not negotiate or settle for any compensation *in extenso* of prospective reliance damages.

## Over-"breach" and undercommitment

The current system of entitlement protection and flexibility in the WTO sets the wrong incentives for injurers and undercompensates victims of escape. What are the systemic consequences of inefficient entitlement protection?

First, parties cannot distinguish whether an injuring party acts in good faith, defaults by mistake or negligence, or behaves opportunistically. This foments suspicion in victims that every de facto flexibility behavior is driven by opportunistic guile. An aura of mistrust must be assumed to pervade the system.

Secondly, as was shown at p. 114 above, whenever a contract, explicitly or implicitly, allows injurers to defect from their previous commitments for less than the real incurred damage (which is the victim's expectation damage), injurers have an incentive to over-"breach" the agreement. Compared to what the hypothetical complete contingent contract would mandate, injurers are inclined to escape inefficiently often. This is opportunistic bad-faith behavior, since it entails welfare-depreciating redistribution to the detriment of the victim and to the benefit of the injurer.

Over-"breach" in the WTO not only creates frustration and discontent among victim parties but also destabilizes the WTO in the long run: the dynamic consequences of overzealous non-performance may be threefold:

(1) Whenever a contract cannot prevent opportunist activity from happening, contracting parties are reluctant to enter into it in the first place. All those contracting parties who may expect to become victims in the course of the contract[88] will liberalize their trade to a lesser extent *ex ante* than would be potentially achievable under the EBC, the politically realistic first-best contract. Rational anticipating actors will drive down the level of participation and cooperation (initially and in future trade liberalization rounds), because they have to assume that they will get "less miles for the buck" should a trade partner "default on them".

(2) Frustration may even lead them to exit the system partially, de facto, or fully.[89]

(3) Alternatively or concomitantly, victims may refrain from utilizing the WTO dispute settlement mechanisms in the first place. Instead of litigating, they may engage in extra-contractual means of retribution and/or aggressive self-help behavior. They may opt for bilateral resolution outside the WTO forum,[90] seek retaliation outside the trade realm (e.g. political coercion), engage in unilateral retaliation (e.g. *Section 301 of the U.S. Trade Act of 1974*), enact retaliatory AD

---

[88] Since the WTO is a long-term repeated-interaction contract where Members trade a myriad of goods day in and day out, practically every country must anticipate assuming the role of the victim at some point in time.

[89] Note that Member exit is not a dichotomous variable. Rather, there are various degrees of exit. We can witness partial exit in the form of engagement in preferential trading agreements and bilateralism, withdrawal from plurilateral agreements and protocols, resort to extra-WTO policies, or non-participation in trade talks.

[90] Examples of bilateral arrangements outside the DSB-ambit include VER-type accords, or an offer of favorable GSP treatment for the victim by the injuring country. These extra-WTO settlements can be win-win solutions for the participating countries to the detriment of non-participating third parties.

action,[91] enter into retaliatory litigation, or design strategic retaliation tactics (e.g. "carousel" retaliation).

Any of these three dynamic consequences can be expected to seriously harm the system and sour the atmosphere and general WTO spirit of trade liberalization.

---

[91] Note that retaliatory dumping has proliferated vastly throughout the last decade (for empirical data on retaliatory AD, see Feinberg and Olsen 2004; Prusa and Skeath 2002).

# PART III

# Flexibility and enforcement in the WTO: towards an agenda for reform

Part I of this study gave an introduction to incomplete contract theory. It stressed the crucial role that contractual flexibility provisions, and default rules in particular, play in incomplete contracts. Part II presented a comprehensive contract-theoretical analysis of the WTO contract. We identified players, utilities, and motives for contracting, and discussed the nature of contractual incompleteness prevalent in the treaty. This was followed by a portrait of basic entitlements exchanged in the WTO today and how they are protected from intra- and extra-contractual *ex post* non-performance. Pursuant to this systematic examination, we assessed in which respects the system of trade policy flexibility and enforcement is flawed in the current-day WTO. The consequences of these shortcomings for the international trading system in general were summarized.

This final part of the study is geared towards an outline of reform. Chapter 6 will conduct the thought experiment of a "hypothetical bargain analysis" (see Scott 1990, p. 598). It theorizes about how reasonably rational, self-interested trade negotiators can be expected to organize and design a system of contractual non-performance in a multilateral trade agreement such as the WTO. Building on the previous analysis, we will search for the most efficient institutional rules for breach, "breach," and remedies trade negotiators will craft for themselves, cognizant of the idiosyncratic contracting context of the WTO. We want to elucidate which intra-contractual (legal) rules of trade policy flexibility best protect the various entitlements traded in the WTO, which enforcement provisions best safeguard compliance with these rules, and what cost injurers should incur for committing illegal behavior.

In short, Chapter 6 will hypothesize about how the WTO would look if it were organized along the precepts of the efficient "breach" contract (EBC). It will lay out a positive benchmark of trade policy flexibility and enforcement. Chapter 7 will conclude with detailed reform suggestions for a better and more viable system of flexibility and enforcement in the WTO.

# 6

# Theorizing about the WTO as an efficient "breach" contract

Seen from a contract-theoretical point of view, the current-day system of entitlement protection, trade policy flexibility, and enforcement in the WTO gives reason for concern. Currently, whenever an unforeseen (and hence unspecified) state of nature occurs, injuring WTO Members can choose between several substitutive (formal and informal) trade policy flexibility mechanisms, all of which are systematically undercompensatory. This results in (opportunistic) over-"breach" *ex post*, and undercommitment *ex ante*. The harm to the international trading system as a whole can be assumed to be significant. Economically weak players especially mistrust the contractual regime. This renders the global trading system dynamically unstable and underperforming.

Finding viable improvements and proposing sustainable reform avenues is imperative. Yet in order to make a meaningful contribution, it seems important that any proposal for reform is directed towards what is *achievable*, not just what seems *desirable*. Many reform proposals currently circulating in WTO scholarship are under a "prescriptive fallacy" (Dunoff and Trachtman 1999, p. 3): authors base their suggestions on what they take to be right, fair, legal, distributively just, globally efficient, or morally apposite. These are often intelligent, convincing, laudable, and well-intentioned endeavors. However, they display one crucial error in their reasoning – they are not incentive compatible with what decision-makers desire. One cannot expect self-interested actors to agree to treaty details that are not conducive to their utility improvement, let alone reforms which might eventually harm them. Indeed, if those individuals who ultimately decide on reforms of the contractual design lose out from a given reform proposal, it stands little to no chance of ever being enacted. Thus, many prescriptions for WTO reform reside in a normative nirvana without hope of serious implementation.

To avoid this pitfall, let us take a step back and engage in a different consideration: "What would the *right* (read: incentive compatible) institutional design of flexibility and enforcement look like? What system of non-performance and enforcement can we expect reasonably rational trade negotiators to draft in the first place, given the trade-offs and constraints surrounding the initial negotiations?" This chapter will conduct a hypothetical bargain analysis of the WTO system of non-performance. It recreates the WTO in a manner that makes political-economic sense by maintaining the same contextual ingredients and inputs as the real WTO treaty – the same number of signatories, same entitlements, same types of uncertainty, same timeline, same transaction costs, etc. Yet the hypothetical treaty will suggest a somewhat different governance structure. The outcome is a model contract of what the best achievable contract between self-interested policy-makers could look like. In absence of the unattainable first-best of the Pareto-efficient complete contingent contract, the contracting ideal is the efficient "breach" contract.[1] The resulting EBC can be seen as an archetype of a multilateral trade agreement, and may therefore serve as a feasible benchmark institution against which to measure the reality of flexibility and enforcement in the contemporary WTO arrangement. This will help us set forth a politically realistic, systemically viable, and comprehensive reform agenda of the WTO system of non-performance in the final chapter.

In order to avoid confusion about what the WTO *is today* and what it *is conceptualized as*, we shall introduce the notation "vWTO" whenever talking about the idealized (hypothetical) version of the World Trade Organization.[2]

Finding the optimal (incentive compatible) design of trade policy flexibility and enforcement in an incomplete multilateral trade agreement entails the following suite of questions:

(1) What is the optimal protection of the market access entitlement, and of the various non-reciprocated multilateral entitlements? Will the

---

[1] As was shown at p. 124 above, the benchmark governance structure for an incomplete contract is given by the achievable first-best, the efficient "breach" contract. The EBC mimics the outcome of the hypothetical complete contingent contract by striking the optimal balance between flexibility and entitlement protection: victims' entitlements are protected such that opportunistic opt-out is deterred by means of punitive extra-contractual remedies.

[2] We wish to make very explicit that the hypothetical version of the WTO does not pretend to *actually be* the WTO in its contemporary form. The notation vWTO is therefore shorthand for "a multilateral trade agreement between reasonably rational, self-interested trade policymakers, such as the WTO".

Members allow for temporary deviation from all previously agreed commitments, or should some of the exchanged entitlements instead be protected by rules of inalienability? Is trade policy flexibility in the WTO best organized as a ready-to-use liability-type escape, or in the form of *ex post* renegotiations between injurer and victim?

(2) How many different flexibility measures will safeguard the most efficient protection of an entitlement?

(3) Should there be any strings attached to enacting a trade flexibility mechanism? In other words, what should be the optimal level of conditionality for making use of trade flexibility?

(4) If liability-type flexibility is the negotiation equilibrium, what is the remedy benchmark, i.e. what is the damage rule of choice for intra-contractual non-performance? Should the victim be put in as good a position as if the injurer had performed? Should the *status quo ante* the "breach" be re-established? Should the *status quo ante* the contract be restored? Or should the victim instead receive a fair share of the efficiency gains incurred by the non-performance of the injurer?

(5) What is the policy instrument of choice for intra-contractual non-performance: tariff compensation or retaliation?

(6) Finally, what kind of an enforcement regime should be in place to protect the contractual system of entitlement protection? Which extra-contractual remedies can safeguard adherence to the contractual rules, given the limitation of self-enforcement in international law?

Our analysis builds on the theoretical findings collected in Chapter 3 on incomplete contracting, and on Chapters 4 and 5, which characterized the nature of the WTO contract. Section 6.1 will give a complete overview of the trade game, and its inherent trade-offs and the constraints that potential WTO signatories are faced with at the beginning of contract negotiations. This is followed by a discussion of the efficient entitlement protection design of the reciprocal market access obligation (section 6.2) and of non-reciprocated multilateral entitlements (section 6.3). Section 6.4 assesses how reasonably rational policy-makers can be assumed to efficiently organize the enforcement regime. Section 6.5 concludes by comparing the institutional design of the hypothetical EBC version of the WTO (the vWTO) with the contemporary trade regime. Since our characterization of the hypothetical first-best contract between selfish policy-makers may clash with what some pundits deem fair, morally just, or normatively desirable, we briefly assess whether the politically efficient archetype of the vWTO is also a "good" contract with respect to general welfare and the needs of non-signatory parties, such as consumers and producers. Our analysis paints a mildly positive picture of the vWTO in this respect: since the hypothetical contract makes the world trading system more stable, more inclusive, and promotes more participation and cooperation, the vWTO results in a globally more efficient contract. Various non-signatory parties will benefit from this improved contractual framework.

## 6.1   The "trade game"

Before characterizing the hypothetical contract, let us give a complete overview of the "trade game" that reasonably rational trade policy-makers are confronted with at the outset of their contract negotiations. Consider Figure 6.1: similar to Figure 4.6, but adapted to the WTO context, it illustrates the trade-offs and constraints that trade negotiators have to take into consideration when sitting down to design the EBC.

Figure 6.1 represents a stylized version of the "trade game" that unfolds after the contracting parties agree to conclude a trade agreement: the vWTO. In stage 1 ($t_1$), various policy-makers representing sovereign states agree to overcome inefficient market access externalities, and to reap transaction cost efficiencies by introducing minimum standard levels. To that end, signatories draft a governance structure: they determine substantive and basic auxiliary entitlements (primary rules), as well as entitlement protection mechanisms (secondary rules), and enforcement provisions (tertiary rules).

In stage 2, depending on the quality of this institutional framework, vWTO Members negotiate the level of mutual commitments, i.e. the depth and breadth of market access concessions, as well as the minimum level of positive integration commitments.[3] The most reluctant liberalizer thereby sets the extent of trade liberalization commitments.

After the level of cooperation is fixed, the repeated-interaction performance phase of the contract begins at stage 3. Countries start interacting according to the terms of the contract (infinite repetition). At some point in time ($t_3$), uncertainty in the environment is resolved: an exogenous or endogenous market access or non-trade contingency hits and may create room for regret in one or more Members.

---

[3] For expositional convenience, stages 1 and 2 are separated here (see Chapter 4, note 122 above).

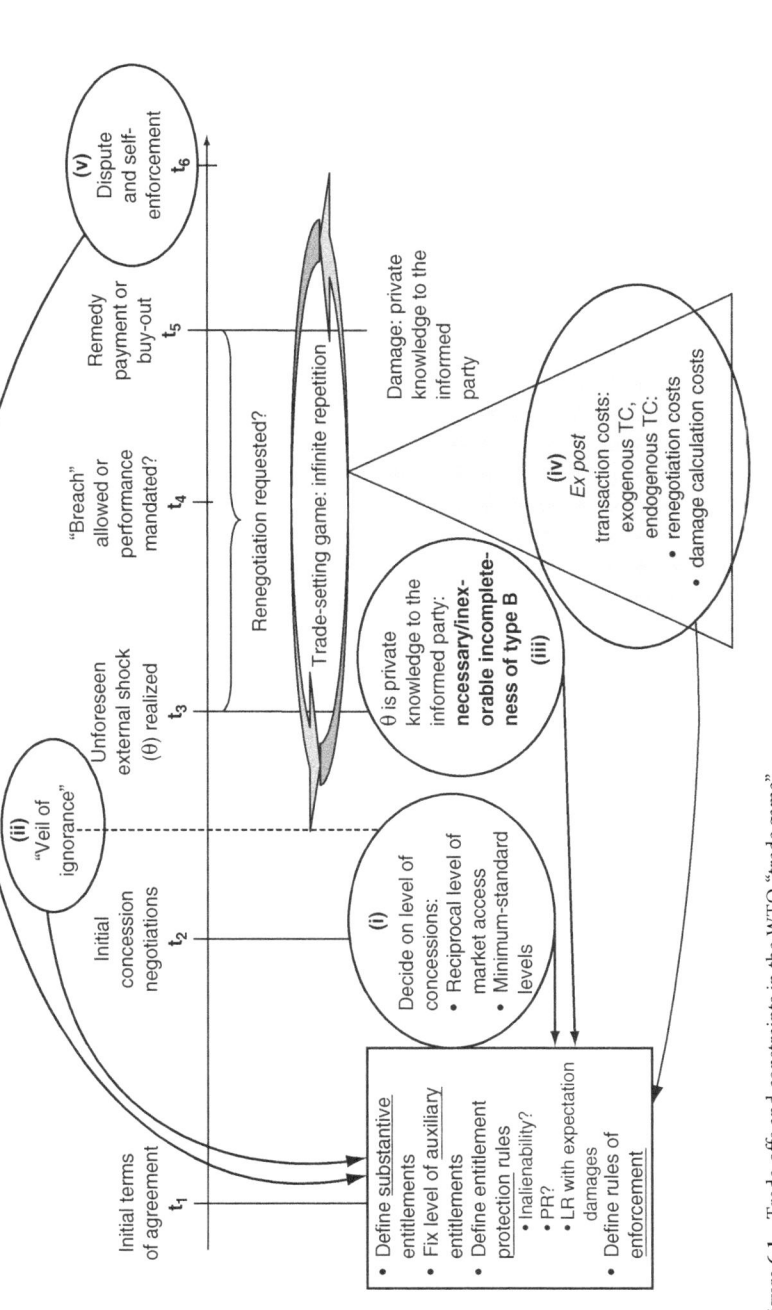

**Figure 6.1** Trade-offs and constraints in the WTO "trade game"

Source: based on Schropp 2007a, Figure 1 Note: This chart represents (from the perspective of one signatory) a stylized version of the contracting game between countries that conclude a trade agreement based on market access externalities and common minimum standards. $t_1$ to $t_6$ mark different points in time. At $t_1$, the time of the conclusion of the agreement, reasonably rational policy-makers draft the optimal governance structure for the incomplete contract. Signatories have to anticipate and bear in mind (i) the nature of the traded entitlements, (ii) the veil of ignorance, (iii) the uncertainty inherent in the trade game, (iv) the transaction costs (TC) in the contract performance phase, and (v) the enforcement capacity constraints due to the absence of a central enforcer. These five constraints fundamentally determine signatories' design of the most efficient governance structure. PR is "property rule"; LR is "liability rule".

In stage 4, depending on the terms of the initial agreement, an affected injurer may be allowed to react to the contingency. If a rule of inalienability is in place, or if the shock was too insignificant to warrant expected compensation payments, the injurer will perform as promised. Whenever the contract provides for a liability rule (LR) of *ex post* discretion, the injurer may default from previously agreed levels of performance at his own initiative. This triggers intra-contractual remedies in stage 5. Alternatively, the injuring Member initiates a lengthy renegotiation phase with victims (which is resolved any time between $t_3$ and $t_5$), aimed at buying off the victim's right to demand performance as prescribed.

A victim country that claims to have detected a nullification or impairment of its vWTO rights can initiate the dispute settlement and enforcement mechanisms in stage 6. An injuring Member refusing to pay its remedies as previously agreed to, or defecting from an entitlement protected by an inalienability rule, also triggers a dispute initiation on the part of the victim country.

When drafting their contractual governance structure at $t_1$, the signatories of the multilateral trade agreement must be conscious of, and take into serious consideration, the trade-offs and constraints that unfold during this trade game. The following impediments to contracting eventually determine the form and design of the optimal governance structure (see numbering in Figure 6.1).

(i) **Nature of entitlements**    The trade negotiators must have a common understanding of the nature of the exchanged entitlements (see at p. 190 above). The market access entitlement is reciprocally owed between country dyads. Hence, the primary promise between every pair of signatories is to have a balanced exchange of market access in place. The common trade liberalization level (depth and breadth of commitments) leading to the balance is secondary. The market access entitlement encompasses a wide range of industries with numerous tariff lines, or services commitments. It also includes a number of auxiliary entitlements geared towards safeguarding that initial balance.

The numerous multilateral entitlements (minimum standard rules, procedural rules, external rules, rules of transparency, and obligations owed to the institution) are *not* reciprocal in nature: there is no balance to speak of. Instead, coordination entitlements are owed *erga omnes partes* – to the entire membership. Many multilateral coordination entitlements are dichotomous (binary) in nature; that is, partial performance is not possible.

(ii) **Veil of ignorance**   The WTO contract is concluded behind a Rawlsian "veil of ignorance" (as Ethier 2001a; 2002; Lawrence 2003; and Sykes 1991 concur). Reasonably rational parties negotiate the vWTO as a long-term commitment. Although they know that trade liberalization is beneficial in the long term, signatories have no full information of their economic significance in the distant future, of the composition of their comparative advantage, of their role as injurers or victims, of the identity of acceding countries, or generally of how future states of the world will impact their wellbeing.[4]

The fact that contracting governments are negotiating trade agreements behind a veil of ignorance is consequential. First, it rules out problems connected with adverse selection (hidden knowledge): if signatories are unsure about their future role, they are not likely to strategically misrepresent it. Secondly, as Ethier (2001a) and Sykes (1991) point out, *ex ante* symmetrically uninformed, reasonably rational actors can be considered to take the choices of a social planner whose aim is to maximize the future wellbeing of all contracting parties. In absence of any information to the contrary, parties anticipate that they will be hit by exogenous and endogenous shocks just as often as any other country.[5] This leads them to craft agreements, and commit to trade liberalization, just as a social planner would do. However, note that the maximand is not general (consumer) welfare, but the welfare of all contracting parties, viz. self-interested policy-makers.

(iii) **Nature of contingencies and incompleteness**   At p. 202 above we reviewed the nature of market access contingencies, which we characterized as political support shocks with spillover potential. Similarly,

---

[4] Readers might have doubts as to how realistic the concept of a "veil of ignorance" really is in trade agreements. Yet consider the following illustration. The GATT as one of the fundamental pillars of today's WTO system was founded in April 1947. Among its original signatories were Burma, Ceylon, Republic of Cuba, Czechoslovak Republic, Lebanon, Southern Rhodesia, and Syria. When signing the Agreement none of the signatories could foresee each others' economic role sixty years down the road. In fact, some of the above countries no longer even exist today (Czechoslovakia), or took quite different economic trajectories due to political upheavals over the last six decades (Burma, Cuba, Lebanon, Rhodesia/Zimbabwe, Syria). According to economic dogma, completely rational policy-makers would have had to take into consideration developments of this sort, and discount them accordingly.

[5] In a situation with two signatories (where one party is "Home" and the other is "Rest of the World"), transactors will assume the roles of victim and injurer of a protectionist back-tracking measure roughly 50 percent of the time.

non-trade contingencies were also shown to be political support shocks which prompt signatories to react by means of (partial) defection from initially agreed obligations (cf. at p. 210 above). The type of uncertainty that besets market access and multilateral entitlements was demonstrated to be such that previously unforeseen political contingencies are revealed asymmetrically to injurers. As shown at p. 206 and p. 210 above, this predestines the vWTO contract to be incomplete: both kinds of entitlements either display necessary incompleteness or inexorable type B incompleteness (depending on whether the probability density function of contingencies is known to signatories or not; see Figure 4.7).

**(iv) Post-contractual transaction costs: costs of renegotiation and quantification**   When deciding on the regime of *ex post* discretion, reasonably rational signatories must take into consideration the exogenous and endogenous transaction costs that unfold during the trade game. As shown at p. 115 above, the choice between a liability rule or a property rule of default is crucially determined by an inherent trade-off between renegotiation costs (pursuant to a property rule (PR)) and damage calculation or quantification costs (pursuant to an LR). The entitlement-specific *ex post* transaction costs (TC) in the WTO will be discussed below.

**(v) Enforcement constraints**   The vWTO is a self-enforcement regime, as is the WTO. In the absence of an external enforcer, vWTO Members are restricted to their own enforcement capacity. However, enforcement does not necessarily have to be purely bilateral. Just as individual citizens of a country overcome collective action problems, join forces, and institute a system of collective policing and enforcement (by dispensing resources to establish bureaucracies, police forces and other executive bodies), vWTO Members are free to bundle their enforcement capacities into certain means of collective enforcement.

## 6.2   Organizing protection of the market access entitlement

When self-interested policy-makers negotiate a reciprocal exchange of market access behind a veil of ignorance, they are motivated by two objectives: to encapsulate the current domestic political support constellation (which determines their favorite (politically optimal) level of trade liberalization); and the drive to design a sustainable institutional system that is fit to deal with an uncertain future. When designing the system of trade policy flexibility and market access entitlement protection, forward-looking policy-makers behave like social planners whose job it is to maximize the welfare of all present and future self-interested trade policy-makers. The analysis will show that policy-makers opt for protecting the market access entitlement with an unconditional liability rule of default.

### 6.2.1 Focusing on default rules

Exposed to necessary or inexorable type B incompleteness, forward-looking policy-makers are conscious of the fact that it is impossible to anticipate every future contingency, even if they invested infinite time and resources into writing the contract (see our discussion at p. 73 above). Therefore, reasonably rational decision-makers do not bother trying: contingencies are private knowledge to the affected party, and cannot possibly be directly anticipated. Negative integration provisions that prohibit certain instruments can easily be replaced by ill-meaning Members with other, previously non-specified instruments – with the same protectionist result. In addition, writing down contingencies and instruments is costly, prone to erratic and ambivalent language, and an additional source of opportunism and disputes. Rational policy-makers can thus be assumed to prefer leaving the market access entitlement completely non-contingent. They content themselves with living in full contractual uncertainty of the future, and with focusing on the efficient design of *ex post* discretion rules.

Acknowledging the inevitable incompleteness of the contract, contractual clauses relating to the entitlement to reciprocal trade hence consist of (i) concession schedules; (ii) rules circumscribing and detailing the market access entitlement (definitions and instructions, non-discrimination titles, rules on non-tariff barriers, exceptions, etc.); and (iii) a single rule of default. The default rule states that whenever a market access-related disturbance occurs, the fallback rule comes into effect. In short, the exchange of market access at the vWTO is organized as an optimally indefinite subcontract. This finding is consequential. It allows us to resort to some formal work conducted on the WTO.[6]

---

[6] For reasons of scientific economy, scholars often model the WTO as a tariff-liberalization agreement where future contingencies are unknown. Contingencies are formalized as protectionist shocks of a commonly known probability density function. In other words, the WTO is modeled as an optimally indefinite market-access contract that is beset by what we defined at p. 72 above as type A or efficient, or as type B or necessary

### 6.2.2 Inalienability or ex post discretion?

When assessing the optimal entitlement protection for the reciprocal market access promise, the first question that needs to be tackled by trade policy-makers is whether *ex post* discretion should be allowed at all, or whether a rule of inalienability is in fact more apt. We argue in favor of discretion in two steps. First, we review the literature that establishes a link between trade policy flexibility and the stability of the world trading system in a repeated-interaction context. Secondly, taking the risk of breakdown of the multilateral trading order as less of a concern, we assess the incentive compatibility of a rule of inalienability in a one-shot game.

### If stability of the system is an issue[7]

A completely non-contingent market access deal negotiated behind the veil of ignorance can be conveniently represented by an infinitely repeated tariff-setting game between two symmetrical, equally uninformed players. Self-interested policy-makers from two symmetrical countries (which only differ in their factor endowments) sit down to negotiate a tariff-liberalization agreement to overcome mutual market access externalities. Uncertainty is introduced in the form of a completely unexpected exogenous political support shock ($\theta$) of a finite size. The shock by definition is unwelcome, i.e. unleashes a desire for a protectionist reaction in the affected party.[8] $\theta$ is a random i.i.d. shock of a commonly known probability density function $p(\theta)$.[9] Shocks are idiosyncratic to each player, and are temporary in nature: they only affect the signatory for a single period.

The tariff-setting game, in which every signatory sets its tariff simultaneously and independently at the beginning of each period, can now be represented as a prisoners' dilemma (PD) between these two parties

---

incompleteness (depending on the underlying assumptions of how previously unforeseen contingencies are revealed to players).

[7] This section is a synthesis of the two outstanding works of Rosendorff (2005) and Herzing (2005, chapter 3). We give an account of the general intuition of these contributions, and leave the details and intricacies of the models to the interested reader.

[8] Another way of seeing it is to assume that the political shock always harms import-competing industries who then exercise their political clout with the self-interested policy-maker.

[9] i.i.d. stands for "independent identically distributed random variables." In probability theory, a sequence of random variables is i.i.d. if each has the same probability distribution as the others and all are mutually independent.

(Home and Foreign, the latter represented by *) with the following payoffs:[10]

|   | C* | D* |
|---|---|---|
| C | $W^C(t^C, t^{C*}; \theta)$, $W^{*C}(t^C, t^{C*}; \theta^*)$ | $W^S(t^C, t^{D*}; \theta)$, $W^{*D}(t^C, t^{D*}; \theta^*)$ |
| D | $W^D(t^D, t^{C*}; \theta)$, $W^{*S}(t^D, t^{C*}; \theta^*)$ | $W^N(t^N, t^{N*}; \theta)$, $W^{*N}(t^N, t^{N*}; \theta^*)$ |

Thereby,[11] $t^C$ is the previously agreed cooperative tariff level; $t^D$ is the defective tariff, namely the best-reaction function to the other player's cooperative payoff ($t_{BR}(t^C)$), and $t^N = t_{BR}(t_{BR})$ is the non-cooperative Nash-tariff, where both countries apply the optimal tariff against each other.

$W^C(t^C, t^C; \theta)$ is each player's per-period payoff in the Cooperative case;
$W^D(t_{BR}(t^C), t^C; \theta)$ is the payoff for the Defector;
$W^S(t^C, t_{BR}(t^C); \theta)$ is the "Sucker's payoff" if the other party defaults;
$W^N(t_{BR}(t_{BR}), t_{BR}(t_{BR}); \theta)$ is the non-cooperative Nash payoff that exists in the absence of any trading agreement.

The general payoff structure of prisoners' dilemmas $W^D > W^C > W^N > W^S$ holds. This infinitely repeated trade-setting game breaks down in a finite time scale, as shown in Figure 6.2.

Figure 6.2, which we came across before in Figure 3.3 panel (a), plots the shock level of the unanticipated state of nature on the horizontal axis, and the injurer's (dis)utility from defecting as the dependent variable. The well-known H&R curve represents the value of one-time defection ($W_\theta^D - W_\theta^C$), whereas the line $CV^{PD}$ is the continuation value of trade

---

[10] The sequence of the per-period trade-setting game is as follows: (i) at the beginning of a period, both countries (Home and Foreign*) experience independent political support shocks that are unobservable to the trading partner; (ii) both countries determine independently what trade policy they will apply, the options being setting either the cooperative tariff or deviation, i.e. applying the optimally defective tariff; (iii) both players implement their policies, and the period begins; (iv) at the end of the period, the implemented policies are verified. Any deviation by one country is regarded as a breach of the agreement and will therefore lead to a breakdown of the cooperative regime.

[11] Note that in a stage-game with symmetrical and equally uninformed players, the expected per-period payoffs are identical. Thus the (*) representing the foreign country can be dropped, which reduces the examination to one single signatory; the other Members' payoffs are equivalent.

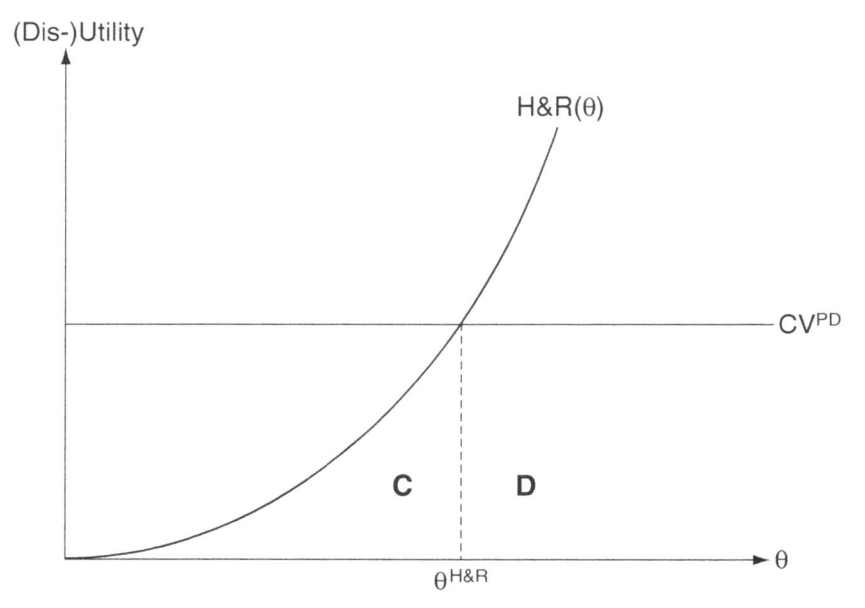

**Figure 6.2**   Breakdown condition for the simple tariff-setting game
Source: author based on Rosendorff 2005, Figure 1
Note: This graph is similar to Figure 3.3, panel (a). It shows the injurer's trade-off in the face of some exogenous shock ($\theta$): the injurer can decide between defecting once and forgoing cooperation payoffs in all future periods, and continued cooperation. The vertical axis plots the disutility from cooperation foregone, and the utility from defection. H&R is "hit-and-run," the difference in payoff between $W^D(\theta)$ and $W^C(\theta)$. $CV^{PD}$ is the continuation value of the repeated PD game. The chart shows the cut-off shock level ($\theta^{H\&R}$) above which the injurer prefers to defect (D) instead of cooperating (C).

cooperation, which the injurer foregoes by defecting.[12] Thus, it can be seen that the prisoners' dilemma stage-game is only sustainable for low realizations of $\theta$ high discount factors, and for low levels of trade liberalization (which flatten the H&R curve). However, whenever the exogenous shock exceeds the threshold level $\theta^{H\&R}$, the contract breaks down. With i.i.d. shocks, this happens in finite time.[13]

---

[12] As shown in Chapter 2, the continuation value is the net present value of the per-period cooperation benefits over the reversion to non-cooperative Nash play. The line is flat in $\theta$, because by assumption future payoffs are independent of the current shock level.

[13] The breakdown condition in each period is $W_\theta^D - W_\theta^C > \delta/1-\delta\ [W^C - W^N]$ where $W_\theta^D - W_\theta^C$ is the hit-and-run payoff in the current period (dependent on the shock), and $\delta/1-\delta\ [W^C - W^N]$ is the continuation value of the game. $\delta$ thereby depicts the discount factor.

If the market access contingency ($\theta$) were to be symmetrically revealed to both parties, the game would have a trivial outcome: no party would have the chance to misrepresent the true state of nature. Consequently, the shock-affected party would be allowed to refrain from full contractual performance for exactly one period, given that it pays commensurate damages to the victims of the resulting protectionist measure (Bagwell and Staiger 1990; Ethier 2001a). This simple tit-for-tat result would replicate the Pareto-efficient complete contingent contract.[14]

Yet whenever shock contingencies are asymmetrically revealed, this offers opportunities for injurers to strategically misrepresent the real size of the shock, and to engage in excessive defection to the detriment of the victim. In order to forestall the possibility of any such opportunistic behavior, the negotiating parties may decide *ex ante* on an inalienability rule of entitlement protection: they might be of the opinion that the losses to victims generated from excessive "breach" outweigh the danger of breakdown of the system. The WTO literature has firmly established that this is not a good idea, and that the introduction of escape clauses Pareto-dominates a rule of mandatory specific performance.

Rosendorff (2005) shows that the inclusion of an escape clause strategy in the action space of the players helps obtain Pareto-superior long-term cooperation in the shadow of the grim trigger. The author extends the above PD game for a third possible action next to cooperation and defection: each party can escape its commitments by partially withdrawing from its obligations in the current period, given that it grants compensation to the victim.[15] Rosendorff assumes that these damage payments are exogenously awarded by a dispute settlement panel, and are proportional (but not commensurate) to the harm caused to the victim. The resulting payoff matrix of this extended prisoners' dilemma game is:

---

[14] Note that symmetrical revelation of contingencies replicates Axelrod's classic result that tit-for-tat is the most viable retaliation strategy in an infinitely repeated prisoners' dilemma (Axelrod 1984; Axelrod and Keohane 1986; Oye 1986).

[15] Whether this escape clause is organized as a liability-type opt-out or tariff-renegotiations obligation (property rule) is inconsequential here.

|  | C* | EC* | D* |
|---|---|---|---|
| C | $W^C(t^C, t^{C*}; \theta)$, $W^{*C}(t^C, t^{C*}; \theta^*)$ | $W^S(t^C, t^{D*}; \theta) + \pi D(\theta^*)$, $W^{*D}(t^C, t^{D*}; \theta^*) - \pi D(\theta^*)$ | $W^S(t^C, t^{D*}; \theta)$, $W^{*D}(t^C, t^{D*}; \theta^*)$ |
| EC | $W^D(t^D, t^{C*}; \theta) - \pi D^*(\theta)$, $W^{*S}(t^D, t^{C*}; \theta^*) + \pi D^*(\theta)$ | $W^N(t^D, t^{D*}; \theta) - \pi D^*(\theta) + \pi D(\theta^*)$, $W^{*N}(t^D, t^{D*}; \theta^*) - \pi D(\theta) + \pi D^*(\theta)$ | $W^N(t^D, t^{D*}; \theta) - \pi D^*(\theta)$, $W^{*D}(t^C, t^{D*}; \theta^*) + \pi D^*(\theta)$ |
| D | $W^D(t^D, t^{C*}; \theta)$, $W^{*S}(t^D, t^{C*}; \theta^*)$ | $W^D(t^D, t^{C*}; \theta) + \pi D(\theta^*)$, $W^{*S}(t^D, t^{C*}; \theta^*) - \pi D(\theta^*)$ | $W^N(t^D, t^{D*}; \theta)$, $W^{*N}(t^D, t^{D*}; \theta^*)$ |

Thereby, D and D* represent the damage done to the victim, and $\pi D(\theta^*)$ and $\pi D^*(\theta)$ represent the damage award to the victim of a protectionist measure.

Rosendorff (2005, p. 393, Proposition 1) proves mathematically that a pair of "structured defection" strategies (shaded cells) is a Nash equilibrium that Pareto-dominates a strategy without temporary escape: a country defects if its partner defected in any period in the past, and otherwise *Cooperates* (if its preference shock is mild), temporarily *EsCapes* (if the shock is strong), or *Defects* (if the shock is enormous). In other words, a policy-maker who can decide in each period whether to cooperate as promised, to escape the obligation once in return for compensation payments, or to defect, will act in a way that is *ex ante* welfare-superior to the 2 × 2 PD game shown above.

To see why this is so, consider Figure 6.3. Starting from the same initial set-up as the previous graph, Figure 6.3 shows that opening up the opportunity to engage in structured one-time defection can often save the trade-setting game from breaking down. Each country affected by a protectionist shock can balance off its incentive to seize the hit-and-run advantage (thereby exiting the system) against escaping its obligations in the present period only and paying proportional indemnity to the victim.[16] For light shocks, where the (expected) compensation payment is larger than the hit-and-run advantage, the injurer cooperates as promised (area C in Figure 6.2). At a threshold level $(\theta^{EC})$, escape-cum-compensation yields higher payoffs for the injurer (the area EC).

---

[16] The damage caused to the victim is indirectly dependent on the injurer's experienced shock, because that contingency shock determines the size of the optimal defection tariff of the injuring country.

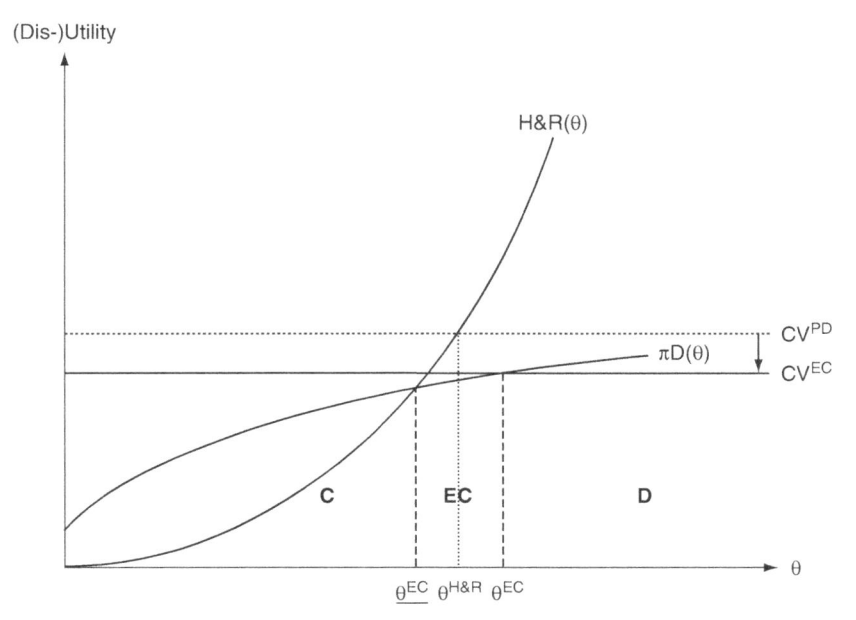

**Figure 6.3**    Stability and breakdown in the escape-clause game according to
Rosendorff 2005
Source: based on Rosendorff 2005, Figure 3
Note: This graph pictures the same initial situation as Figure 6.2. This time, however,
the injurer has the opportunity to choose an escape action, and to compensate the
victim for that one-time defection. The $\pi D(\theta)$ curve represents an exogenously given
compensation function that is proportional to the harm caused to the victim ($\pi$ is the
proportionality factor). The trade-off that the injurer faces is thus between
Cooperating (in situations where the protectionist shock, and therewith the hit-and-
run gain, is mild); choose escape (EC) and pay damages (in situations where the
proportional compensation is less than future payoffs); or Defect and exit the contract
(where the experienced shock is enormous). Since escape behavior reduces the
expected per-period cooperation, the continuation value ($CV^{EC}$) is assumed to
decrease for every future period compared to the simple PD game of Figure 6.2.

Whenever the current shock is larger that a cut-off level ($\theta^{EC}$), the
opportunistic hit-and-run advantage outweighs the continuation value
of cooperating. The injurer exits the trade game.

Comparing the outcomes of Figures 6.2 and 6.3, two things can immediately be noticed. First, the game of structured defection is more robust
against breakdown and exit (Rosendorff 2005, p. 395, Proposition 2): while
under inalienability the injurer remains cooperative in the presence

of shocks up to ($\theta^{H\&R}$) and exits thereafter, injurers with the option to escape only exit pursuant to higher shocks ($\theta^{EC}$). The trade game provided with an escape clause is more stable.

Secondly, the continuation value of the game is reduced, because *real* cooperation (i.e. contractual exchange that reaps the transaction efficiencies for which the vWTO was concluded in the first place) happens less often ($\theta^{EC}$ instead of $\theta^{H\&R}$). This brings down the expected per-period payoffs and consequently the value of the entire game.

In addition to those directly visible results, Rosendorff proves formally that adding an escape-cum-damage option has additional advantages over a rule of inalienability – a wider variety of countries will join the agreement. Whereas in conventional PD games only the most patient players (those with relatively high discount rates) will sign on to the self-enforcing agreement, an opt-out clause effectively lowers the threshold level of discount factors necessary to sustain a cooperative outcome. Thus, a wider variety of countries with lower discount factors can enter the agreement (Rosendorff 2005, p. 395, Corollary 1).

Furthermore, an initial agreement will be easier to strike (Rosendorff 2005, p. 389, and Rosendorff and Milner 2001, p. 850). Fearon (1998) warns that the longer the shadow of the future stretches in infinitely repeated games, the fiercer the initial bargaining is expected to be. The *ex ante* negotiated terms of the agreement "lock in" the uncertain future distributional gains and losses that occur in the course of the repeated game. This in turn gives rise to strategic hold-out behavior by negotiating parties.[17] The inclusion of an escape mechanism, significantly reduces this lock-in effect, and makes initial bargaining less fierce and thus initial agreement easier to strike.

Herzing's contribution (2005, chapter 3) is in many ways an improvement on Rosendorff's article. Most notably, Herzing overcomes the two main weaknesses encumbering Rosendorff's paper, namely the assumptions that compensation be exogenously awarded and proportional to the damage, and that tariff commitments be fixed.[18] Herzing endogenizes both decisions, and so provides for a richer picture of the tariff-setting PD between two countries behind the veil of ignorance.[19]

---

[17] See the discussion on hold-outs in Chapter 3 p. 64, note 9, and at p. 118, note 100 and accompanying text.

[18] The result of those two exogenous assumptions is that Rosendorff is only concerned with the role of the injurer while neglecting any considerations on the part of potential victims.

[19] Herzing's improvements, however, come at the price of added complexity and incomprehensibility for non-specialists.

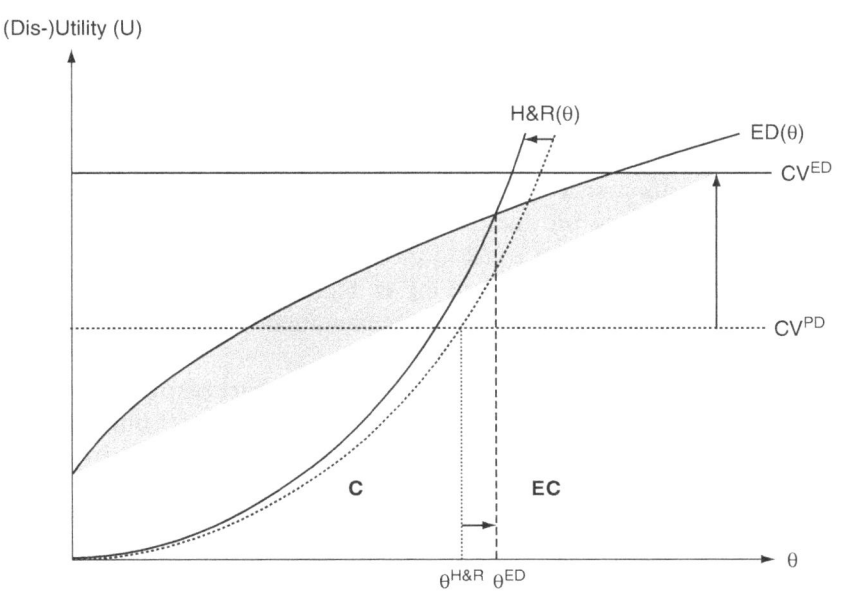

(Dis-)Utility (U)

H&R($\theta$)

ED($\theta$)

$CV^{ED}$

$CV^{PD}$

C

EC

$\theta$

$\theta^{H\&R}$  $\theta^{ED}$

**Figure 6.4**   Stability in the escape-clause game according to Herzing 2005
Source: based on Herzing 2005, chapter 3
Note: This graph pictures the identical initial situation of Figure 6.2 and 6.3, but illustrates Herzing's (2005) findings. Behind the veil of ignorance, signatories negotiate a trade agreement that never breaks down. This implies a compensation schedule (shaded area) which either compensates the victim country for its expectation damages or amounts to the injurer's entire continuation value, whichever constraint is binding. The ED($\theta$) curve represents the victim's expectation damages (that indirectly depend on the injurer's shock). Compared with a rule of inalienability, the signatories commit to higher trade liberalization levels under the optimal compensation schedule. This skews the H&R curve to the left, and increases the continuation value of the game (upwards shift of the $CV^{ED}$ line). In general, more pure cooperative behavior occurs under an expectation damage-backed escape clause (marked by a rightwards shift from $\theta^{H\&R}$ to $\theta^{ED}$).

Herzing uses the same $3 \times 3$ matrix of the extended prisoners' dilemma but has the two symmetrical parties bargain over the right size of compensation and the *ex ante* mutual trade liberalization. In other words, he replaces $\pi D(\theta^*)$ and $\pi D^*(\theta)$, respectively, for a reciprocally negotiated compensation ED($\theta$). Figure 6.4 illustrates Herzing's key findings.

In his highly sophisticated model, Herzing confirms all of Rosendorff's findings: the enactment of an escape clause regime leads to more stability, less exit, more inclusiveness, and less *ex ante* bargaining. In addition, Herzing sets forth the following results. First, reasonably rational parties may design a framework under which the contract never breaks down (2005, p. 86, Proposition 1). This set-up requires the introduction of an intricate compensation scheme triggered by the use of an escape clause. The compensation schedule under which cooperative behavior is always sustained condemns the injurer either to pay the victim's expectation damages, or to pay a sum equal to the injurer's entire continuation value of the game (whichever constraint is binding; Herzing 2005, p. 89, Proposition 3).[20] In Figure 6.4, this compensation schedule is represented by the shaded area.

Secondly, the inclusion of an escape clause backed by the optimal compensation scheme facilitates more far-reaching tariff liberalization than under a rule of inalienability (Herzing 2005, p. 94, Proposition 6).[21] In other words, the introduction of trade policy flexibility enhances *ex ante* cooperation.[22] Thirdly, a well-designed escape clause makes pure cooperation more likely (instead of less likely, as Rosendorff claims): since the injuring country is forced to internalize the externalities it creates, it is hesitant to invoke the escape clause too often (Herzing 2005, p. 93, Proposition 5). Thus, pure cooperation is chosen by injurers for higher shocks than under the no-escape regime (see Figure 6.4 where $\theta^{ED}$ lies to the right of $\theta^{H\&R}$).

Fourthly, an intuitive implication of deeper *ex ante* trade liberalization concessions and more pure cooperation in the face of protectionist shocks is that the expected per-period payoff under an escape clause regime is strictly larger than under a rule of inalienability. $CV^{ED}$ is located above $CV^{PD}$, which indicates a higher continuation value for the trade game with expectation damages (Herzing 2005, p. 96, Proposition 8 and p. 97, Lemma 8).[23]

---

[20] The victim's expectation damages are indirectly dependent on the political support shock experienced by the injurer, since the latter's optimal defection reaction is a function of the nature and size of the contingency.

[21] In addition, the mutually agreed tariffs are lower for every discount factor countries may be endowed with (Herzing 2005).

[22] Higher tariff liberalization commitments make defection more attractive and skew the H&R curve leftwards, as Figure 6.4 shows.

[23] "Since in addition to the benefit from increasing possibilities from liberalization [i.e. more *ex ante* tariff commitments], the efficiency-enhancing effect under the optimal compensation costs scheme is sufficiently strong to increase per-period payoffs in relation to when there is no escape clause, an agreement on integrating an escape clause

This last finding stands in contrast to the contentions of influential IR scholars (e.g. Downs and Rocke 1995; Rosendorff 2005; Rosendorff and Milner 2001; Setear 1997), who maintain that the inclusion of flexibility instruments in a trade agreement leads to a loss of credibility in the system and to fewer reciprocal market access concessions than an agreement without escape clauses.[24] This is wrong.

As Herzing has demonstrated, a well-crafted escape regime with truly commensurate remedies replicates full compliance by the injurer. Receiving the exact replacement value basically insures the victim of an escape measure. Hence one should not expect a loss of trust in the system, measured in terms of the continuation value of per-period cooperation.

Rosendorff's contention (2005, p. 396) that the inclusion of an opt-out mechanism lowers the value of the agreement for its members is an outflow of his reductionist modeling – not of the logic of escape clauses. Intuitively, agreements with an optimal flexibility mechanism adhering to the proportionality principle of efficient "breach" suffer no loss in cooperativeness, and thus do not generate less welfare for two reasons. First, there are instances in which decision-makers use opt-outs where before they had exited the agreement for good. This fact per se has intrinsic value. Secondly, using the opt-out mechanism is no more than witnessing efficient "breach" at work: in regimes without escape provisions, policy-makers must decide between the continuation value of the game, and the temptation to cheat once and then revert to non-cooperation forever after. That means they are confronted with the one-off choice of staying in the agreement or aborting it. Yet under a commensurate compensation scheme, policy-makers are faced with a new kind of trade-off which now reads: Will a breach be efficiency-enhancing for the general welfare, or will it not? Since victims are fully insured by the contractual escape, they do not value the opt-out game any less. Injurers, hoping to achieve gains (net of compensation payments) certainly value the escape game more than not having this option. The opt-out scheme should thus be strictly welfare-enhancing, not welfare-depreciating. It is hence a codified Pareto principle.

To conclude this discussion on the inalienability of escape: in a non-stationary world a trade agreement concluded for reasons of overcoming

under the optimal compensation scheme will yield an unambiguously better outcome than when there is no escape clause" (Herzing 2005, p. 97).

[24] Setear (1997) argues that trade policy flexibility is a step backwards in the process towards greater cooperation, since its relative ease of use increases opportunities for non-cooperation and the likelihood of defection.

a market access-induced PD may break down in finite time under a rule of inalienability. The introduction of an escape clause allowing for temporary deviation from cooperation gives rise to more cooperative behavior, even as shocks increasing the one-period gain from deviating occur. In order to prevent injurers from capitalizing on their private information as to the nature of the protectionist shock, some form of cost must be incurred each time the escape clause is enacted. The best results are achieved if this cost equals the expectation damages incurred by the victim country.

### If stability of the system is not an issue

If we are not concerned with the stability of the world trading system, and tacitly assume that the agreement is enforceable because every Member has a vital interest in not letting the world trading system break down, it is even more straightforward to demonstrate the Pareto-superiority of an escape clause over a rule of mandatory specific performance in the tariff-setting game.[25]

To see this, let us revisit the formal illustration of incomplete contracting given at p. 110 above.[26] The general model introduced above is convenient at this point, since it is exactly applicable to our situation of an optimally non-contingent incomplete contract. We assume that two risk-neutral, self-interested, and reasonably rational players negotiate the trade deal behind a veil of ignorance. They design a governance structure for a single-transaction, one-shot PD game (or, equivalently, but more realistically, a series of unrelated future periods). In the presence of necessary incompleteness, the agreement is rationally organized as a non-contingent, perfectly indefinite contract that consists only of a

---

[25] The underlying assumption hereby is that the WTO exists in the "shadow of the grim trigger": the threat of a grim-trigger punishment and thereby retreating to a highly protectionist past tacitly supports the system's equilibrium path. Since no Member has an interest in returning to a non-cooperative Nash equilibrium, "all actual trade disputes, punishments, and defiances [sic] of DSP rulings have been just parts of the equilibrium path" (Ethier 2001a, p. 4). Neglecting concerns over system breakdown brings with it significant modeling convenience: issues of non-performance, remedies, and *ex ante* commitment are not constricted by the narrow confines of an infinitely repeated trade-setting game. Instead, they can be modeled within a one-shot game, whose outcomes are assumed to be supported by the threat of reverting to a grim-trigger punishment. This allows for more structure in the model (additional decisions and actions).

[26] See Ethier 2001a and Sykes 1991, Appendix A. Both models demonstrate that the introduction of an escape clause into an incomplete (but enforceable) contract Pareto-dominates a rule of inalienability. However, both models assume that contingencies are symmetrically observable.

description of the level of market access concessions (assume tariff cuts for simplicity), and the agreed-upon rule of escape-cum-remedies (see section 6.2.1).

After the details of the governance structure are sealed, the two parties negotiate the (discrete) reciprocal level of tariff liberalization, whereby the most reluctant liberalizer sets the common standards of commitments applicable to both parties. Let us define:[27]

| | |
|---|---|
| c | as level of cooperation, agreed to *ex ante* by each player. Here, c can be understood as the trade liberalization level generated from reciprocal tariff cuts. $c \in [0,1]$, whereby 1 equals full trade liberalization. The level of mutual cooperation is endogenously determined (negotiations are not modeled), whereby the most reluctant liberalizer sets c; |
| $\theta$ | as unforeseen contingency that hits exactly one player. Behind the veil of ignorance the players are ignorant as to which party is affected. $\theta \in [1, \infty]$ is an exogenous protectionist political support shock of some magnitude.[28] The player affected by the shock may experience regret, and consequently assumes the role of the injurer. The revelation of the shock is private knowledge to the affected party. |
| B | as "breach" set, that is, {θ | the contract will not be performed}; |
| Δ | as damage measure (a monetary compensation, for simplicity) payable by the injurer to the victim; |
| $W^C(c,\theta)$ | as value enjoyed by the injuring country if it is hit by the exogenous shock, but performs the contract as promised (*Cooperation payoff*); |
| $W^D(c,\theta)$ | as value enjoyed by the injuring country if it is hit by the exogenous shock and escapes from certain contract obligations (*Defection payoff*); |
| $W^D(c,\theta) - \Delta$ | as value enjoyed by the injurer, given "breach" and subsequent damage payment; |

[27] For details of variables and economic microfoundations of the model, see Schropp 2007a, Appendix, sections A, C, D.
[28] θ is a random i.i.d. shock. The probability density function of θ, p(θ), is common knowledge. p(θ) is exogenous, differentiable, and stable over time.

| | |
|---|---|
| $V^C(c)$ | as value enjoyed by the victim country if the injurer performs his obligations as promised (*Cooperation* payoff); |
| $V^S(c)$ | as value enjoyed by the victim country if the injurer escapes from certain contract obligations ("Sucker's" payoff); |
| $V^S(c) + \Delta$ | as value enjoyed by the victim country, given "breach" by the injurer and subsequent damage payment; |
| $V^N(c)$ | as value enjoyed by the victim in the pre-contractual non-cooperative past ("Nash" payoff).[29] |

Behind the veil of ignorance, that is, unaware of which party is going to be hit by a protectionist shock in any given period, each policy-maker aims at maximizing her expected welfare $E[Z(c,\theta, B(c))]$:

$$E(Z) = \frac{1}{2}\left[\int_{\tilde{B}} W^C(c, \theta)p(\theta)d(\theta) + \int_B W^D(c, \theta)p(\theta)d(\theta)\right]$$
$$+ \frac{1}{2}\left[\int_{\tilde{B}} V^C(c)p(\theta)d(\theta) + \int_B V^S(c)p(\theta)d(\theta)\right]$$

where B is the "breach" set and $\tilde{B}$ the non-"breach" (i.e. performance) set. Note that by maximizing $E[Z(\cdot)]$ each signatory *ex ante* acts as if it were maximizing the common welfare, or the general efficiency of the entire game. This is consequential, because it gives us a social planner's approach to the issue. The benchmark for the two reasonably rational policy-makers is thus the unachievable Pareto-efficient complete contingent contract (CCC), which maximizes the sum of the expected values of the contract to the injurer and the victim.[30]

Whenever reacting to a large protectionist shock is apt to generate joint welfare gains (which is indubitably the case in a tariff-setting game – think of the shock as e.g. a balance-of-payments crisis), the CCC will prescribe non-performance. More precisely, the Pareto efficient "breach" set equals $B^{opt}(c)$, where:

---

[29] As in every PD, $W^D(c,\theta) > W^C(c,\theta)$, and $V^C(c) > V^N(c) > V^S(c)$.
[30] See Mahlstein and Schropp 2007, section D.

$$B^{opt}(c) = \{\theta | V^S + W^D \geq V^C + W^C\}$$

or equivalently:

$$B^{opt}(c) = \{\theta | W^D - W^C \geq V^C - V^S\}$$

Thus, in the hypothetical world of a CCC, the injuring country's regret contingency (the anticipated protectionist political support shock) must be large enough such that its regret $(W^D - W^C)$ outweighs the harm done to the victim $(V^C - V^S)$. Wherever shocks exist that satisfy this constraint, non-performance is permissible, indeed obligatory. Since the CCC is the first-best contract, it also induces the optimal reciprocal trade liberalization level $(c^\star)$.[31]

In the absence of complete rationality and foresight, the CCC must remain a distant ideal for the two signatories. In the presence of uncertainty, the contracting parties must decide whether *ex post* discretion should be permissible or not. A rule of mandatory specific performance is no more than a prohibition of any kind of *ex post* non-performance. The "breach" set is the empty set, $B^{IR}(c) = \{\}$, whereby IR is "inalienability rule." It is intuitive to see that under a rule of inalienability an injurer (the better nomenclature here would be "party affected by an external shock"), barred from seizing *ex post* regret contingencies, will experience a loss of expected welfare every time a political support shock of substantial size occurs. This condemns the injurer to engage in under-"breach." Inefficiently, little room for escape will naturally reduce injurers' *ex ante* willingness to liberalize. Since behind the veil of ignorance every signatory must anticipate assuming the role of the injurer at least half of the time, an empty "breach" set and the resulting under-"breach" will equally induce fewer *ex ante* trade liberalization commitments.

The Pareto-inferiority of a rule of mandatory performance becomes even more pronounced if we compare the expected payoffs under the inalienability regime with a liability rule of default accompanied by expectation damages. Under a rule of mandatory specific performance:

$$E(Z^{IR}) = \frac{1}{2}\left[\int_{\tilde{B}} W^C(c,\theta)p(\theta)d(\theta)\right] + \frac{1}{2}\left[\int_{\tilde{B}} V^C(c)p(\theta)d(\theta)\right]$$

---

[31] Cf. at p. 111 above; see also Mahlstein and Schropp 2007, section D. Indeed, $c^\star$ is the politically optimal tariff for both policy-makers, given the symmetry of the game set-up.

since *ex post* escape is prohibited. Under a liability rule the expected payoff for each signatory equals:

$$E(Z^{LR}) = \frac{1}{2}\left[\int_{\tilde{B}^{opt}} W^C(c,\theta)p(\theta)d(\theta) + \int_{B^{opt}} W^D(c,\theta)p(\theta)d(\theta) - \Delta\right]$$

$$+ \frac{1}{2}\left[\int_{\tilde{B}^{opt}} V^C(c)p(\theta)d(\theta) + \int_{B^{opt}} V^S(c)p(\theta)d(\theta) + \Delta\right]$$

The damage payment $\Delta$ cancels out and yields:

$$E(Z^{LR}) = \frac{1}{2}\left[\int_{\tilde{B}^{opt}} W^C(c,\theta)p(\theta)d(\theta) + \int_{B^{opt}} W^D(c,\theta)p(\theta)d(\theta)\right]$$

$$+ \frac{1}{2}\left[\int_{\tilde{B}^{opt}} V^C(c)p(\theta)d(\theta) + \int_{B^{opt}} V^S(c)p(\theta)d(\theta)\right]$$

Since the expectation damage measure induces the optimal "breach" decision ($B^{opt}$) on the part of the injurer,[32] and since it holds that:

$$W^D(c,\theta) > W^C(c,\theta)$$

and

$$[W^D(\cdot) - W^C(\cdot)] > [V^C(\cdot) - V^S(\cdot)] \; \forall c, \theta \text{ under } B^{opt},$$

the expected payoff under a liability rule $E(Z^{LR})$ is strictly larger than expected payoffs under a rule of inalienability $E(Z^{IR})$.

To conclude: behind the veil of ignorance any signatory will opt for escape-cum-expectation damages instead of a rule of inalienability, since the former strictly Pareto-dominates the latter in terms of expected future payoffs.

### 6.2.3   *A property or liability rule of escape? A question of transaction costs*

The last section demonstrated that the provision of a rule of post-contractual escape Pareto-dominates a situation where performance is

---

[32] See equation (4) at p. 113 above.

always mandated, no matter what the contingency. This section now delves into the issue of efficient non-performance design in a trade agreement based on market access externalities: is a liability rule or a property rule of entitlement protection more likely to precipitate efficient *ex post* performance and optimal *ex ante* trade liberalization concessions?

As a preliminary factor, signatories will want to know which remedy measure best complements a liability rule. The results generated at p. 113 above feed into the situation at hand, as confirmed by Mahlstein and Schropp 2007, and Schropp 2007a, Appendix, section E. Behind a veil of ignorance, and in a situation of an optimally indefinite, non-contingent tariff liberalization agreement, and where political support shocks are asymmetrically revealed, signatories will opt for the expectation damage measure. Expectation damages yield Pareto-optimal non-performance decisions: not only do these then generate an optimal "breach" set, they also effectuate the politically largest possible reciprocal trade liberalization commitments *ex ante*.[33] In other words, only remedies amounting to the expectation damages can replicate the outcome of the first-best of the CCC.[34]

This leaves us with the sole question of whether the market access entitlement in the hypothetical vWTO should be protected by liability-cum-expectation damages or by a rule of renegotiation. As explained at p. 115 above, the answer can be found in the inherent trade-off between the transaction costs of renegotiation and the TC of damage calculation. Indeed, that section listed a catalog of criteria that reasonably rational trade negotiators should observe when deciding on the relevant rule of flexibility.

## Transaction costs of damage calculation

When deliberating whether to put in place an LR to protect the reciprocal market access entitlement, trade negotiators must be wary of the fact that both the original contingency and the damage caused by a protectionist measure are private knowledge to the injuring and victim government, respectively. *Ex post facto*, that is, after the injurer has performed partial withdrawal of previously made market access commitments, the victim

---

[33] Economics aside, as Mavroidis (2000) shows, the international legal benchmark for remedies of *restitutio in integrum* is equivalent to expectation damages. Hence, public international law would mandate that the victim of a measure in question is compensated by expectation damages.

[34] The intuition behind this result is the same as that given at p. 111 above.

has no incentive whatsoever to reveal its true expectation damages. This is the task of an impartial arbitrator. A number of exogenous TC in connection with calculating damages must be taken into consideration.

**Cost of arbitration**   Having an arbitration entity in place is costly. Although dispute panels can be recruited to assume the job of calculating damages, the vWTO DSB may have to stock up its technical competence; calculation of the damage is essentially a quantification exercise best conducted by experienced economists.

**Monetization of expectation damages**   One distinct difficulty for the vWTO arbitrators lies in putting a "price tag" on the political, inherently subjective, harm incurred by the victim government. This is a complicated but by no means impossible task. First, arbitrators are dealing with a tangible issue, namely a market access balance. Mandating that trade damages and lost market access opportunities be offset by additional access in other industries is a doable task, and probably a reliable proxy for the subjective impairment suffered by victim policy-makers. DSU panels have collected ample experience of how to deal with market access infringements in the last sixty years. Secondly, as Kaplow and Shavell (1996a, p. 726) have shown, an independent arbitrator neither needs to be omniscient nor operate flawlessly in order to be effective. As long as its judgment is neither completely incompetent nor systemically biased against victims or injurers, arbitrators can succeed in producing satisfying outcomes.[35]

**Implicit calculation of expectation damages by the injurer**   Before the injurer decides to enact a protectionist measure, it will have to assess the likely circle of victims, and the harm which its actions can be expected to cause to these countries. The injuring Member is faced with the same problem as the arbitrators later on: they have to put a price tag on the likely nullification and impairment to victims' market access entitlement, and cannot count on honest support by the victim(s). For the injuring government this means investing time and resources in research, prior to

---

[35] By explicitly mandating expectation damages that completely insure the victim country and replicate full compliance on the part of the injurer, the vWTO avoids the one systematic error that is prevalent in the current WTO system. As we set out at p. 243 above, WTO arbitrators must be reproached for having misinterpreted commensurate damages as reliance instead of expectation damages.

enacting policies that it might regret thereafter. On the positive side, the uncertainty involved may prompt injuring governments to opt out only in those cases where the political support shock is definitely large enough to justify escape.

It is noteworthy that endogenous TC, or strategic behavior, on the part of the victim or injurer are not present under a remedy-backed LR. We hinted at p. 119 above at the problem of over-investment (or overcommitment) by the victim in situations of an asymmetrical revelation of contingencies. Yet behind a veil of ignorance where parties do not know their future role before concluding the contract, over-investment by the victim is not an issue.[36]

## Transaction costs of tariff renegotiations

The choice for renegotiation as a trade flexibility tool, on the other hand, brings with it a different set of TC-induced problems.

**Implicit calculation of damages and non-performance gains by injurer and victim**   When the party experiencing regret and the potential victim(s) sit down to renegotiate the terms of their mutual market access balance, both governments have to invest in serious up-front preparations. As is the case under an LR, the injuring party must spend time and effort researching the likely consequences of its actions for the victim(s). In addition, however, each victim government will want to investigate the potential non-performance gains of the injurer in the hope of appropriating as much of these gains as possible. To that end, victim countries must necessarily detect the original political support contingency which hit the injurer. Eliciting the original contingency and (based on that conjecture) calculating the efficiency gains from non-performance is a complex business, and one which by far eclipses the task that arbitrators have to master under a liability rule of escape. Also, calculation errors by one party may be prone to holding up the entire renegotiation process.[37]

---

[36] The reason is that behind a veil of ignorance all signatories take decisions in the manner of a social planner (see Mahlstein and Schropp 2007). The commitment to trade liberalization is made *before* the veil of ignorance is lifted. Since overcommitment is inefficient behavior, no rational signatory will choose that option.

[37] Depending on whether renegotiation takes place in a hub-and-spoke manner with victims sequentially engaging in bilateral negotiations with the injurer, or whether it takes place in a convention-style meeting involving all victims, a calculation error on the part of one victim may inadvertently hold out the entire settlement process.

284 TOWARDS AN AGENDA FOR REFORM

**Costs of renegotiation** Even if vWTO Members are benevolent and do not engage in strategic gamesmanship, renegotiation is a costly endeavor. Manpower and other negotiation resources are expended, which could be used more efficiently elsewhere. The more victims involved in the renegotiations, and the more heterogeneous these players are, the longer the deliberations will last.

**Opportunity costs of time** Renegotiations are also costly in terms of opportunities foregone: whenever an injurer is hit by a significant regret contingency, every moment that lapses without the affected Member reacting is costly. With every minute devoid of a modification agreement, more efficiency gains from escape are lost. Depending on the nature and size of the political support shock, a negotiation-induced delay can completely frustrate all these non-performance gains. Victims thereby do not necessarily have to be malevolent or opportunistic. It just lies in the nature of renegotiations that the time lapsed between experience of shock and the decision to act is larger than under a liability rule of opt-out.

**Double-sided hold-out** In addition to the exogenous (objective) TC listed above, there are serious endogenous (behavioral) *ex post* TC involved in the renegotiation game. Since both the regret contingency and the damage caused are private information to injurer and victim respectively, both parties have a strong incentive to misrepresent the true state of nature. A victim government, on the one hand, will try to misconstrue its likely damage so as to appropriate as much as possible of what it thinks are the injurer's gains from non-performance.

The injuring Member, on the other hand, is very likely to engage in reverse hold-out: since it has proprietary knowledge, the injurer has an incentive to misconstrue both the actual size of the exogenous shock and the extent of expected efficiency gains from non-performance.[38]

This double-sided hold-out may lead to a war of attrition, both parties mistrusting each other's assertions, and consequently rejecting the other party's settlement offers. Wars of attrition take very long to resolve and are hence very costly.[39] Neither party will be able to convince the other that it is telling the truth. For fear of establishing a reputation as a soft

---

[38] Mahlstein and Schropp 2007, in a tariff-setting model with common knowledge of damage done to the victim (when the original contingency is private information for the injurer), formally show the non-trivial efficiency losses that result from sequential bargaining under a renegotiation provision of flexibility.

[39] See above discussion, especially in Chapter 3, p. 121, note 106).

negotiator, neither party wants to come out as a "loser" of this game, either. In addition, Fearon (1998, p. 278) argues that those distribution fights, if resolved at all, are paradoxically won by the party with the *lowest* stakes in the matter, i.e. the country with the lowest discount factor (see also Rosendorff and Milner 2001, p. 850). Knowledge of this last fact is not good news for injurers. Anticipating such a disappointing result, injurers may refrain from participating in welfare-enhancing renegotiations right away, since in the marginal case their entire *ex post* gains from non-performance could be appropriated by victims.

**Redistribution disputes**    A final drawback of a PR of flexibility is the occurrence of turf wars between multiple victims. Once victims (think to) have an idea of the size of the injurer's non-performance gains, they will want to secure the biggest possible share of that pie. They do so by holding out the other victims by deliberately procrastinating the renegotiation process. A strategic victim thereby hopes that its competitors settle early and for less, so that it itself can secure the lion's share of these spoils.

### Conclusion: a rule of liability Pareto-dominates a rule of renegotiation as default rule of the market access entitlement

The presence of *ex post* transaction costs impedes vWTO signatories and renders impossible a truly efficient system of policy flexibility in the market access argument. The liability rule accompanied by expectation damages entails much lower post-contractual TC than a rule of renegotiation. Although the maintenance of a competent vWTO arbitrator is costly, and the monetization of expectation damages not a trivial issue, an LR of default surpasses the alternative of tariff renegotiations by far: a key advantage of the LR is that it can be enacted immediately without any opportunity losses. Another important factor is that granting unilateral opt-out does not give way to strategic behavior, whereas under a PR both the party experiencing regret and all potential victims of a suggested measure have an incentive to misrepresent the truth, to play for time, to procrastinate, or to engage in other opportunistic strategies. This is a recipe for trouble: it undermines the spirit of togetherness and cooperation, makes mischief, and is generally apt to sour the relations between contracting parties. Since the vWTO (and more so, the actual WTO) is a relational contract that crucially relies on the benevolence and goodwill of its Members, mechanisms that bring out opportunistic traits in signatories must be avoided.

In conclusion, a property rule of flexibility produces higher costs *ex post*, which prompts less efficient non-performance decisions by potential injurers.[40] Anticipating this, signatories behind the veil of ignorance will adjust their *ex ante* trade liberalization concessions accordingly. The provision of an LR-cum-expectation damages, on the other hand, though not a perfect tool, prompts relatively more efficient decisions by both injurers and victims.

### 6.2.4   Specifics of the default rule

The liability rule is the single default rule protecting the market access entitlement. This section will discuss the specifics of this rule of default. In particular, it assesses whether the enactment of the LR should be connected to some sort of conditionality, and how issues of non-violation should be treated.

#### Level of conditionality: enactment threshold and application scope limitations?

Should the LR be linked to any kind of precondition, or enactment threshold? From the perspective of efficient "breach," this would seem a foolish idea. First, enactment conditions are sunk costs (signaling costs without efficiency-enhancing value), and as such do not bear any inherent value other than that of a signaling device: the injurer signals its resolve to comply in the future and to return to the cooperative path once the shock has subsided (Rosendorff 2005, note 20; Rosendorff and Milner 2001, p. 831). However, paying the victim its expectancy under the optimal DR should be enough for the injuring country to demonstrate its cooperative zeal. Secondly, a high level of contingency is an additional burden for the injurer on top of expectation damages payable to the victim. But everything *in extenso* of expectation damages violates the precept of efficient "breach," and reduces injurers' willingness to default in situations where it is actually efficient to do so. Sunk-cost preconditionality is tantamount to demanding overcompensation from the injurer. Overcompensation leads to insufficiently little non-performance, or under-"breach," and ultimately to inefficient

---

[40] In anticipation of later costs connected to a PR, injurers will refrain from choosing non-performance in the marginal non-performance decision. These are situations where the ideal CCC would prescribe *ex post* escape, but the injurer, in anticipation of *ex post* costs connected to this decision, will just abstain from engaging in contractual default.

*ex ante* investments behind the veil of ignorance. Therefore, parties must be expected to refrain from prescribing any sort of enactment threshold.[41]

Is it sensible to limit the application scope of the liability default rule? Mandating "MFN'ed" non-performance is not advisable: protectionism should be allowed on a selective, discriminatory basis, just as the accompanying remedy payments are bilateral and commensurate. Since the victim(s) are compensated for their loss(es), non-discrimination would only expand the circle of victims, and therewith the damages to be shouldered by the injuring Member. A maximum period of escape (as in SGA Art. 7.1, for example) does not seem reasonable, either: as long as injurers comply with paying expectation remedies, their escape is efficient and therefore deserves to be endorsed.

However, two limitations on using the liability opt-out are crucial. First, protectionist back-tracking in reaction to market access shocks should be limited to tariff barriers only. Tariffs are the most direct measure with the fewest externalities and dead-weight losses (Krugman and Obstfeld 1994, chapter 9). Also, import taxes are a transparent measure (readily observable by all parties), and easily adjustable.

Secondly, the damage remedy should consist of compensation only. Tariff compensation offers by the injuring Member to the victim country/countries politically and economically Pareto-dominate the countermeasure of retaliation: compensation avoids the negative political-economic implications of the suspension of concessions, such as the small-country bias, the economic dubiety, and the contract-defeating nature of retaliation.[42] More importantly, tariff compensation does not drive down the negotiated market access balance (a second-order effect of retaliation), but instead keeps it on the same (presumably politically optimal) level that was initially negotiated.[43]

---

[41] In the same vein, it should be evident that special concessions granted to the injurer are equally ineffective. SGA Art. 8.3 currently confers a three-year grace period for injurers invoking the safeguard of GATT Art. XIX. There is no logical reason why compensation payments by the injurer should set in with a latency of three years. This is another violation of the efficient "breach" principle.

[42] See our discussion on the weaknesses of the countermeasure of retaliation at p. 242 above.

[43] Paying compensation remedies in the form of monetary fees, as championed by some authors (Barfield 2001, p. 131; Bronckers and van den Broek 2005, p. 109; Davey 2005b; O'Connor and Djordjevic 2005; Pauwelyn 2000, p. 345; WTO 2004, chapter VI.D) seems a less attractive option from the point of view of self-interested policy-makers. Although monetary fines are more fungible than tariff liberalization offers, it should be remembered that the currency of the WTO contract is political support, not consumer welfare.

## Non-violation claims and the default rule of flexibility: two concepts apart?

As stated at p. 202 above, WTO and vWTO Members may inadvertently close their partners' market access at times. For that situation, the current WTO Agreement allows for non-violation claims, though they have hardly ever been used. Reasonably rational policy-makers can be expected to staff the vWTO with a workable NVC that can be appealed to whenever a country feels that its market access balance is out of synch subsequent to any kind of non-reported protectionist escape – be it inadvertent or not. The affected country approaches a vWTO arbitrator, who consequently assesses if and how much harm occurred. An NVC is substantially equivalent to a DR, with the sole difference that the initiative does not come from the injurer, but from the victim's side. Thus, in contrast to the current system where the relationship between NVC and GATT Art. XXVIII is somewhat dubious (cf. at p. 235 above), under the vWTO they emanate from the same basic concept of liability default.

### 6.2.5 *Conclusion: an unconditional liability rule as optimal protection of the market access entitlement*

The optimal institutional design which rational trade negotiators will negotiate in ignorance of their future role in the trade game consists of two components: an optimally indefinite, completely non-contingent definition of the reciprocal market access obligation, and a single rule of default. In the presence of contractual incompleteness of the necessary or inexorable type B sort, neither contingency measures nor negative integration provisions add anything to contractual efficiency: future states of nature are left undescribed. The mutually granted right to compete in trade partners' markets is protected by a simple liability rule of protection: the provision features an unconditional opt-out clause, and a stipulation of commensurate tariff compensation amounting to the expectation damage measure.

To policy-makers, seeing new market access opportunities may be worth more than monetary fees. Also, monetary fees may imply negative political-economic consequences for the injuring government, such as public outcry ("selling indulgences" to trade rivals) or having to involve the domestic legislature. A more differentiated analysis of the political economy aspects of providing monetary compensation, however, is warranted and seems like an interesting field of future research.

This single rule of default, accompanied by the expectation damage remedy, is able to replicate the outcomes of the complete contingent contract: escape from the previously agreed market access level ("breach") is only performed in situations where it is globally efficient. The injurer internalizes all the harm caused to the victim, and makes the latter indifferent between performance and escape. The injuring Member appropriates all efficiency gains from non-performance, and thus has an incentive to seize regret whenever it occurs. Yet the institutional design precludes the injuring Member from enacting any inefficient redistributive measure, i.e. opportunistic *ex post* back-tracking. This safeguards optimal *ex ante* commitment by all parties behind the veil of ignorance.

This unconditional intra-contractual LR is contractually fixed within the GATT/GATS Agreements, but not within the DSU. For the liability-rule regime to work, vWTO Members need binding third party arbitration, the procedures of which have to be contractually specified. Whether the arbitration will be performed by WTO panels or the AB, or some other body of the WTO Secretariat, is inconsequential. What is important is that this arbitration function is not to be conflated with any adjudicatory role or court-like procedures. Arbitration is not about assessing right or wrong, or settling disputes. It is about finding the right price for a legitimate escape from previously agreed contractual market access obligations.

### 6.3   Organizing the protection of multilateral entitlements

The next step of our hypothetical bargain exercise is to assess how reasonably rational policy-makers are organizing the protection of the various multilateral entitlements that are exchanged in the WTO and vWTO. Before the true state of nature is revealed to the vWTO Members, they are ignorant about the nature and size of possible non-trade contingencies, about which country will be hit, for how long, and to what extent. Therefore, again, reasonably rational signatories search for the institutional design that maximizes the common welfare of all participating trade policy-makers.

#### 6.3.1   Focusing on default rules

For the same reason that applies to the market access entitlement, it is not rational for policy-makers to strive for contractual completeness in a situation of necessary or inexorable incompleteness of type B that all multilateral, or coordination entitlements are beset with (cf. at p. 210 above). Hence, trade policy-makers can be expected to concentrate on the drafting of default rules for the protection of multilateral entitlements. Forward-looking and vigilant drafters examine every multilateral entitlement, and assign it its own default rule.

### 6.3.2   Optimal design of default rules protecting multilateral entitlements

Not all multilateral entitlements are of similar type; there are major qualitative differences. Some entitlements are minor procedural obligations, some are far-reaching commitments to abide by certain minimum standards of regulation, others are external codes of conduct integrated into the contract. Negotiating policy-makers should classify coordination entitlements in three groups. Group 1 consists of entitlements where *ex post* discretion is impermissible for moral or systemic reasons. Those entitlements are to be protected by mandatory specific performance, i.e. a rule of inalienability. Group 2 are those entitlements whose infringement is not welcome, but causes only minor nuisance to the community as a whole. These are to be protected by liquidated damages. Group 3 consists of all other multilateral entitlements which are reasonably protected by a property rule of flexibility. We shall explain each in turn.

#### If *ex post* discretion is impermissible: an inalienability rule of default

As discussed at p. 105 above, rules of inalienability are apposite in situations where *ex post* non-performance is immoral, contract-annihilating, or welfare-depreciating. All these situations can occur with respect to some multilateral entitlements.

*Ex post* default is immoral with respect to some external entitlements, such as *ius cogens* norms. Peremptory norms of international law supersede every treaty provision in international law. Sovereign countries must not "contract around" them. They must not deviate from these entitlements, either. Back-tracking is also immoral with respect to the voting rights of Members: no injuring party should be able to infringe upon the voting rights owned by other Members. In the same vein, no Member should ever be allowed to relinquish its voting right.

A rule of inalienability has to be put in action whenever contractual escape crowds out the cooperative drive by other signatories. This is especially the case for entitlements where partial performance is not possible,[44] and back-tracking is always tantamount to completely nullifying the previously made commitment. In certain cases, some kind of domino effect is triggered if a single party defects from its multilateral entitlement: the prospect and anticipation of one signatory stepping out of line frustrates the drive of (some or all) other parties to commit *ex ante* to some level of regulation, or some minimum standard. The result of temporary non-performance by an injurer is not *less* regulation, but *no* regulation. Take, for example, the multilateral obligation to protect patents for twenty-five years. If that entitlement can legally be reneged upon *ex post,* and country A decides to grant only two years of patent protection, A's neighboring countries will not want to protect any longer than the defector.[45] Anticipating several countries abandoning a rule of extended patent protection, no other country will want to commit to the full twenty-five years. The same logic applies to the protection of copyrights. If countries collectively commit to grant extended copyright to software codes, but, say, China "opts out" of that obligation, other vWTO Members must anticipate that many plagiarist companies will settle down in China and undermine the entire system. To avoid a collapse of the regulation from the start, multilateral copyright provisions are best protected by rules of inalienability.

In summary, when drafting the terms of entitlement protection, signatories should think hard about which multilateral entitlements are best protected by a rule of inalienability. In particular, dichotomous, far-reaching, commitment-intensive regulation promises warrant mandatory specific performance at all times so as to avoid a crowding out of *ex ante* cooperation concessions.

---

[44] It is not possible to partially overstep a deadline; it is not feasible to protect copyrights a little, to have half a patent office in place, or to only minimally infringe upon *ius cogens*. Compare this to the non-dichotomous (discrete) market access entitlement, where partial non-performance (e.g. temporary protectionist increase of the United States' tariffs of hot-rolled steel from 10 to 35 percent) is the norm.

[45] Patent protection creates monopoly rents for the patent holder, and thus prevents economy-wide technological spillovers. Patents hamper technological progress. Consequently, governments may be reluctant to grant extensive patent protection. Offering less protection may give a country a technological head-start in global competition (see e.g. Romer 1996, chapter 3).

## If *ex post* discretion causes minor damage: a liquidated damages rule of default

Following the nature of multilateral entitlements, *ex post* violation is presumably rarely welfare-enhancing. The regret contingency must be substantial enough to make up for the harm done to all other signatories. Thus, post-contractual non-performance should generally not come too easily for signatories. However, there may be multilateral entitlements whose (possibly inadvertent or negligent) infringement will not cause a great deal of harm to affected Members. Take for example instances of minor misdemeanor, such as an overstepped deadline, an omission to report or notify, or a late payment. These administrative or regulatory offences may be perceived as petty infringements in the grand scheme of things. They cause minor nuisance to the system as a whole, but hardly affect any contracting party in particular.

An entitlement protection in the form of an LR or PR is then not warranted, simply because the transaction costs connected to lengthy renegotiations or arbitrated liability easily outweigh the damage done. Yet infringements should not be ignored, either. For that reason, in situations of minor nuisance, a liquidated damage rule of default seems the most sensible and expeditious action. Liquidated damages should be made in cash and be payable to the Organization.[46]

## If *ex post* discretion is permissible: a property rule of default

For all those multiple entitlements which neither fall in the category of immutable protection, nor are bagatelle provisions, *ex post* discretion should be permissible. We find strong evidence that multilateral entitlements of this third group are best protected by a property rule of renegotiation. Consider the following reasons.

**A rule of liability is a slippery slope**    Contracts on the scale of the WTO and vWTO need some form of institutional spine. Multilateral entitlements are the structural backbone of the WTO and vWTO contract. Without the unfailing presence of numerous procedural obligations, timelines, or general rules of *modus operandi*, predictability and

---

[46] This is not to suggest that any deadline, statutory guideline, or notification provision should be "up for grabs" using a simple violation-cum-liquidated damages mechanism. Many multilateral entitlements might be outright annihilated by such a provision. The point is merely that reasonably rational contracting parties should carefully assess which of the many multilateral entitlements should really fall under a relaxed remedy rule.

constancy of the international trading regime suffers. If most of these entitlements were "up for grabs" by means of a liability rule, the system would be in danger of destabilization: if no country could ever be sure that its trading partners would stick to their obligations owed to the entire membership, and instead had to learn *ex post facto* that a liability-type opt-out had occurred, trust and confidence in the contract would suffer. A liability rule for nearly every entitlement would render the idea of a binding agreement futile, and dissolve the very nature of the contract.

**Strong presumption of opportunism**　As stated above, the regret contingency for multilateral entitlements must be significant, since it should exceed the harm done to all signatories that benefit from *erga omnes partes* obligations. The exercise of a unilateral opt-out is generally welfare-depreciating, i.e. opportunistic. Opportunism may happen whenever damages cannot easily be calculated (on this point see below). Signatories can be expected to foreclose any possibility of opportunism up-front by demanding renegotiations instead of unilateral opt-out accompanied by remedy payments.

Also, if the injuring Member is guided by discontent with some systemic defect of the contract rather than opportunistic guile, its desire for *ex post* non-performance is akin to a modification request. Modifications of systemic flaws are better addressed by renegotiation than by escape-cum-remedy.

**Liability damages are difficult to measure**　This is an important argument against a liability rule of default for multilateral entitlements: it is very difficult to calculate damages caused by a unilateral opt-out of a multilateral entitlement. As pointed out above (see especially Chapter 5, note 36 and accompanying text), the quantification of damage caused by an *erga omnes* obligation entails logical and practical problems. Any encroachment from a multilateral entitlement by one signatory harms the system as a whole. But how can damages to the system be measured?

Assessing damages pursuant to an escape from an *erga omnes* entitlement is hypothetical, next to impossible to assign and apportion, and difficult to "monetize." Any vWTO arbitrator would be charged with the non-trivial task of assessing how trade in the international trading system would have evolved had the escaping party performed as promised. Further, the arbitrator would also have to establish to what extent every single contracting party suffered as a result of the non-performance, and how the opt-out affected the competitive relationship between all signatories. Apart from the difficulty connected with the counterfactual nature of that calculation, the damage can be assumed to be profoundly subjective for every victim.[47] In addition, every systematic calculation error by the arbitrator is multiplied 152-fold in effect, since all of the 153 WTO or vWTO Members (except the injurer) would receive the wrong expectation damage.

In summary, having an arbitrator assess and apportion damages caused by multilateral entitlement infringements is likely to create tremendous discontent among the membership. A PR of default, on the other hand, would relieve an impartial bystander of this unmanageable task. Under a renegotiation provision the injurer sits down with all interested parties, explains its problem, and negotiates a solution with its trade partners. This provides victim Members with time to reflect on the implications of a possible back-tracking measure, and on the expected harm the measure in question is likely to cause them.

**Probability of strategic victim behavior is small**    While damage calculation is notoriously difficult, the transaction costs of renegotiation can be assumed to be minor for cases of escape from multilateral entitlements. Harm done through ill-meaning strategic behavior is of less concern. First, since non-trade contingencies are usually not imminent emergencies that could threaten the existence of countries (or rather, the political survival of the policy-makers in charge), injurers are under less time pressure, and may not easily be held out by victims applying procrastination strategies in order to carve out a better deal for themselves.

Secondly, although all vWTO Members can potentially partake in the renegotiation of multilateral entitlements, few victims will be interested in participating, and those who do will have less interest in behaving strategically. The individual damage to every country is often minor and

---

[47] For example: an arbitrator would have to calculate what the counterfactual level of world trade would have been, had Norway in the *Norway – Trondheim Toll Ring* case from 1991 publicly tendered the construction work (see Chapter 5, note 36). This calculation should include general equilibrium considerations, second-order ripple effects, and third party externalities. The arbitrator would also have to assign expectation damages to the United States, Burkina Faso, Vanuatu and all other vWTO Members and argue convincingly as to why the remedy amounts differ. Things get more difficult if a defection from a multilateral entitlement does not cause palpable harm, but intangible damage. How can the subjective harm to Canada following, say, a refusal by the United States to pay the yearly financial contribution to the WTO be measured?

of little interest to many players (what is the damage to Vietnam if Chile fails to pay its membership fees to the vWTO?).

Thirdly, if the renegotiation request concerns an important topic, concerned parties will think twice before engaging in strategic games-manship: due to the repeated nature of the trade game, every country must reckon on having to escape from multilateral obligations at some point in time. Holding out the injurer, or vetoing a non-performance request, will be remembered within the membership. And since every Member can take part in every renegotiation, the formerly impeded injurer may easily pay back the "new" injurer commensurately. Thus, the consensus principle of renegotiations could be a blessing: few signa-tories will want to have the reputation of being a recalcitrant or oppor-tunistic victim.

### 6.3.3   Conclusion: mixed default rules of protection for multilateral entitlements

Reasonably rational trade negotiators ought to concentrate their efforts on designing workable default rules for multilateral entitlements rather than on drafting elaborate contingency rules. We have shown that the exercise of *ex post* trade policy flexibility should not be made easy for injurers when it comes to multilateral entitlements. It is reasonable to divide the vast number of coordination entitlements into three groups: one for cases where *ex post* discretion must be considered as immoral or welfare-depreciating; one for those entitlements where non-performance is a mere nuisance; and one for those where post-contractual non-performance is permissible and protected by a rule of renegotiation.

Thus, the vWTO Charter should include an article comprising of at least three rules of default. Multilateral entitlements throughout the contract can then refer back to this provision. Alternatively, every treaty article listing a non-market access entitlement should also contain in a final paragraph the applicable rule of default. Special attention should be directed to the issue of how entitlements can be protected by the relatively weak liquidated damage rule, as well as by the rigid rule of inalienability.

## 6.4   A two-tier system of enforcement

We have characterized the intra-contractual entitlement protection rules for the trade and coordination entitlements in the form of simple default rules. This system of DR ensures that any substantial political support regret experienced by self-interested policy-makers during the performance phase of the contract can be seized, if doing so enhances the general welfare of the contracting parties. Thus, every vWTO Member acting in good faith can use the contractual safety valves, provided it abides by the rules of non-performance attached to the entitlement it wants to withdraw from. By virtue of the efficient "breach" provisions, no country is forced to use violation of the Agreement in order to liberate itself from untenable commitments.

What remains for this hypothetical trade agreement to deal with are bad-faith and haphazard clashes between countries. Haphazard clashes are provoked by unintentional and inadvertent instances of default, and accidental contractual gaps (textual ambiguities, ambivalent formulations, omissions, erratic provisions). Reasonably rational contracting parties cherish no illusion that their contract will feature these inadvertent gaps. An elaborate system of enforcement should be able to separate good-faith clashes pursuant to inadvertent gaps from bad-faith clashes motivated by sheer opportunistic guile. Clarifying contractual ambiguities and filling inadvertent gaps has an intrinsic positive value for the vWTO membership as a whole: eliminating haphazard gaps leads to transaction cost efficiencies and makes trading easier and more predictable. The institutional framework should encourage signatories to bring those issues to light, and under no circumstances should it dissuade Members from openly questioning problematic or erratic provisions.

Reasonably rational trade policy-makers should craft a two-tier system of enforcement. Designed as an escalation scheme, enforcement rules deal with extra-contractual behavior in two stages: a *dispute* stage and a *punishment* stage.[48]

The first tier is aimed at eliminating welfare-enhancing good-faith trade disputes, and at solving them in an amicable manner. This dispute stage gives parties the opportunity to demand clarification of the treaty language where they see fit, and to subsequently resolve the dispute harmoniously. Whenever a signatory feels that its entitlements are nullified or impaired by the actions of another Member, it can appeal to a

---

[48] We stated at p. 32 above that contractual enforcement always consists of two phases: a dispute or litigation phase, in which issues of enforceability (observability, verifiability, quantifiability) are paramount, and a punishment or remediation phase, in which enforcement capacity plays a crucial role. Many scholars equate enforcement with punishment and thereby ignore (or assume away) that detecting, defining, and recognizing contractual deviation is not at all a clear-cut case.

Dispute Settlement Body. The DSB hears the litigating parties, collects the facts of the case, and interprets contractual provisions according to the object and purpose of the entitlement.[49] In its ruling, a dispute panel clarifies ambiguities and fills inadvertent gaps.[50]

If it turns out that the claimant indeed witnessed a nullification or impairment of its rights, or that the defendant infringed upon a multi-lateral entitlement, the DSB in this first phase of enforcement treats the incident like a contractual DR, where the injurer failed to notify the victim(s). For the market access entitlement protected by an LR of default, the arbitrator (after having given the litigants the opportunity to reach a mutually agreed solution) will calculate the expectation damages, including foregone profits during the litigation phase, and the litigation costs incurred by the victim. The injurer is then instructed to settle these remedies in the form of tariff compensation offers.[51]

For those entitlements protected by a property rule, the solved dispute is handed back to the two disputing parties with a request for them to reach a renegotiation solution, just as is required by the initial property rule of contract entitlement. To that end, disputing (or involved) parties are granted a certain timeframe. But since renegotiation *ex post facto* is a difficult business (the defection has already occurred, so the injurer may have little incentive to cover the real price of escape), compensation negotiations may break down, or remain inconclusive during the period granted by the DSB. Therefore, after the lapse of the renegotiation period, the arbitrator calculates the expectation damages incurred by the victim(s) from the point of defection to the end of the renegotiation period, and adds half of the non-performance gains (or its best estimate thereof) on top.[52] After all, this sum is equally able to uphold the efficient

---

[49] We are aware that dispute panels and the AB are required by WTO and international law to primarily interpret ambiguous passages in light of the object and purpose of the provision. However, the vWTO is of such a simple structure that finding the objective of the provision is tantamount to finding out the nature of the relevant entitlement.

[50] On the gap-filling role and competence of the WTO DSB, see Keck and Schropp 2008, section D.5.

[51] Note that tariff compensation amounting to expectation damages is used for intra-contractual escape and in the dispute stage of vWTO enforcement. A resemblance to non-violation claims (see at p. 288 above) is not coincidental. The dispute phase of vWTO enforcement is actually following the same concept.

[52] The intuition behind adding half of the efficiency gains from non-performance is simple. Under a PR of escape, victims stand a good chance of appropriating some of the efficiency gains from non-performance gains (see at p. 119 above). If, pursuant to an infringement of an entitlement protected by a PR, the arbitrator only awarded

"breach" principle just as well as renegotiations do. Entitlements protected by inalienability may not be infringed upon, and any defection on the side of the injurer is *ipso facto* interpreted as being driven by bad faith.

The dispute stage of vWTO enforcement is apt to resolve any ambiguity that existed between vWTO Members without introducing any punitive element to the system. Any party that has been driven by good faith up to this point should be satisfied: injurers may engage in efficient "breach," and victims may bring actions for nullification and impairment. If thus far a trade dispute has not been resolved, the strong presumption holds that the injurer acted in bad faith from the start.

Hence, in case inalienable entitlements are infringed, or an injurer Member steadfastly refuses to abide by the rules of the game, despite the opportunity to resolve the dispute amicably, the punishment stage of vWTO enforcement sets in as a second line of defense for the victim. In this stage, enforcement has more "teeth." First, since the risk remains that non-compliant Members disregard their duty to compensate, the countermeasure of retaliation is the ultimate means of enforcement. Retaliation has the incontrovertible advantage of not being controlled by the offender.[53] Secondly, there is no logical reason for signatories to stay within a "rebalancing" logic, or to keep a dispute bilateral. In order to protect the previously agreed rules of the game, to induce compliance with the panel ruling as quickly as possible, and to deter extra-contractual bad-faith behavior by future injurers, punishment in the second stage of enforcement is punitive in nature. The size of retaliation is fixed by a DSB arbitrator who makes sure that the retaliation amount is strictly (and substantially) higher than the victim's expectation damages.

Two other key ingredients additionally ensure the effectiveness of vWTO enforcement: one is collective enforcement, the other punishment escalation. In collective enforcement, the suspension of concessions leaves the bilateral realm of complainant vs. defendant. Instead,

---

expectation damages (which grant all the gains from non-performance to the injurer), no injurer would ever choose the route of renegotiation in the first place. Instead, the injuring Member would wait to be sued and receive a higher reservation utility from reimbursing the victim with expectation damages.

[53] Strengthening the use of cross-retaliation thereby seems apposite. However, in order to make cross-retaliation a workable tool, the DSB's restrictive, "superficial and inconsistent" (Hudec 2002, p. 90) interpretation of DSU Art. 23.3(c), originating from the *EC – Bananas* adjudication, must be revised (see Schropp 2005, note 47 and accompanying text).

retaliation becomes an issue of concern to the entire vWTO membership. Complaining, affected, and concerned parties alike pool their retaliation capacities to overcome the problem of constituting too small a market to cause noticeable pain to the perpetrator (see Hudec 2002; Maggi 1999b; Pauwelyn 2000). Enforcement, hence, is a real "sanction" to speak of, since it is free from any rebalancing constraint, and does not bear a bilateral notion.

The second ingredient to lend substance to enforcement is an intricate escalation scheme geared to bringing the recalcitrant vWTO Member into compliance: the longer the obstinate injurer refuses to comply with the panel ruling, the more its punishment is ratcheted up. Collective retaliation claims by the membership grow at an increasing rate.[54] At the end of the escalation scheme there are additional penalties in the form of the suspension of certain membership rights, such as the right to attend meetings, to use the DSM, or to receive technical assistance.[55]

In summary, the vWTO – the WTO reconceptualized by rational policymakers – needs procedures and rules for dealing with disputes. Contrary to what some WTO scholars suggest, a binding third party adjudication, such as the DSB, is not epiphenomenal to a liability rule. Mechanisms of dispute settlement must be in place to deal with good-faith clashes (due to contractual ambiguity, interpretative problems, unintentional contract infringements) as well as bad-faith clashes (blatant disregard of vWTO rules for opportunistic gains). vWTO Members will thereby negotiate a two-tier system of treaty enforcement. The first protective belt is apt to deal with good-faith disputes. Remedies at this stage are weak and strictly commensurate to the damage caused. The second layer of protection is punitive and collective in nature. Ultimately, contract enforcement must protect against extra-contractual behavior, not invite it. Given that there is always an efficient safety valve in place for benevolent injurers, vWTO enforcement must protect the contract with high penalties.

This two-step escalation scheme of enforcement is both fair and effective. It is fair since it protects efficient *ex post* escape, and does not

---

[54] With every day the injurer fails to comply, victims' expectation damages increase. The idea of the escalation scheme is to introduce a punitive element, whereby retaliation damages increase over and above the amount of expectation losses. Similar to interest rates, retaliation awards grow as long as the injurer stays non-compliant.

[55] The positive aspect of the suspension of membership rights is that they do not entail negative trade effects. Experiences in that area have already been gathered in the IMF, the Montreal Protocol for the Protection of the Ozone Layer, and the ILO (Charnovitz 2001; Lawrence 2003).

---

discourage interpretative disputes over textual ambiguities, contractual ambivalence, and contractual flaws. It is effective since it insures victims' expectancy under the bargain, guarantees the re-establishment of the balance of concessions, and punishes unambiguous bad-faith behavior. For ill-meaning injurers, the incentive structure of the game has changed in comparison to the real-life WTO: violation of the Agreement is no longer a substitute for using contractual flexibility mechanisms. It is no longer a comfortable fallback that injurers can resort to at any time. Perpetrating extra-contractual bad-faith behavior is now a painful experience for injurers. The rational anticipation of functioning punitive retaliation makes prospective injurers amenable to engaging in serious renegotiations and striving for mutually agreed solutions. In light of coercive punishments, letting renegotiations break down is no longer an attractive option.

### 6.5  The vWTO as an efficient "breach" contract: a "better" trade agreement?

Based on the findings gathered from previous chapters, Chapter 6 conducted a hypothetical bargain analysis of the WTO, giving rise to the concept of a theoretical benchmark contract, the vWTO. This contract is an image of what the WTO could look like if it were organized along the principles of the efficient "breach" contract. We opened this chapter with a series of questions concerning the vWTO's governance structure. Let us provide a summary of findings.

The hypothetical bargain analysis of the vWTO contract depicts a bare-bone contract, consisting of the definition and characterization of the exchanged (substantive and auxiliary) entitlements, as well as of one single intra-contractual protection rule for each entitlement. These entitlements are completely non-contingent in the face of the unbridgeable uncertainty the contract is encumbered with.

An efficient "breach" of trade commitments emerges endogenously when rational policy-makers negotiate the trade agreement. Contractual flexibility mechanisms in the vWTO capture all gains from non-performance: the market access entitlement is best protected by an unconditional liability rule of default and backed by expectation damages. Expectation damages are payable in additional tariff commitments only. They replicate full compliance of the injurer and put the victim in as good a position as if the injuring country had performed. Coordination entitlements are protected by default rules of inalienability, liquidated damages, or renegotiation, depending on the damage that *ex post* discretion provokes in victim countries.

Enforcement has a dual role of addressing good-faith disputes triggered by inadvertent contractual gaps, and of safeguarding compliance with the rules of the game. The precursory dispute stage is geared towards precipitating an amicable resolution of the conflict, and features no punitive element. The subsequent punishment stage is aimed at deterring bad-faith injurers from defecting and causing inefficiencies. An escalatory "sanctions" scheme includes collective suspension of concessions or other obligations, which can be enriched and ratcheted up by the temporary withdrawal of some of the injurer's membership rights.

To conclude this chapter, we briefly compare the current WTO governance structure with that of the hypothetical vWTO, both in terms of organization (section 6.5.1) and efficiency outcomes (section 6.5.2). This is followed by a discussion of the stakeholders for whom the benchmark treaty vWTO constitutes the "better" contract (section 6.5.3).

### 6.5.1    How do the WTO and the vWTO differ?

With respect to trade policy flexibility and enforcement, the current-day WTO and the hypothetical vWTO share important elements: both institutional frameworks demand strict compliance with the contractual rules and with dispute panel rulings. Both favor mutually agreed solutions over official third party arbitration; both contracts prefer tariff compensation over retaliation. Yet a consequential difference is that the system of non-performance in the vWTO works. The governance structure of the hypothetical bargain is such that it sets the right incentives in order to put into effect these contractual stipulations. The institutional design of the vWTO is an incentive compatible arrangement which manifests itself in four important organizational differences between what the WTO should look like and what it looks like today.

**The vWTO is simpler**    The provisions of the vWTO contract are less circumstantial, yet not less precise than what we find in the WTO today. The vWTO dispenses with anticipating regret contingencies, prohibiting policy instruments, and drafting elaborate contingency measures. Instead, the vWTO gets by with a definition and explanation of the relevant entitlements, one default rule of protection per entitlement, and a set of enforcement rules and procedures. Less treaty language and fewer contractual provisions create less room for ambiguity, informal opt-outs, legal loopholes – and therewith fewer possibilities for opportunistic maneuvering.

**The vWTO features different rules of default**    A striking difference between the trade policy flexibility design of WTO and vWTO lies in the definition of what constitutes intra-contractual behavior. This is particularly relevant with respect to rules of default. As analyzed in section 5.1.1 and section 5.2 above, the WTO's de iure protection of market access and coordination entitlements is organized by means of renegotiation rules (GATT Art. XXVIII, GATS Art. XXI, WTO Charter Art. X). Our hypothetical bargain analysis showed that it is more efficient for self-interested policy-makers to grant a rule of unconditional liability (backed by expectation remedies) to market access entitlements, and to protect multilateral entitlements with a property rule (featuring negotiated remedies), a rule of inalienability, or liquidated damages, depending on the nature of the multilateral entitlement at hand. When it comes to cases where *ex post* discretion is immoral, a strict rule of inalienability should be formulated.

The contractual default rules in the hypothetical vWTO are apt to capture all room for regret, while discouraging opportunistic opt-out. As elaborated in detail at p. 234 above, the same is *not* true for the contemporary system of "breach" and remedy in the WTO.

**Nature and calculation of damages are different**    As discussed at p. 234 above, the interpretation of "substantially equivalent" damages by WTO arbitrators is strictly undercompensatory. Equivalent damages payable to the victim pursuant to a liability-type opt-out must be interpreted as expectation gains foregone. Hence, the expectation damage measure, which puts the victim in as good a position as had the injurer performed, is the only remedy to safeguard efficient "breach" and adequate *ex ante* commitments. This not only requires a novel calculation method on the part of arbitrators, but also gives procedural precedence to the countermeasure of tariff compensation over that of retaliation.

**Violation of the Agreement is no longer a substitute for using intracontractual flexibility**    A consequential difference between WTO and vWTO is that the current arrangement fails to discriminate effectively between permissible non-performance (flexibility tools) and a flat-out violation of the contract. Some Members experiencing regret are barred from acting in good faith due to rigidities in the current trade policy flexibility regime, while violation is often the "cheapest" non-performance solution for injurers. De iure flexibility clauses and violation are thus *substitute* mechanisms of escape. This is illogical and dangerous for the entire system.

The hypothetical vWTO, on the other hand, uses enforcement provisions as a second line of contractual defense; it turns trade policy flexibility and enforcement into complementary instruments. The vWTO displays a two-tier enforcement system that effectively protects its Members against ill-meant extra-contractual behavior. Given that there are efficient default rules of flexibility in place, and with contractual misunderstandings smoothed out by a preceding dispute phase, the second stage of WTO enforcement protects the contract with coercive collective penalties, without doing harm to the world trading system.

### 6.5.2  Efficiency edge of the vWTO over the WTO

What would be the likely consequences if the world trading system were organized along the lines of the hypothetical vWTO? We foresee four important advantages.

(i) **Clear separation between good faith and bad faith: opportunism curbed**    At p. 128 above, we inched our way towards a theory of disputes in incomplete contracts. We called attention to the important difference between good-faith and bad-faith disputes. Acts of good faith can be efficiency-enhancing and should be supported by any efficient contract. Bad-faith behavior is opportunistic, and thus by definition welfare-depreciating, and must be forestalled by robust enforcement mechanisms. The difficulty in drawing the line between good- and bad-faith clashes lies not in the presence of contractual uncertainty but in deficiently drafted contracts. Section 3.5 above distinguished four types of contracting errors: ambiguous and ambivalent language, insufficient language, rigidity, and suboptimal remedies.

The hypothetical vWTO is free from the problems of rigidity and suboptimal remedies: every intra-contractual use of flexibility mechanisms is per se well-intentioned, and every well-intentioned escape is possible. Violation of the Agreement is thus either inflicted by contracting errors (ambiguities, ambivalence, or insufficient language) or driven by bad faith. The dispute stage of vWTO enforcement is able to identify and weed out good-faith disputes generated by contracting flaws, and passes malevolent arguments on to the punishment stage.

This is an important advantage over the current system of WTO enforcement. A clear separation between good intentions and bad-faith disputes fully enables and justifies punitive sanctions for recalcitrant WTO Members. Coercive punishments, in turn, deter Members from circumventing the contract by using extra-contractual, informal opt-out avenues. Curbing the opportunistic behavior of injurers is hence an important improvement on the current WTO system.

(ii) **More stability, more compliance**    As was shown in the course of the discussion of Herzing's (2005) model in section 6.2.2, the introduction of optimal flexibility mechanisms in trade agreements based on market access externalities substantially increases the contract's resistance to a wide range of exogenous political support shocks. Member exit (be it partial or full) and complete breakdown of the international trading system are less likely to occur under the efficient "breach" principle.

At the same time, an optimal system of trade policy flexibility like the hypothetical vWTO leads to more compliance with the letter of the Agreement (read: performance as promised). The prospect of punitive damages for bad-faith behavior should deter Members from deliberately defecting from the Agreement. Increased compliance should be the natural consequence.[56]

(iii) **More cooperation, deeper integration**    The vWTO is an efficient "breach" contract and as such largely replicates the outcome of the unachievable Pareto-efficient complete contingent contract. The prospect of increased compliance through the inclusion of the optimal escape scheme in a trade agreement will induce all contracting policy-makers to consent to the politically optimal level of trade liberalization in the initial negotiations, as was shown in sections 6.2.2 and 6.2.3, respectively. This result, generated in a simple tariff-setting model, can quite possibly be generalized to include all entitlements traded in the WTO and vWTO.

Policy-makers participating in the initial negotiations do not risk much but gain a lot from including additional and more sensitive issue areas (i.e. sectors that are more likely to be affected by political support

[56] This finding is in disagreement with various IR scholars (e.g. Goldstein *et al.* 2000; Goldstein and Martin 2000; Smith 2000; Yarbrough and Yarbrough 1987; 1997), who contend that there exists a "domestic political trade-off between treaty compliance and policy discretion" (Smith 2000, p. 138).

shocks) into the Agreement. A broader range of trade topics and industries can thus be included into the efficient trade deal of the vWTO.

**(iv) Fewer disputes, increased trust in the system, freer trade, and more expected welfare**    A trade agreement which is selective between good- and bad-faith behavior, which is more stable, fosters broader and deeper cooperation between trading partners, and induces increased compliance with the rules, will necessarily yield fewer disputes, more trust, higher levels of welfare, and freer trade. We explain each in turn.

The vWTO allows its Members to engage in efficient "breach" whatever the underlying contingency. This reduces the DSB caseload, since previous opt-outs in the form of violation-cum-retaliation can now be dealt with intra-contractually. So far, violation of the Agreement is being abused as an informal flexibility mechanism for reasons of opportunistic guile, and for want of an intra-contractual alternative. The vWTO, however, dispenses with such behavior. Only interpretative problems in connection with contracting errors can be expected to be brought before the DSB. Since the vWTO's structure is much simpler than the current-day Agreement (no contingent language, negative integration provisions, or contingency measures), the remaining interpretative problems will be less numerous. The workload of the DSB is reduced.

Trust in the system is generated by the injurers' certainty of being able to seize regret contingencies whenever they occur. Victims can be sure they will not suffer from the exercise of trade policy flexibility mechanisms. Disputes are less frequent, and flat-out non-cooperative behavior rare. The vWTO surpasses the current contractual framework in all these aspects. A virtuous circle is initiated: trust in the system is rewarded by freer trade (more depth and breadth of *ex ante* cooperation commitments). A higher *ex ante* promise leads to higher per-period payoffs, which increases the expected welfare that parties can hope to reap, which again fosters Members' trust in the trading order.

### 6.5.3   The vWTO: a "better" contract?

Does this mean that the hypothetical vWTO constitutes an objectively "good" contract? There are two points to make. First, the vWTO is the most *efficient* contract for self-interested and reasonably rational policymakers, given the contractual circumstances, constraints, and trade-offs that the bargaining context entails. The vWTO is the first-best treaty that policy-makers can achieve. This makes it a "good" contract from the selfish point of view of the negotiating policy-makers.

Secondly, whether the outcome of the vWTO can be referred to as good, fair, equitable, or just, lies in the eye of the beholder. These terms are not only inherently subjective, but also relative concepts, and this is not the place to delve into a discussion of justice or fairness.[57] If by "good contract" the observer means to say that the vWTO should be conducive to the *general global welfare* of non-signatories (such as consumers and producers worldwide) then we must leave the design of a "good contract" to future research. We can only offer conjectures here: the fact that the hypothetical vWTO makes the contract more stable, more reliable, more incentive compatible, and induces country governments to be more compliant, cheat less, liberalize more industries, make bigger tariff cuts, and include more issue areas in the trade deal, would suggest that the vWTO contract should at least not be judged as outrightly pernicious to global welfare.

However, a couple of caveats have to be taken into account. For one, in a contract like the vWTO, where governments can step back from nearly any entitlement they have previously committed to, the predictability and stability of market access, and a level playing field of competition for all non-signatory actors, must suffer. The exercise of *ex post* discretion, and the occurrence of possible tariff retaliations, severely affect the international trading activity. Consumers and producers cannot easily foresee which political support contingencies will prompt self-interested policy-makers to withdraw from which commitments. This volatility in the global trading order may induce the private sector to invest less, trade less, or consume less than would be efficient.

Also, the optimal *ex ante* trade liberalization levels for policy-makers are potentially a far cry from what would constitute optimal general-welfare

---

[57] The benchmark for our construction of the hypothetical vWTO was efficiency, as seen from the perspective of self-interested policy-makers. If this concept of Pareto-efficiency clashes with someone's notions of fairness and justice, they may overlook that both efficiency and fairness are best understood as relative, rather than absolute concepts in this situation. It is the power of the factual – unalterable contextual real-life constraints – that sets the limits for what is ultimately achievable, and hence efficient *and just*. If one accepts that the ideals of fairness, equity, justice, etc., just like the one of efficiency, have to obey a set of inevitable constraints, all of the former principles must collapse with the notion of efficiency. If one is not willing to discount the concepts of fairness, equity, or distributional justice for factual parameters, then one must accept that these ideals "must take a back seat" (Downs, Rocke, and Barsoom 1996, p. 386) in the face of real-life constraints, and agents' selfish preferences in particular.

levels of commitment. Consumers may see trade liberalization concessions from political trade agreements as overzealous or insufficient,
depending on the nature of their utility functions.[58] Finally, any sort of
remedy payment in the form of tariff compensation, or punishment in
the form of retaliation taken in response to a trade policy flexibility
measure, does not benefit the harmed export sector (nor, for that matter,
the sector which is liberalized as compensation). Hence, any rebalancing
of commitments occurs with an eye to the concerned policy-makers, but
not necessarily for the benefit of the involved industries.[59]

In summary, non-signatory stakeholders (especially consumers and
exporters) generally benefit from the improved contractual framework of
the vWTO. However, more research should be conducted in this area.

---

[58] This, however, equally goes for the current WTO regime, where trade protection is even
higher than in the hypothetical vWTO.

[59] This flaw is also inherent in the contemporary WTO system, and can only be overcome
by means of monetary compensation dispensed to the victim industries.

# 7

# Towards an efficient "breach" contract: an agenda for reform

Having assessed in the previous chapter what the WTO would look like as an EBC and how reasonably rational governments would optimally design a system of contractual non-performance, we can now proceed to suggesting an agenda for reform. This chapter provides a conclusion to the entire study, precisely because without the detailed analysis of previous chapters this reform agenda would be just another *ad hoc* change request to join the ranks of the many that WTO scholarship has seen so far. The following reform proposals are built on firm foundations, since they lay out a politically realistic (read: incentive compatible), systemically viable, and efficient system of flexibility and enforcement in the WTO.

The following presents ways in which the contemporary WTO could be shifted onto the trajectory of the achievable first-best: the efficient "breach" contract. The results of Chapter 6, which characterized the hypothetical bargain of the vWTO, can be operationalized and put into effect by changing the text of the current contract. We have worked out a "shortlist" and a richer catalog of reform suggestions. The shortlist (section 7.1) contains those improvements towards an efficient "breach" contract which are most urgent and/or possess the largest reform leverage. The extensive catalog (section 7.2) sketches comprehensive and long-term changes and amendments required to develop a coherent and sustainable institutional system of non-performance in the WTO. Section 7.3 concludes and presents a research outlook.

## 7.1 The shortlist of reform

Chapter 6 characterized how the WTO would look, if it were rigorously geared towards efficiency from the point of view of self-interested policymakers: each entitlement would be optimally indefinite, and protected by a single operable rule of default and by the DSU as a second line of defense. We are aware that turning the current WTO into an EBC is a long-term (and probably very idealistic) endeavor. This section presents the three most pressing reform steps which can deliver the largest "reform traction." These steps are:

(i) the institution of a default rule of liability for the market access entitlement;
(ii) the implementation of a common default rule for all multiple coordination entitlements;
(iii) a reform of the current system of enforcement.

With this shortlist, which involves GATT Art. XIX (and GATS Art. X), a novel Art. Xbis in the WTO Agreement, and DSU Art. 22, the WTO should establish some progress towards an efficient system of non-performance.

### 7.1.1 Establish a revised GATT Art. XIX[1]

A crucial first step in the reform proposal is to refashion GATT Art. XIX, which currently serves as a contingency measure for economic emergencies, into Art. XIX(rev.), the default rule for the market access entitlement. Modeled on the specifications of the vWTO (section 6.2 above) the liability rule of flexibility should display the following characteristics.

*No preconditions and a minimum of constraints on the application scope.* In an incomplete contract a default rule of flexibility should not be impeded by a high level of conditionality (cf. at p. 286 above). Every injurer should be able to enact the revamped GATT Art. XIX(rev.) for any reason and at any time, inasmuch as the country is willing to grant tariff compensation amounting to victims' expectancy. The use of the DR is to be regulated by a minimum of constraining provisions. Apart from the obligation that protectionism be confined to an increase in tariff instruments only, few conditions apply to the enactment of Art. XIX(rev.). Resort to *ex post* escape can happen at short notice, be discriminatory in nature, be enacted on a temporary or medium term, and be invoked following any fathomable contingency.

*Compensation, not retaliation, as the remedy of choice.* For reasons of efficiency, remedies payable to victim(s) are to be made in the form of tariff compensation (see at p. 287 above). Therefore, any reference to

---

[1] GATS Art. X should be reformed in a similar way for the trade in services. For reasons of space we only discuss the reform of trade policy flexibility here for trade in goods.

the suspension of concessions, such as in Art. XIX.3(a) of the contemporary GATT, is to be eliminated.

*Binding arbitration.* An important component of GATT Art. XIX(rev.) is the introduction of mandatory arbitration that sets in if no swift mutually agreed solution is reached. The WTO arbitration authority, which may be composed of dispute panelists (although acts of opt-out pursuant to Art. XIX(rev.) are not to be conceived of as disputes), must be impartial, competent, and enjoy general authority.

*Insert a mandate for expectation damages.* Article XIX.3(a) of the contemporary GATT speaks of "substantially equivalent" damages that the victim of a safeguard measure can assert. As explained at p. 234 above, WTO arbitrators have wrongly interpreted this term as prospective direct trade damages, i.e. remedies roughly satisfying the reliance damage definition. To avoid substantial flaws of this sort, and to institute the incentive compatible remedy of expectation damages (cf. at p. 280 above), GATT Art. XIX(rev.) must put into unambiguous terms that the benchmark for remedies is the expectation damage measure only.

GATT Art. XIX revised according to the above principles could read as follows:[2]

> Article XIX(rev.) (*Special Action on Imports of Particular Products*)[3]
>
> 1. A Member shall be free to temporarily withdraw or modify concessions in respect of any product by resorting to a tariff measure.
>
> 2. Before a Member can take the special action pursuant to provisions of Paragraph 1 of this Article, it shall give notice in writing to the Members as far in advance as may be practicable and shall provide adequate opportunity for prior consultations with those Members having a substantial interest as exporters of the product concerned. In critical circumstances where delay would cause damage difficult to repair, action under Paragraph 1 of this Article may be taken provisionally without prior consultation, on the condition that consultations shall be effected immediately after taking such action.
>
> 3. If agreement among the interested Members with respect to the action is not reached, the Member which proposes to take or continue the action shall, nevertheless, be free to do so, if it maintains a general level of reciprocal and mutually advantageous market access concessions not less favourable to trade than that provided for in this Agreement prior to such negotiations. To achieve this precept, the Member shall provide means of

---

[2] Some passages follow Roitinger's suggested diction (Roitinger 2004, p. 194).

[3] Please note that the following suggestions do not fulfill the formal requirements of an official amendment proposal. Our representation is driven by reading convenience, not by legalistic revision criteria.

trade compensation which put the adversely affected Members in as good a position as had the Member applying the measure performed as promised. This includes nullification and impairment that has accrued since the date of the enactment of the measure in question. Compensation is mandatory and shall be consistent with the covered agreements.

    4. (a)  A standing arbitrator[4] is established. Resort to arbitration can be requested by any Member involved whenever no agreement on trade compensation is reached between the Member applying the measure in question and the exporting parties which are affected by such a measure.

    (b)  The arbitrator grants tariff compensation awards according to Paragraph 3, Sentence 2, of this Article.

    (c)  The parties shall accept the arbitrator's decision as final.

GATT Art. XIX(rev.) allows WTO Members to capture any type of regret contingency. Injuring countries can act independently of the confining language of other GATT contingency measures.[5] The term "temporarily" in paragraph 1 is chosen to distinguish Art. XIX(rev.) from GATT Art. XXVIII, a relationship that will have to be clarified in the course of a broader revision of the GATT (more on that below). Paragraph 2 of the modified GATT Art. XIX(rev.) leaves room for WTO Members to reach mutually agreed solutions. In renouncing any timelines, and granting any involved Member the right of instantaneous appeal to arbitration, strategic hold-out games by victims or injurers during this negotiation phase are eliminated. Mandatory compensation amounting to (prospective) expectation damages indemnifies victims adequately for their harm suffered (see paragraph 3 above). Compensation must be in compliance with the general rules of the WTO, but there is no obligation to offer compensatory liberalization on an MFN basis. Compensation is owed to the victim(s) of the measure only.[6]

---

[4] "The expression 'arbitrator' shall be interpreted according to the specifications laid down in Art. 22 of the Understanding on Rules and Procedures Governing the Settlement of Disputes."

[5] Note that GATT Art. XIX(rev.) would replace the entire Agreement on Safeguards.

[6] We believe that authors like Anderson (2002); Charnovitz (2001); Pauwelyn (2000); Roitinger (2004); and Schropp (2005) are wrong in arguing that the wording "Compensation ... if granted, shall be consistent with the covered agreements" (DSU Art. 22.1(3)) means that compensation must be offered on a *non-discriminatory MFN* basis. The covered Agreements often provide for exceptions to the MFN principle (e.g. GATT Art. XXIV, the enabling clause, DSU Art. 22.2), yet these provisions are equally consistent with the covered Agreements. This sentence means that compensation must be in line with the general rules of the game, and it excludes prohibited behavior such as quantitative restrictions, VERs, OMAs, or export subsidies.

## 7.1.2    Add Art. Xbis to the WTO Agreement

It is not easy to discern a clear default rule protecting the numerous multilateral entitlements in the current WTO system. As we discussed at p. 248 above, it is not at all certain whether WTO Charter Art. X actually constitutes a rule of default, and if so, what it really means. Thus, step two of our reform agenda is to put in place an unambiguous default rule that covers all coordination entitlements. At p. 290 above, we showed that WTO Members should ideally examine every single multilateral entitlement for optimal protection, which can be a rule of inalienability, liquidated damages, or a property rule of renegotiation. However, cognizant of the fact that demanding an immediate enactment of this ideal design would overburden WTO Members in a first stage of WTO reforms, we propose a robust transitional solution. A novel Art. Xbis is to be added to the WTO Charter. That novel article stipulates a general default rule of renegotiation. Every Member which feels concerned is to veto temporary changes of multilateral entitlements.[7] Hence, Art. Xbis of the WTO Agreement could read like this:

> Article Xbis (*Modification Requests and Emergency Escape Measures*)
>
> 1. Any Member may, by negotiation and agreement with every Member affected or concerned, modify or withdraw a concession of this Agreement or the Multilateral Trade Agreements in Annexes 1, 2, and 3. Exempt from this provision are those concessions whose modifications and emergency escape measures are regulated directly in Annexes 1A and 1B.
>
> 2. In such negotiations and agreement, which may include provision for compensatory adjustment with respect to tariff liberalization in goods and services, the Members concerned shall endeavour to maintain a general level of reciprocal and mutually advantageous concessions not less favourable to the international trading system than provided for in this Agreement and its Annexes prior to such negotiations.
>
> 3. Any Member rejecting a modification or emergency escape request mentioned under Paragraph 1 of this Article shall deposit an instrument of rejection with the Director-General of the WTO within a period of 90 days after the beginning of the initial negotiations.
>
> 4. Modification and emergency escape requests of a Plurilateral Trade Agreement shall be governed by the provisions of that Agreement.

---

[7] Anticipatory and sophisticated Members will realize which multilateral entitlements are rationally protected by a rigid rule of inalienability, and will veto any corresponding request to escape, even if they do not feel directly affected by the requested measure. Bagatelle opt-outs (ideally protected by a liquidated damages rule), on the other hand, will not concern them.

The newly added Art. X*bis* of the WTO Agreement institutes a general rule of renegotiation for any entitlement, except for the market access entitlement, whose protection is regulated separately in the GATT/ GATS (see paragraph 1, sentence 2). The Member requesting escape has ninety days to come to terms with all those signatories which are affected by, or concerned about, the *ex post* escape request. Compensation offers by injuring Members are not limited to tariff measures, but can offer higher commitments in other obligations (e.g. higher minimum standards), as the wording in paragraph 2 suggests ("may include..."). Note that explicit consensus is not required for the measure to be enacted; a Member refusing the outcome of the renegotiations must officially submit a letter of rejection (see paragraph 3). This way, silent acquiescence can be achieved for minor cases of nonperformance.

### 7.1.3 Revise DSU Art. 22

The third pillar of the reform proposal is a reorganization of the WTO enforcement regime. We discussed at p. 242 above the problems inherent in the contemporary WTO system of enforcement, while at p. 295 above, we laid out in detail how enforcement should ideally be organized in the hypothetical vWTO. Our reform proposal is straightforward. Fortunately, the DSU deals with issues of enforcement in Art. 22 only. A revised version of that article should display the following characteristics.

*Introduction of hierarchy* and *chronology of enforcement instruments.* Enforcement under the current DSU Art. 22 displays a chronology of mutually accepted compensation, followed by the complainant's retaliation request, and (in case of objections against the requested retaliation schedule by the defendant) arbitration. Chronology, however, is not equivalent to hierarchy. Under the current DSU regime, defendants have little interest in either a mutually agreed solution or in serious compensation negotiations (see our discussion at p. 242 above, and Schropp 2005, section 3.4). Thus, the defendants' incentive structure has to be changed. This is achieved by a two-step procedure. As laid out at p. 295 above the first stage of enforcement (the dispute stage) is driven by the goal of achieving a mutually agreed solution after the panel report is circulated, or at least an amicable resolution of the dispute. Therefore, if negotiations over a mutually agreed solution break down after a period of thirty days, mandatory arbitration sets in. At this first stage, the arbitrator is confined to awarding tariff compensation amounting to full expectation damages to the complaining party, which the defendant is encouraged to accept.

If the defending party stays recalcitrant, the second stage of enforcement (the punishment stage) sets in. The arbitrator is authorized to award punitive damages. How best to bring the recalcitrant injurer into compliance is the subject of an elaborate escalation scheme, which is to be designed at a later stage of the larger reform agenda (see below). This two-prong enforcement scheme gives effect to the chronology of compensation and retaliation by establishing an incentive hierarchy of instruments.

An overhauled DSU Art. 22(rev.) could read like this:

> Article 22(rev) (*Compensation and Suspension of Concessions*)[8]
>
> 1. Compensation and the suspension of concessions or other obligations are temporary measures available in the event that the recommendations and rulings are not implemented within a reasonable period of time. However, neither compensation nor the suspension of concessions or other obligations is preferred to full implementation of a recommendation to bring a measure into conformity with the covered agreements. Compensation is *mandatory* and, if granted, shall be consistent with the covered agreements.
>
> 2. If the Member concerned fails to bring the measure found to be inconsistent with a covered agreement into compliance therewith or otherwise comply with the recommendations and rulings within the reasonable period of time determined pursuant to paragraph 3 of Article 21, such Member shall, if so requested, and no later than the expiry of the reasonable period of time, enter into negotiations with any party having invoked the dispute settlement procedures, with a view to developing mutually acceptable compensation. If no satisfactory compensation has been agreed within 30 days after the date of expiry of the reasonable period of time, *any party having invoked the dispute settlement procedures shall refer the matter of compensation to arbitration. Such arbitration shall be carried out as determined in paragraph 3 of this Article.*
>
> 3. (a) *Arbitration shall be carried out by the original panel, if panel members are available, or by an arbitrator appointed by the Director-General and shall be completed within 60 days after the date of expiry of the reasonable period of time.*
>
>    (b) *The arbitrator shall present to the Member concerned a compensation package taking into consideration voluntary compensation concession offers granted under letter (d) of this Article.*

---

[8] DSU Art. 22(rev.) in parts uses the same wording as the original DSU Art. 22. For the ease of reading, novel wording is shown in italics to distinguish it from the current language.

(c) *The arbitrator* shall not examine the nature of *compensation* but shall determine whether the level of such *trade compensation puts the adversely affected Members in at least as good a position as if the Member applying the measure had performed as promised. This includes nullification and impairment that has accrued since the date of request for consultations, as well as litigation costs incurred, and benefits foregone due to the violating measure. Punitive compensation awards that put the Member applying the measure into a worse position than had it performed shall be avoided.*

(d) *In considering compensation, the Member concerned may provide the DSB and the arbitrator with a compensation package apt to re-establish the general level of reciprocal and mutually advantageous market access concessions not less favourable to trade than that provided for in this Agreement prior to the nullification and impairment. Compensation offers must be in accordance with the rules and regulations of the covered Agreements.*

(e) *The parties shall accept the arbitrator's decision as final and the parties concerned shall not seek a second arbitration.*

4. *If the Member concerned fails to implement the arbitrator's decision and to bring the measure found to be inconsistent with a covered agreement into compliance therewith or otherwise to comply with the recommendations and rulings within, the matter shall again be referred to arbitration. The arbitrator authorizes the suspension of concessions or other obligations under the covered agreements. Concessions or other obligations shall not be suspended during the course of the arbitration.*

5. (a) *The arbitrator acting pursuant to paragraph 4 shall not examine the nature of the concessions or other obligations to be suspended but shall determine the adequate level of such suspension.*

(b) *The level of the suspension of concessions or other obligations authorized by the DSB shall be no less than what is needed to put adversely affected Members in at least as good a position as if the Member applying the measure had performed as promised.*

(c) The parties shall accept the arbitrator's decision as final and the parties concerned shall not seek a second arbitration.

6. [see original DSU Art. 22.3, except for the chapeau, which reads: In considering what concessions or other obligations to suspend, *the arbitrator* shall apply the following principles and procedures:]

7. [see original DSU Art. 22.5]

8. (a) *Suspension of concessions or other obligations authorized by the DSB can be enacted by the party having invoked the dispute settlement procedures, by Members affected by the measure in question, or by Members concerned with the functioning of the world trading system.*

(b) *If pursuant to the enactment of suspension of concessions or other obligations authorized by the DSB the Member concerned remains in default and declines to bring the measure found to be*

> *inconsistent with a covered agreement into compliance therewith*
> *or otherwise to comply with the recommendations and rulings*
> *within, the DSB by consensus can decide to withdraw certain*
> *membership rights.*

DSU Art. 22(rev.) sets in place an enforcement hierarchy that actually works: the *dispute stage* (paragraphs 1 to 4) leaves enough room to clarify ambiguities and to settle the dispute amicably, whilst the *punishment stage* sanctions the injuring Member's recalcitrance and coerces it into swift compliance.

Paragraph 1 is to strengthen the procedural role of tariff compensation by making it mandatory (see Lindsey *et al.* 1999; Schropp 2005, section 4.2). Whenever settlement negotiations break down, paragraph 3 prescribes mandatory arbitration, which is basically to proceed as in GATT Art. XIX(rev.) (see discussion above). Paragraph 3(c) stipulates a "compensation floor" of expectation damages for the complainant by explicitly mentioning retroactivity, litigation costs, and profits foregone. This compensation floor allows the arbitrator to include in its damage calculation the victims' share of the injurer's efficiency gains from non-performance. As discussed earlier (see Chapter 6, note 52 and accompanying text), adding some of the spoils from non-performance is important for the protection of multilateral entitlements backed by a property rule. However, paragraph 3(c) also puts a "compensation cap" on the arbitrator's quantification efforts: punitive elements are contained in the dispute stage of enforcement. Paragraph 3(d) provides the defendant with the opportunity to voluntarily submit a pre-selected list of compensation commitments.[9] When calculating the compensation awards, it is up to the arbitrator to decide whether to take into consideration the compensation package offered and whether trade liberalization in those respective industries is apt to suit the complainant's rebalancing needs.

Paragraphs 4 to 8 of DSU Art. 22(rev.) specify the punishment stage of enforcement. As opposed to the current design of DSU Arts. 22.2 and

---

[9] The reader might be reminded of Lawrence's suggestion of "contingent liberalization commitments" (see Lawrence 2003, chapter 5). The present proposal, however, is of a different nature: we do not suggest that Members negotiate their precommitted sectors up-front in a multilateral setting. Rather, a losing defendant can unilaterally submit an ad hoc list of "liberalizable" sectors to a specific complainant in the dispute at hand. Strategic and political deliberations on the part of the defendant under Lawrence's and our own proposal will be quite different (not to speak of the practical and organizational consequences that affect the entire system under Lawrence's proposal).

22.3, we do not interpose the (largely futile) step of a formal retaliation request to the DSB by the complainant. Instead, whenever the convicted defendant Member chooses to ignore its obligation in the dispute stage of enforcement, the arbitrator re-enters the scene immediately. The arbitrator sanctions retaliation awards and determines the mix of sectors to be targeted according to paragraph 6. Punitive damages are possible, with expectation damages as the remedy floor (see paragraph 5(b)). The collective nature of retaliation is regulated in paragraph 8(a), while further escalation is possible under paragraph 8(b).

## 7.2 Long-term reform proposals

The reform of only three articles in the WTO contract yields substantial mileage. It would pave most of the way towards turning the current system of trade policy flexibility and enforcement into an EBC. WTO Members experiencing a political support shock would prefer to use the readily available DR instead of most (in)formal tools of escape, and especially the strategy of violation-cum-retaliation. Tariff compensation amounting to the expectation damage remedy would be instituted and would insure victims optimally. Stricter enforcement would deter opportunistic Members from overtly infringing upon the rules of the game.

However, more work needs to be done to eventually convert the current WTO contract into the vWTO, the contracting ideal of the EBC as portrayed in Chapter 6 above. Various grander-scale reform schemes need to be tackled, and remaining loopholes and inconsistencies of the current institutional framework must be closed in the long term. More research must flow into an endeavor of that dimension. We sketch the broad contours of a grander long-term reform agenda concerning the market access entitlements (section 7.2.1), multilateral entitlements (section 7.2.2.), and WTO enforcement (section 7.2.3).

### 7.2.1 *Reforming the protection of the market access entitlement*

There are three long-term reform endeavors concerning the market access entitlement:

(i) make the GATT and GATS leaner;
(ii) overhaul the current system on antidumping and countervailing duties;
(iii) clarify the relationship between GATT Arts. XIX(rev.) and XXVIII, and GATS Arts. X and XXI, respectively.

(i) **Make the GATT and GATS leaner** The contemporary WTO is far from the optimally non-contingent contract that the hypothetical ideal of the vWTO stipulates. The GATT, with its appending Agreements in particular, features various contingency measures and negative integration provisions that must be seen as insufficient and unwise attempts to fight contractual incompleteness (see Chapter 5, p. 238, at note 61 and accompanying text). Goods and services Agreements should become leaner. Trade negotiators should carefully examine whether in light of the unconditional rules of default, contingency measures like GATT Arts. XXII, XVIII, or XX are still relevant. In the same vein, negative integration provisions as featured in the TBT, SPS, or GPA should be tested for relevance.

(ii) **Revise AD and CvD regimes**[10] An important objective of the trading community should be a fundamental reform of the AD and CvD codes of the WTO. As stated at p. 226 above, it seems evident that AD and CvD actions today are predominantly used as opt-out tools for protectionist reasons, and that the recourse to them as "unfair trade remedies" is a barely veiling fig-leaf.[11] In fact, AD and CvD can be accurately described as a property rule of protection *granted to the injurer*. It is time Members tackled the reform of the two codes in a manner that fits the WTO's mandate and original intent.

A fundamental overhaul of AD and CvD regimes would consist of (a) an agreed-upon set of core definitions and principles;[12] (b) a minimum of technical reforms;[13] (c) a serious reduction of national discretion, a less lenient standard of deference, and a consideration of basic economic reasoning (cf. discussion at Chapter 5, p. 226, note 32 and accompanying

---

[10] This paragraph is adapted from Schropp 2005, section 4.1.

[11] According to Messerlin (2000, p. 163), less than 10 percent of all antidumping cases have even the slightest chance of being considered as "predatory" or "strategic dumping," the two only economically noxious categories (Willig 1998). According to the authors, the vast majority of AD measures are driven by protectionist motivation, and thus constitute protectionist escape actions.

[12] A binding set of definitions and principles could finally give answers to important questions like: What is dumping and why is it harmful? What are fundamental objectives and justifications for AD and CvD action? What exactly constitutes remediable "unfair trade"? Nowhere in the AD Agreement or elsewhere in the GATT is there an attempt to define the basic economic and social precepts, principles, and objectives that would justify AD action. There is mention of how "dumping" is determined, but not what exactly makes it pernicious.

[13] See Schropp 2005, note 59 for explanations.

text). Since both AD and CvD have hardly any economic basis anyway,[14] it would be best eventually to do away with the two codes completely and integrate AD and CvD into domestic competition law.[15]

**(iii) Clarify the relationship between GATT Arts. XIX(rev.) and XXVIII** A final long-term project that needs to be tackled by trade negotiators once GATT Art. XIX is revised is the relationship between the default rule and the provision of permanent modification of tariff schedules (GATT Art. XXVIII).[16] Under a DR as proposed, an article on tariff renegotiation may be superfluous. WTO Members would benefit from a further examination of this point.

### 7.2.2 Reforming the protection of multilateral entitlements

With regard to the efficient protection of the various multilateral entitlements, we suggest two long-term reform topics. First, as explained at p. 295 above, not every multilateral entitlement is best protected by the same default rule. It seems crucial that trade negotiators convene and analyze every multilateral entitlement for its optimal protection rule. As stated in Chapter 6, there are three ways of protecting those coordination entitlements: by inalienability, by liquidated damages, and by a rule of renegotiation. The new Art. X*bis* added to the WTO Charter, albeit a robust interim solution, should be redrafted to comprise three sections, one for each default rule. Entitlements in the Agreements should then explicitly refer back to one of those three sections, so that every multilateral entitlement traded in the entire WTO is protected by a clear and unambiguous rule of default.

A second task for WTO negotiators is to clarify (define) the relationship between WTO Charter Art. X (dealing with amendments of the

---

[14] "Although economic theory identifies a few plausible scenarios in which antidumping measures might enhance economic efficiency, the law remains altogether untailored to identifying them or limiting the use of antidumping measures to plausible cases of efficiency gain" (Sykes 1998, p. 2).

[15] Antitrust agencies deal with anticompetitive and monopolistic tendencies on a daily basis and thus would appear to be the obvious candidates for assessing unfair practice in international trade (Barfield 2005; Messerlin 2000). Profound reform proposals of WTO laws on AD and CvD can be found in Bown (2002b); Hoekman and Mavroidis (1996); and Lindsey and Ikenson (2003). Most of these authors discuss the substitution of AD by antitrust regulation. Horlick and Palmer (2002) focus on the relationship between CvD and antitrust. Roitinger (2004, p. 193) offers an extensive literature review.

[16] The same goes for the relationship between GATS Arts. X and XXI.

contract) and Art. X*bis* (dealing with modification and emergency measures). It is not yet clear how these two rules can be reconciled sensibly to function side by side.

### 7.2.3   Reforming the WTO enforcement regime

Once WTO enforcement has been changed by virtue of DSU Art. 22(rev.), in the long run WTO Members should convene to improve the protection of multilateral entitlements. Clearly, if an inalienable entitlement is infringed upon, the entire dispute phase of enforcement must be skipped. In the same vein, the way arbitrators deal with compensation calculations in the dispute stage, pursuant to infringement of a multilateral entitlement, needs to be clarified, elaborated, and cast into treaty language. A second important long-term goal is the design of efficient guidelines for collective retaliation. These guidelines should include suggestions concerning which Members/Member groups should participate in the suspension of concessions, at what stage, and to what extent.[17] As a third step, signatories should draft guidelines that contain details of the escalation scheme design of retaliation and sanctions.[18]

### 7.3   Final remarks and future research

In Shakespeare's *Hamlet*, astonished Horatio inquires whether drunken revels are a common pastime pleasure at the Danish Court. Prince Hamlet disapproves of the frequent binge-drinking of his compatriots, and proclaims that, albeit a Danish native himself (and hence "to the manner born), it is a custom / More honour'd in the breach than the observance."[19] In today's parlance the Shakespearean dictum "more honored in the breach than the observance" has lost its negative connotation and is used to express that sometimes a practice, convention,

---

[17] We should think of an arrangement which stipulates that only affected Members retaliate collectively in a first stage. If that proves ineffective (or inoperable, if only developing countries are the affected victims), large industrialized Members such as the United States, European Union, and Japan join the ranks of sanctioning countries. Details of these guidelines need to be contractually fixed in the long term.

[18] Issues here include the progression of sanctions over time. The longer the offending Member stays recalcitrant the more penalties are ratcheted up. Also, the question must be tackled as to whether (and if so, when) essential membership rights should be suspended in order to bring the injurer into compliance.

[19] William Shakespeare, *Hamlet*, Act I, Scene 4 (available at www.gutenberg.org/etext/2265).

rule, or belief is better ignored (breached) than observed – even though it may have been previously deemed to be desirable. This study has dealt with the question when, under which circumstances, and at what price, a "breach" of WTO rules is more beneficial to the international trading order than strict adherence to the original commitments.

We provided an introduction to incomplete contracts; performed a comprehensive contract-theoretical analysis of the World Trade Organization; established the WTO as a necessarily incomplete contract; assessed the flaws of the contemporary system of entitlement protection, trade policy flexibility, and enforcement in the international trading order; conducted a hypothetical bargain analysis of what the WTO could look like if it were properly designed; and suggested concrete steps of reform towards turning the WTO into an efficient "breach" contract.

The study stressed and clarified the intricate connection between contractual incompleteness, intra-contractual trade policy flexibility mechanisms, contract enforcement, and Members' willingness to commit to trade liberalization. We gave substance to the concept of efficient "breach" (better: "efficient non-performance"), and elaborated what that concept means in the international trade context and how it can be effectuated in the WTO. We identified the weaknesses of the current regime of trade flexibility and enforcement in the WTO, including the systemic and dynamic consequences thereof. The resultant reform agenda is concrete, substantiated, politically realistic, and systemically viable.

A lot of theoretical ground was covered in the course of this study. We are aware that we often painted with a broad brush and at times slurred over issues which deserve greater attention and closer consideration. In order to focus on the most salient questions, and due to the natural limitations of such a study, we left open numerous issues. Among those there are four unresolved, which must be passed on to WTO scholarship. These challenges would make worthwhile subjects of future research.

**Rationale for trade agreements** No examination of a contract is complete without a clear understanding of what drives signatories to strike an agreement in the first place. Our analysis at p. 181 above revealed that current trade scholarship is unfortunately far from answering comprehensively why sovereign countries engage in trade cooperation. Whilst economic, political, and legal explanations seem able to elucidate facets of the cooperative motivation, scholarship has not captured the whole picture. More work needs to be done that produces testable results as to which of the numerous approaches (or which combination of approaches) best manages to explain countries' resolve to engage in trade cooperation in the form of a written treaty. Cross-disciplinary work seems a fruitful and promising avenue for future research.

**Coordination entitlements**    We perceive a relative neglect of non-market access entitlements in trade scholarship. Pauwelyn (2006) stated that the WTO contains more than just reciprocal market access entitlements. It was our aim to put this finding into practice by dismantling the WTO contract into its constituent entitlements. We showed that the WTO is best conceptualized as a bundle of single-issue contracts, consisting of the prominent market access entitlement but also of substantive minimum standard entitlements, as well as of various auxiliary entitlements. While much work in WTO scholarship has concentrated on the reciprocal exchange of market access and tariff liberalization concessions, it is remarkable that research on the multilateral entitlements exchanged in international trade agreements is scarce. Formal economic work in particular should be welcomed. It is high time for political economists to leave behind the prisoners' dilemma set-up and to dedicate energy into alternative collective-action games of strategy in order to explain other facets of trade cooperation.

**Nature of trade disputes**    As discussed at p. 128 above, any trade scholar whose object of research is "enforcement mechanisms" or "dispute settlement" ought to have a proper theory of disputes. How can anybody propose novel tools and improved instruments for settling disputes, if he or she does not demonstrate an understanding of the very nature of disputes? For WTO experts, academics, practitioners and policy-makers alike, learning more about how disputes arise and why they escalate should be an issue of great importance. We have proposed a few tentative steps towards a more coherent theory of disputes; much more work needs to be done.

**How to measure expectation damages?**[20]    Measuring expectation damages will be a tough call for WTO arbitrators: all trade agreements are inherently *political* deals designed and concluded by self-interested policy-makers. Hence, the initial balance of concessions and the entire metric of the WTO is presumably profoundly political. Yet arbitrators

---

[20]  This paragraph draws in parts on Schropp 2005, section 4.4.

can neither observe nor measure the political harm done to a victim government by its trade partner's unilateral policy adjustment. How can arbitrators ever claim to be able to calculate, in tangible currency, political expectation damages? How then can they credibly assert to be able to re-establish a profoundly political balance of welfare if political expectation damages are unverifiable?

There is no immediate solution to this conundrum. A couple of comments are nevertheless in order. First, the restoration of expectation damages to the injured party is the correct instrument to measure remedies. It would be imprudent to condemn the endeavor of quantification and monetization of efficiency losses just because it seems challenging.[21] Secondly, novel approaches to the quantification of victims' harm have recently been undertaken.[22] The quality of these attempts remains to be seen.

One promising way of calculating expectation damages could be to check the work of the neighboring fields of competition and antitrust. Competition authorities have a long track-record of applying coherent economic reasoning when defining relevant markets, market potentials, and damages, including profits foregone (cf. Neven 2000). Another possibility is more heuristic in nature: WTO scholars could assess how Members actually proceed when engaging in tariff renegotiations under GATT Art. XXVIII. Although parties do not thereby issue exact figures and numbers, they nevertheless come up with tangible results which take into account the expected harm done by the protectionist impact of a tariff bound increase. The insights generated from studying how the involved WTO Members manage to generate objective outcomes from this subjective renegotiation task may well lead to a general quantification framework.

---

[21] As Mavroidis (2000, p. 769) concurs: "The fact though that full recovery [i.e. expectation damages] is, in practice, sometimes hard to calculate, does not render the reparation exercise meaningless ... Although assessment of damages is the task of the judge, calculation of the damage is essentially a quantification exercise, that is, essentially the task of the economist." Ultimately, the calculation of expectation losses is a technical and empirical task to be conducted by specialists. If WTO arbitrators are not prepared to execute economic analyses of this kind today, the WTO should improve its economic competence rather than drop the task for reasons of practicality. The fact that the DSB could benefit more from the resources of the WTO Economic Research and Statistics Division and puts insufficient effort into economic and econometric reasoning is a different story, and one that could be remedied quite easily.

[22] See Breuss 2004; Josling 2004; Keck 2004; Spamann 2006; Trachtman 2006. See also the forthcoming edited volume on the calculation of trade damages in WTO dispute settlement (Bown and Pauwelyn 2009).

# BIBLIOGRAPHY

Abbott, K. and Snidal, D. 1998. "Why States Act through Formal International Organizations," *Journal of Conflict Resolution* 42(1): 3–32

Adler, E. 2002. "Constructivism in International Relations," in W. Carlsnaes, B. Simmons, and T. Risse (eds.), *Handbook of International Relations* (London/Thousand Oaks/New Delhi: Sage), pp. 95–118

Aggarwal, V. K. and Dupont, C. 1999. "Goods, Games and Institutions," *International Political Science Review* 20(4): 393–409

2004. "Collaboration and Coordination in the Global Political Economy," in J. Ravenhill (ed.), *Global Political Economy* (Oxford: Oxford University Press), pp. 28–49

Aghion, P., Dewatripont, M., and Rey, P. 1990. "On Renegotiation Design," *European Economic Review* 34(2–3): 322–329

1994. "Renegotiation Design with Unverifiable Information," *Econometrica* 62 (2): 257–282

Allison, G. 1971. *Essence of Decision: Explaining the Cuban Missile Crisis* (Boston, MA: Little Brown)

Anderson, K. 2002. "Peculiarities of Retaliation in WTO Dispute Settlement," CEPR Discussion Paper no. 3578

Axelrod, R. 1984. *The Evolution of Cooperation* (New York: Basic Books)

Axelrod, R. and Keohane, R. 1986. "Achieving Cooperation under Anarchy: Strategies and Institutions," *World Politics* 38(1): 226–254

Ayres, I. and Gertner, R. 1989. "Filling Gaps in Incomplete Contracts: an Economic Theory of Default Rules," *Yale Law Journal* 99(1): 87–130

1992. "Strategic Contractual Inefficiency and the Optimal Choice of Legal Rules," *Yale Law Journal* 101(4): 729–773

Ayres, I. and Talley, E. 1995a. "Distinguishing between Consensual and Nonconsensual Advantages of Liability Rules," *Yale Law Journal* 105(1): 235–253

1995b. "Solomonic Bargaining: Dividing a Legal Entitlement to Facilitate Coasean Trade," *Yale Law Journal* 104(5): 1027–1117

Bagwell, K. 2007. "Remedies in the WTO: an Economic Perspective." *Mimeo*

Bagwell, K., Mavroidis, P. C., and Staiger, R. W. 2002. "It's a Question of Market Access," *American Journal of International Law* 96(1): 56–76

2003. "The Case for Auctioning Countermeasures in the WTO," NBER Working Paper Series no. 9920

2005. "The Case for Tradeable Remedies in the WTO," in S. Evenett and B. Hoekman (eds.), *Economic Development and Multilateral Trade Cooperation* (Washington, DC: Palgrave/Macmillan and World Bank), pp. 56–76

Bagwell, K. and Staiger, R. W. 1990. "A Theory of Managed Trade," *American Economic Review* 80(4): 779–795

1997. "Multilateral Tariff Cooperation during the Formation of Free Trade Areas," *International Economic Review* 38(2): 291–319

1999. "An Economic Theory of GATT," *American Economic Review* 89(1): 215–248

2002a. "Economic Theory and the Interpretation of GATT/WTO," *American Economist* 46(2): 3–19

2002b. *The Economics of the World Trading System* (Cambridge, MA: MIT Press)

2005a. "Enforcement, Private Political Pressure and the GATT/WTO Escape Clause." *Mimeo*

2005b. "Enforcement, Private Political Pressure, and the General Agreement on Tariffs and Trade/World Trade Organization Escape Clause," *Journal of Legal Studies* 34: 471–513

Baird, D. G. 1990. "Self-Interest and Cooperation in Long-Term Contracts," *Journal of Legal Studies* 19(2): 583–596

Baldwin, D. A. (ed.) 1993. *Neorealism and Neoliberalism: the Contemporary Debate* (New York, NY: Columbia University Press)

Baldwin, R. 1987. "Politically Realistic Objective Functions and Trade Policy," *Economic Letters* 24: 287–290

1989. "The Political Economy of Trade Policy," *Journal of Economic Perspectives* 3(4): 119–135

Baran, P. A. 1967. *The Political Economy of Growth* (New York: Monthly Review Press)

Barfield, C. E. 2001. *Free Trade, Sovereignty, Democracy: the Future of the World Trade Organization* (Washington, DC: The AEI Press)

2005. "Anti-dumping Reform: Time to Go Back to Basics," *World Economy* 28 (5): 719–737

Barton, J. H., Goldstein, J., Josling, T. E., and Steinberg, R. H. 2006. *The Evolution of the Trade Regime* (Princeton and Oxford: Princeton University Press)

Barzel, Y. 1997. *Economic Analysis of Property Rights* (Cambridge: Cambridge University Press)

Battigalli, P. and Maggi, G. 2002. "Rigidity, Discretion, and the Costs of Writing Contracts," *American Economic Review* 92(4): 798–817

Bello, J. H. 1996. "The WTO Dispute Settlement Understanding: Less is More," *American Journal of International Law* 90(3): 416–418

Bernhardt, W., Broz, L., and Leblang, D. 2002. "Special Issue on the Political Economy of Monetary Institutions," *International Organization* (Autumn): 693–860

Bhagwati, J. 1988. *Protectionism* (Cambridge, MA: MIT Press)

2002. "The Unwinnable War," *Financial Times*, January 29

Bhandari, J. S. and Sykes, A. O. 1998. *Economic Dimensions in International Law: Comparative and Empirical Perspectives* (Cambridge: Cambridge University Press)

Blonigen, B. A. and Bown, C. P. 2003. "Antidumping and Retaliation Threats," *Journal of International Economics* 60(2): 249–273

Bown, C. P. 2001. "Antidumping Against the Backdrop of Disputes in the GATT/WTO System." *Mimeo*

2002a. "The Economics of Trade Disputes, the GATT's Article XXIII, and the WTO's Dispute Settlement Understanding," *Economics and Politics* 14(3): 283–322

2002b. "Why are Safeguards under the WTO So Unpopular?," *World Trade Review* 1(1): 47–62

2004. "On the Economic Success of GATT/WTO Dispute Settlement," *Review of Economics and Statistics* 86(3): 811–823

Bown, C. P. and Hoekman, B. 2005. "WTO Dispute Settlement and the Missing Developing Country Cases: Engaging the Private Sector," *Journal of International Economic Law* 8(4): 861–890

Bown, C. P. and Pauwelyn, J. 2009. *The Law, Economics and Politics of Trade Retaliation in WTO Dispute Settlement* (Cambridge: Cambridge University Press, forthcoming)

Brainard, L. S. and Verdier, T. 1994. "Lobbying and Adjustment in Declining Industries," *European Economic Review* 38(3–4): 586–595

Brander, J. 1987. "Rationales for Strategic Trade and Industrial Policy," in P. R. Krugman (ed.), *Strategic Trade Policy and the New International Economics* (Cambridge, MA: MIT Press), pp. 23–46

1995. "Strategic Trade Policy," in G. Grossman and K. Rogoff (eds.), *Handbook of International Economics* (Amsterdam: North Holland), pp. 1395–1455

Brander, J. and Spencer, B. 1985. "Export Subsidies and Market Share Rivalry," *Journal of International Economics* 18(1–2): 83–100

Breuss, F. 2004. "WTO Dispute Settlement: an Economic Analysis of Four EU–US Mine Trade Wars," *Journal of Industry, Competition and Trade* 4(4): 275–315

Bronckers, M. and van den Broek, N. 2005. "Financial Compensation in the WTO: Improving the Remedies of WTO Dispute Settlement," *Journal of International Economic Law* 8(1): 101–126

Bütler, M. and Hauser, H. 2002. "The WTO Dispute Settlement Mechanism: a First Assessment from an Economic Perspective," *Journal of Law, Economics, and Organization* 16(2): 503–533

Calabresi, G. and Melamed, A. D. 1972. "Property Rules, Liability Rules, and Inalienability: One View of the Cathedral," *Harvard Law Review* 85(6): 1089–1128

Carr, E. H. 1939. *The Twenty Years' Crisis, 1919–1939* (New York: Harper and Row)

Cass, D. Z. 2005. *The Constitutionalization of the WTO* (Oxford: Oxford University Press)

Charnovitz, S. 2001. "Rethinking WTO Trade Sanctions," *American Journal of International Law* 95(4): 792–832

2002a. "Should the Teeth be Pulled? An Analysis of WTO Sanctions," in D. L. M. Kennedy and J. D. Southwick (eds.), *Political Economy of International Trade Law: Essays in Honor of Robert E. Hudec* (Cambridge: Cambridge University Press), pp. 602–635

2002b. "Triangulating the World Trade Organization," *American Journal of International Law* 96(1): 28–55

2002c. "The WTO's Problematic 'Last Resort' Against Non-Compliance," *Aussenwirtschaft* 57(4): 409–440

Charny, D. 1991. "Hypothetical Bargains: the Normative Structure of Contract Interpretation," *Michigan Law Review* 89(7): 1815–1879

Chase-Dunn, C. 1998. *Global Formation: Structures of the World-Economy*, 2nd edn. (Lanham, MD: Rowman and Littlefield)

Chayes, A. and Chayes, A. H. 1990. "From Law Enforcement to Dispute Settlement," *International Security* 14(4): 147–164

1993a. *The New Sovereignty: Compliance with International Regulatory Agreements* (Cambridge, MA: Harvard University Press)

1993b. "On Compliance," *International Organization* 47(Spring): 175–205

1998. "The Constructivist Turn in International Relations Theory," *World Politics* 50(2): 324–348

Checkel, J. T. 1998. "The Constructivist Turn in International Relations Theory," *World Politics* 50(2): 324–348

Cheung, S. N. S. 1992. "On the New Institutional Economics," in L. Werin and H. Wijkander (eds.), *Contract Economics* (Oxford and Cambridge: Basil Blackwell), pp. 48–65

Chung, T.-Y. 1991. "Incomplete Contracts, Specific Investments, and Risk Sharing," *Review of Economic Studies* 58(5): 1031–1042

Coase, R. H. 1937. "The Nature of the Firm," *Economica, New Series* 4(16): 386–405

Cohen, G. M. 1999. "Implied Terms and Interpretation in Contract Law," in B. Bouckaert and G. de Geest (eds.), *Encyclopedia of Law and Economics* (Ghent: Edward Elgar/University of Ghent), pp. 78–99

Copeland, B. 1990. "Strategic Interaction Among Nations: Negotiable and Non-Negotiable Trade Barriers," *Canadian Journal of Economics* 23(1): 84–108

Craswell, R. 1993. "The Relational Move: Some Questions from Law and Economics," *Southern California Interdisciplinary Law Journal* 3: 91–114

1999. "Contract Law: General Theories," in B. Bouckaert and G. de Geest (eds.), *Encyclopedia of Law and Economics* (Ghent: Edward Elgar/University of Ghent), pp. 1–24

Dam, K. W. 1970. *The GATT: Law and International Economic Organization* (Chicago, IL: University of Chicago Press)

Davey, W. J. 2005a. "Evaluating WTO Dispute Settlement: What Results Have Been Achieved through Consultations and Implementation of Panel Reports?," paper presented at the Conference on the WTO at 10, Tokyo, Japan, October 25

2005b. "The Sutherland Report on Dispute Settlement: a Comment," *Journal of International Economic Law* 8(2): 321–328

de Bièvre, D. 2004. "Governance in International Trade: Judicialisation and Positive Integration in the WTO" (Bonn: Max Planck Institute for Research on Collective Goods), pp. 1–23. *Mimeo*

Diego-Fernandez, M. 2004. "Compensation and Retaliation: a Developing Country's Perspective." *Mimeo*

Dixit, A. 1987. "Strategic Aspects of Trade Policy," in T. F. Bewley (ed.), *Advances in Economic Theory: Fifth World Congress* (New York: Cambridge University Press), pp. 329–362

2007. *Lawlessness and Economics: Alternative Modes of Governance* (Princeton, NJ: Princeton University Press)

Downs, G. W. and Rocke, D. 1995. *Optimal Imperfection? Institutions and Domestic Politics in International Relations* (Ann Arbor, MI: University of Michigan Press)

Downs, G. W., Rocke, D. M., and Barsoom, P. N. 1996. "Is the Good News about Compliance Good News about Cooperation?," *International Organization* 50(3): 379–406

Drake, W. J and Nicolaïdis, K. 1992. "Ideas, Interests and Institutionalization: 'Trade in Services' and the Uruguay Round," in P. M. Haas (ed.), *Knowledge, Power, and International Policy Coordination* (Columbia: University of South Carolina Press), pp. 37–100

Dunoff, J. L. and Trachtman, J. P. 1999. "Economic Analysis of International Law," *Yale Journal of International Law* 24(Winter): 1–55

Eaton, J. and Grossman, G. 1986. "Optimal Trade and Industrial Policy under Oligopoly," *Quarterly Journal of Economics* 51(2): 383–406

Edlin, A. S. and Reichelstein, S. 1996. "Holdups, Standard Breach Remedies, and Optimal Investment," *American Economic Review* 86(3): 478–501

Ethier, W. J. 1998. "Regionalism in a Multilateral World," *Journal of Political Economy* 106(6): 1214–1245

2001a. "Punishments and Dispute Settlement in Trade Agreements," PIER Working Paper no. 01–21

2001b. "Theoretical Problems in Negotiating Trade Liberalization," *European Journal of Political Economy* 17(2): 209–232

2002. "Escape and Entry Mechanisms in the Multilateral Trading System," PIER Working Paper no. 02–009

2004a. "Intellectual Property Rights and Dispute Settlement in the World Trade Organization," *Journal of International Economic Law* 7(2): 449–457

2004b. "Political Externalities, Nondiscrimination, and a Multilateral World," *Review of International Economics* 12(3): 303

2004c. "Trade Policies Based on Political Externalities: an Exploration," PIER Working Paper no. 04–006

2006. "Selling Protection for Sale," PIER Working Paper no. 06–14

Fearon, J. D. 1998. "Bargaining, Enforcement, and International Cooperation," *International Organization* 52(2): 269–305

Feinberg, R. and Olsen, K. 2004. "The Spread of Antidumping Regimes and the Role of Retaliation in Filings." *Mimeo*

Finger, J. M. 1991. "The GATT as an International Discipline over Trade Restrictions," in R. Vaubel and T. D. Willett (eds.), *The Political Economy of International Organizations* (Boulder, CO: Westview Press), pp. 121–145

1998. "GATT Experience with Safeguards: Making Economic and Political Sense of the Possibilities that the GATT Allows to Restrict Imports," World Bank Policy Research Working Paper no. 2000

2002. "Safeguards: Making Sense of GATT/WTO Provisions Allowing for Import Restrictions," in B. Hoekman, A. Mattoo, and P. English (eds.), *Development, Trade and the WTO* (Washington, DC: World Bank), pp. 195–205

Finger, J. M. (ed.) 1993. *Antidumping: How It Works and Who Gets Hurt* (Ann Arbor, MI: University of Michigan Press)

Finger, J. M., Hall, H. K., and Nelson, D. R. 1982. "The Political Economy of Administered Protection," *American Economic Review* 72(3): 452–466

Finger, J. M., Ng, F., and Wangchuck, S. 2001. "Antidumping as Safeguard Policy." *Mimeo*

Finger, J. M. and Winters, A. L. 2002. "Reciprocity in the WTO," in B. Hoekman, A. Mattoo, and P. English (eds.), *Development, Trade and the WTO* (Washington, DC: World Bank), pp. 50–59

Finger, J. M. and Zlate, A. 2003. "WTO Rules that Allow New Trade Restrictions: the Public Interest is a Bastard Child," paper prepared for the UN Millenium Project Task Force, April

Finnemore, M. 1996. *National Interests in International Society* (Ithaca and London: Cornell University Press)

Finnemore, M. and Sikkink, K. 1998. "International Norm Dynamics and Political Change," *International Organization* 52(4): 887–918

2001. "Taking Stock: the Constructivist Research Program in International Relations and Comparative Politics," *Annual Review of Political Science* 4: 391–416

Frank, A. G. 1969. *Capitalism and Underdevelopment in Latin America: Historical Studies of Chile and Brazil* (New York: Monthly Review Press)

Friedman, D. 1989. "The Efficient Breach Fallacy," *Journal of Legal Studies* 18(1): 1–24

Fudenberg, D. and Tirole, J. 1990. "Moral Hazard and Renegotiation in Agency Contracts," *Econometrica* 58(6): 1279–1319

Furusawa, T. 1999. "The Optimal Penal Code vs. Infinite Nash Reversion in Trade Liberalization," *Review of International Economics* 7(4): 673–681

Gardner, R. N. 1980. *Sterling-Dollar Diplomacy in Current Perspective: the Origins and the Prospects of our International Economic Order* (New York: Columbia University Press)

Gerhart, P. 2003. "The Two Constitutional Visions of the World Trade Organization," *Pennsylvania Journal of International Economic Law* 24(1): 1–74

Gilpin, R. 1987. *The Political Economy of International Relations* (Princeton, NJ: Princeton University Press)

Goetz, C. and Scott, R. E. 1981. "Principles of Relational Contracts," *Virginia Law Review* 67(2): 1089–1150

Goldberg, V. P. 1976. "Regulation and Administered Contracts," *Bell Journal of Economics* 7: 426–448

Goldstein, J. 1996. "International Law and Domestic Institutions: Reconciling North American Unfair Trade Laws," *International Organization* 50: 541–564

1998. "International Institutions and Domestic Politics: GATT, WTO, and the Liberalization of International Trade," in A. O. Krueger (ed.), *The WTO as an International Organization* (Chicago/London: University of Chicago Press), pp. 133–152

Goldstein, J. and Gowa, J. 2002. "US National Power and the Postwar Trading Regime," *World Trade Review* 1(2): 153–170

Goldstein, J., Kahler, M., Keohane, R., and Slaughter, A.-M. 2000. "Introduction: Legalization and World Politics," *International Organization* 54(3): 385–399

Goldstein, J. and Martin, L. L. 2000. "Legalization, Trade Liberalization, and Domestic Politics: a Cautionary Note," *International Organization* 54(3): 603–632

Gowa, J. 1989. "Bipolarity, Multipolarity, and Free Trade," *American Political Science Review* 83(4): 1245–1256

Gowa, J. and Mansfield, E. D. 1993. "Power Politics and International Trade," *American Political Science Review* 87(2): 408–420

Grané, P. 2001. "Remedies under WTO law," *Journal of International Economic Law* 4(4): 755–772

Grieco, J. M. 1988. "Anarchy and the Limits of Cooperation: a Realist Critique of the Newest Liberal Institutionalism," *International Organization* 42(3): 485–507

1990. *Cooperation among Nations: Europe, America and Non-Tariff Barriers to Trade* (Ithaca, NY: Cornell University Press)

Grieco, J. M. and Ikenberry, G. J. 2003. *State Power and World Markets: the International Political Economy* (New York/London: W. W. Norton and Co.)

Grossman, G. 1987. "Strategic Export Promotion: a Critique," in P. R. Krugman (ed.), *Strategic Trade Policy and the New International Economics* (Cambridge, MA: MIT Press)

Grossman, G. M. and Helpman, E. 1994. "Protection for Sale," *American Economic Review* 84(4): 833–850

1995a. "The Politics of Free-Trade Agreements," *American Economic Review* 85(4): 667–690

1995b. "Trade Wars and Trade Talks," *Journal of Political Economy* 103(4): 675–708

2001. *Special Interest Politics* (Cambridge, MA: MIT Press)

Grossman, G. M. and Maggi, G. 1998. "Free Trade Versus Strategic Trade: a Peek into Pandora's Box," in R. Soto, R. Ramachandran, and K. Mino (eds.), *Global Competition and Integration* (Dordrecht: Kluwer Academic Press)

Grossman, G. M. and Mavroidis, P. C. 2004. "United States – Section 110(5) of the Copyright Act, Resource to Arbitration under Article 25 of the DSU: Would've or Should've: Impaired Benefits due to Copyright Infringement," in H. Horn and P. C. Mavroidis (eds.), *The WTO Case Law of 2001* (Cambridge: Cambridge University Press)

Grossman, S. J. and Hart, O. D. 1986. "The Costs and Benefits of Ownership: a Theory of Vertical and Lateral Integration," *Journal of Political Economy* 94 (4): 691–719

Grossman, S. J. and Perry, M. 1986. "Perfect Sequential Equilibrium," *Journal of Economic Theory* 39(1): 97–119

Gruber, L. 2000. *Ruling the World: Power Politics and the Rise of Supranational Institutions* (Princeton, NJ: Princeton University Press)

Gruenspecht, H. K. 1988. "Dumping and Dynamic Competition," *Journal of International Economics* 25(3–4): 225–248

Guzman, A. 2002a. "The Political Economy of Litigation and Settlement in the WTO." *Mimeo*

2002b. "A Compliance-Based Theory of International Law," *California Law Review* 90(6): 1823–1887

Guzzini, G. 2002. "A Reconstruction of Constructivism in International Relations," *European Journal of International Relations* 6(2): 147–182

Haas, P. M. 1992. "Introduction: Epistemic Communities and International Policy Coordination," in P. M. Haas (ed.), *Knowledge, Power, and International Policy Coordination* (Columbia, SC: University of South Carolina Press), pp. 3–35

Hadfield, G. K. 1990. "Problematic Relations: Franchising and the Law of Incomplete Contracts," *Stanford Law Review* 42(4): 927–993

1994. "Judicial Competence and the Interpretation of Incomplete Contracts," *Journal of Legal Studies* 23(1): 159–184

Haggard, S. and Simmons, B. A. 1987. "Theories of International Regimes," *International Organization* 41(3): 491–517

Hardin, G. 1968. "The Tragedy of the Commons," *Science* 162(3859): 1243–1248

Harms, P., Mattoo, A., and Schuknecht, L. 2003. "Explaining Liberalization Commitments in Financial Services Trade," World Bank Policy Research Paper Series no. 2999

Hart, O. D. 1995. *Firms, Contracts, and Financial Structure* (Oxford: Clarendon Press)

Hart, O. D. and Holmström, B. 1987. "The Theory of Contracts," in T. R. Bewley (ed.), *Advances in Economic Theory, Fifth World Congress* (Cambridge: Cambridge University Press), pp. 396–398

Hart, O. D. and Moore, J. D. 1988. "Incomplete Contracts and Renegotiation," *Econometrica* 56(4): 755–785

Hasenclever, H., Mayer P., and Rittberger V. 1997. *Theories of International Regimes* (Cambridge: Cambridge University Press)

2000. "Integrating Theories of International Regimes," *Review of International Studies* 26(1): 3–33

Hauser, H. 1986. "Domestic Policy Foundation and Domestic Policy Function of International Trade Rules," *Aussenwirtschaft* 41(2/3): 171–184

2000. "Die WTO-Streitschlichtung aus einer Law and Economics Perspektive," in H. Berg (ed.), *Theorie der Wirtschaftspolitik: Erfahrungen, Probleme, Perspektiven* (Berlin: Verlag Duncker & Humblot), pp. 79–111

Hauser, H. and Roitinger, A. 2003. "Renegotiation in Transatlantic Trade Disputes," in E.-U. Petersmann and M. A. Pollack (eds.), *Transatlantic Economic Disputes* (Oxford: Oxford University Press), pp. 487–506

2004. "Two Perspectives on International Trade Agreements," *Zeitschrift für ausländisches öffentliches Recht und Völkerrecht* 64(3): 641–658

Hendricks, K. and Wilson, C. 1985. "The War of Attrition in Discrete Time," *International Economic Review* 29(4): 663–680

Hermalin, B. E. and Katz, M. L. 1993. "Judicial Modification of Contracts between Sophisticated Parties: a More Complete View of Incomplete Contracts and their Breach," *Journal of Law, Economics and Organization* 9(2): 230–255

Herzing, M. 2005. *Essays on Uncertainty and Escape in Trade Agreements*, dissertation (Stockholm University, Stockholm, Sweden)

Hillman, A. L. 1982. "Declining Industries and Political-Support Protectionist Motives," *American Economic Review* 72(5): 1180–1190

Hillman, A. and Moser, P. 1996. "Trade Liberalization as Politically Optimal Exchange of Market Access," in M. Canzeroni, W. J. Ethier, and V. Grilli, *The New Transatlantic Economy* (Cambridge: Cambridge University Press), pp. 295–312

Hillman, A. L. and Ursprung, H. W. 1988. "Domestic Politics, Foreign Interests, and International Trade Policy," *American Economic Review* 78(4): 729–745

1994. "Domestic Politics, Foreign Interests, and International Trade Policy: Reply," *American Economic Review* 84(5): 1476–1478

Hillman, A., van Long, N., and Moser, P. 1995. "Modelling Reciprocal Trade Liberalization: the Political-Economy and National-Welfare Perspectives," *Swiss Journal of Economics and Statistics* 131(3): 505–515

Hoekman, B. M. and Kostecki, M. 1995. *The Political Economy of the World Trading System* (Oxford: Oxford University Press)

Hoekman, B. M. and Mavroidis, P. C. 1996. "Dumping, Antidumping and Antitrust," *Journal of World Trade* 30(1): 27–52

Holmes, P., Rollo, J., and Young, A. R. 2003. "Emerging Trends in WTO Dispute Settlement: Back to the GATT?," World Bank Policy Research Working Paper no. 3133

Holmström, B. and Tirole, J. 1989. "The Theory of the Firm," in R. Schmalensee and R. D. Willig, *Handbook of Industrial Economics* (New York: Elsevier Science Publishing), pp. 61–133

Horlick, G. N. and Palmer, C. R. 2002. "Subsidies, Antidumping and Countervailing Duties in the ALCA/FTAA." *Mimeo*

Horn, H. 2006. "National Treatment in the GATT," *American Economic Review* 96 (1): 394–404

Horn, H., Maggi, G., and Staiger, R. W. 2005. "The GATT/WTO as an Incomplete Contract and the Role of Dispute Settlement Procedures." *Mimeo*

2006. "The GATT/WTO as an Incomplete Contract." *Mimeo*

Horn, H. and Mavroidis, P. C. 2003. "What Should be Required of a Safeguard Investigation? A Comment on *US – Lamb*," in H. Horn and P. C. Mavroidis, *The WTO Case-Law of 2001: the American Law Institute Reporters' Studies* (Cambridge: Cambridge University Press), pp. 72–114

2006a. "The WTO Dispute Settlement Data Set: User's Guide Version 1.0." *Mimeo*

2006b. "The WTO Dispute Settlement System 1995–2004: Some Descriptive Statistics." *Mimeo*

Horn, H. and Mavroidis, P. C. (eds.) 2004. *The WTO Case Law of 2001* (Cambridge: Cambridge University Press)

2005. *The WTO Case Law of 2002* (Cambridge: Cambridge University Press)

Howse, R. and Mavroidis, P. C. 2003. *The Law of the World Trade Organization*

Howse, R. and Nicolaïdis, K. 2001. "Legitimacy and Global Governance: Why Constitutionalizing the WTO is a Step too Far," in R. B. Porter *et al.* (eds.), *Efficiency, Equity, Legitimacy: the Multilateral Trading System at the Millennium* (Washington, DC: Brookings Institution Press)

Howse, R. and Staiger, R. W. 2005. "United States Recourse to Arbitration by the United States under 22.6 of the DSU, WT/DS136/ARB, 24 February 2004," *World Trade Review* 4(2): 295–316

Hudec, R. E. 1990. *The GATT Legal System and World Trade Diplomacy* (New York: Praeger)

　1993. "Circumventing Democracy: the Political Morality of Trade Negotiations," *NYU Journal of International Law and Politics* 25: 311–322

　2002. "The Adequacy of WTO Dispute Settlement Remedies: a Developing Country Perspective," in B. Hoekman, A. Mattoo, and P. English, *Development, Trade and the WTO* (Washington, DC: World Bank), pp. 81–91

Hufbauer, G. C. and Goodrich, B. 2003a. "Next Move on Steel: Revocation or Retaliation?," IIE Policy Briefs no. 03-10

　2003b. "Steel Policy: the Good, the Bad, and the Ugly," IIE Policy Brief no. 03-1

Hull, C. 1948. *The Memoirs of Cordell Hull* (London: Hodder and Stoughton)

Hungerford, T. L. 1991. "GATT: a Cooperative Equilibrium in a Noncooperative Trading Regime?," *Journal of International Economics* 31(3–4): 357–369

Hviid, M. 1999. "Long-Term Contracts and Relational Contracts," in B. Bouckaert and G. de Geest (eds.), *Encyclopedia of Law and Economics* (Ghent: Edward Elgar/(University of Ghent), pp. 46–72

Ikenberry, G. J., Lake, D. A., and Mastanduno, M. 1989. "The State and American Foreign Economic Policy," *International Organization* 42(1): 1–14

Irwin, D. A. 1996. *Against the Tide: Intellectual History of Free Trade* (Princeton, NJ: Princeton University Press)

　2005. *Free Trade under Fire* (Princeton, NJ: Princeton University Press)

Irwin, D. A., Mavroidis P. C., and Sykes A. O. 2008. *The Genesis of the GATT* (Cambridge: Cambridge University Press, forthcoming)

Jackson, J. H. 1969. *World Trade and the Law of GATT* (New York: Bobbs-Merrill)

　1997a. *The World Trading System* (Cambridge, MA: MIT Press)

　1997b. "The WTO Dispute Settlement Understanding: Misunderstandings on the Nature of Legal Obligation," *American Journal of International Law* 91 (1): 60–64

　2004. "International Law Status of WTO Dispute Settlement Reports: Obligation to Comply or Option to 'Buy Out'?," *American Journal of International Law* 98(1): 109–125

Jawara, F. and Kwa, A. 2004. *Behind the Scenes at the WTO: the Real World of International Trade Negotiations: Lessons of Cancun* (London/New York: Zed Books)

Johnson, H. G. 1953. "Optimum Tariffs and Retaliation," *Review of Economic Studies* 21(2): 142–153

Johnston, J. S. 1990. "Strategic Bargaining and the Economic Theory of Contract Default Rules," *Yale Law Journal* 100: 615–664

Jolls, C. 1997. "Contracts as Bilateral Commitments: a New Perspective on Contract Modification," *Journal of Legal Studies* 26(January): 203–238

Jones, K. 2004. "The Safeguards Mess Revisited: the Fundamental Problem," *World Trade Review* 3(1): 83–91

Josling, T. E. 2004. "WTO Dispute Settlement and the EU–US Mini Trade Wars: a Commentary on Fritz Breuss," *Journal of Industry, Competition and Trade* 4(4): 337–344

Kahnemann, D. 2003. "Maps of Bounded Rationality: Psychology for Behavioral Economics," *American Economic Review* 93(5): 1449–1475

Kaplow, L. and Shavell, S. 1994. "Accuracy in the Determination of Liability," *Journal of Law and Economics* 37(1): 1–15

 1995. "Do Liability Rules Facilitate Bargaining? A Reply to Ayres and Talley," *Yale Law Journal* 105(1): 221–233

 1996a. "Accuracy in the Assessment of Damages," *Journal of Law and Economics* 39(1): 191–210

 1996b. "Property Rules versus Liability Rules: an Economic Analysis," *Harvard Law Review* 109(4): 713–790

Keck, A. 2004. "WTO Dispute Settlement: What Role for Economic Analysis?," *Journal of Industry, Competition and Trade* 4(4): 365–371

Keck, A. and Schropp, S. A. B. 2008. "Indisputably Essential: the Economics of Dispute Settlement Institutions in Trade Agreements," *Journal of World Trade* 42(5): 785–812

Kenney, R. W. and Klein, B. 1983. "The Economics of Block Booking," *Journal of Law and Economics* 26(3): 497–540

Keohane, R. O. 1984. *After Hegemony: Cooperation and Discord in the World Political Economy* (Princeton, NJ: Princeton University Press)

 1993. "Institutional Theory and the Realist Challenge after the Cold War," in D. A. Baldwin (ed.), *Neorealism and Neoliberalism: the Contemporary Debate* (New York: Columbia University Press), pp. 269–300

 2002. *Power and Governance in a Partially Globalized World* (London/ New York: Routledge)

 2005. *After Hegemony: Cooperation and Discord in the World Political Economy* (Princeton, NJ/Oxford: Princeton University Press)

Kindleberger, C. P. 1973. *The World in Depression, 1929–1939* (Berkeley, CA: University of California Press)

Kirchgässner, G. 2000. *Homo Oeconomicus* (Tübingen: Mohr Siebeck)

Kleen, P. 1989. "The Safeguard Issue in the Uruguay Round: a Comprehensive Approach." *Journal of World Trade* 23(5): 73–92

Klein, B. 1996. "Why Hold-ups Occur: the Self-Enforcing Range of Contractual Relationships," *Economic Enquiry* 34: 444–463

Klein, B., Crawford, R. G., and Alchian, A. A. 1978. "Vertical Integration, Appropriable Rents, and the Competitive Contracting Process," *Journal of Law and Economics* 21(October): 297–326

Klimenko, M., Ramey, G., and Watson, J. 2002. "Recurrent Trade Agreements and the Value of External Enforcement." *Mimeo*

Koremenos, B., Lipson, C., and Snidal, D. 2001. "The Rational Design of International Institutions," *International Organization* 55(4): 761–799

Kovenock, D. and Thursby, M. 1992. "GATT, Dispute Settlement, and Cooperation," *Economics and Politics* 4: 151–170

Krasner, S. D. 1976. "State Power and the Structure of International Trade," *World Politics* 28(2): 317–347

　　1999. *Sovereignty: Organized Hypocrisy* (Princeton, NJ: Princeton University Press)

Kratochwil, F. V. 1989. *Rules, Norms, and Decisions: On the Conditions of Practical and Legal Reasoning in International Relations and Domestic Affairs* (Cambridge: Cambridge University Press)

Kratochwil, F. V. and Ruggie, J. G. 1986. "International Organization: a State of the Art on an Art of the State," *International Organization* 40(4): 753–775

Krauss, M. I. 1999. "Property Rules vs. Liability Rules," in B. Bouckaert and G. de Geest (eds.), *Encyclopedia of Law and Economics* (Ghent: Edward Elgar/ University of Ghent), pp. 782–793

Krishna, P. and Mitra, D. 1999. "Reciprocated Unilateralism: a Political Economy Perspective." *Mimeo*

Krugman, P. R. 1991. "The Move Toward Free Trade Zones," *Federal Reserve Bank of Kansas City Economic Review* (November): 5–25

　　1993. "What Do Undergrads Need to Know about Trade?," *American Economic Review* 83(2): 23–26

　　1997. "What Should Trade Negotiators Negotiate About?," *Journal of Economic Literature* 35: 113–120

Krugman, P. R. and Obstfeld, M. 1994. *International Economics: Theory and Policy* (New York: HarperCollins College Publishers)

Kucik, J. and Reinhardt, E. 2007. "Does Flexibility Promote Cooperation? 'Efficient Breach' in the Global Trade Regime." *Mimeo*

Kydland, F. and Prescott, E. 1977. "Rules Rather than Discretion: the Inconsistency of Optimal Plans," *Journal of Political Economy* 85(3): 473–491

Lang, A. T. F. 2006. "Reconstructing Embedded Liberalism: John Gerard Ruggie and Constructivist Approaches to the Study of the International Trade Regime," *Journal of International Economic Law* 9(1): 81–116

Lapan, H. E. 1988. "The Optimal Tariff, Production Lags and Time Consistency," *American Economic Review* 78(3): 395–401

Lawrence, R. Z. 2003. *Crimes and Punishments? Retaliation under the WTO* (Washington, DC: Institute for International Economics)

Lee, Y.-S. and Mah, J. S. 1998. "Reflections on the Agreement on Safeguards in the WTO," *World Competition* 21(6): 25–31

Levy, P. I. 1997. "A Political-Economic Analysis of Free Trade Agreements," *American Economic Review* 87(4): 509–519

  1999. "Lobbying and International Cooperation in Tariff Setting," *Journal of International Economics* 47: 345–370

  2003. "Non-Tariff Barriers as a Test of Political Economic Theories," Economic Growth Center, Yale University, Center Discussion Paper no. 852

Lindsey, B. 2000. "The U.S. Antidumping Law: Rhetoric versus Reality," *Journal of World Trade* 34(1): 1–38

Lindsey, B., Griswold, D. T., Groombridge, M., and Lukas, A. 1999. "Seattle and Beyond: a WTO Agenda for the New Millenium," CATO Center for Trade Policy Studies no. 8

Lindsey, B. and Ikenson, D. J. 2002. "Reforming the Antidumping Agreement: a Road Map for WTO Negotiations," Cato Institute Briefing Paper no. 21

  2003. *Antidumping Exposed: the Devilish Details of Unfair Trade Law* (Washington, DC: Cato Institute)

Ludema, R. 2001. "Optimal International Trade Agreements and Dispute Settlement Procedures," *European Journal of Political Economy* 17(2): 355–376

Macaulay, S. 1985. "An Empirical View of Contract," *Wisconsin Law Review* 5: 465–482

MacLeod, W. B. 2006. "Reputations, Relationships and the Enforcement of Incomplete Contracts," Center for Economic Studies and Ifo Institute for Economic Research (CESifo) no. 1730

Macneil, I. 1978. "Contracts: Adjustment of Long-Term Economic Relations under Classical, Neoclassical, and Relational Contract Law," *Northwestern University Law Review* 72(6): 854–905

  1981. "Economic Analysis of Contractual Relations: Its Shortfalls and the Need for a 'Rich Classificatory Apparatus,'" *Northwestern University Law Review* 75(6): 1081–1063

  1982. "Efficient Breach of Contract: Circles in the Sky," *Virginia Law Review* 68 (5): 947–969

Maggi, G. 1999a. "The Role of Multilateral Institutions in International Trade Cooperation," *American Economic Review* 89(1): 190–214

  1999b. "Strategic Trade Policy under Incomplete Information," *International Economic Review* 40(3): 571–594

Maggi, G. and Rodriguez-Clare, A. 1998. "The Value of Trade Agreements in the Presence of Political Pressure," *Journal of Political Economy* 106(3): 574–601

2005. "A Political Economy Theory of Trade Agreements," CEPR Working Paper no. 5321

Mahlstein, K. and Schropp, S. A. B. 2007. "Optimal Rules for Escape and Remedy in Trade Agreements," HEI Working Paper 27–2007 (available at www.hei. unige.ch)

Mahoney, P. G. 1999. "Contract Remedies: General," in B. Bouckaert and G. de Geest (eds.), *Encyclopedia of Law and Economics* (Ghent: Edward Elgar/ University of Ghent), pp. 117–140

Malanczuk, P. 1997. *Akehurst's Modern Introduction to International Law* (London: Routledge)

Martin, A. and Vergote, W. 2004. "A Case for Strategic Antidumping," Columbia University Working Paper

Martin, L. L. 1993. "The Rational State Choice of Multilateralism," in J. G. Ruggie (ed.), *Multilateralism Matters: the Theory and Praxis of an Institutional Form* (New York: Columbia University Press), pp. 91–121

Martin, L. L. and Simmons, B. A. 1998. "Theories and Empirical Studies of International Institutions," *International Organization* 52(4): 729–775

Maskin, E. and Newberry, D. 1990. "Disadvantageous Oil Tariffs and Dynamic Consistency," *American Economic Review* 80(1): 143–156

Maskin, E. and Tirole, J. 1999. "Unforeseen Contingencies and Incomplete Contracts," *Review of Economic Studies* 66(1): 83–114

Masten, S. E. 1999. "Contractual Choice," in B. Bouckaert and G. de Geest (eds.), *Encyclopedia of Law and Economics* (Ghent: Edward Elgar/University of Ghent), pp. 25–45

Matsuyama, K. 1990. "Perfect Equilibria in a Trade Liberalization Game," *American Economic Review* 80(3): 480–492

Mavroidis, P. C. 1993. "Government Procurement Agreement; the Trondheim Case: the Remedies Issue," *Aussenwirtschaft* 48(1): 77–94

2000. "Remedies in the WTO Legal System: Between a Rock and a Hard Place," *European Journal of International Law* 11(4): 763–813

2005. "Enforcement of WTO Obligations: Remedies and Compliance." *Mimeo*

2006. "Remedies in the WTO: a Framework of Analysis." *Mimeo*

2007. *Trade in Goods* (Oxford: Oxford University Press)

Mayer, W. 1994. "Optimal Pursuit of Safeguard Actions over Time," in A. Deardoff and R. Stern (eds.), *Analytical and Negotiating Issues in the Global Trading System* (Ann Arbor, MI: University of Michigan Press), p. 629

McGinnis, J. O. and Movsesian, M. L. 2000. "The World Trade Constitution," *Harvard Law Review* 114: 511–605

McLaren, J. 1997. "Size, Sunk Costs and Judge Bowker's Objection to Free Trade," *American Economic Review* 87(3): 400–420

2002. "A Theory of Insidious Regionalism," *Quarterly Journal of Economics* 117 (2): 571–608

Meade, J. 1942. *The Economic Basis of Durable Peace* (London: G. Allen & Unwin Ltd.)

Mearsheimer, J. J. 1995. "The False Promise of International Institutions," *International Security* 19(3): 5–49

Medrado, R. G. 2004. "Re-negotiating Remedies in the WTO: a Multilateral Approach." *Mimeo*

Menard, C. (ed.) 2004. *The International Library of the New Institutional Economics* (Cheltenham: Edward Elgar)

Messerlin, P. 2000. "Antidumping and Safeguards," in J. Schott (ed.), *The WTO After Seattle* (Washington, DC: Institute for International Economics), pp. 159–183

Miller, J. N. 2000. "Origins of the GATT: British Resistance to American Multilateralism," Jerome Levy Economics Institute, Bard College no. 318

Milner, H. V. 1997. *Interests, Institutions, and Information: Domestic Politics and International Relations* (Princeton, NJ: Princeton University Press)

Milner, H. V. and Rosendorff, P. B. 1997. "Democratic Politics and International Trade Negotiations: Elections and Divided Government as Constraints on Trade Liberalization," *Journal of Conflict Resolution* 41(1): 117–146

Mitra, D. 1999. "Endogenous Lobby Formation and Endogenous Protection," *American Economic Review* 89(5): 1116–1143

Morgenthau, H. 1948. *Politics Among Nations: the Struggle for Power and Peace* (New York: Knopf)

Morrow, J. D. 1994. "Modeling the Forms of International Cooperation: Distribution versus Information," *International Organization* 48(3): 387–423

Moser, P. 1990. *The Political Economy of the GATT* (Grüsch: Verlag Ruegger)

Neufeld, I. N. 2001. "Anti-Dumping and Countervailing Procedures: Use or Abuse? Implications for Developing Countries," UNCTAD Policy Issues in International Trade and Commodities Study Series no. 9

Neven, D. 2000. *Evaluating the Effects of Non-Tariff Barriers: the Economic Analysis of Protection in WTO Disputes* (World Bank)

Nöldeke, G. and Schmidt, K. M. 1995. "Option Contracts and Renegotiation: a Solution to the Hold-up Problem," *Rand Journal of Economics* 26(2): 163–179

North, D. C. 1990. *Institutions, Institutional Change, and Economic Performance* (New York: Cambridge University Press)

  1991. "Institutions," *Journal of Economic Perspectives* 5(1): 97–112

  2005. *Understanding the Process of Institutional Change* (Princeton, NJ: Princeton University Press)

O'Connor, B. and Djordjevic, M. 2005. "Practical Aspects of Monetary Compensation, the *US – Copyright* Case," *Journal of International Economic Law* 8(1): 127–142

Odell, J. and Sell, S. 2006. "Reframing the Issue: the Coalition on Intellectual Property and Public Health in the WTO, 2001," in J. Odell (ed.), *Negotiating Trade: Developing Countries in the WTO and NAFTA* (New York: Cambridge University Press)

Ordover, J. A. and Rubinstein, A. 1986. "A Sequential Concession Game with Asymmetric Information," *Quarterly Journal of Economics* 101(4): 879–888

Osborne, M. J. 1985. "The Role of Risk Aversion in a Simple Bargaining Model," in A. E. Roth (ed.), *Game-Theoretic Models of Bargaining* (Cambridge: Cambridge University Press)

Ostrom, E. 2003. "How Types of Goods and Property Rights Jointly Affect Collective Action," *Journal of Theoretical Politics* 15(3): 239–270

Oye, K. 1986. *Cooperation under Anarchy* (Princeton, NJ: Princeton University Press)

Palmeter, D. 1991a. "The Antidumping Law: a Legal and Administrative Non-Tariff Barrier," in D. Kennedy and J. Southwick (eds.), *The Political Economy of International Trade Law* (Cambridge: Cambridge University Press), pp. 646–666

  1991b. "The Rhetoric and the Reality of the United States' Anti-Dumping Law," *World Economy* 14(1): 19–36

  1996. "A Commentary on the WTO Antidumping Code," *Journal of World Trade* 30(4): 43–69

  2000. "The WTO as a Legal System," *Fordham International Journal* 24(2000/2001): 444

Palmeter, D. and Alexandrov, S. A. 2002. "'Inducing Compliance' in WTO Settlement," in D. L. M. Kennedy and J. D. Southwick (eds.), *The Political Economy of International Trade Law* (Cambridge: Cambridge University Press), 646–666

Pauwelyn, J. 2000. "Enforcement and Countermeasures in the WTO: Rules are Rules – Toward a More Collective Approach," *American Journal of International Law* 94(2): 335–347

  2001. "The Role of Public International Law in the WTO: How Far Can We Go?," *American Journal of International Law* 95(3): 535–578

  2003. *Conflicts of Norms in Public International Law: How the WTO Relates to Other Rules of International Law* (Cambridge: Cambridge University Press)

  2006. "How Strongly *Should* We Protect and Enforce International Law?." *Mimeo*

Penrose, E. F. 1953. *Economic Planning for the Peace* (Princeton, NJ: Princeton University Press)

Petersmann, E.-U. 1986. "Trade Policy as a Constitutional Problem," *Aussenwirtschaft* 41(2/3): 405–439

  1991. "Non-Violation Complaints in Public International Trade Law," *German Yearbook of International Law* 34: 175–231

  1995. "The Transformation of the World Trading System through the 1994 Agreement Establishing the World Trade Organization," *European Journal of International Law* 6: 1–61

1998. "From the Hobbesian International Law of Coexistence to Modern Integration Law: the WTO Dispute Settlement System," *Journal of International Economic Law* 1: 175–198

2002. "Constitutionalism and the WTO: from a State-Centered Approach Towards a Human Rights Approach in International Economic Law," in O. Kennedy and J. Southwick (eds.), *The Political Economy of International Trade Law* (Cambridge: Cambridge University Press)

2003. "Human Rights and the Law of the World Trade Organization," *Journal of World Trade* 37(2): 241–281

2005. "Addressing Institutional Challenges to the WTO in the New Millennium: a Longer-Term Perspective," *Journal of International Economic Law* 8(3): 647–665

2006. "Multilevel Trade Governance in the WTO Requires Multilevel Constitutionalism," in C. Joerges and E.-U. Petersmann (eds.), *Constitutionalism, Multilevel Trade Governance and Social Regulation* (Portland, OR: Hart Publishing)

Posner, R. A. 1988. *Economic Analysis of the Law* (Boston, MA: Little, Brown and Co.)

Powell, R. 1994. "Anarchy in International Relations Theory: the Neorealist-Neoliberalist Debate," *International Organization* 48(2): 313–344

Prusa, J. and Skeath, S. 2002. "The Economic and Strategic Motives for Antidumping Filings," NBER Working Paper no. 8424

Putnam, R. D. 1988. "Diplomacy and Domestic Politics: the Logic of Two-Level Games," *International Organization* 42(3): 427–460

Rawls, J. 1971. *A Theory of Justice* (Cambridge, MA: Harvard University Press)

Regan, D. 2006. "What are Trade Agreements For? Two Conflicting Stories Told by Economists, with a Lesson for Lawyers," *Journal of International Economic Law* 9(4): 951–988

Reus-Smit, C. 1997. "The Constitutional Structure of International Society and the Nature of Fundamental Institutions," *International Organization* 51(4): 555–589

Rodrik, D. 1995. "Political Economy of Trade Policy," in G. Grossman and K. Rogoff (eds.), *Handbook of International Economics* (Amsterdam: New Holland), pp. 1457–1494

1997. *Has Globalization Gone Too Far?* (Washington, DC: Institute for International Economics)

Rogerson, W. P. 1984. "Efficient Reliance and Damage Measures for Breach of Contract," *Rand Journal of Economics* 15(1): 39–53

Roitinger, A. 2004. *The Institutional Design of Trade Policy Flexibility in the World Trade Order: Analysis and New Direction for Reform*, Dissertation at Universität St. Gallen (HSG)

Romer, D. 1996. *Advanced Macroeconomics* (New York: McGraw Hill)

Rosendorff, B. P. 1996. "Voluntary Export Restraints, Antidumping Procedure, and Domestic Politics," *American Economic Review* 86(3): 544–561

2005. "Stability and Rigidity: Politics and Design of the WTO's Dispute Settlement Procedures," *American Political Science Review* 99(3): 389–400

Rosendorff, B. P. and Milner, H. V. 2001. "The Optimal Design of International Trade Institutions: Uncertainty and Escape," *International Organization* 55 (4): 829–857

Rubinstein, A. 1982. "Perfect Equilibrium in a Bargaining Model," *Econometrica* 59(4): 777–793

1998. *Modeling Bounded Rationality* (Cambridge, MA: MIT Press)

Ruggie, J. G. 1982. "International Regimes, Transactions, and Change: Embedded Liberalism in the Postwar Economic Order," *International Organization* 36 (2): 379–415

1998. *Constructing the World Polity: Essays on International Institutionalization* (London/New York: Routledge)

Ruggie, J. G. (ed.) 1993. *Multilateralism Matters: the Theory and Praxis of an Institutional Form* (New York: Columbia University Press)

Salanié, B. 1997. *The Economics of Contracts* (Cambridge, MA: MIT Press)

Sandler, T. 1992. *Collective Action: Theory and Applications* (Ann Arbor, MI: University of Michigan Press)

Schermers, H. and Blokker, N. 1995. *International Institutional Law: Unity within Diversity*, 3rd rev. edn. (Cambridge, MA: Kluwer Law International)

Schropp, S. A. B. 2005. "The Case for Tariff Compensation in WTO Dispute Settlement," *Aussenwirtschaft* 60(4): 485–528

2007a. "Efficient 'Breach', Adequate Remedies and Optimal Trade Liberalization: Theorizing about Trade Policy Flexibility in the WTO," paper presented at the NCCR Democracy Module 1 Workshop (on file with the author)

2007b. "Revisiting the 'Compliance-vs.-Rebalancing' Debate in WTO Scholarship: Towards a Unified Research Agenda." *Mimeo*

Schuknecht, L. 1992. *Trade Protection in the European Community* (Reading: Harwood Academic Publishers)

Schwartz, A. 1992. "Relational Contracts in the Courts: an Analysis of Incomplete Agreements and Judicial Strategies," *Journal of Legal Studies* 21(2): 271–318

Schwartz, W. F. and Sykes, A. O. 1996. "Toward a Positive Theory of the Most Favored Nation Obligation and its Exceptions in the WTO/GATT System," *International Review of Law and Economics* 16(1): 27

2002a. "The Economic Structure of Renegotiation and Dispute Resolution in the WTO/GATT System," John M. Olin Law and Economics Working Paper no. 143

2002b. "The Economic Structure of Renegotiation and Dispute Resolution in the WTO/GATT System," *Journal of Legal Studies* 31(1): 170–204

Scott, R. E. 1987. "Conflict and Cooperation in Long-term Contracts," *Californian Law Review* 75(6): 2005–2054

1990. "A Relational Theory of Default Rules for Commercial Contracts," *Journal of Legal Studies* 19(2): 597–616

Setear, J. K. 1997. "Responses to Breach of a Treaty and Rationalist International Relations Theory: the Rules of Release and Remediation in the Law of Treaties and the Law of State Responsibility," *Virginia Law Review* 83: 1–150

Shavell, S. 1980. "Damage Measures for Breach of Contract," *Bell Journal of Economics* 11(2): 466–490

1984. "The Design of Contracts and Remedies for Breach," *Quarterly Journal of Economics* 99(1): 121–148

Simmons, B. A. and Martin, L. L. 2002. "International Organizations and Institutions," in W. Carlsnaes, B. Simmons, and T. Risse (eds.), *Handbook of International Relations* (London/Thousand Oaks/New Delhi: Sage), pp. 192–211

Simon, H. A. 1955. "A Behavioral Model of Rational Choice," *Quarterly Journal of Economics* 69(1): 99–118

Skyrms, B. 2003. *The Stag Hunt and Evolution of Social Structure* (Cambridge: Cambridge University Press)

Smith, A. and Venables, A. 1991. "Counting the Cost of Voluntary Export Restraints in the European Market," in E. Helpman and A. Razin (eds.), *International Trade and Trade Policy* (Cambridge, MA: MIT Press), pp. 187–220

Smith, J. M. 2000. "The Politics of Dispute Settlement Design: Explaining Legalism in Regional Trade Pacts," *International Organization* 54(1): 137–180

Snidal, D. 1997. "International Political Economy Approaches to International Institutions," in J. S. Bhandari and A. O. Sykes (eds.), *Economic Dimensions in International Law: Comparative and Empirical Perspectives* (Cambridge: Cambridge University Press), pp. 477–512

2002. "Rational Choice and International Relations," in W. Carlsnaes, B. Simmons and T. Risse (eds.), *Handbook of International Relations* (London/Thousand Oaks/New Delhi: Sage), pp. 73–94

Spamann, H. 2006. "The Myth of 'Rebalancing' Retaliation in WTO Dispute Settlement Practice," *Journal of International Economic Law* 9(1): 31–79

Srinivasan, T. N. 2005. "Non-Discrimination in GATT/WTO: Was there Anything to Begin With and is there Anything Left?," *World Trade Review* 4(1): 69–95

Staiger, R. W. 1995. "International Rules and Institutions for Trade Policy," in G. Grossman and K. Rogoff (eds.), *Handbook of International Economics* (Amsterdam: North Holland), pp. 1495–1551

Staiger, R. W. and Tabellini, G. 1987. "Discretionary trade policy and excessive protection," *American Economic Review* 77(5): 823–837

1989. "Rules and Discretion in Trade Policy," *European Economic Review* 33 (6): 1265–1277

1999. "Do GATT Rules Help Governments Make Domestic Commitments?," *Economics and Politics* 11(2): 109–144

Stein, A. 1983. "Coordination and Collaboration Regimes in an Anarchic World," in S. D. Krasner (ed.), *International Regimes* (Ithaca, NY/London: Cornell University Press), pp. 115–140

Steinberg, R. H. 2002. "Consensus-based Bargaining and Outcomes in the GATT/ WTO," *International Organization* 56(2): 339–374

Stigler, G. 1971. "The Theory of Economic Regulation," *Bell Journal of Economic Management and Science* 2: 3–21

Stirling, A. 1999. *On Science and Precaution in the Management of Technological Risk* (Seville: Institute for Prospective Technological Studies)

Sykes, A. O. 1989. "Countervailing Duty Law: an Economic Perspective," *Columbia Law Review* 89(2): 199–263

1991. "Protectionism as a "Safeguard": a Positive Analysis of the GATT 'Escape Clause' with Normative Speculations," *University of Chicago Law Review* 58 (1): 255–305

1998. "Antidumping and Antitrust: What Problems Does Each Address?," in R. Z. Lawrence (ed.), *Brookings Trade Forum: 1998* (Washington, DC: Brookings Institution), pp. 1–43

1999. "International Trade," in B. Bouckaert and G. de Geest (eds.), *Encyclopedia of Law and Economics* (Ghent: Edward Elgar/University of Ghent), pp. 1114–1132

2000. "The Remedy for Breach of Obligations under the WTO Dispute Settlement Understanding: Damages or Specific Performance?," in M. Bronckers and R. Quick (eds.), *New Directions in International Economic Law* (Cambridge, MA: Kluwer Law International), pp. 347–357

2003. "The Safeguards Mess: a Critique of WTO Jurisprudence," *World Trade Review* 3(3): 261–295

Tarullo, D. 2002. "Book Review: the EU and the WTO: Legal and Constitutional Issues," *Journal of International Economic Law* 5(4): 941–943

Tharakan, P. K. M. 1995. "Political Economy and Contingent Protection," *Economic Journal* 105(433): 1550–1564

Tharakan, P. K. M. and Waelbroeck, J. 1994. "Antidumping and Countervailing Duty Decisions in the EC and in the US: an Experiment in Comparative Political Economy," *European Economic Review* 38(2): 171–193

Thompson, A. and Snidal, D. 2005. "Guarding the Equilibrium: Regime Management in the WTO," Working Paper presented at the Annual Meeting of the American Political Science Association

Tirole, J. 1994. "Incomplete Contracts: Where Do We Stand?," *Econometrica* 67 (4): 741–781

Tornell, A. 1991. "Time Inconsistency of Protectionists Programs," *Quarterly Journal of Economics* 106(August): 963–974

Trachtman, J. P. 1999. "The Domain of WTO Dispute Resolution," *Harvard Journal of International Law* 40: 333–363

    2006. "Building the WTO Cathedral." *Mimeo*

Trebilcock, M. and Howse, R. 2006. *International Trade Regulation* (London: Routledge)

Tumlir, J. 1985. "Conception of the International Economic and Legal Order," *World Economy* 8(1): 85–87

Vazquez, C. M. and Jackson, J. H. 2002. "Some Reflections on Compliance with WTO Dispute Settlement Decisions," *Law and Policy in International Business* 33(4): 555–567

Wallerstein, I. 1974. *The Modern World-System: Capitalist Agriculture and the Origins of the European World-Economy in the Sixteenth Century* (New York: Academic Press)

Waltz, K. 1954. *Man, State, and War: a Theoretical Analysis* (New York: Columbia University Press)

Wendt, A. 1999a. "On the Via Media: a Response to the Critics," *Review of International Studies* 26(1): 165–180

    1999b. *Social Theory of International Politics* (New York: Cambridge University Press)

Williamson, O. E. 1979. "Transaction-Cost Economics: the Governance of Contractual Relations," *Journal of Law and Economics* 22(October): 233–261

    1985. *The Economic Institutions of Capitalism* (New York: Free Press)

    2000. "The New Institutional Economics: Taking Stock, Looking Ahead," *Journal of Economic Literature* 38(3): 595–613

Willig, R. D. 1998. "Economic Effects of Antidumping Policy," in R. Z. Lawrence (ed.), *Brookings Trade Forum: 1998* (Washington, DC: Brookings Institution), pp. 57–79

Wolfe, R. 2003. "Regulatory Transparency, Developing Countries and the WTO," *World Trade Review* 2(2): 157–182

WTO 2004. *The Future of the WTO: Addressing Institutional Challenges in the New Millennium,* Report by the Consultative Board to the Director-General Supachai Panichpakdi (Geneva: World Trade Organization)

    2005. *Trade, Standards and the WTO,* World Trade Report 2005 (Geneva: World Trade Organization)

    2007. *Sixty Years of Multilateral Trading System: Achievements and Challenges,* World Trade Report 2007 (Geneva: World Trade Organization)

Yarbrough, B. V. and Yarbrough, R. M. 1987. "Institutions for the Governance of Opportunism in International Trade," *Journal of Law, Economics, and Organization* 3(1): 129–139

1997. "Dispute Settlement in International Trade: Regionalism and Procedural Coordination," in E. D. Mansfield and H. V. Milner (eds.), *The Political Economy of Regionalism* (New York: Columbia University Press) pp. 134–163

Zimmermann, T. A. 2006. *Negotiating the Review of the WTO Dispute Settlement Understanding* (London: Cameron May)

# INDEX

ABM (Anti-Ballistic Missiles Treaty)
106–107
added value, in WTO calculations 233
agency theory *see* methodological
individualism
ambivalence/ambiguity, contractual
68, 71, 77–78, 91, 129
benefits of avoidance, impossibility
of quantifying 94
Anderson, Kym 25
antidumping measures 5, 78, 223,
226–227, 318–319
level of precondition 226
proposed reforms 318–319
prosecutions 247
scope of application 227
antitrust law 319, 323
application, scope of 4
Arrow, Kenneth 57–58
assurance, role in contract/
commitment 31–32, 42, 58
asymmetrical information 64, 66–68,
69–70, 73–74, 86–87, 89, 117–118,
119–121, 208, 210, 269
attrition, war of 120–121, 284–285
auxiliary entitlements
balancing against substantive 45
defined 44
dependent (*vs.* general) 45, 48–49, 88
in WTO 191, 192–193, 194–196,
197, 215
Axelrod, Robert 269
Ayres, Ian 95

bad-faith clashes/disputes 296, 303–304
Bagwell, Kyle 23, 40, 144, 150, 151–152,
153–154, 158, 237

balance-of-payments measures 204,
208, 220, 279
balancing 169
Baldwin, Richard 139
bandwagoning 169
Barfield, Claude 21
Barton, John H. 25
Battigalli, Pierpaolo 72
"battle-of-the-sexes" game 55, 189
"beggar-thy-neighbor" policies *see*
opportunism
"binding overhang" 222
blackmail *see* crowding out
bounded rationality *see* reasonable
rationality
Bown, Chad P. 25, 223, 246
Brander, James A. 224
breach
definition/use of term 8
in game theory 110
*see also* "efficient breach"; escape;
violation
Buchanan, James 149

Calabresi, Guido 43, 107, 190
C&C (court and copper) *see* third-party
enforcement
CCC (complete contingent claims
contract) 57–59, 105, 111–112, 128
as benchmark for real-life
contracts 85, 86–87, 98–99,
102, 104, 109, 124, 127, 213,
278–279, 304
impracticability 60, 84, 211
Charnovitz, Steve 238
cheating, benefits of *see* hit-and-run
advantage

international law, norms of 195–196, 248–249, 290
IR (international relations) theory 143–144, 162–173, 177, 179, 180–181, 275
   approaches to decision-making 163–165, 166
   principal schools 166–173
   theories on locus of decision-making 165–166
Irwin, Douglas A. 155
ius *cogens* 107, 196, 249, 290

Johnson, Harry 143, 150
joint welfare maximization, as contractual aim 42, 102
Jolls, Christine 106
*jus cogens see* peremptory norms

Kaplow, Louis 51, 52, 116, 282
Keohane, Robert 166–167
Keynes, John Maynard 173
Kleen, Peter 21
Klein, Benjamin 91
Koremenos, Barbara 23
Kovenock, Dan 23
Krugman, Paul R. 142, 221

large countries, manipulation of trading system 150–151, 169
Lawrence, Robert Z. 316
L&E (law and economics) theories 16, 61, 76, 92–93, 127
Lee, Yong-Shik 21
legal fees *see* litigation: costs
legal theory 143–144, 173–177, 180
Lerner symmetry 153
liability rule(s) 19–20, 47, 48, 52–54, 104, 107–115, 126–127
   advantages 121, 285–286, 288–289
   arbitration requirement 115–116
   best complementary remedy 115, 281
   compared with property rule 108, 115–122, 280–286
   pitfalls 119, 120, 292–294

scope of application 287
specifics 286–288
types 108
in vWTO 235–236, 247, 279–288, 302, 309
liberalism 167
   "embedded" 171
liberalization 1–2, 11–12, 39, 306–307, 321
   commitments 191–192, 316
   optimal level, means of achieving 304–305
   policy-makers' motives for 143
   scholarship 24–25
Lindsey, Brink 21, 319
liquidated damages 54 *see* damages
litigation
   costs 63, 233
   petty, risk of 91–92
loopholes 78–80

Maggi, Giovanni 72–73, 144, 148–149, 157, 207, 216, 217
Mah, Jai S. 21
Mahlstein, Kornel 24–25, 110, 121, 281, 284
Mahoney, Paul G. 2, 102–103, 109
market access
   impact of vWTO on 306
   reciprocal balance 182–183
market access approach (to economic theory) 144, 149–155, 179–180
   arguments for 183–187
   central argument 149–150
   *see also* political externalities school; terms-of-trade school
market access contingencies 203–211
   compared with multilateral 210–211
   exogenous *vs.* endogenous 204
   foreseeability 206–207, 217
   political nature 205
   predictability of outcomes 207
   probability of occurrence 207–208
   symmetrically/asymmetrically revealed 208
   in trade game 269–276
   trade-relatedness 205
   urgency of response 210–211

WTO flexibility mechanisms (cont.)
  political economy 241
  (preferred) structure 13
  proposed reforms 3, 14, 19–20,
    257–258, 308–320; long-term
    317–320
  *see also* market access entitlement;
    WTO entitlements
WTO violation(s) 6, 227, 230

means of discouragement 295–296,
  302–303, 304
sanctions 20, 227–228; inadequacy
  242–244, 251–252
scholarship 24
*see also* violation-cum-retaliation;
  WTO: contravention of letter/spirit

zero-damage rule 108, 113–114

For EU product safety concerns, contact us at Calle de José Abascal, 56–1°, 28003 Madrid, Spain or eugpsr@cambridge.org.

www.ingramcontent.com/pod-product-compliance
Ingram Content Group UK Ltd.
Pitfield, Milton Keynes, MK11 3LW, UK
UKHW020351060825
461487UK00008B/612